W9-BYB-560

# THE
# PROJECT
# MANAGER'S
## DESK REFERENCE

# THE
# PROJECT
# MANAGER'S
## DESK REFERENCE

PROJECT PLANNING • SCHEDULING
EVALUATION • CONTROL • SYSTEMS

**THIRD EDITION**

## JAMES P. LEWIS

### McGraw-Hill

New York    Chicago    San Francisco    Lisbon    London
Madrid    Mexico City    Milan    New Delhi    San Juan
Seoul    Singapore    Sydney    Toronto

This publication is designed to provide accurate and authoritative information in regard to the subject matter covered. It is sold with the understanding that neither the author nor the publisher is engaged in rendering legal, accounting, or other professional service. If legal advice or other expert assistance is required, the services of a competent professional person should be sought.

> —*From a Declaration of Principles jointly adopted*
> *by a Committee of the American Bar*
> *Association and a Committee of Publishers*

McGraw-Hill books are available at special quantity discounts to use as premiums and sales promotions, or for use in corporate training programs. For more information, please write to the Director of Special Sales, Professional Publishing, McGraw-Hill, Two Penn Plaza, New York, NY 10121-2298. Or contact your local bookstore.

The Lewis Method is a registered trademark of The Lewis Institute, Inc. PMI, PMBOK, and PMP are registered trademarks of the Project Management Institute. Mind Map is a registered trademark of Tony Buzan. HBDI is a trademark of Herrmann International. The grid containing a thinking profile is also copyright by Herrmann International, and all such figures in this book are used by permission.

This book is printed on acid-free paper.

*This book is dedicated to the memory of my late wife,*

Lea Ann McDowell.

*This is the first of my books that
she has not worked on with me.*

*It is also dedicated to the memory of*

Eunice Belbin

*Late wife of Meredith Belbin
my new friend.*

*They are lost to us in this lifetime, but never forgotten.*

# Empty House
## by James P. Lewis

*I* come home to this empty house,
Tired and jet-lagged from my flight;
The silence strong and undiminished
By Leo's purrs of joy.

*F*irst time in over 30 years
That you aren't here to greet me.
Patient, waiting, whatever the time,
To say, "I'm glad you're home."

*I* fall in bed, exhausted;
Sad and lonely in my pain and grief.
But Leo doesn't let me sleep,
So glad is he it's not an empty house tonight.

# Nature's Way
By Meredith Belbin

It's Nature's way that leaves are shed
   and cover what was green.
It's Nature's way that 'neath the leaves
   new shoots appear unseen.
It's Nature's way that what was gained
   comes at a heavy cost.
It's Nature's way that 'mid the gloom
   all is never lost.

# CONTENTS

**Chapter 25**

## How to Apply Systems Thinking in Managing Projects   471

**Chapter 26**

## Problem Solving in Projects   481

**Chapter 27**

## Solving Close-Ended Problems   487

**Chapter 28**

## Solving Open-Ended Problems   497

# PREFACE

**W**elcome to this third edition of the *Project Manager's Desk Reference*. Although it was written to be a quick reference guide for busy project managers, the desk reference has been widely used as a textbook in university courses. It is customary to include everything but the "kitchen sink" in books of this type, but I have chosen to make the desk reference a (hopefully) useful guide for working project manager who need a quick refresher on the more common topics of project management.

Much of the material in the book has been stable for a number of years—such as critical path method, how to develop the work breakdown structure, and so on. What is changing most about project management is actually the number of people who are adopting the methods for their organizations. Project management is finally becoming a recognized discipline.

I hope you will find this new revision useful in managing your projects, whether you are a student or practicing project manager.

**Jim Lewis**
Vinton, Virginia

October 2006

SECTION ONE

# INTRODUCTION AND OVERVIEW

# CHAPTER

# Overview of Project Management

## THE NEED FOR SHARED UNDERSTANDING

Until everyone in an organization has a shared understanding of what is meant by projects and project management, misunderstandings, conflicts, and miscommunication are bound to exist. One of my associates conducted training for a government agency and found that they were using the term "program management" to mean what most people would call department management. Furthermore, many senior managers will tell you that they understand project management, because they used to manage projects. What they don't realize is that they followed no formal, structured approach, and they don't really understand what project management *should* be. This is not meant as a criticism, but simply as an observation that such points of view prevent organizations from achieving real competence in project management, because executives don't recognize the need for a formal approach.

Projects are people.

This chapter will establish definitions of important terms and introduce general concepts about project management.

## THE AUTHORITY FOR PROJECT MANAGEMENT

The authority for any discipline is generally the professional association that represents practitioners in that discipline. In the case of project management, that would be the Project Management Institute (PMI®) in the United States, and although there are other professional associations around the world, PMI was one of the first established, and most others follow their lead. For that reason, in this book I will subscribe to the definitions and terms outlined in the Project Management Body of Knowledge, or PMBOK®, published by PMI. These definitions are by no means absolute, nor is there universal acceptance of them, but they provide a general starting point from which we can diverge as necessary.

> A project is a temporary endeavor undertaken to produce a unique product, service, or result.
> —PMBOK 2004, p. 20.

## DEFINITION OF A PROJECT

There are many possible definitions of a project, but the one PMI chose appears in the text box. The definition implies that a project has a definite starting and ending point, but this is often not the case. Some projects seem to never end, often because people keep asking for changes to the job. In addition, the project produces a unique outcome—something that has not been done before. To say that building a house is a project, when that same design has been built before, may seem incorrect, but the conditions are different, the people involved are probably different, and so the definition can be applied.

Below are some examples of projects, followed by a list of activities that do not qualify as projects:

### Examples

- Developing a new product or service
- Building a bridge, house, road, runway, or other structure
- Writing software
- Installing a new manufacturing process, cell, or assembly line
- Writing a book
- Developing a new marketing plan

### Counter Examples

- Processing insurance claims, orders, or invoices
- Manufacturing something
- Cooking in a restaurant
- Driving a delivery truck over the same route every day
- In short, anything of a purely repetitive nature

## An Alternative

Quality expert Dr. J. M. Juran (1989) offered another definition of projects that I like: "A project is a problem scheduled for solution." This definition makes us realize that project management is problem solving on a large scale. However, the word "problem" invariably means something bad. When people tell you they have a problem, you know bad news will follow.

I am using the word "problem" in a much broader sense. Developing a new product or software program is a problem, but a very positive one. So "problem" does not always mean something negative, although sometimes it will , such as in an environmental cleanup project.

One of the common difficulties in running projects is that insufficient time is spent at the beginning defining exactly what problem to solve. This can lead to the unfortunate situation in which the right solution has been developed, but for the wrong problem. Guidelines will be presented in the planning chapters of this book on how to avoid this error.

## PROJECT STAKEHOLDERS

Before we go any further, it might be useful to examine the stakeholders involved in any project. First of all, note the definition of stakeholder—anyone who has a vested interest in the project. This includes customers, suppliers, contributors, the project sponsor, managers, and sometimes the citizens of an area when the project is a public-works job.

> **stakeholder:** Anyone who has a vested interest in the project.

A customer is the user of the project deliverables. In some cases the customer will have ordered the project and will pay for it, as in the case of construction of a building, home, or road. In other cases, the customer is the person who buys products developed by the project and later manufactured by the company. The quality-improvement movement stressed the importance of meeting customer needs as a condition for success in business, and I would contend that this is still an issue for many projects—not truly meeting customer needs. More on this in the chapter on project planning.

> **customer:** The user of project deliverables.

The project sponsor is the person who actually orders the project in the first place. This person could be the customer, but in many cases it will be a third party, such as someone in the marketing department who orders that a new product be developed. The sponsor is responsible for ensuring that the project is properly budgeted, that the schedule is acceptable, and that the team has the resources needed to achieve the desired results.

> **sponsor:** The person who orders that a project be done.

The project manager should have overall responsibility for making sure the project is completed on time, within budget, within scope, and at the desired level of performance. In too many cases, the role of the project manager is too weak to permit him/her to control these outcomes fully, which means that the project manager cannot really be held accountable for results.

> **project manager:** The person who has total responsibility for ensuring that the project is completed on time, within budget, within scope, at the desired performance level.

## DEFINITION OF PROJECT MANAGEMENT

To cite the 2004 edition of the PMBOK again, it defines project management as ". . . application of knowledge, skills, tools and techniques to project activities to meet project requirements. Project management is accomplished through the application and integration of the project management processes of initiating, planning, executing, monitoring and controlling, and closing" (op cit., p. 23). These processes are further defined in the PMBOK. The objective of this book is to explain how to accomplish these in practice.

I think it is important to mention that these processes do not fully capture the essence of project management. Much of project management consists of dealing with people, trying to get team members to perform at the required level, negotiating for scarce resources, and dealing with political issues. These activities are not really captured by the PMBOK processes, and no document can do justice to the true complexity of project management.

### A Performing Art

Project management is not just scheduling.

It is not just tools.

It is not a job position or job title.

It is not even the sum total of all of these. Project management should be considered a *performing art*. And a performing art is more than tools or systems. But my experience shows that not many people understand this. A lot of managers believe that project management is mostly scheduling, and that if a person can do some technical job (using the word "technical" in a very broad sense), then that individual can manage.

I have found that there is an almost inverse correlation between individuals who are technical experts and those who are excellent managers. One reason for this may be that technical expertise is a largely left-brain function, whereas being an excellent manager may be a largely right-brain function. In fact, management professor Henry Mintzberg has advocated that we should ". . . plan on the left and manage on the right" [side of the brain] (Mintzberg, 1989).

This is a pervasive problem. I have been teaching project management since 1980—more than 25 years—and I am convinced that not many people understand what management is. This goes also for project management.

Perhaps no person has thought more about management than Peter Drucker, who attempted to define management in his book, *Management: Tasks, Responsibilities, Practices* (Drucker, 1973). The book contains 839 pages, and explores general aspects of managing outside the scope of this book. However, in chapter two, Drucker begins discussing what management is all about, and it is very instructive to examine what he says.

> . . . managers practice management. They do not practice economics. They do not practice quantification. They do not practice behavioral science. These are the tools for the manager (op. cit., p. 17).

He goes on to say:

> One implication is that there are specific managerial skills which pertain to management, rather than to any other discipline. . . . Management is a practice rather than a science. In this, it is comparable to medicine, law, and engineering. It is not knowledge, but *performance* [italics added] (op. cit., p. 17).

What is important about this is to realize that attorneys, physicians, and engineers all study intensively for many years in a university, but the practice of their discipline is not learned in the classroom. It is only learned on the battlefield—in the trenches, so to speak. Can you imagine a surgeon learning how to perform an operation strictly by reading a book or attending a lecture? Of course not! In fact, a retinal surgeon once told me that you learn surgery by watching someone do it, then doing it yourself, and finally by teaching someone else how to do it. The real learning takes place in the final step—when you teach it.

I believe this explains why much of management training fails to turn out skilled managers. The training itself focuses on knowledge. MBA programs, for example, teach would-be managers how to understand balance sheets, what the law says about various issues, and so on. They do not teach the *performing art* of management! That must be learned—like surgery—in the trenches, from someone who already knows how it is done.

However, all too many managers have never had anyone teach them the practice of management. They gain their knowledge and are left to figure out for themselves how to apply it. And this can be a formidable problem. I know that if I have a cavity in a tooth, it should be filled. But for me to pick up a drill and some filling and actually fill a tooth is another matter altogether.

The net result is that we have thousands of managers who have only a textbook understanding of the job, and are therefore not very good at what they do. This is why so many organizations succeed in spite of themselves, rather than because of their actions. The reality, in too many cases, is that the first myth of management is that it exists.

> The first myth of management is that it exists.

## The Tasks of Management

Drucker points out that an organization does not exist for its own sake, but to fulfill a specific social purpose and to satisfy a specific need of society. "Management, in turn, is an organ of the institution" (op. cit., p. 39). He goes on to say that management is defined by the tasks performed, and that there are three primary tasks of management.

1. To achieve the specific purpose and mission of the institution, whether business enterprise, hospital, or university;
2. To make work productive and the worker achieving;
3. To manage social impacts and social responsibilities (op. cit., p. 40).

## Purpose and Mission

To elaborate on these, Drucker points out that for a business enterprise, the primary purpose is economic performance. The responsibility of management then is to ensure that economic performance comes first. He is quick to point out, however, that if you do not meet the needs of customers, there will be no economic performance. I have always thought of purpose and mission in this way: the purpose of a business is economic performance, that is, the make a profit. Its mission is to meet the needs of customers. And these two must be kept in balance all the time. When a business puts economic performance above meeting the needs of customers, it eventually fails. Similarly, if a business concentrates solely on meeting the needs of customers, but does not make a profit, it too will fail.

## Making Work Productive and Workers Achieving

An institution has only one true resource—human beings. It performs by making human resources productive. This is done through work, and making work productive is an essential function. To do this, we must make work suitable for human beings to perform, and the way this is done is different than making a process suitable for a machine. Failing to understand the "technology" of human beings leads to a failure to make workers achieve, whether they run machines, design products, or work as executives.

## Managing Social Impacts and Social Responsibilities

Drucker points out that "business exists to supply goods and services to customers, rather than to supply jobs to workers and managers, or even dividends to stockholders. For a management to forget this is mismanagement" (op. cit., p. 42). A business impacts society in many ways. It provides needed goods and services to customers, who may also be employees. It provides a quality of life that has become increasingly important over the years. It may discharge waste that must be disposed of properly—thus the need to be environmentally "friendly." As Drucker says, ". . . mismanaging social impacts eventually will destroy society's support for the enterprise and with it the enterprise as well" (op. cit., p. 43).

## The Three Tasks and Project Management

While these three tasks apply to managers in general, it is reasonable to ask if they apply to project managers. I believe the answer is a definite "yes." The purpose and mission of a project should always be aligned with the purpose and mission of the enterprise. In fact, while project managers are usually not involved in project selection, alignment of project purpose with organization purpose should be one of the primary criteria by which a project is selected. Furthermore, prioritization of projects should be based on how closely they conform to the purpose and mission of the enterprise, and how well they contribute to it.

As for making work productive and enabling workers to achieve, this seems so obvious as to require no comment. How could you possibly have a successful project when work is unproductive and project team members are unable to achieve? Is it the project manager's responsibility to ensure that these conditions are met? Yes. However, in matrix organizations, this responsibility may fall largely to functional managers, from whose departments team members are drawn. It seems reasonable that project managers cannot be successful if functional managers fail to discharge their own responsibilities regarding productive work and worker achievement.

Finally, I believe that project managers must be just as concerned as general managers about the social impacts of their projects. In some situations, the impact of a project will be primarily within the organization, while in others it will be largely outside. Public works projects are good examples of the latter. In addition, when you consider that many projects are global in scope, there are social impacts in other countries, and these impacts contribute to the perception of those individuals of the country of origin of the project.

## PROJECT CONSTRAINTS

As Drucker has pointed out, one of the major tasks of a manager is to ensure that the purpose and mission of the enterprise are achieved. The same can be said for project managers. To do this, project managers engage in five processes aimed at achieving project objectives: initiating, planning, executing, controlling, and closing. Each of these activities will be treated in major sections of this book. For now, we will only examine the primary constraints or objectives that exist in all projects. We say that project work must be completed:

- ◆ At the desired **P**erformance level. A bridge must carry a certain load. A car must achieve certain fuel economy, speed, and so on. Performance defines what the output of the project must accomplish.

- ◆ Within **C**ost or budget constraints. This refers to the *project* budget, not to the *product* cost. Note that there are several cost components to a project: labor, capital equipment, outside services, and supplies or materials.

- ◆ On **T**ime. Most projects come with a deadline.

◆ For a given magnitude or **S**cope of work. Note that how big the job is may not relate directly to performance requirements. For example, in designing a new airplane, the company may design every single component or it may contract some of the design work to other companies. The technical performance expected of the airplane does not change in either case, but the magnitude of the work to be done by the airplane company does vary.

The first three of these are referred to as the *P*, *C*, and *T* aspects of project management. Some people call them good, cheap, and fast (*P* = good; *C* = cheap; *T* = fast), and refer to them as the *triple constraints* of a project.

As pointed out above, however, scope is the size of the project. Unfortunately, in the past it has been common to combine scope and performance and call them "good." As I have shown, they are not the same, so there are actually four constraints rather than three.

The relationship among these four variables can be illustrated by a mathematical relationship:

$$C = f(P, T, S)$$

The equation says that cost is a function of performance, time, and scope. I generally recommend that for this relationship, you consider labor costs only, because they are directly related to the other three, whereas other cost categories are not. (This does not mean that we can forget about capital equipment or materials cost, but that they do not have a direct relationship to the other variables. They are generally tracked separately from labor costs.) Ideally, the functional relationship could be expressed as a specific mathematical equation, such as:

$$C = 2P + 3T + 4S$$

However, the exact relationship is almost never known. The values for all four constraints are estimated. Nevertheless, we know that they are related, because if you try to change one of them, at least one of the others will change. For example, if you increase the scope of the project while holding $P$ and $T$ constant, you will certainly increase the cost to do the job.

One way to illustrate the relationship is shown in Figure 1.1. Note that performance, cost, and time are the sides of the triangle, while scope is the area. From geometry, we know that if the lengths of the sides are given, we can determine the scope, or area of the triangle. Alternatively, if we know the lengths of two sides and the area, we can determine the length of the third side. This leads to a very important practical aspect of managing projects: Values for any three of the variables can be dictated, but the value of the fourth one will be determined by the "equation" for the triangle.

**F I G U R E  1.1**

Triangle Showing Relationship of $P$, $C$, $T$, and $S$

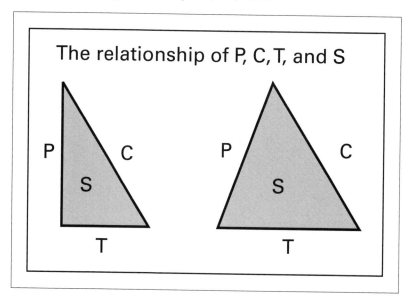

I like to say it this way: Whoever assigns the project to me (usually the project sponsor) can specify three of the variables, but I get to pick the fourth one. For example, if the sponsor tells me that the job must be completed by a certain date, at a specific performance level, and also defines the scope, then I should be allowed to tell the sponsor what I need (cost) in order to achieve those results. If the sponsor replies that this is more than he can afford, then a tradeoff must be made in one of the other variables—usually scope. If we reduce scope, we can do the project for a lower cost. When the sponsor insists that the job be done for a cost less than the project manager specifies, we are headed for possible failure. We can certainly try to find ways to do the project for less money, and that is always a challenge for a project manager, but to have all four targets dictated arbitrarily is a recipe for disaster—for everyone involved.

Generally speaking, the cost of the project will increase as $P$, $T$, and $S$ increase, except in the case of trying to crash the project. To crash a project means to try to complete it in the absolutely minimum time possible. Naturally, the usual approach to getting projects done really fast is to apply more resources. This can be done by adding people, or if no more people are available, by having the existing staff work more hours per day (overtime). Doing so then leads to a time-cost trade-off curve like the one shown in Figure 1.2.

Notice that crashing a project results in a curve that rises very sharply. This is because you quickly reach a point of diminishing returns as you add more people to the project —people get in each other's way, the work can't be subdivided so much, you need more communication as you add people, and so on. Furthermore, there is a lower boundary below which you can't go, no matter how many people you add. I call this the "forbidden zone."

Not only that, but if you add people to an already late project, you are likely to make it later, because the new people must be trained, and someone on the project has to do

## F I G U R E  1.2

Time-Cost Trade-off Curve

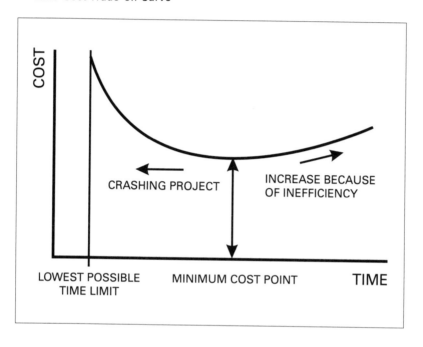

that. This causes their productivity to drop, which makes them have to work overtime to keep up, which results in fatigue, which causes their productivity to drop, which . . . As you can see, this is a vicious loop, which rapidly spirals out of control. This principle was

> Adding people to an already late project may only make it later.
> — Brooks' Law

originally expounded by Brooks in his book on software development, and I believe it applies to a lot of projects besides software (Brooks, 1975).

One of the most common problems project managers face is that the scope of the project may increase as time passes. People think of things that did not initially occur to them. Or they did not take enough time at the beginning of the job to properly define the problem being solved. Unfortunately, the scope tends to increase in small increments rather than in large ones, making such changes almost invisible. Such incremental changes are called *scope creep*. The difficulty is that many people suffer from amnesia at the end of a project. They forget about all the scope changes, and they try to hold you accountable for original targets. For everyone's protection, you have to control scope creep. This will be covered in the control chapters.

Another issue is that organizations are demanding that project managers find ways to cut the time it takes to do the job, while simultaneously reducing the cost—while leaving performance and scope alone. In many cases, the cut is by as much as 50 percent or more. For example, auto makers have been challenged repeatedly to reduce the time required to design a car. At one time they needed six to eight years. Then some Japanese firms reduced the cycle to about three years, and American companies had to follow suit.

We have just seen that when you crash a project by throwing resources at it, that increases costs significantly. Yet we are being challenged to reduce both time and cost! Is this an impossible demand?

Not at all.

To see why this is true, consider an old saying from behavioral science: "If you always do what you've always done, you'll always get what you always got." In other words, if what you have been doing does not get the desired result, change the process. In fact, that is what formal project management is all about.

No doubt you know managers who have been getting projects completed successfully for years, without using this formal project management stuff. The problem is, you don't know how much better they could have done with formal methods.

According to the six-sigma experts, most organizations run at a three-sigma quality level, which means that 20 to 40 cents of every dollar they spend is waste. The same thing applies to projects. Some managers have estimated that one-third of the labor cost in projects is rework. In other words, one of every three individuals on the job spends full time just redoing what the other two people did wrong in the first place! If you reduce the rework, you have just improved productivity by a corresponding amount.

Formal project management can help you achieve that result.

How? By recognizing that much of the rework is caused by poor project planning. If you do a better job planning, you will see a drop in rework.

This is, in fact, one of the fastest ways to show that you are making progress with project management. Unless you have reliable baseline data for previous projects, it is hard to show that you are getting better at managing them. However, if you start measuring rework, you should be able to show a decline over time, which is a good sign that you are making progress.

## The Performance Objective

The often-forgotten objective in project management is the performance target. This target is not just a technical specification. It is a translation of the customer's needs into performance criteria, and that translation may be a technical specification. As I stated previously, failing to meet the customer's needs is a recipe for failure, even if you meet your schedule, budget, and scope requirements.

## THE PROJECT LIFE-CYCLE

As a general rule, projects have a life-cycle consisting of three or more phases. A six-phase model is shown in

Figure 1.3. This model might be appropriate for product development. The phases in this model are called concept, definition, design, development or construction, application, and post-completion. The character of the program changes in each life-cycle phase (see the life-cycle illustration in Figure 1.3).

There are two major pitfalls in the life-cycle of a project. First, the concept for the project is accepted as the definition, leading to the outcome mentioned previously, i.e., the right solution is developed for the wrong problem.

The second pitfall is at post-completion. Note that a final review should be conducted for the project. The aim is to learn what was done well in the job and what might need to be improved. However, this stage is often aborted. At the 1998 Frontiers Conference on project management, the keynote speaker asked an audience of 400, "How many of you have a mandate that you must do a lessons-learned review at the end of your projects?"

One Possible Life-Cycle Model for a Project

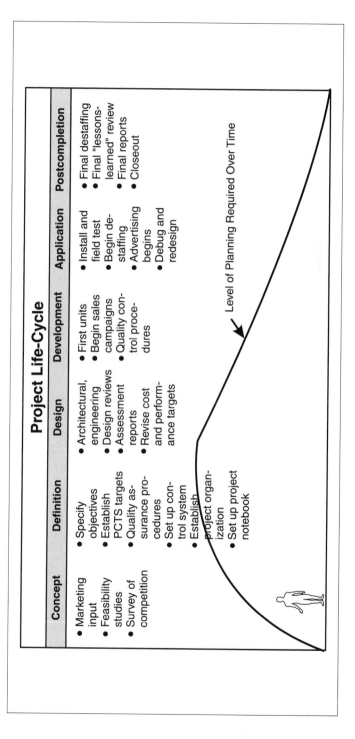

## Project Life-Cycle

| Concept | Definition | Design | Development | Application | Postcompletion |
|---------|-----------|--------|-------------|-------------|----------------|
| • Marketing input<br>• Feasibility studies<br>• Survey of competition | • Specify objectives<br>• Establish PCTS targets<br>• Quality assurance procedures<br>• Set up control system<br>• Establish project organization<br>• Set up project notebook | • Architectural, engineering<br>• Design reviews<br>• Assessment reports<br>• Revise cost and performance targets | • First units<br>• Begin sales campaigns<br>• Quality control procedures | • Install and field test<br>• Begin destaffing<br>• Advertising begins<br>• Debug and redesign | • Final destaffing<br>• Final "lessons-learned" review<br>• Final reports<br>• Closeout |

Level of Planning Required Over Time

About 10 or 12 people raised their hands.

He then asked a very poignant question: "How many of you are required to show management how you will avoid making the same mistakes on your next project that you made on your last one?"

Only two hands went up.

This is tremendously important! As the old adage goes, "People who do not know history are doomed to make the same mistakes again."

I think there are a couple of reasons why people don't do lessons-learned reviews. One is that by the time they finish the project, they are eager to get on with the next job (or maybe they already have). Secondly, they may be reluctant to face the fact that some areas need improvement. In our win-at-all-costs, take-no-prisoners culture, admitting that you need to do better is almost unthinkable. Perhaps, too, failure to face such issues may be caused by not wanting to embarrass anyone. Nevertheless, no matter how well a job has been done, there is always room for improvement, and a lessons-learned review should be conducted in that spirit. Naturally, any climate of blame or punishment simply increases the likelihood that no one will conduct an "honest" evaluation of a project.

## THE PROJECT MANAGEMENT SYSTEM

The project management system consists of seven components, as shown in Figure 1.4. If any one of these is defective, then the management of projects will suffer.

### The Human System

The human system is placed at the bottom of the pyramid because it forms the foundation for everything else. A project manager must deal with all of the "people issues." This includes communication, team building, conflict manage-

**F I G U R E  1.4**

The Project Management System

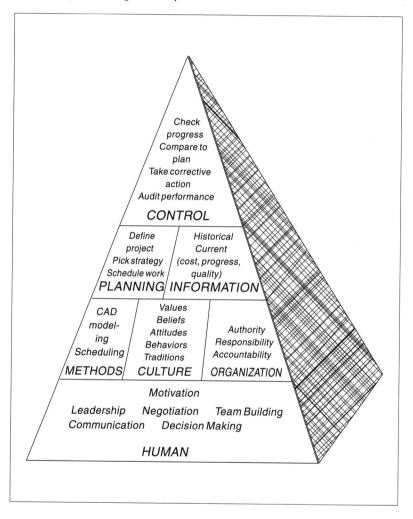

ment and resolution, motivation, and, yes, that "dirty word" *politics!* I have included only a handful of the issues that must be handled.

I can almost hear the groaning now from the techies. As a former engineer, I know this is not typically one of our strong suits. In fact, some techies complain bitterly that they hate the people problems they have to deal with. To them, I suggest that they rethink their careers. They don't want to be project managers. Or any other kind of manager for that matter. You are not likely to be good at something you hate, and in my view, life is too short to spend doing something you hate. And you can't get away from it.

Dealing with people is a major function that a project manager must perform. This is partly because you have a lot of responsibility and (usually) very little authority (or none at all). That is almost a given in project management. So the only way you get anything done is through using people skills. These include persuasion, influence, negotiating, and sometimes just plain begging.

If you hate dealing with people, I suggest you have a heart-to-heart talk with your boss and tell him or her that you don't want to be a project manager. You would rather be a techie for the rest of your life. If that doesn't work, change jobs! I'm serious. But then it's your life, and your career, and you have to make your own choices.

If you are one of those individuals who don't actually hate dealing with people, but feel that you need to improve your skills, then hang in there. Everything listed in the box can be learned—even leadership. That is, it can all be learned if you really want to. So set for yourself a career objective to develop those skills, and read Chapter 19, by my colleague Bob Wysocki, on how to go about it.

## Culture

Related to people issues is culture. Every organization has a culture, which is the sum total of everything in the box—this includes values, beliefs, attitudes, behaviors, and traditions. In fact, one way you can tell when people are talking about culture is that they will say, "We don't do it that way around here."

Broadly speaking, there is nothing inherently right, wrong, good, or bad about cultures. But when people from different cultures interact, it often results in misunderstandings, conflict, and downright fighting. Perhaps a few examples will help.

My wife and I have hosted exchange students from several different countries, for ten months at a time, partly because we are interested in cultures. Our first student was a Japanese girl named Yukiko. When she arrived, I asked her how to say things in Japanese. "Well, 'yes' is *hai* and 'no' is *e-a*," she said, "but we don't like to say 'no' very much."

At the time, I didn't fully appreciate what she was telling me. Later I learned that the Japanese consider saying "no" directly to be fairly rude. For instance, I was in a Japanese restaurant one evening and a fellow came in and ordered a beer by name. The waitress, who was Japanese, said, "Maybe we don't have that kind. Maybe you'd prefer a different kind." Now she knew very well that she did not have the beer he asked for, but she could not say so directly. She had to soften it a bit.

This is very mystifying to Americans, who are used to being direct. So we sometimes get into trouble with Japanese people. "I thought we agreed on this," says the American, who finds some violation of what he thought was agreed to. "Oh, we agreed on this," says his Japanese colleague. Such misunderstandings can be a serious source of conflict.

Another example: I once knew an engineer from India who refused to do technician work, even though it was common practice in the lab for all engineers to do their own technician work, because there were never enough techs to go around. He thought this was demeaning, because in India an engineer would never be asked to do technician work—it was beneath his position.

Finally, my favorite experience was one in Malaysia. I had taught for Petronas, the oil company, and they had a company driver take me to the airport. He was driving a van, and I started to get into the back seat, which is common in the United States. He looked back at me and said, "Sir, you're kind of fat. You'd be more comfortable up here in the front."

It was all I could do to keep from laughing. Fortunately, I had done my homework and I knew that to many people from Asian cultures, being fat is not a stigma like it is in our American "twiggy" society. It is actually a sign of affluence, because over several thousand years, unless you were wealthy, you couldn't afford to eat foods that would cause you to be fat.

What I found funny was to imagine my driver coming to the U. S. to get a job as a limo driver and saying to some unwary person what he said to me. The person complains and he gets fired for insulting the customer. He is totally bewildered. "What happened?" he says. "I was only trying to be helpful." Which he was.

## Organization

Every organization must define the authority, accountability, and responsibility conferred on each member of that organization. As I mentioned previously, project managers always have a lot of responsibility and little authority. It has almost always been that way, and probably will continue.

However, there are two kinds of authority. One is to tell people what to do and expect them to do it. That one you will never have. And it doesn't matter very much in the first place. Ask any CEO of any company, "You have a lot of authority, don't you?" And he will say "Yes." Then ask, "Does your authority guarantee that people do what you want done?" and he will say, "No." Then what does get people to do what a CEO wants done? Every one that I have asked has said, "In the end analysis, the person has to want to do it, and my job is to get them to want to do it."

> Every
> organization
> must define
> authority,
> responsibility,
> and
> accountability.

I call that influence.

And if a CEO has to use influence to get things done, you and I can hope to do no better. That's why you need those people skills listed at the bottom of the pyramid.

The second kind of authority is decision-making authority. This one I consider a major problem for many project managers, especially when it comes to decisions to spend money. I frequently ask project managers how much they can spend without approvals, and it is less than 100 dollars. Yet they have project budgets of hundreds of thousands of dollars.

Their companies are giving these project managers mixed messages. On the one hand, they are told, "We trust you, because we've put you in charge of a project that will cost us a lot of money." The second message, however, is, "If you want to spend any of it, you have to get it approved first." To me, this message means, "We don't trust you."

Now, when two messages differ, the negative one takes priority over the positive one. In other words, these managers are being told that the company doesn't trust them.

If you follow my process for managing projects, you will find that the implementation plan must be approved, and this plan will include a budget for the project. After that, as long as the project manager is spending in accordance with the already approved plan, why should any more approvals be needed? Doing so is a total waste of everyone's time.

## Methods

This refers to the "tools of the trade," so to speak. For project managers, the only issue that usually comes up here is scheduling software. I am going to say here that I understand the need for some standardization in organizations, because IS departments cannot support but so many software programs. However, one size does not always fit all in clothing or in software, and insisting that everyone must use a low-end package will cause major problems for project managers who deal with very large construction projects. Alternatively, insisting that everyone use a high-end package because a few people manage large projects is to provide everyone with a sledge hammer when what they need is a small hammer to drive nails.

There is one solution to this problem that a few companies have found—have one person do all scheduling for a group of project managers. That way the scheduler can become intimately familiar with the high-end package and the project managers only have to know its capability. This works very well and saves a lot of money. Furthermore, it frees project managers from the drudgery of sitting at a computer all the time trying to massage a schedule and allows them to concentrate on the important things that they should be doing, such as dealing with political issues, and so on.

## Control

For the moment, we will skip to the top of the pyramid and then backtrack. When you get right down to it, the reason for managing is always to maintain control. You are expected to control the application of scarce resources to achieve desired objectives. The question is, how is this done?

The answer is partly provided by the definition of control. You exercise control by comparing where you are to where you are supposed to be, and taking corrective action when you find discrepancies. It is clear that this is a feedback system definition of control, as opposed to a power or authority definition.

> **control:** You exercise control by comparing where you are to where you are supposed to be, then taking corrective action when you find discrepancies.

This means that the two boxes under the control box play a vital role in allowing a project manager to control a project.

## Planning

The plan tells where you are supposed to be in the first place. Without a plan, you have no idea if you are doing okay or not. Thus, if you have no plan, you have no control. I consider this to be one of the most important principles

> If you have no plan, you cannot have control—by definition!

of project management, because it clearly explains why planning is not an option—it is a necessity.

## Information

If you don't know where you are, you certainly can't exercise control. This is a problem for most organizations. They have

> If you don't
> know where
> you are, you
> certainly
> can't exercise
> control.

excellent information systems for inventory control, order tracking, and so on, but nothing for tracking projects. The reason is simple—they didn't know they needed one. For the time being, you will most likely have to track your project manually. That isn't too big a problem for most project managers.

You also need historical data on what happened in previous projects. Again, most organizations don't have history databases. If you want to estimate how long a task will take, your best starting point is data on how long it took previously. All too often, this information exists only in the memories of individuals, and these are notoriously faulty. I can hardly remember what I did yesterday, much less what I did three months ago. So historical data really must be captured and recorded. We will discuss this issue more in the control chapters of the book.

# 2
# CHAPTER

# A Model for Managing Projects

## DOES ONE SIZE FIT ALL?

We saw in Chapter 1 that the PMBOK defines project management as ". . . application of knowledge, skills, tools and techniques to project activities to meet project requirements. Project management is accomplished through the application and integration of the project management processes of initiating, planning, executing, monitoring and controlling, and closing" (PMBOK 2004, p. 23). However, we are still left to determine how you initiate, plan, control, and close a project. Executing is a function of the work being done, and is not

> Project management is a disciplined way of thinking about a job, and this way of thinking should be followed in all projects, regardless of content, size, or complexity.

strictly a part of project management. Rather, project management monitors execution steps and tries to ensure that the work stays on track with the project plan.

Having said this, it is fair to ask if there is one approach to managing projects that will work for all jobs, regardless of content. Can the same approach be used in construction, research and development, marketing, and product development? This is equivalent to asking if you follow the same approach to initiate a construction project that you do to initiate a research project. The answer is "yes and no."

There are definitely common elements, such as developing a problem statement, vision, and mission statement for a project. This should be done for all projects, regardless of work content or nature.

Many organizations develop a project charter, but this is *not* universal. In many product development projects, a stage-gate approach is followed. As the product progresses through feasibility to design to release, each stage is followed by a gate in which status of the design is reviewed. Does it meet technical requirements? Can it be produced for the target market cost? Can enough be sold to meet required return on investment (ROI)? If the answer to any of these questions is "no," then the development project may be stopped. Such a process is not so common in construction projects. Once they are started, they are completed eventually, although you may see them slow down compared to the original schedule.

In spite of these differences, however, I believe that a uniform high-level approach can be used to manage all projects. What will differ will be the low-level details. The reason I say this is that project management is a disciplined way of thinking about a job, and that thinking process should be followed in any project, regardless of the content, size, or complexity.

During the past 30 years, I have looked at projects of all kinds and developed a method of managing them that I call The Lewis Method® of project management. It is represented by the flow chart shown in Figure 2.1.

**F I G U R E  2.1**

The Lewis Method® of Project Management

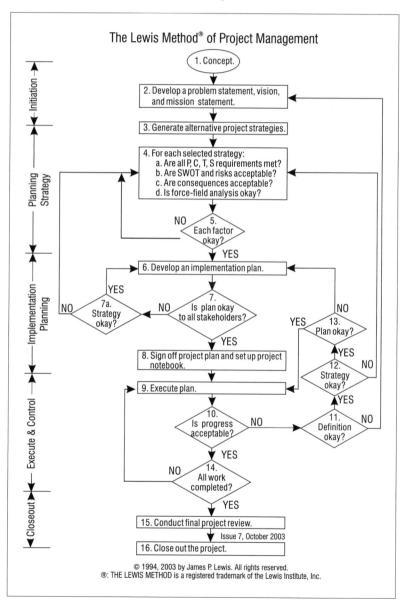

Before discussing the flow chart, I think it might be useful to differentiate between my method and a project management methodology. My method represents the overall process of managing a project. It is robust because it specifies or includes the principles that guide the project manager in his or her practice.

A methodology, however, must be specific to an organization, and spells out the nitty gritty procedures to be followed in carrying out the overall process defined by the *method*. The methodology specifies what forms are to be filled out, who must sign approvals, what meetings must be held, and so on. This means that the methodology will differ from organization to organization, while the overall process remains the same.

One thing that seems to confuse some people is that many projects contain other projects within them. One term that helps relieve the confusion is to call these smaller jobs subprojects. Or, alternatively, you can think of the total job as a program and all of the components as individual projects. You will see this terminology in the section on work breakdown structures (Chapter 6).

Consider a research and development (R&D) project. You could actually deal with this as two projects—the first is a research project with its own goals, deliverables, project team, and so on, and the second is a development project with different goals, deliverables, and perhaps even a different team.

You will notice that the first action a project team takes is to develop a definition of the problem to be solved by the project (see step 2 in the flowchart). This can be a project in itself! The mission is to define the problem. In a case like this, the definition of the problem to be solved might be stated as, "We don't know the problem that we are dealing with at this point," and the mission is, "To define the problem to be solved." The deliverable would then be a crisp definition of the problem that everyone could agree with.

## OVERVIEW OF THE MODEL

Because the model in Figure 2.1 represents the complete process of managing a project, explaining the steps in detail would require writing the entire book as a single chapter. Therefore, I will offer only a general overview of the steps in this chapter, and subsequent chapters will flesh them out in detail.

Steps 1 through 8 constitute the overall planning process, including project scheduling. Steps 9 through 16 specify how to execute the work, as well as how to monitor and control progress, followed by how to close out the project. The model is designed to prevent common problems that seem to occur in projects, but cannot capture the complexity of the entire process without becoming unwieldy. You will note that the PMBOK processes of initiating, planning, executing, controlling, and closeout are shown down the left side of the model.

### Steps 1 and 2: The Initiating Process

As shown in the project life-cycle model presented in Chapter 1, a project begins as a concept. Someone identifies a need for something. Unfortunately, a concept can be very vague. The identified need has not been thought through very thoroughly. For that reason, the concept stage is followed by the definition stage.

The next step is to develop a good definition of the problem to be solved by the project. This is probably the single greatest hurtle to overcome in the entire process. Insistence on writing a problem statement is usually met with skepticism, the reaction being, "We all know what the problem is. Let's get on with it. This is a waste of time!"

Many examples have been described in the literature to show that this is often not the case. I will cite only one. In their book, *Breakthrough Thinking,* Nadler and Hibino (1990) tell of a company that received complaints from its distributors that it was sending them damaged goods. The company hired an efficiency expert to investigate, and she accepted the definition of the problem as offered—to reduce damage to goods. To solve the problem, the expert designed a computer-controlled conveyor to load trucks. She estimated that the conveyor system would cost around $60,000 per warehouse location, with savings yielding a payback of about eight months. Because the company owned 24 warehouses, the total investment was to be $1.44 million.

> A project is a problem scheduled for solution.

The vice president was inclined to accept the consultant's recommendation, but decided (perhaps for political reasons) to ask the internal industrial engineering group for a second opinion. The assignment was given to a staff engineer who was a recent college graduate. He studied the situation. However, rather than accept the definition of the problem as given, he asked a new question: What are we really trying to achieve? His answer was, "We are trying to find the best way of distributing our products to the marketplace." Based on that problem statement, he completed the study and prepared a presentation for management.

When time came for the presentation, the vice president asked, "Well, do we go ahead and spend the $1.44 million?"

The young engineer responded, "No sir. I think you should sell most of the warehouses."

The company ultimately followed his recommendation and sold all but a few regional warehouses, each stocked by air shipments directly from the company's manufacturing plants. Eliminating local warehouses simplified freight transfers so there were fewer physical handling points for each shipment, and consequently less likelihood of damaging goods. The solution saved the company hundreds of millions of dollars each year, and eventually forced their competitors to restructure along the same lines.

This example drives home a most important point about problem solving:
The way a problem is defined determines the solution possibilities. It is this fact that makes it so important to

> **The way a problem is defined determines the solution possibilities.**

define the problem correctly before any planning is done. Chapters 25 to 27 present more complete approaches to problem-solving methods that should be applied at this step.

## Step 3: Generate Alternative Project Strategies

At this step, we move into the overall planning process as defined in the PMBOK. There are actually three aspects to planning—strategy, tactics, and logistics. In step 3, we begin looking at project strategy.

As the old saying goes, "There is more than one way to skin a cat." With most projects, there will be more than one approach that can be applied to achieve the desired result. For example, a house can be built from the ground up and by constructing every single element at the site, or it can be assembled from prefabricated parts. Further, it can be built entirely by one contractor or various parts can be subcontracted (for example, plumbing, wiring, roofing).

In technological projects, the approach may involve using proven technology to reduce risk. Or "cutting-edge" technology may be used to achieve a competitive advantage, despite the fact that risk increases.

The common approach would be to brainstorm a list of available strategies and then select one. Creativity-enhancing methods can be employed to increase the likelihood of developing a good strategy. Edward de Bono is considered by many to be the world's leading expert on creativity, and his book, *Serious Creativity* (1992), presents his approach in detail. The interested reader should consult that book.

## Step 4: Select and Evaluate the Strategy

After developing a list of strategies, one must be selected. A strategy will only be considered suitable if it passes four tests. The answers to these questions may not always be derived quantitatively, nor will each answer be certain, but the analysis is important, for it will identify potential problem areas before time is wasted developing a detailed plan.

Initially, it is a good idea to rank the list of brainstormed ideas based on your intuition—that is, you probably have an idea which one will be best without doing detailed analysis. If this is not true, then you may have to do more work than I am suggesting in the following text to rank them. I will go into more detail on how this is done in Chapter 5.

Once you have the list, choose the top-ranked strategy and subject it to the following analysis. If it fails any test, subject your second-ranked strategy to the same analysis. This continues until you find a strategy that should work.

### Step 4a: Are All $P$, $C$, $T$, $S$ Requirements Met?

The first question is whether the approach meets all performance, cost, time, and scope requirements. In other words, will it do the job? Naturally, this is a judgment call, but experience can usually guide you to answer the question. However, it may be necessary to do some broad-brush implementation planning before you answer the question definitively. For that reason, when step seven is reached, if the implementation plan is not okay, examine the strategy to determine if it is acceptable, and if not, develop a new one and repeat the process.

### Step 4b: Are Identified Risks Acceptable?

This step is intended to identify any risks that might cause the approach to fail. Some managers think doing a risk analysis is a bad idea because it causes people to begin thinking negatively, and they fear that will create morale problems.

That might be the case if such an analysis is not done correctly. To simply ask what could go wrong and leave it at that would very likely cause people to doubt the viability of the approach. However, I do not let people do a risk analysis in that manner. For any risks that are considered serious, I ask, "What might we do if it happens?" In other words, we must identify contingencies for every risk, if at all possible. By following this approach, risks are being managed, rather than just being identified. Chapter 17 covers how to do this in detail.

### Step 4c: Are consequences acceptable?

By taking any action to solve a problem, peripheral effects may occur. These can be called unintended consequences of the steps taken. These unintended consequences create new problems. The question is, then, can we live with those consequences? If not, then we must consider a different approach to the project.

As an example of unintended consequences, legislation was enacted some years ago in the U.S. to make streets more accessible to handicapped people. The law required that

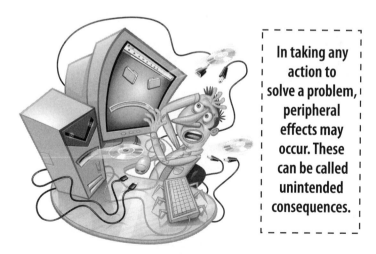

In taking any action to solve a problem, peripheral effects may occur. These can be called unintended consequences.

ramps be placed at street corners, to make it possible to get a wheelchair across the street without having to negotiate difficult curbs.

This solved the problem for wheelchair-bound individuals, but created problems for blind people, who use their canes to search for the intersection by feeling for the curb—which has now been removed! It also makes sidewalks more hazardous for sighted individuals, because sudden drops in pavement level are not always easily seen.

Another example of unintended consequences is the result of having a sale to reduce inventory levels. When the sale ends, some customers perceive the product to be of lower value than it was previous to the sale.

In a project context, we know that projects may have environmental impacts that are undesirable. Or in a product development situation, pursuing "safe" technology may achieve a speedy time-to-market, but result in a competitive disadvantage. In addition, it may cause the organization to fall behind in the development of its technological capability.

As mentioned previously, if such consequences are not acceptable, then a different approach (strategy) for the project should be considered.

### Step 4d: Does it pass a force-field analysis?

Of the four tests that a strategy must pass, the force-field analysis is probably the hardest to quantify. Nevertheless, it is well worth doing.

As Figure 2.2 shows, a force-field analysis looks a little like a risk analysis, but is very different. On the right side of the page are listed forces in the environment that might assist in the implementation of the project, while on the left side are forces that might hinder or resist its implementation.

Notice that these are social forces. They result from the attitudes that people have toward certain approaches. For example, we sometimes hear people say in organizations, "We don't do things that way around here." If a project manager

**F  I  G  U  R  E   2.2**

Force-Field Analysis

is attempting to run a project using an approach that a powerful member of management considers out of line with "how things are done around here," then it is likely that the manager's resistance may cause the approach to fail.

The factor labeled NIH means "not invented here." Sometimes individuals resist a particular approach simply because they did not think of it. Although this may be petty, such resistance can sabotage a project and should not be underestimated.

Once both positive and negative forces have been identified, the method calls for estimating and tallying up the strengths of all forces, with the understanding that the sum of the positive forces must be greater than the sum of the negatives or the approach will not work. The usual approach to measuring the forces is to rate them on a 10-point scale, then multiply by a weighting factor (assuming that they are not all of equal importance), and sum them.

In my opinion, this is an exercise in futility. It appears to give a measurement to something that I believe usually is unmeasurable. For that reason, I do not advocate the practice. Rather, I suggest simply trying to deal with the negative forces.

There are three approaches that can be used to deal with forces identified in the analysis. They are:

1. Strengthen the positive forces so they are definitely stronger than the negatives.
2. Find ways to get around the negatives.
3. Find some way to weaken or eliminate the negatives.

What we find people doing in case after case is choosing option one. They try to overcome the negative forces with stronger positive forces. This is in spite of countless experiences that teach that the harder you try to overcome a negative force, the stronger it becomes! Systems theorists have understood this for years, yet it does not seem to be well understood by most of us. The "push-resist" interaction typifies all conflict and competitive situations, and the stronger one side pushes, the more the other side resists. All you have is escalation.

The most helpful way to deal with forces is to try to neutralize them. Find some way to make them go away. For example, if someone thinks the selected strategy is bad, ask that person, "What would I have to do to convince you that this is a good approach?"

There are two possible responses. The person can tell you to "forget it." You will never be able to convince him/her that the approach is sound. If so, you may have to forget trying to convince the person and decide whether to proceed or choose a different option.

However, I will always ask the person, "Are you sure there is *nothing* I can do? That's pretty heavy." Usually this gets the second response, which is for the person to say, "Well, I suppose if you can do this (they explain what it will take) I would be convinced." The nice thing about this approach is that you now know what it takes to "make the sale." You no longer have to hunt for the selling proposition. If you can do what the person suggests, you are "home free."

## Step 5: Decide Whether the Above Factors Are All Okay

If you have passed each of the four tests, you can consider the selected strategy to be tentatively acceptable. It is still possible that during implementation planning you may find problems with the approach and have to reject it, but this is not highly likely. There is one caution: Very analytical individuals sometimes go into "analysis paralysis" at this step in planning a project. The purpose of these steps is not to identify every single risk or consequence that may exist, but to assess some of the most likely ones. Project managers may have to assert this a number of times with skeptical or negatively oriented members of the proposed project team.

## Step 6. Develop an Implementation Plan

Up to this point, the planning process has answered the broad question of what strategy will be employed to manage the project. Now the strategy must be translated into specific steps to get the job done. These steps will define what is done, by whom, for how long, at what cost, etc. An overriding concern will be deciding how to translate customer needs into solutions. During this stage, a work breakdown structure will be developed, a schedule using CPM or PERT will be

formulated, resources will be allocated, responsibilities assigned, control systems developed, and so on. Chapters 3
through 10 address how this is done.

## Step 7. Check That All Stakeholders Agree with the Plan

A stakeholder is defined as anyone who has a vested interest in the project. This will include suppliers, contributors,
customers, senior management, financial contributors,
sometimes the community, and so on. In the case of contributors, we need to ensure that they can make their contributions when required at the desired level of quality. If the
customer(s) is considered, we want to be sure the work
done will meet his/her needs. If the answer is "no," then we
must examine strategy (step 7a). If strategy is considered
unacceptable at this point, the model routes us back to step
4, where a new strategy is selected, tested, and new planning is done.

　　If only the implementation plan is at fault, the loop
routes back to step 6, meaning that the working plan must be
fixed to the satisfaction of all stakeholders.

## Step 8. Sign off the Project Plan and Set Up a Project Notebook

Stakeholders indicate their approval of the plan by signature.
This also represents their okay for the execution phase to begin. Use a notebook to hold all project documentation.

## Step 9. Execute the Plan

At this point work begins. The detailed implementation plan
will guide the steps during the execution phase. One pitfall that
is sometimes observed in projects is that the plan is not followed during execution of the work. This is especially true
when problems are encountered. It is tempting to forget the

plan and just start trying to correct the problem. Note, however, that steps 10 through 13 are designed to handle problems.

## Step 10. Check Progress

As work is performed, it should be monitored. One of the principal tools for doing this is earned-value analysis, which is discussed in Chapter 13. However, it is important to remember that earned-value analysis can only be used properly if the performance objective is being met. That is, work can only be said to be on target if it meets customer requirements. The fact that what has been done functions correctly according to a technical specification does not mean that the project is on target. The Edsel may have functioned correctly according to its engineering specs, but it was not accepted by the market. If the answer at this step is "no," the model routes into control steps.

## Step 11. Re-Check Definition

This step ensures that we are still trying to solve the correct problem, rather than the wrong one. If the answer is "no," the model routes all the way back to step 2, meaning the project must be totally replanned. This won't happen very often, but must be considered as a possibility.

## Step 12. Strategy Okay?

As in step 7a, it is important to ask whether an implementation difficulty is caused by a defective strategy. If it is, the model routes back to step 4, so another strategy can be selected.

## Step 13. Plan Okay?

If the answer to this question is "no," then we have to change the implementation plan. However, if the answer is "yes," then that means the plan is not being followed. In many cases, the reason will be that insufficient resources have been provided. If not, then they must be forthcoming or the project will have to be planned all over again. Note that resources can be increased through the use of extra people or overtime.

## Step 14. All Work Complete?

This just keeps looping back to the execution step, meaning that during execution we monitor progress, take corrective action when necessary, and so on. Once we are sure all work has been completed, we are ready to do step 15.

## Step 15. Final Lessons-Learned Review

This is an important step in closing out a project. Before the project can be considered complete, a lessons-learned review should be conducted. This review is for the purpose of learning what was done well and what could be improved, so that progress can be made in future projects. See Chapter 11.

## Step 16. Close Out Project

Final reports are written, the project notebook containing all documentation is placed in a central file, and the project is considered complete.

SECTION TWO

# PROJECT PLANNING

# 3

CHAPTER

# General Aspects
# of Project Planning

## AN INTRODUCTION TO PROJECT PLANNING

This chapter will introduce project planning and establish
guidelines for what a formal project plan should contain.

### Project Planning and Customer Needs

As the quality movement emphasizes, the first order of business in today's world must be meeting the needs of customers. If project management is to accomplish this, the customer
must be identified and his/her needs defined.

This is often easier said than done. First of all, we must
identify just who the customer is in the first place. In customer-funded projects, the answer is clear. But in product development projects, it is not. We also sometimes consider group
leaders to be customers for software system-development
projects, when it might be more appropriate to consider their

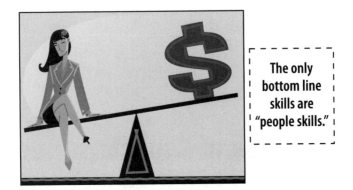

The only bottom line skills are "people skills."

direct reports the real customers, because they are the people who will ultimately use the system. I have been told more than once about systems that were turned over to users who complained that the system did not meet their needs.

The information systems (IS) person is bewildered. "We talked to your boss," she says. "She told us this was what you needed."

To which the user replies, "Why did you talk to her? She doesn't know what we do!"

This is often true. Group leaders can be so busy that they do not really know what their people do anymore. So you really need to talk to that user to get a clear understanding of his needs.

This, too, can be a significant problem. Often, customers have an "itch" that they want "scratched." That is the best definition they can offer. They want the product to be "easy to use." They want "convenience." These basic "itches" must be translated into product or service features. We can say that solutions are developed for customer needs.

One important point is that we want to do more than the bare minimum necessary to satisfy customer needs—we want to actually delight the customer. To do so requires that you actually exceed his expectations. If you can do this, you can build customer loyalty and, in a competitive situation, defend against competition.

One approach used to translate customer needs into product or service features is quality function deployment (QFD). It is outside the scope of this book to cover QFD in depth, but a short overview will be given. For those readers interested in learning more, consult *The QFD Handbook* (ReVelle, Moran, and Cox, 1998).

Figure 3.1 depicts an example of a QFD matrix, stripped down to its bare essentials. Down the left side is a list of customer requirements. Across the top are some of the features of the product (in this case, a hotel) that are expected to satisfy those customer requirements. In those cells containing a plus

**F I G U R E   3.1**

QFD Matrix for a Hotel

| + =CORRELATION<br>* =STRONG CORRELATION<br>0 =NO CORRELATION | Individual Temp. Control | Lighting | Furnishings | Cable TV | Room Service Menu | Courteous Staff | Airport Courtesy Van | Rank |
|---|---|---|---|---|---|---|---|---|
| Comfort | * | + | * | 0 | * | 0 | + | 2 |
| Service | 0 | 0 | 0 | 0 | * | * | * | 3 |
| Price for Value | * | * | * | * | * | * | * | 5 |
| Security | 0 | 0 | 0 | 0 | 0 | 0 | 0 | 1 |
| Able to Read or Work Comfortably | 0 | * | * | 0 | 0 | 0 | 0 | 4 |
| Access to Telephone / Computer | 0 | 0 | + | 0 | 0 | 0 | 0 | 6 |
| Convenience | 0 | 0 | 0 | 0 | * | 0 | * | 7 |
| In-Hotel Entertainment | 0 | 0 | 0 | * | + | 0 | 0 | 8 |

sign (+), there is a positive correlation between the feature and the requirement. Where an asterisk (*) is shown, the correlation is still positive and very strong. A zero means no correlation. Although there can be negative correlations, none are shown in this example.

Finally, on the right side of the matrix is a ranking of the customer's requirements, with number one being most important. This ranking is obtained through customer surveys, interviews, etc.

The idea is to give the customer those features that have positive correlations with requirements that rank highly and to avoid providing those features that have no correlations or that correlate only with very lowly ranked features. As you can see for the hotel matrix, the team that initially set up this matrix has missed the fact that security is the most important customer requirement. They need to go back to the drawing board.

## THE PROJECT NOTEBOOK

Steps 1 through 8 of the model for managing projects help you develop and ultimately sign off. This plan is usually housed in a loose-leaf notebook (or notebooks, in the case of very large projects). As the project is executed, progress reports, correspondence, quotations, revisions, and so on will be placed in the notebook, so that when the job is finally closed out, the notebook provides a complete "track record" of the job from start to finish. This notebook is then placed in a central file so that anyone can refer to it as an aid in planning subsequent projects.

Following are the items that should be part of every project plan and should be in the notebook when it is first set up:

- ◆ A problem statement.
- ◆ Project mission statement (formal for large projects; informal for smaller ones). See Chapter 5 for developing a formal mission statement.

- Project strategy, together with a SWOT analysis supporting it.
- Project objectives.
- Documentation of QFD analysis or other means of translating customer needs into solutions.
- Statement of project scope.
- Contractual requirements: a list of all deliverables, including reports, hardware, software, and so on.
- End-item specifications to be met: including building codes, government regulations, etc.
- Work breakdown structure.
- Schedules: both milestone and working schedules should be provided.
- Required resources, including people, equipment, materials, and facilities. These must be specified in conjunction with the schedule. Loading diagrams are helpful.
- Control system.
- Major contributors: Use a linear responsibility chart for this.
- Risk analysis with contingencies when available.
- Statements of work (SOW)—this is optional.

## Sign Off of the Plan

Once the plan has been prepared, it should be submitted to stakeholders for their signatures.

- A contributor's signature indicates that individual is committed to her contribution, agrees with the scope of work to be done, accepts the specs as valid, etc., It is not considered a guarantee, as no one has 20/20 foresight or complete control over their time.

However, it is considered a commitment, a promise to do everything within reason to meet project objectives.

♦ The customer's signature indicates that he agrees with what the project will accomplish and that it will meet his needs.

♦ A financial officer's signature indicates her agreement that the project can be funded at the rate indicated over time.

The plan should be signed in a project plan review meeting, not by mail!

People should be encouraged to "shoot holes in the plan" during the review meeting, rather than waiting until problems develop later.

I suggest requiring signatures only by stakeholders who are taking responsibility for some aspect of the project, but not for people with no responsibility for any aspect of the project. This eliminates the situation in which 27 signatures are required to get anything done, which sets up tremendous organization inertia.

## Changing the Plan

It would be nice to think that a plan, once developed, would never change. However, that is unrealistic. Unforeseen problems are almost certain to arise. The important thing is to make changes in an orderly way, following a standard change-control procedure. Without exercising change control, the project may wind up over budget, behind schedule, and hopelessly inadequate, with no warning until it is too late.

> The first rule of planning is to be prepared to replan!

Following are some guidelines that should be helpful.

◆ Make changes only when a significant deviation occurs. A significant change will usually be specified in terms of percent tolerances relative to the original targets.

◆ Exercise change control to protect everyone from the effects of scope creep.

◆ Document causes of changes for reference in planning future projects.

## Definition of Planning

When I first started teaching project management, I consulted a number of books on planning to learn more about how it is supposed to be done. What I found is that many books on planning seem to assume that readers already know how to do it, so the texts are descriptive rather than prescriptive. Furthermore, I struggled with the definition of planning until I realized one day that planning requires answering the following questions:

◆ What must be done?

◆ How should it be done?

◆ Who will do it?

◆ By when must it be done?

◆ How much will it cost?

◆ How good does it have to be?

## Suggestions for Effective Planning

I have found that not many people know how to conduct a planning session. This is understandable, as there are very few schools that teach planning, and few companies provide guidance or training in the subject. I hope the following

Don't plan in more detail than you can manage.

suggestions will be helpful, as they are based on my 40 years experience in planning projects.

1. Plan to plan. It is always difficult to get people together to develop a plan. The planning session itself should be planned or it may turn into the type of totally disorganized meeting that plagues many organizations.

2. The people who must implement a plan should participate in preparing it.

3. The first rule of planning is to be prepared to replan. Unexpected obstacles will undoubtedly crop up.

4. Because unexpected obstacles will crop up, always conduct a risk analysis to anticipate the most likely ones. Develop a Plan B just in case Plan A doesn't work. Why not just use Plan B in the first place? Because Plan A is better, but has a few weaknesses.

Plan B has weaknesses also, but its weaknesses must be different than those in Plan A, or there is no use in considering it a backup.

5. Begin with a definition of the purpose of accomplishing whatever is to be done. Develop a problem statement. All actions in an organization should be taken to achieve a result, which is another way of saying, "solve a problem." If you skip this step, you may find yourself developing the right solution to the wrong problem.

6. Use the work breakdown structure to divide the work into smaller "chunks" with accurate estimates developed for duration, cost, and resource requirements.

## Phased Planning

When a project spans a long period of time, or when considerable uncertainty exists about the approach to take (as in some research projects), it is impossible to plan long-term activities in much detail. The approach is to plan near-term work in detail, and as each phase is completed, to plan the next phase in detail. Although this is a valid approach, the politics of your organization may prohibit its application.

# 4

C H A P T E R

# Planning: Developing the Project Mission, Vision, Goals, and Objectives

## DECIDING WHAT MUST BE DONE: DEFINING YOUR MISSION, VISION, GOALS, AND OBJECTIVES

I have already pointed out in an earlier chapter that projects do not fail at the end; they often fail at the beginning. We are now moving to step 2 of the Lewis Method (see Figure 4.1), and this is where it can all go wrong. There are two fairly common reasons why this is true. One is that people are convinced that they know what is supposed to be done, so they don't think there is any reason to take time clarifying problem, mission, and vision.

The second reason is a communications problem. The project manager communicates the mission to the team and thinks they all understand, when in fact, they don't.

There are many possible causes for the first instance, in which people think they understand, but don't. One is that they are not good at defining problems. They mistake symptoms

**F I G U R E  4.1**

Step 2 of The Lewis Method

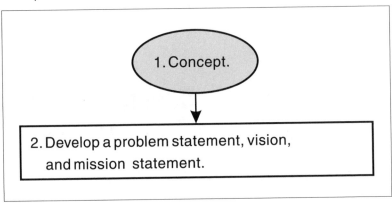

for causes, or accept the first definition that someone offers without questioning whether it is valid. As an example, if I say, "I have a headache," I have just expressed a symptom. I do not know what the problem is. It could be stress, something I ate, or a brain tumor. One thing is certain: I could take painkillers and make the headache go away, but if I have a brain tumor, the pain will return. By taking a painkiller, I would have treated the symptom without addressing the underlying cause of the pain.

Or suppose the electrically operated window in my car won't go down. The dealer says the motor is burned out and replaces it. A few weeks later, the window won't go down again. The dealer says the motor is burned up. It seems suspicious, doesn't it, that two motors burned up? I challenge the dealer to see if there is a reason why the motor has burned up. It turns out that my voltage regulator is defective and my alternator voltage is running too high. Until the regulator problem is corrected, the motor will continue to burn up. Determining that the regulator is the cause of the problem is called identifying the root cause.

In the second instance, the communication problem is often the result of the false consensus effect, which Jerry Harvey (Harvey, 1988) calls the Abilene Paradox. Harvey wrote a story that illustrates how this effect gets groups into trouble. Briefly, a family is sitting around a farmhouse one Sunday morning in 100-degree heat. They have nothing to do, and when someone asks, "What would you like to do to-day?," another person suggests that they drive to Abilene and have lunch at the cafeteria.

Soon they are on their way, in an old car with no air conditioning, and it is about 90 miles to Abilene. By the time they get there, they are pretty grungy because of the heat. They have lunch, which turns out to be mediocre, then walk around Abilene for awhile. It turns out there is nothing to do in Abilene, so they are bored again. They get back into the car and head home.

When they get home, they park the car and start toward the house.

"Boy, that was a waste of time," someone says. "Can you believe that we just drove 180 miles for that meal?"

"I thought you wanted to go," Pa says.

"No, I just went because the rest of you wanted to go," the person replies.

They look at each other in surprise. Then they take a poll. They find that no one wanted to go to Abilene. Each person believed that all the others wanted to go, and complied, not wanting to be the sole dissenter.

Now there is a very subtle point here. This sounds like a failure to manage agreement. It is not! It is a failure to manage *disagreement*. This happens because there is a cultural belief that if nobody dissents, each person must be in agreement with the others—or, to put it another way, silence means consent. In addition, in many cultures, if a person does dissent, the rest of the team or group see the individual as being difficult, so we learn not to disagree when we think we are in the minority on an issue.

> Without a shared
> understanding of
> the problem, vision,
> and mission of the
> team, you cannot
> possibly be
> successful.

For this reason, a project manager must be very careful to ensure that there truly is a shared understanding and agreement with the project mission. This requires taking specific steps to ensure such consensus, which will be explained later in this chapter.

## What Is the Difference between Mission and Vision?

I said earlier that projects begin as someone's concept. That individual has an idea that something is needed or would be nice to have—the first step in bringing about something new. Whether or not the person could describe a clear picture of what he has in mind, it is true that the concept could be called an image in his head. For example, before airplanes and helicopters were invented, people dreamed of being able to fly using some kind of mechanical device. They visualized being able to do this—thus the word vision.

Quite simply, the genesis of any project is a vision. The mission of the project is to bring about a result that is in line with the person's vision. Thus, the mission of a project is always to achieve the vision. The problem is, if the vision is cloudy or vague, then the result will be as well. It is also true that if all members of the project team don't understand the vision—even when it is a clear one—then the result will be confusion and wasted effort.

For that reason, a project manager's first responsibility is to ensure that the sponsor's vision for the project is clear and shared by all members of the team. That vision—if it evolves through the life of the project—must be recommunicated to everyone. Otherwise, at the end of the project, there will be a lot of dissatisfied people.

In some cases, a vision is a dream that is simply based on desire—a felt need. It would be nice to send a person to the moon to see what is actually up there. That is one example.

In other cases, a problem exists that must be solved. We want to fly because it takes forever to go a long distance using ground transportation. The problem leads someone to visualize being able to fly using some kind of mechanical device and the mission then becomes to develop such a device.

Here again, people seem to have difficulty defining problems, so I want to focus on that aspect of project management now. Remember, a project can be thought of as a problem scheduled for solution.

## Defining the Problem

Most teams are not given a problem statement by the project sponsor. They are given a mission statement. "Your assignment," says the sponsor, "is to go forth and conquer." The thing

**problem:** A gap between where you are and where you want to be, that is confronted by obstacles that prevent easy movement to close the gap.

is, the sponsor has identified a problem and has decided that it can be solved by having the team go forth and conquer. If she has misdefined the problem, however, then achieving the mission will not solve the problem at all.

For that reason, a team must begin by gaining a clear understanding of the problem to be solved before starting to polish the mission statement. Furthermore, the only good way to achieve a shared understanding of the problem is through participation in developing a formal statement of the problem.

Yes, I know this sounds like overkill. You, as project manager, should not have to go through this laborious process. You should just be able to get the team together, explain the problem to them, and then they can go forth and conquer.

Unfortunately, it doesn't work that way.

Project managers are probably more frequent victims of the Abilene Paradox than anyone else on earth. The only way around this problem is to work with the group in such a way that every member has an opportunity to test his or her understanding of what is going on. This process will be described later in this chapter.

## Importance of the Mission Statement

As is true for an organization as a whole, a mission statement for a project gives it a sense of purpose and direction. It is a broad statement, from which all subsequent planning can proceed. It can be developed using a very formal procedure that I present later in this chapter, or it can be more informally stated.

> A mission statement provides the basis for which goals and objectives can be set and for making decisions, taking actions, hiring employees, etc.

The mission statement should be used to set goals and objectives, to make decisions, and to determine what goods and services the organization should provide, whether it be a project group or the overall company.

## Developing the Mission Statement

A project is always conducted to achieve some purpose, solve a problem, or meet a need for the organization. Unless the problem, need, or purpose is clearly understood, then the mission itself cannot be clear. A later chapter introduces a technique for solving problems that is called the "Five Whys." Any time something is supposed to be done, if you ask the question, "Why?" five times, you will arrive at the root purpose of performing the activity.

For example, suppose someone suggests holding a meeting. By asking, "Why?" several times, you get the following:

"Why should we have this meeting?"

"Because people in the project team need information on some changes we are going to make."

"Why do they need this information?"

"Because they may do their jobs incorrectly without the information."

"Then the purpose of the meeting is to give people information that they need to prevent them from doing their jobs wrong?"

"Right!"

In this case, we only had to ask, "Why?" twice to arrive at the true purpose of having the meeting. In other cases, it may be necessary to go the full distance, but you almost never have to ask, "Why?" more than five times.

Note also that the real issue concerning the word "mission" is to identify the purpose of the project. This is, to me, the heart of the matter. If you can't state the purpose of a project, then something is wrong. You may, in fact, be undertaking a project that shouldn't be done.

Consider now the following example. Suppose I have just taken a job in a distant city. I plan to move there, and the first thing I realize is that I have no place to live. This is a problem to be solved or a need to be met. I might say, then, that my mission is to find a place to live.

True, but will just any place do? I could live under a bridge. There are homeless people who do that. Or I could live at the YMCA. Some people do. But as I think about it, neither of these will do. I have in mind some specific requirements for the kind of place where I want to live. So I make a list of the characteristics or requirements that this place must have. Figure 4.2 shows one way to do this.

I also no doubt have an idea in mind of roughly what the place should look like. I might prefer modern architecture, more traditional, or something very old. I might want a one- or two-story house. Collectively, the must, want, nice-to-have, and my mental image of the appearance of the house constitute a vision of the place I am looking for. I may not find exactly what I am looking for, or I might find something that I like better than my original concept, but that concept is the starting point. Without this you can flounder hopelessly.

In addition, if you are hunting for a place to live with a family or significant other, you have an entirely different problem than if you are doing it alone. When you compare your lists of musts, wants, and nice-to-haves, you find that they are not the same. Your must-have features are not even on his or her list! And vice-versa. Naturally, until you can make the major details of these two lists match, you will never be able to agree on a selection. This is called achieving a shared vision, and is what every project manager must achieve in the project team, or chaos will result. In addition, I suggest that for projects, you burn the list of nice-to-haves. The 80/20 principle says that 80 percent of our time will be spent on 20 percent of project requirements. That means the nice-to-haves. We should spend 80 percent on the must-have components, of course, so the safe thing to do is be absolutely unmerciful in tossing out that nice-to-have list. The road to project hell is paved with that list.

Chevron Showing Requirements

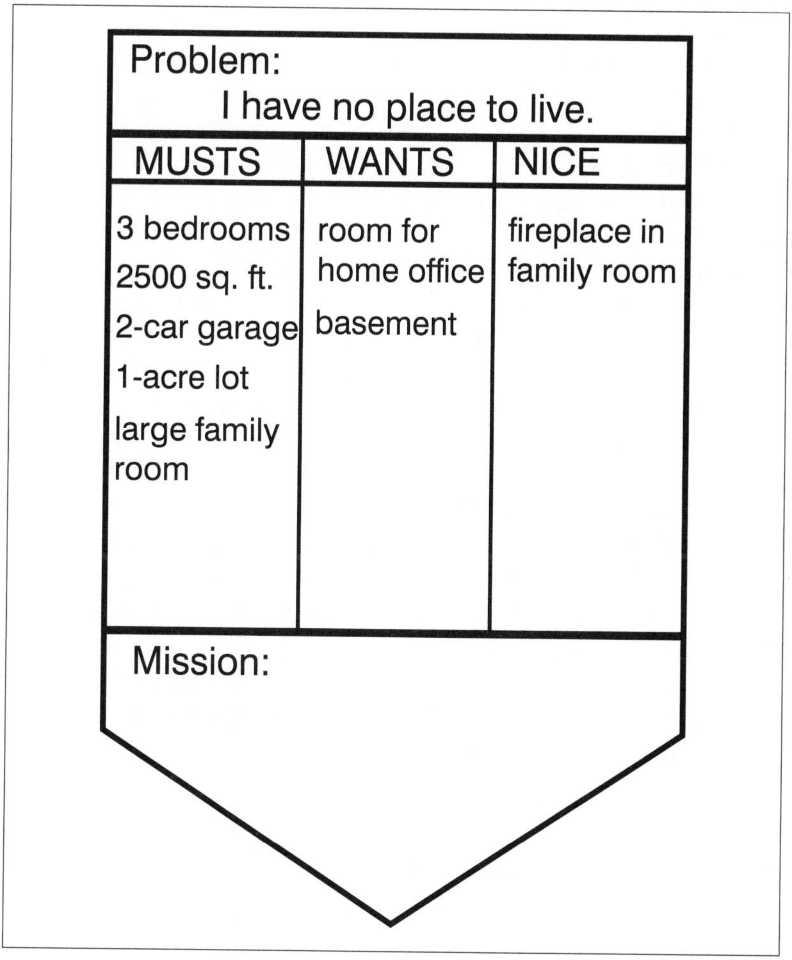

| Problem: I have no place to live. | | |
|---|---|---|
| MUSTS | WANTS | NICE |
| 3 bedrooms 2500 sq. ft. 2-car garage 1-acre lot large family room | room for home office basement | fireplace in family room |

Mission:

Koch (1998) suggests that the way to do this is to set for the team an almost impossible deadline. That way, they don't have time to fool with the nice-to-haves. I know of one team that found themselves faced with an impossible deadline, which they met, and I can assure you that they did not include any nice-to-have features in the product! I don't think Koch's suggestion should literally be practiced, as I think it is too severe, but there is merit in the intent of the recommendation.

Now, if we combine the statement of need with the vision, we arrive at the mission: My mission is to find a place to live that conforms to my vision. This is shown in Figure 4.3.

Note that if I find a place to live that conforms to the vision, I will have met my need or solved my problem. Otherwise, I have not. Note also that many people will say, "My problem is to find a place to live." It is because we use the word problem in so many ways that we become confused about the meaning of the word. To simplify, confining yourself to the following meaning will help you clarify mission and vision: A problem is a gap between where you are and where you want to be, that is confronted by obstacles that prevent easy movement to close the gap.

It is the obstacles that actually create the problem. If you had no obstacles, you would have no problem. As an example, if I am at one end of a long hallway and I want to be at the other end, and all I have to do is walk to the other end, then I have no problem, just a goal. On the other hand, if I cannot walk, or if someone has placed a big alligator in the hall and he is going to bite my leg off as I try to go by, then I have a problem. Solving problems always involves overcoming obstacles.

### The Formal Mission Statement

A mission statement should answer two questions:

1. What are we going to do?
2. For whom are we going to do it?

Some people suggest that a third question be answered: How do we go about it? To me, this is asking that the team decide on strategy at the same time they are trying to decide

F I G U R E  **4.3**

Chevron Showing Mission, Vision, Problem

| Problem: I have no place to live. | | |
|---|---|---|
| **MUSTS** | **WANTS** | **NICE** |
| 3 bedrooms 2500 sq. ft. 2-car garage 1-acre lot large family room | room for home office basement | fireplace in family room |

Mission:
To find a place that meets all musts and as many of the others as possible.

on their mission. I believe this question should be reserved for step 3 in my project management method.

Note that, in the case of finding a place to live, it is not necessary to answer the second question, since I am the "for whom." In most cases, however, it is important to identify who the customer is.

As an aid to answering these questions, it is useful for the team to work through the process outlined in Figure 4.4.

As you can see, the process generates active involvement in developing a working mission statement, so that the Abilene Paradox is avoided. By following this approach, you will find in step 2 that some individuals may not have a clear understanding of the team's mission. This procedure should get everyone on board with a common understanding.

If you are working on a very important, long-duration project, you might also want to take your team through the steps in Table 4.1. By doing so, you will collectively address issues that the team must deal with over the long run, and you will also achieve a greater shared understanding of the team's situation than might be possible through any other means.

## F I G U R E  4.4

### Steps in Writing a Mission Statement

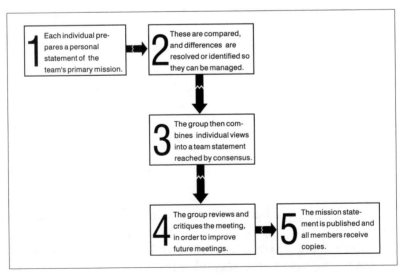

## T A B L E  4.1

### Developing a Mission Statement

| STEP TO FOLLOW | COMMENTS |
| --- | --- |
| 1. List all of the team's *stakeholders*. | A stakeholder is *anyone* who has a vested interest in what the team is doing—customers, suppliers, senior management, and so on. |
| 2. Highlight the team's *customers* from within the list of stakeholders just generated. | A customer is a *user* of the team's output. |
| 3. Check the three most important stakeholders—at least one of them should be the team's major customer. | This step will generate much discussion and debate. Do not cut it off prematurely. |
| 4. Make a list of those things your three most important stakeholders want from the team. | The objective is to ensure that you satisfy the customer's **needs!** Don't *guess*—find out! |
| 5. When the team has finished its job, how will members know they were successful? List those *criteria for success* that will be used to judge the team's performance. | Criteria can be hard or soft. Budgets, schedule, and quality might be measured as hard. Learning, satisfaction, and other criteria are soft. They can be as important as the hard measures. |
| 6. Determine what critical events might occur in the future that could affect the team's success either positively or negatively. | Examples include a merger, hostile takeover, recession, technology breakthrough, and population change. |
| 7. Write the mission and purpose statement. | Follow the steps in the model presented above. |

Once you have written your mission statement, make sure everyone has a copy of it and that everyone uses it! How? Before taking every step, you should ask how to take that step in such a way that it supports achieving your mission. These actions include solving problems, making decisions, recruiting team members, and so on. By following this procedure, the mission statement becomes operational. Otherwise, you probably will have the mission-statement-in-the-drawer effect: A statement was written, then filed neatly in someone's desk drawer and forgotten.

## Guidelines for Developing Good Objectives

Once the project mission is written, and before detailed planning can be carried out, specific objectives should be established.

Those objectives should be written! There are at least three reasons for this.

First, the discipline of writing your objectives will force you to clarify them in your own mind. I have found that when I start to write out my objectives, I am sometimes not too clear on them myself. Second, if they are in writing, everyone in the team has access to them and can refer to them periodically. Third, being able to refer to them in written form

| Objectives may be to: |
| --- |
| ◆ Develop expertise in some area |
| ◆ Become competitive |
| ◆ Improve productivity |
| ◆ Improve quality |
| ◆ Reduce costs |
| ◆ Modify an existing facility |
| ◆ Develop a new sales strategy |
| ◆ Develop a new product |

should help members of the team resolve differences of opinion about what they are supposed to do. You can achieve clearly defined objectives by meeting the following conditions:

- They should be **specific**—that is, not fuzzy, vague statements, such as "I want to be the best." What does that mean?

- They should be **realistic.** That is, they should be objectives that contribute to achieving the team's overall purpose.

- They should be **measurable** when possible. This can be very difficult to achieve. How can you measure performance improvement of knowledge workers, for example? See the following section for ideas on units of measurement for quantifying targets.

- They should **align** with the strategic objectives of the organization.

- They should be stated in terms of *deliverable items,* if possible. Deliverable items may be assessment reports, written recommendations, etc.

- They must be **comprehensible**—that is, *understandable*—stated in such a way that other people will know what you are trying to achieve. Have you ever left a meeting and wondered what everyone was supposed to do? Chances are the objectives were not stated clearly or in understandable language.

- They should be **realistic**—something that we should be doing. If the objective is not in line with the overall project mission, then it should be challenged.

- They should be **time limited** if possible. Remember this rule when setting performance-improvement objectives for employees: If such targets are not time limited, they will never happen!

**Objectives
should be
attainable!**

- ◆ Objectives should be **attainable.** That means that
  they should be both realistic and achievable. When
  appropriate, objectives should be assigned a risk
  factor so others in the organization will be aware of
  such risk.

- ◆ They should also specify a **single** end result. When
  multiple objectives are combined into one statement,
  it becomes difficult to sort out what is being said.

## A POINT ABOUT DEFINITIONS

People tend to confuse tasks and objectives. An objective is a
desired end state. You are presently at point A and want to
get to point B. Tasks are those actions that you take to arrive
at the final destination. Determining which tasks or actions
you must take to reach an objective is part of problem solving
and/or planning. Note that no statement of objective should
specify how it will be achieved, as this may lock you into a

method that is not the best to pursue. Keep the problem-solving process separate from setting objectives.

## ESTABLISHING PRIORITIES

In a project, many objectives will be sequenced strictly by logical considerations. However, others may have priorities that are a function of other important factors. Such importance may be determined by need, economics, or social desirability. Exercise care that less important objectives do not sidetrack progress

> Doing the right things is more important than doing things right.
> — Peter Drucker

toward more important ones. Objectives that must be accomplished before some other target can be reached are called feeder objectives. To prioritize your objectives, it may be enough to simply group them into categories A, B, and C with "A" being most important, etc. On the other hand, you may actually need to rank-order your list. If you try to rank more than 10 objectives, the task is very difficult. To make the job easier, you may want to use the method of paired-comparisons.

Suppose I have four objectives that I want to rank-order. They are listed below:

1. Replace roof on house.
2. Enter the MBA program at local college.
3. Learn to play golf.
4. Take a trip to Europe.

Rather than trying to rank these by "brute force," I compare all possible pairs, and put an asterisk beside the objective

in each pair that is most important to me. The number pairs
are listed following:

1✓   2
1✓   3
1✓   4
2✓   3
2    4✓
3    4✓

As you can see, objective one is more important, with
three votes, than objective four, with two votes, than objective two, and objective three.

## THE PRIORITY MATRIX

Because there are so many comparisons to make for a large
number of objectives, the method of paired-comparisons can
be greatly simplified using a priority matrix like the one
shown in Figure 4.5. Consider six alternatives, which must be
ranked. The matrix makes the comparison very straightforward. Following are the objectives to be ranked:

1. Install new grinder.

2. Develop standard test procedure for product X.

3. Recruit person for position Y.

4. Do performance appraisal for Charlie.

5. Find second source for part Z.

6. Review standards document for quality department.

To enter data into the matrix, work across the rows. We
begin with objective one, which is to install a new grinder.
Working across row one, we ask if objective one is more important than objective two. It is, so we insert a 1 into row one,
column two. Next, is objective one more important than objective three? It is not, so we place a zero in row one, column

**F I G U R E  4.5**

Priority Matrix

| | 1 | 2 | 3 | 4 | 5 | 6 | Total | Rank |
|---|---|---|---|---|---|---|---|---|
| 1 | | 1 | 0 | 0 | 1 | 1 | 3 | 3 |
| 2 | 0 | | 0 | 0 | 0 | 0 | 0 | 6 |
| 3 | 1 | 1 | | 0 | 1 | 1 | 4 | 2 |
| 4 | 1 | 1 | 1 | | 1 | 1 | 5 | 1 |
| 5 | 0 | 1 | 0 | 0 | | 1 | 2 | 4 |
| 6 | 0 | 1 | 0 | 0 | 0 | | 1 | 5 |

The vertical axis is more
important than the horizontal axis.

three. We continue in this way until all cells have been filled in across row one.

In row two, the first question would be if objective two is more important than objective one, but we answered that question when we worked across row one, so whatever was placed in row one, column two, will be the reverse (or inverse) now. In fact, you can fill in column one below the diagonal with the inverse of what you placed in row one above the diagonal. In this way, you only fill in the rows above the diagonal, then fill in the columns below the diagonal with the inverse of the corresponding row.

Once you total the rows, the row with the highest total will be ranked one, next-highest will be two, and so on. If you have a tie between two rows, simply examine the matrix to see what has already been said about those two objectives.

For example, if rows one and three had tied in this matrix, you would examine row one and ask if objective one is more important than objective three. The answer is "no," so objective three would be one rank higher than objective one.

An extension of this method is the analytical hierarchy. A number of software packages can help you perform complex paired-comparisons. One of the best that I know is Expert Choice. If you do a Google® search for this product, you should find a supplier on the Web.

# 5
CHAPTER

# Planning Project Strategy

## PLANNING PROJECT STRATEGY AND STRATEGIC PLANNING

Strategic planning is an attempt to define where an organization would like to be several years in the future. Planning project strategy tries to figure out the best way to achieve a project mission. Strategic planning is the responsibility of senior managers, while planning project strategy is the job of the project manager and key team members.

### We Need a Good Game Plan!

The word *strategy* was originally a military term. The *Oxford English Dictionary*, considered to be the authoritative source of definitions, offers the following:

> *strategy:* the art of projecting and directing the larger military movements and operations of a campaign. The mode of executing tactics.

┌ ─ ─ ─ ─ ─ ─ ─ ─ ─ ─ ─ ─ ┐
¦   **Divide and Conquer**   ¦
└ ─ ─ ─ ─ ─ ─ ─ ─ ─ ─ ─ ─ ┘

*tactics:* the art of handling forces in battle or in the immediate presence of the enemy.

In colloquial terminology, we sometimes call strategy a "game plan," an overall approach to achieve our major objectives. The important point here is that strategy can only be decided upon after an organization's mission and objectives have been determined. All planning is done to meet objectives, and strategy is only the broad outline of the plan.

One example of military strategy is "divide and conquer." In business, we have JIT, concurrent or simultaneous engineering, and self-directed work teams as ways of achieving business objectives. Another example is that many organizations have decided to reduce their number of employees and to contract out work previously done by those employees. By doing so, they avoid the problem of seasonal downturns in the economy that might force them to lay off excess employees, only to have to rehire them when the economy bounces back. Another example of strategy was related to me by a friend who is a military historian. During World War II,

it was imperative that ships and planes be built at an accelerated rate, so manufacturers devised a number of approaches
that would speed up the process. One of these manufacturers, Avondale Shipyards, devised a new way of building
ships. For centuries, shipbuilders have followed a basic approach, which is to build the ship in the position that it ultimately occupies when placed in the water. That is, the keel is
on the ground and the decks are above. Avondale discovered
that it was far easier to weld steel when the ship was upside
down. In its normal position, welding in the keel area required welders to stand on their heads. By building the ship
upside down, they could stand upright. Naturally, they had
to devise a way to turn the ship over once the assembly was
complete up to the decks, and they did. This strategy was so
much more efficient than traditional approaches that Avondale created a significant competitive advantage over shipyards that employed the old method. See Figure 5.1.

To emphasize the importance of these building strategies, Liberty ships were being built at the rate of one every 10
to 12 days. They were put to sea with the painters on board,

**F I G U R E  5.1**

Building Ships Upside Down

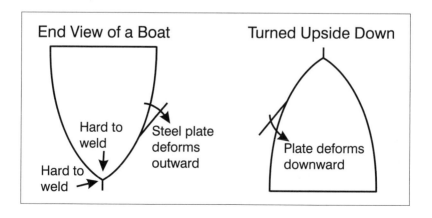

End View of a Boat                Turned Upside Down

Hard to weld
Hard to weld
Steel plate deforms outward
Plate deforms downward

and painted on the way across the Atlantic. And B-24 bomb-
ers were being built at the rate of one every 55 minutes at the
height of the war! They had pilots waiting to test-fly them as
soon as they came off the assembly line. In developing project strategy, the project team must answer two fundamental
questions:

- What are we going to do?
- How are we going to do it?

In the model for managing projects presented in Chapter 2, the first major step is to define the problem to be
solved. That is, we must understand what the project is intended to do for the organization and the end user. Because
the need to clearly define the problem is stressed in that
chapter, it will not be emphasized here.

Once you know what the project is supposed to achieve
(problem, mission, and vision are clear), then you can develop a strategy. The strategy planning phase must be a distinct part of the process, as shown in steps 3 and 4.
Implementation planning must be deferred until a clear strategy has been devised. Timing is very important. If strategy
planning is done too soon, it may be so vague (because of
lack of sufficient definition) as to be useless. If it is too late,
decisions may have been made already that will limit possible alternatives. To keep the overall model simple, strategy
planning is shown as steps 3 and 4. These steps, however,
consist of a number of activities, as shown in Figure 5.2.

## The Strategy Planning Model

The activities in the strategy planning model are not in any
particular sequence. In fact, they are to some degree interac-
tive, so that the information derived from one analysis might
require going back to another step and digging out more information. Two of the components in the strategy planning
model are contained in the model for developing a mission

Activities Involved in Planning Strategy

**The Database**

Past performance
Current situation
Forecasts

**Evaluation of:**

Organization's
Strengths
Weaknesses
Environmental
Opportunities
Threats

**Expectations of Major
Outside Interests**

Local community
Society
Customers
Suppliers
Stakeholders
Creditors

**Expectations of Major
Inside Interests**

Senior managers
Middle managers
Hourly workers
Team members
Staff

Implementation
Plan

Strategic Plan

Mission, Goals
Objectives

statement, presented in Chapter 4. These are the identification of the expectations of major inside and outside interests, called stakeholders, in the mission-development model. This means that, if a mission statement has been developed in accordance with the model, stakeholder expectations have already been identified. Also, for a project team, some of those stakeholders listed in the strategy planning model may be relevant while others may not. However, one should be careful not to dismiss a party as irrelevant without verifying whether that conclusion is correct. Stakeholders are identified by whether the project may impact them in some way or whether they may have an impact on the project. If either is true, they should be considered important to the analysis.

Conducting the database analysis is limited in some organizations by a lack of good historical data. In that case, the analysis depends on the memories of individuals, and is subject to all of the biases and inaccuracies to which human beings are prone. Those limitations should be noted in making use of remembered data. Analysis of the current situation should be easier, assuming that the project team members have access to vital information on the business, its competitors, and so on. Forecasts are based on environmental scanning. They should include examination of technological developments, economic trends, pending government regulations, social trends, and so on. Naturally, forecasting is very difficult, and is limited by what information is available about competitors and other key entities. Finally, we have the evaluation of environment and company for some specific variables. This evaluation is generally called a SWOT analysis. It prescribes that the team examine the company's strengths and weaknesses as well as the opportunities and threats presented by the environment.

These factors are clearly not independent. For example, forecasting is based on evaluations of the external environment and understanding the expectations of stakeholders. The current situation is also influenced by the environment

and expectations of stakeholders. For that reason, the model
is drawn to indicate that interdependence.

## CONDUCTING THE ANALYSES

### Environmental Factors

The major environmental factors that may affect a project are
economic, technological, government or legal, geographic
(including weather or terrain), and social. The economic variable can affect a project in many ways. During a recession
companies tend to run "leaner" than in more prosperous
times, making resources scarcer and conflicts among projects
almost inevitable. When the project spans national borders,
currency fluctuations can be a significant factor. In addition,
the economy in both the host country and home country will
be considerations. For those projects that span long time
frames, will inflation affect the project and, if so, what parts?

Technological changes can be the most difficult to forecast and deal with. In one of my own projects, for example,
we wanted to design a new 1,000-watt linear amplifier with
totally solid-state devices (no vacuum tubes). However, a feasibility study showed that current devices were not capable
of meeting all of the technical requirements, so a conventional vacuum-tube design had to be implemented.
E. F. Schumacher (1989) has observed that westerners are inclined to execute all projects with the highest technology
available, when that might not be the best approach for projects in developing nations. He suggests that employing the
right level of technology is important, if the project is to be
judged a success. Projects are increasingly affected by government regulations and legal issues. Product liability suits
in the United States have grown to such an extent that companies are very cautious in their handling of new products,
construction, and so on. No one wants to make sports helmets,

for example, because of the possibility of being sued if a player is injured. Environmental regulations have forced many businesses to change their way of running projects. At the NASA test facility near Las Cruces, NM, for example, a test engineer told me that they once tested rocket components with minimal concern for the effluents. However, because of population growth near the test facility, they have had to take measures to contain toxic gases, so that no danger is posed to nearby residents. Geographic factors certainly play a part in how some projects are run. Many companies are now global, and co-location of project participants is impossible. Fortunately, with modern communications technology, they are able to achieve what is called virtual co-location, whereby members of the team "meet" as often as necessary through teleconferencing. Naturally, geography also affects strategy in construction projects in terms of terrain, material resources available, and so on. The other influence is human resource availability. I once saw the construction of a large Shell refinery in Bintulu, Sarawak. Ten years before, Bintulu was a small fishing village of about 6,000. At the time I visited, almost 60,000 people lived there—naturally, most of them were imported.

It may be, of course, that key members of a project team will not want to spend long periods in very inhospitable locations, so this may require the recruitment and training of local personnel for the duration of the job.

Social factors are sometimes overlooked, especially by technical people, in planning project strategy. Social factors include an assessment of the values, beliefs, traditions, and attitudes of people—in short, the culture of the people who are stakeholders in the project. Religious and other significant holidays must be factored into project scheduling. In January people in the Far East celebrate Chinese New Year much more than westerners do our new year. Everything may come to a halt for a few days while people get ready to celebrate this important event.

By the same token, ignorance of the social taboos of a culture can create embarrassment and cause projects to fail. As an example of this, an engineer from Germany was visiting a company in the United States. He went to the men's restroom and saw a sign at the entrance saying it was being cleaned. He went inside and there was a woman cleaning the facility. In Germany, women will come into the restrooms to clean, and it does not matter that men are using the facility. So he went ahead with his business.

The woman cleaning the restroom was horrified by this. It simply is not done in the U. S. She filed a complaint alleging that he had deliberately used the facility to harass her. The president of the German company had to write a formal letter of apology to the U. S. company to resolve the issue!

In looking at all of the environmental factors, one may ask, do they represent an opportunity or a threat to the success of the project? Technological developments, for example, can be either, depending on circumstances. If a design is frozen with a certain technology and a new technology cannot be integrated with the design, then that change represents a threat to the success of the project, because acceptance by customers is likely to be low. Anyone designing conventional record players must certainly have been alerted by the development of CD players that there was a limited market for record players. Those who were on their toes took steps to enter the CD market. Otherwise, they might have experienced the same decline that manufacturers of buggy whips did when the automobile displaced the need for their product.

## Organizational Factors

Assessing an organization's strengths and weaknesses is a key element in strategy planning. Unfortunately, biases too often discredit the analysis. Managers are inclined to be optimistic about the strengths and a bit blind to the weaknesses of the organization. Nevertheless, the analysis must be done.

Assessing an organization's strengths and weaknesses is a key element in strategic planning.

Factors to examine include expertise of personnel, labor relations, physical resources, experience with the kind of project being planned, company image, senior management attitudes, morale of employees, market position of the organization, tendencies to overdesign or miss target dates, commitment of the organization to supply resources to the project as promised. Naturally, you want to capitalize on strengths and minimize the impact of weaknesses. Further, the team's strengths must be capable of offsetting those identified environmental threats, and a conscious effort should be made to take advantage of opportunities presented by the environment.

### Expectations of Stakeholders

Expectations of senior managers can be a major influence on the success or failure of a project. When those expectations for project performance are unrealistic, the impact is almost always negative. One of the more common expectations is that all target dates will be met. Such expectations lead to conflict.

The expectations of other stakeholders can also make or break a project. As an example, members of the community hear about the project and believe that it will create job opportunities for them. The project manager considers the skills needed for project success to be missing from the local community and recruits outsiders. There is public outrage, followed by unpleasant altercations, which results in senior management being pressured to abandon the project. Numerous examples exist of public pressures to abandon construction of hazardous waste facilities, nuclear power plants, and other projects considered by the community to be a threat to their security.

On the positive side, construction of the Saturn plant in Tennessee was undoubtedly aided by positive public reaction.

## FORMULATING PROJECT STRATEGY

Once all of these factors have been identified and examined, the project team will be ready to develop a number of alternative methods of project implementation. These methods must meet external threats and take advantage of opportunities. Usually strategy will be a combination of several elements, such as contracting out part of the work, developing a creative financial plan, partnering with another organization, and so on.

Coxon (1983) lists twelve possible strategies for projects:

1. **Construction-oriented:** an example of this would be the Avondale Shipyards approach to building ships.

2. **Finance-based:** this might involve some creative way of funding a project, perhaps through the use of bonds or grants; it might also involve special attention to cash flow and cost of capital.

3. **Governmental:** this involves taking into account government requirements and working closely with appropriate agencies to assure that no pitfalls will block progress.

4. **Design:** when certain design techniques have an advantage over others, this strategy may offer an advantage.

5. **Client/contractor:** this might include forming partnerships between client and contractor.

6. **Technology:** employing a cutting-edge technology might present certain risks, but offer greater competitive advantages. As mentioned previously, choosing the right level of technology might be important in developing countries.

7. **Commissioning:** if the commissioning aspects of the project are considered to be especially difficult or complex, then this strategy might be employed.

8. **Cost, quality, or time:** because these are interrelated, emphasizing one will be at the expense of impacting another. For example, when speed is of the utmost importance, and quality standards must be simultaneously maintained, then cost must increase. Nevertheless, if there is a significant market advantage to be gained through speed, the cost may well be offset by the profits made.

9. **Resource:** a resource strategy would be necessary when a particular resource is limited or abundant. For example, in Indonesia, Thailand, and other eastern countries, labor costs are so low that many construction projects are labor-intensive by western standards.

10. **Size:** it may be that for certain kinds of projects, economies of scale are only obtained once the size of the job exceeds a certain level.

11. **Contingency:** the strategy goes only so far as planning what to do if certain things happen.

12. **Passive:** this is a situation in which the project manager decides (consciously or unconsciously) to have

no strategy at all (paradoxical, since this is in itself a strategy). It might be appropriate when the future is believed to be very stable or, conversely, to be so chaotic that developing a strategy is virtually impossible. This is also called "flying by the seat-of-the-pants."

## CONDUCTING A SWOT ANALYSIS

Following are the questions asked in conducting a SWOT analysis. The form on page 92 should also help simplify the process. The questions that must be answered are:

- ◆ What **S**trengths do we have? How can we take advantage of them?

- ◆ What **W**eaknesses do we have? How can we minimize the impact of these?

- ◆ What **O**pportunities are there? How can we capitalize on them?

- ◆ What **T**hreats might prevent us from getting there? (Consider technical obstacles, competitive responses, values of people within your organization, and so on. Note that threats are not necessarily the same as risks.)

- ◆ For every obstacle identified, what can we do to overcome or get around them? (This helps you develop contingency plans.)

# SWOT Analysis Form

**Project:**

**Date:**

**Prepared by:**

Strategy, goal, or objective being considered:

| List strengths of your team | How can you best take advantage of these? | List weaknesses of your team | How can you minimize the impact of these? |
|---|---|---|---|
| | | | |
| What opportunities does this project/strategy/goal present? | How can you best take advantage of them? | List those threats that might keep you from succeeding | How can you deal with each identified threat? |
| | | | |

# 6

CHAPTER

# Implementation Planning

Once a suitable strategy has been chosen for a project, details about how to execute the strategy must be developed. Strategy answers the broad question, "How are we going to go about this job?" while implementation planning dots all of the *i's* and crosses all of the *t's*. In other words, implementation planning deals with nitty-gritty details about how the job will be done.

One of the mistakes that people make in planning projects is to begin implementation planning before they have developed a solid strategy. Of course, a strategy is implied by an implementation plan, but if you don't have the strategy clearly in mind, your detailed execution plan will almost certainly contain "holes."

In any case, once implementation planning starts, the most important tool of project management is the work breakdown structure (WBS). The WBS lists all of the project tasks that must be done to achieve desired results. The next section outlines how to create and use a WBS.

Planning is vital

- What must be done?
- How much will it cost?
- How long will it take?

## DEVELOPING AND USING THE WORK BREAKDOWN STRUCTURE

In Chapter 3, I said that planning is answering some questions, such as: "What must be done?," "How long will it take?," and "How much will it cost?" The WBS helps you identify what must be done, who will do it, how long it will take, and what it will cost. In doing so, the WBS ties the entire project together.

Some projects do not need a critical path or Gantt schedule, perhaps because the job is so small, but every project will benefit from doing a WBS. One reason is that forgetting a critical task is one of the 12 major causes of project failure. The WBS identifies all tasks and can be reviewed for completeness by all stakeholders, before proceeding with further planning. In my opinion, this makes it the most valuable tool for managing projects.

## Estimating Time and Cost

Estimating how long a task will take and what it will cost is always a major part of managing a project. Estimates are used for several purposes. One is to decide whether a project should be done at all. Another is to determine total impact on the organization, in the event that the project is not discretionary, but is mandated by law or necessity. Finally, estimates are used to determine resource requirements, task and project completion, and total cost.

Although project managers generally are not involved in deciding whether projects are viable, such decisions are usually made based on estimates that project managers make. One of the most common of these is the "ballpark" estimate. This term is an American one that refers to baseball. When we say that an estimate is in the ballpark, it is believed to be about right. This means that it is good enough to make a decision about whether to proceed or not.

To make a ballpark estimate, a project manager (or project team) will look at the history of a similar project. If a previous project had cost $100,000 and the new project involves a similar level of work, then the project manager may use that number as the basis for the current project, add a contingency for unknowns (say 10 percent) and therefore provide an estimate of $110,000 to the person requesting it.

If the degree of similarity between the two projects is very close, then the estimate may prove fairly accurate. However, we often find that such similarity is extremely poor, and this can result in the ballpark estimate being in error by a large amount. This means that a decision to do the project may be wrong. The project should not have been done. For this reason, ballpark estimates can cause major problems for organizations.

It is important for everyone involved to understand how an estimate is to be used, including how accurate the estimate must be for the intended use, to arrive at an estimate of the required accuracy. Limitations of estimating accuracy seem to be very poorly understood. To put this in perspective, imagine that you want to build a home, and you ask a builder how much your proposed house will cost. In most areas of the United States, a builder can look at the plan for the house and give you a rough estimate simply based to the total area of the house and the location in which it will be built.

As an example, the builder may tell you that the proposed house will cost about $100 per square foot. For a typical 2,000-square-foot house, this would be about $200,000. This cost does not include the land, only the house itself. If you ask the builder how accurate the estimate is, he will probably tell you that it is about ±10 percent. This is about as good as you will get based on a square-foot-based estimate. If you ask for a more accurate estimate, the builder will ask you to leave the plans for a few days, and he will use the plan to determine material costs at current market value and add this to labor costs and his profit margin to arrive at a final cost. If you now ask about the accuracy of the estimate, it will generally be no better than ±5 percent. And this is as good as it gets!

## All Estimates Are Based on History

Construction work is fairly well defined. The industry has huge amounts of historical data on which to base its estimates. When you consider disciplines like engineering design or biotech product development—or any situation in which you are doing something for the first time, meaning, of course, that you have no history—then you are never going to achieve 5 percent tolerances on estimates. Such tolerances are likely to be in the 25-to-50 percent range, at best, and if project sponsors don't understand this, everyone is going to get burned eventually.

I started this discussion by describing the ballpark estimate, which is made using a similar project as the starting point. Ballpark estimates often have huge tolerances, but they are usually not symmetrical. They may be in the range of –10 percent to +100 percent! One of the major causes of project failure is that these ballpark estimates become targets, which the project managers are expected to meet.

There is nothing wrong with doing ballpark estimates to determine whether or not a job is worth doing at all, but these should never be used as actual targets. As an example, if your car has a problem and you are undecided whether to invest a lot in repairs, or whether you should just get rid of it and buy a new one, you may ask a mechanic for a ballpark estimate of repair costs. If the figure is too high, you may decide to trade the car. If it is fairly low, you may go ahead with repairs.

## Improving Estimating Accuracy

By breaking a complex project down into small units of work, more accurate estimates can be made than those achieved by ballpark estimates. The best tool for doing this is the work breakdown structure (WBS).

## Work Breakdown Structure Format

There are two popular forms of the WBS. One looks similar to an organization chart (Figure 6.1), and might even be thought of as such, except that the boxes represent work activities rather than reporting structures. The second form of

**F I G U R E   6.1**

Standard Work Breakdown Structure

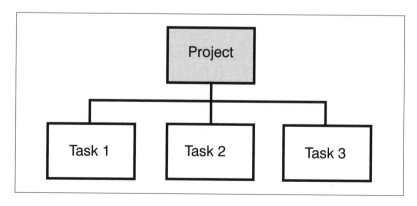

**F I G U R E   6.2**

Line-Indented Work Breakdown Structure

## Write Project Management Book

**1. Develop Proposal**
    1.1 Survey competition
    1.2 Estimate market potential
    1.3 Identify publishers

**2. Do Research**
    2.1 Review literature
    2.2 Interview experts
    2.3 Interview project managers

**3. Write Text**
    3.1 Develop first draft
    3.2 Revise
    3.3 Submit to publisher
    3.4 Approve edited copy

**4. Develop Illustrations**
    4.1 Roughs
    4.2 Final drafts
    4.3 Print-ready files

**5. Index**
    5.1 Make word list
    5.2 Master document
    5.3 Generate

WBS is the line-indented form (Figure 6.2). It is a straightforward list of project activities, with each new indentation being a lower level—but higher degree of detail (smaller unit of work to be performed). This is a convenient format, which can be produced entirely in text format on a computer, complete with line numbering. However, it does not visually show the scope of the project as well as the graphic form.

F I G U R E  6.3

WBS-Level Names

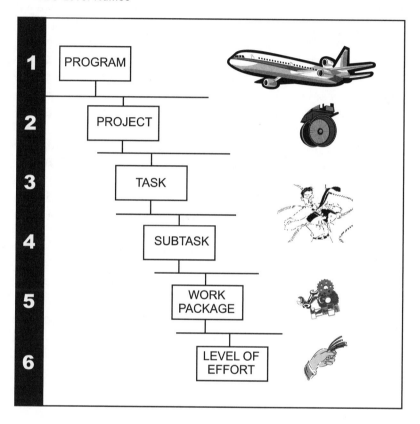

A commonly used format for the WBS has six levels, which appear in Figure 6.3. It is perfectly acceptable to use more than six levels, but you will find it almost impossible to devise names for the lowest levels. After the sixth level, most people just use the word task or activity to designate the work.

The main reason for using names is for communication purposes. If everyone uses common terminology, then you can inquire about a work package, and everyone would know that you are referring to level five of the structure.

Note that level one is called a program and level two is called a project. This will clarify the difference between program and project management. A program is a very large job that consists of a number of projects. An example would be the design of an airplane (Figure 6.4). Designing an engine, avionics, or a fuselage would be components large enough to be called projects. In fact, engine and avionics designs are usually carried out by companies other than the aircraft manufacturer. This means that the program manager is responsible for managing those subcontractors.

One of the traps that people fall into when they are learning to develop the WBS is that they turn it into a grocery list. For example, suppose that I have taken off a week to do a number of projects around my home, such as yard landscaping, repairing the roof, and restocking the pantry. I make a WBS like the one shown in Figure 6.5.

You will notice that on the major task labeled "shop for groceries," I have listed buy eggs, buy bread, buy potatoes, and so on. I have actually put my grocery list on my WBS. This is not what I should do.

Instead, I should list those activities that must be performed to buy groceries. These include drive to store, load cart, pay, drive home, and so on. Figure 6.6 illustrates this.

Here is how you test it. When all of the activities in Figure 6.6 have been completed, the box above, labeled "shop for groceries," will have been done. In the previous figure, however, after having bought bread, eggs, and potatoes, I am still standing in the store, and I don't know how I got there. Furthermore, the box above (labeled "shop for groceries") is not complete in this case!

Another thing that tricks people is that they try to think sequentially when doing the WBS and place underneath one box something that must be done before the box above can be done. This is a predecessor arrangement, and is actually confusing the WBS with critical-path scheduling. Again, the test is whether the box above is completed in the process of doing the tasks below. When a predecessor is placed below another

**F I G U R E  6.4**

Tiny Portion of a WBS for an Airplane

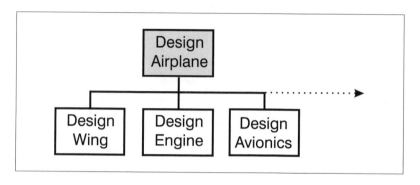

**F I G U R E  6.5**

A WBS for a Home Project

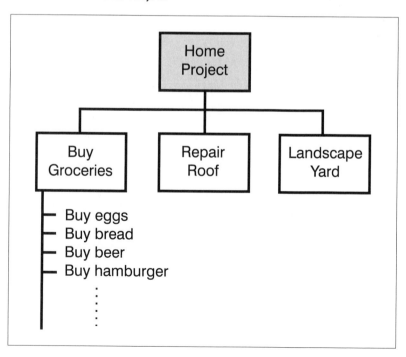

**F I G U R E  6.6**

The Correct Approach to the Home Project

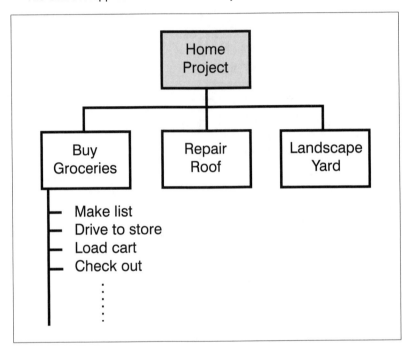

task, completing that predecessor will not leave the task above completed.

It is very hard not to think sequentially when doing the WBS. I don't know if we are born with that mind-set or if we learn to adopt it later in life, but it seems that almost everyone does it. You simply have to keep reminding yourself that you are not worrying about the order in which things get done at this step.

## General Aspects of Work Breakdown Structures

Following are some general aspects of the WBS that you need to keep in mind:

- Up to 20 levels can be used. More than 20 is considered overkill. For smaller projects, four to six levels will generally be adequate.

- All paths on a WBS do not have to go down to the same level. That is, you don't have to force the structure to be symmetrical. On any given branch, when you arrive at a level that will produce an estimate of the required accuracy, you stop.

- The WBS does not show sequencing of work except in the sense that all level-five work packages hanging below a given subtask must be complete for the subtask to be complete, and so on. However, work packages below that subtask might be performed in series or parallel. Sequencing is determined when schedules are developed.

> ☞ A work breakdown structure does not show the sequence in which work is performed! Such sequencing is determined when a schedule is developed.

- A WBS should be developed before scheduling and resource allocation are done.

- The objective is to identify all the work to be done first, then think about who will do it, how long it will take, and how much it will cost.

- The WBS should be developed by individuals knowledgeable about the work. This rule applies to projects that involve many disciplines, such as designing an airplane, as we saw in Figure 6.4. There we said that the engine and avionics would be developed by subcontractors. They each would put together a WBS for their projects, then these would be consolidated with the rest to provide an overall structure.

- ◆ Break down a project only to a level sufficient to produce an estimate of the required accuracy. This needs elaboration. While there is a danger that ballpark estimates may become targets, there is a need for them. Ballpark estimates help you decide whether to do a project or not. In such cases, it is helpful to break the work down a couple of levels.

> ☞ Don't plan in more detail than you can manage.

For detailed working estimates, however, the question is when to stop. The basic guideline is that you stop when you have identified work that you can manage. For example, in doing maintenance work, such as overhauling a big power generator, project managers often have history that allows them to schedule to the nearest hour. Such a level of detail would be far too fine for most activities, however. In many cases, you can't control work to better than the nearest day—or even the nearest week—so when you reach a level at which tasks have durations of a day, you stop.

> ☞ No task should have a duration greater than four to six weeks.
>
> ☞ Engineering and programming tasks should have durations no greater than one to three weeks.

The opposite side of this is planning in too little detail. Generally speaking, task durations should not exceed four to six weeks, and in the case of engineering or software programming, the duration should not exceed one to three weeks. In other words, there must be balance between too much and too little detail.

Furthermore, there must be some way of knowing that work is done. Otherwise, there is a tendency for work to reach 80 or 90 percent "complete" and stay there forever. This is because of the difficulty of tracking progress with knowledge work—programming, engineering design, and so on. In general, such work should be shown as either complete or simply started. No attempt should be made to say it is 20 percent, 50 percent, or 80 percent complete.

## Estimating Time, Cost, and Resource Requirements

Every project manager is faced with the same problem: how do you estimate how long it will take to do something? After you have done something once, estimating how long it will take to do the next job is easier, but that does not mean you

> Principle: An
> exact estimate
> is an
> oxymoron!

can give an exact determination of time, cost, and resources. It will still be an estimate, and an estimate is not exact! In fact, it is a guess, and everyone should understand this.

Estimating is never simple, and the higher the stakes, the more anxiety-provoking the job is. However, unless the estimating problem can be managed, projects will never come in on time or on budget.

The question is, how does a project manager know how long it will take to do a project, even if she knows how many human resources are available to do the work? The standard answer is, from experience! However, it is not at all clear exactly what that means. Let us examine what we mean by experience and its relationship to estimating activity durations. As an example, if you have been driving to the same workplace from the same home for several years, using the same route each time, you know about how long it takes to get to work. In large metropolitan areas, people report times like those shown in Table 6.1.

When asked, "What is your best estimate of how long it will take you to get to work tomorrow?" most people give the typical driving time (in the example above, 45 minutes). When the driving time follows a normal distribution curve, the typical time is an average, and the probability of achieving that time or less is 50 percent. If the distribution is skewed, which is the most common situation, and is shown in Table 6.1, then the probability may be ±50 percent. As-

**T A B L E  6.1**

Driving Times in Urban Areas

| Best Case | Typical Time | Worst Case |
|-----------|--------------|------------|
| 30 minutes | 45 minutes | 90 minutes |

F I G U R E  6.7

Normal Distribution Curve

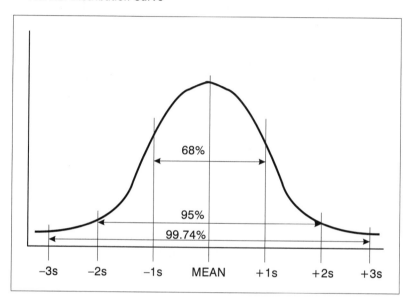

sume for now that the distribution is almost normal, as shown in Figure 6.7. If you are unfamiliar with statistics you should consult a basic text, such as the one by Walpole (1974), cited in the reading list, to see why this is true.

People are generally not too concerned that their typical time for driving to work has a 50-50 likelihood of success. But ask them the same question for a project activity, and they don't like to give numbers that have such low probability. The reason is that there are penalties for taking longer than you say it will take. (You get yelled at, if nothing else!)

Note that, even in the case of driving to work, say you ask, "How long would you *allow* yourself to get to work, if you had to meet with the president of your company and being late would be career suicide?" Most people are likely to answer with the upper limit (in this case, one hour), just in case they encounter an accident or some other traffic event that causes their time to approach the upper limit. That way, they will be sure to get to work on time, unless the situation is extreme and the time exceeds the one-hour upper limit. What they are doing, of course, is increasing their probability of success from 50 percent to 99.9 percent.

In a project, much the same process is involved. If a task has been performed a large number of times, the average duration is known, given a certain level of human resources to do the work, and this average can be used as the basis for an estimate.

However, if people are punished for taking longer than the estimated time to do a task, they will not give average durations. As in driving to work, they will allow more time. This is called padding the estimate, and it is an attempt to increase probability of success and to prevent punishment.

As the normal distribution curve in Figure 6.7 shows, there is an 84 percent probability that a duration one standard deviation above the mean can be met, 98 percent for two standard deviations, and 99.9 percent for three standard deviations. Thus, by padding, the individual can greatly increase the probability that the work can be completed in the estimated time.

**PRINCIPLE:** As the probability of success approaches 100 percent, the probability of getting the project funded approaches zero.

Unfortunately, safety carries a price. Increasing the allowed time will increase the probability of a successful scheduled completion, but it also increases the budgeted cost of the project, often to the point that the job will not be funded.

For this reason, project estimating assumes average durations, unless specified otherwise. The idea is that, for a project consisting of a large number of activities, some of the work will take longer than the average estimated duration, while other tasks will take less than the average. Therefore, the total project completion time will gravitate toward the average expected time for the critical path! The exception is the activities actually on the critical path. In this case, if any task takes longer than estimated, the project end date will slip, so on the critical path, it is important to make sure that you meet estimated durations.

In some organizations, there are pressures that keep people from completing work sooner than specified. That is, while you might expect that some tasks would be completed early, they aren't. There is one common reason for this: if you complete a task early, you will be expected to do so the next time. This is insane! It is the same as saying that if a person who averages 45 minutes driving to work gets there in 30 minutes one day, he should always get there in 30 minutes. A sample of one has set the expectation that all future times

PARKINSON'S LAW: Work expands to take the time allowed.
~ C. Northcote Parkinson

will be the same. This ignores factors outside the driver's control that may cause her driving time to vary.

All processes vary! This is a law of nature, and it cannot be set aside. You can reduce variation. This is what much of technological progress aims to do. But you can never reduce variations to zero. Until this is understood, people will follow Parkinson's Law and take as long or longer than allowed to complete their work, meaning that those projects cost more than necessary.

Does this mean that estimates should never be padded? Absolutely not! There are situations in which failure to allow for uncontrollable events would represent poor project management practice. Construction is one example. We know how long various activities will take because we have good history. However, the time taken will be a function of how many days we have bad weather and can't work. By consulting weather history for the area, we can estimate how many days of weather delay we will probably encounter and pad the schedule accordingly. This is called risk management, and more detail will be given on this subject in Chapter 17.

While padding is certainly justified to reduce risk, I believe it must be done aboveboard, on a task-by-task basis. Otherwise, the project manager might incorrectly assume that every member of the team has provided average-duration estimates. Then when he puts some padding into the project at the top level, he ends up adding fat on top of the fat that individuals have already included in their estimates, and the project estimate is sure to be too expensive.

This is one reason not to get into "game playing" in an organization. Sometimes a manager asks for an estimate, and when it is provided, the manager cuts the estimate by 10 or 15 percent, based on the belief that the estimate contains at least that much fat. Note that the probability of achieving a time that is one standard deviation below the mean is only 16 percent, so cutting an estimate that was an average expected duration severely reduces the probability that the time can be met.

If the project manager gets burned because his estimates were averages and they were cut, then the next time he is asked for an estimate, he will indeed pad, based on his experience that estimates will be cut. This time, however, the manger cuts 20 percent, so the next time the project manager pads 25 percent, and so on. Such games are hardly productive.

The objective of all project planning should be to develop a plan that is realistic, so that managers can decide whether to do the work. The objective should not be to try to "get" the project manager when he is unable to meet unrealistic deadlines.

## Other Factors in Estimating

You can only develop an average expected duration for an activity by assuming that the work will be nearly identical to work previously done and that the person(s) assigned to the task will have a certain skill level. If a less-skilled person is

Adjustments must be made for experience or skill of the resource assigned to the task.

assigned to the work, you can expect the work to take longer, and conversely, a more-skilled person could probably do the job faster. Thus, adjustments must be made for experience or skill of the resources assigned to the task.

However, we also know that there is no direct correlation between experience and speed of doing work. It may not actually be true that the more experienced person can do the job faster than the person with less experience. And putting pressure on the individual will pay dividends only up to a point. I remember once when I was pressuring one of my project team members to get a job done faster, he got fed up with the pressure. Finally, he said, "Putting two jockeys on one horse won't make him run any faster." And he was right.

Then there was a project manager who told me that when his boss doesn't like an estimate of how long it will take to perform a task, he tells him to use a more productive person! That was his solution to all scheduling problems (Figure 6.8).

Another factor is how much productive time the person will apply to the task each day. It is not uncommon in some organizations for people to spend an average of 25 percent of each day in meetings, on the phone, waiting for supplies, and other activities, all of which reduce the time available to spend on project work. Allowances must be made for such nonproject time.

In addition, if experience with a task is minimal, the expected duration might be adjusted upward, compared to the closest task for which experience exists. If virtually no experience can be used as a basis for estimating, then it might be appropriate to use PERT techniques (see Chapter 10). Another possibility is to use consensual estimating.

## Consensual Estimating

In consensual estimating, several people who know something about the work to be done are asked to estimate task durations independently of each other. They then meet and compare their estimates. When these are clustered very closely together, they may take an average of them. How-

More Productive Person

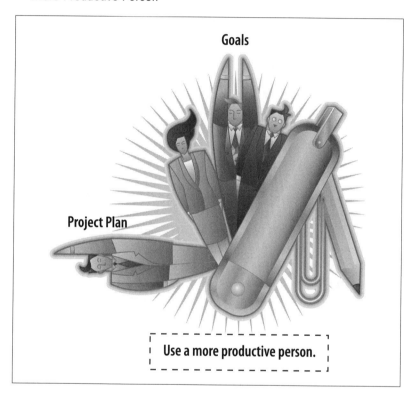

ever, when there is a significant discrepancy between their estimates, they discuss the differences and try to determine what each person was thinking that accounts for the spread. An example of such a spread is shown in Figure 6.9.

In this discussion, they try to decide if the majority should agree with the person who had the significantly different number, or whether that person should modify her estimate to be in line with the others. This should not be a strong-arming discussion, but an open discussion with mutual respect for differing points of view. The objective is to reach a consensus on what the number should be.

**F I G U R E   6.9**

Estimates with Significant Disparity

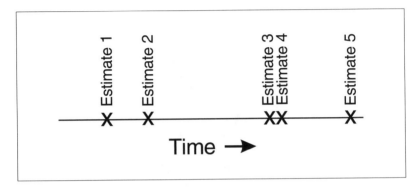

In this case, the word "consensus" means that each person must be able to say, "Although I don't entirely agree with the rest of you, I am fully willing to support the majority position." Notice that we don't use majority voting alone, because doing so gains compliance but not necessarily support for the majority position. If any member of the group has strong objections to the majority position, then the group can continue the discussion until a consensus has been reached or they can overrule the minority person as a last resort.

There are several advantages to this approach. One is that various points of view are brought into the discussion, which reduces the probability that something will be overlooked. Second, no one person is on the hook for the estimate, so no one gets "blamed" if the time actually required misses the target. The third advantage is that everyone learns more about estimating through this process.

## Means Tables

For construction projects, there are books containing means tables, which list the average expected durations for typical construction activities, together with multipliers to adjust those times to compensate for geographic location, weather, and so on. A source of means tables is listed in Chapter 32.

For other types of projects, unfortunately, there are no means tables available, so you must develop historical data by keeping records on previous project work. This is, perhaps, one of the most important benefits of developing a standardized project management methodology—by doing the work in specified ways and by keeping records of actual working times, an organization can develop a database that can be used to greatly improve future project estimates.

## Using Charts of Accounts for WBS Numbering

Ultimately, it will be necessary to compare actual progress of the project to the plan. In particular, labor costs will be charged back to the project, and accomplishment of work will be compared to the plan. The device for tracking costs is the chart of accounts. A sample is shown in Figure 6.10.

Each scheduled task in the project will be assigned a chart-of-accounts number, and as people work on that task, they fill out a time report that tells how many hours they spent on it, as well as how much of it they completed. This allows for good project control as well as for building a historical database over time.

## The Linear Responsibility Chart

Once the WBS has been completed, a linear responsibility chart (LRC) can be filled out to show who has responsibility for which tasks. The standard organizational chart is of the pyramid variety. It portrays the organization as it is "supposed" to exist at a given point in time. However, the pyramidal organization chart is insufficient for projects, because it does not display the nonvertical relations between members in the team. Although not normally defined, the interaction

**F I G U R E   6.10**

## Chart of Accounts

| Account Number | Activity Description | Account Number | Activity Description |
|---|---|---|---|
| 000 * | | 032 | Camera work |
| 001 | Development of concepts | 033 | Office layout |
| 002 | Preliminary design | 034 | Reserved |
| 003 | Computer analysis | 035 | Reserved |
| 004 | Environmental tests | 036 | Contract administration |
| 005 | Alternative selection | 037 | Contractor payroll |
| 006 | Delphi technique | | certification |
| 007 | Systems analysis | 038 | Reserved |
| 008 | Reserved | 039 | Reserved |
| 009 | Field investigation | 070 * | |
| 010 * | | 071 | Project management |
| 011 | Final design | 072 | Project planning & |
| 012 | Draft specifications | | scheduling |
| 013 | Drafting/graphics | 073 | Project coordination |
| 014 | Checking drawings | 074 | Reserved |
| 015 | Specifications review | 075 | Client meetings & |
| 016 | Maintenance work | | conferences |
| 017 | Technical writing | 076 | Public meetings & hearings |
| 018 | Cost estimating | 077 | Reserved |
| 019 | Bid preparation | 078 | Reserved |
| 020 * | | 079 | Project review meetings |
| 021 | Quality control checks | 080 * | |
| 022 | Reserved | 081 | Administrative services |
| 023 | Reserved | 082 | Clerical support |
| 024 | Computer data preparation | 083 | Composing & editing |
| 025 | Computer analysis | 084 | Typing |
| 026 | Computer keypunching | 085 | Reproductions/printing |
| 027 | Reserved | 086 | Training |
| 028 | Shop drawing review | 087 | Marketing & sales |
| 029 | Reserved | 088 | Reserved |
| 030 * | | 089 | Reserved |
| 031 | Prepare visual aids | 090 * | |

between people in a working environment affects the success of the effort and cannot be overlooked.

One of the common problems of interaction in a project is that someone makes a unilateral decision about something that affects one or more other individuals in the project. For example, capital equipment may be purchased without consulting other users to determine their needs, and the purchased equipment may be lacking. Or in designing a product, one designer may do her work without consulting another designer about aspects of the design that concern both of them.

LRCs help by showing requirements such as who must be consulted or notified. Following on page 118 is an example of a linear responsibility chart. The empty form on page 119 can be copied and used in your own projects.

**F I G U R E 6.11**

Linear Responsibility Chart (Sample)

Project: Notebook for Proj. Mgrs.  Date Issued: 01-Dec-90  Sheet 1 of 1
Manager: Jim Lewis  Date Revised: 13-Dec-92  Filename: LRCSAMP

## PROJECT CONTRIBUTORS

| TASK DESCRIPTIONS | Lea Ann | Susi | Jim | Norm S. | Carolyn | | | | | |
|---|---|---|---|---|---|---|---|---|---|---|
| Design forms | 2 | | 1 | | | | | | | |
| Final layout of forms | 1 | 2 | | | | | | | | |
| Write guidelines for use | | | 1 | 2 | | | | | | |
| Design package | 1 | | 2 | 2 | | | | | | |
| Develop sales plan | | | 1 | 2 | 2 | | | | | |
| Production coordination | 1 | 2 | 2 | | | | | | | |
| | | | | | | | | | | |
| | | | | | | | | | | |
| | | | | | | | | | | |
| | | | | | | | | | | |
| | | | | | | | | | | |
| | | | | | | | | | | |

Codes: 1 = Actual responsibility || 2 = Support || 3 = Must be notified || Blank = Not involved

© 1991 by James P. Lewis

**F I G U R E 6.12**

Linear Responsibility Chart

| | Date Issued: | 13-Dec-92 | Sheet _____ of _____ |
| | Date Revised: | 13-Dec-92 | Filename: LRCSAMP |

Project: _____
Manager: _____

## PROJECT CONTRIBUTORS

| TASK DESCRIPTIONS | | | | | | | | | | | | |
|---|---|---|---|---|---|---|---|---|---|---|---|---|
| | | | | | | | | | | | | |
| | | | | | | | | | | | | |
| | | | | | | | | | | | | |
| | | | | | | | | | | | | |
| | | | | | | | | | | | | |
| | | | | | | | | | | | | |
| | | | | | | | | | | | | |
| | | | | | | | | | | | | |
| | | | | | | | | | | | | |
| | | | | | | | | | | | | |
| | | | | | | | | | | | | |
| | | | | | | | | | | | | |

Codes: 1 = Actual responsibility ‖ 2 = Support ‖ 3 = Must be notified ‖ Blank = Not involved

© 1991 by James P. Lewis

# PROJECT SCHEDULING

# 7

# Developing a Project Schedule

Project scheduling is both art and science. The science comes from determining where in a network the critical path is and how much slack or float there is on the noncritical paths. It also involves determining calendar dates, by dropping out nonworking days, such as holidays, weekends, and individual contributors' vacation periods. When used, the science also involves leveling the application of resources so that large peaks and valleys do not occur. And finally, programs such as @Risk™ can do Markov process analysis of various paths through the project to determine worst-case scenarios, so that managers can plan for uncontrollable things that can wreck a project.

> The real emphasis on scheduling is in finding ways to parallel as many activities as possible to complete projects in minimum times.

The *art* is in constructing a workable schedule. Although we talk about critical path method (CPM) and performance evaluation and review technique (PERT), which is a variation of CPM that uses statistics to determine probabilities of completion times, the real emphasis of scheduling involves finding ways to parallel as many activities as possible to complete projects in minimum times.

In my experience, the main struggle with scheduling is in the art, not the science. For most projects there will be a lot of schedule networks to help get the job done, but some are better than others (depending on the criteria used to determine *best*) and you can never be certain that you have realized the *one best network* for your project.

The resource leveling involved in the science part of project management is done by a computer algorithm, and many of these exist. However, the result is only as good as the art applied in assigning people to the project in the first place. As an example, novice schedulers sometimes assign personnel to projects on a 100 percent basis, and this is bound to fail. No one is available to work on anything 100 percent of the time. We know that the maximum is usually around 80 percent, because people must have breaks (a *personal* factor), they get tired and productivity drops (called *fatigue*), and they are held up while waiting for other people (*delays*). These are called the PF&D factors that reduce worker availability.

> No one is available to work on *anything* 100 percent of the time!

In most instances, the 80 percent figure is too high, especially for knowledge workers, who have to attend meetings that don't contribute directly to getting work done. They also must talk with customers, do nonproject work, and so on. For these people, availability is seldom better than 50 percent.

> **Unless you know the actual availability of your personnel, your schedule is likely to be optimistic.**

Unless the project manager knows the actual availability of personnel, the schedule is likely to be very optimistic. One example of this was related to me at a nuclear power plant. During a refueling operation, workers must go down into the cavity that normally contains the fuel. It is still hot down there, and they have to wear shielded suits. The outside temperature may be 85 to 90 degrees, and inside the suit it is much higher. Because of the temperature and the cramped space, they can only work for a few minutes at a time, thereby stretching out the total time required to do the work.

This is one industry that has made major gains in scheduling. Only a few years ago, a refueling job required about six months to complete. Through skillful scheduling, this has been reduced to as few as 30 days.

Another example. In 1983 the San Diego Building Industry sponsored a contest to see how fast a 2,000-square-foot, single-story house could be built. Normally a builder will require several months to do a job like this. They spent several months planning the job (developing the schedule), and were able to build the house in two hours and 45 minutes! They had 350 workers on the job. They poured the cement slab, using chemicals to make the concrete cure in only 45 minutes, and while that was being done, crews were building the wall structures, the roof, and other parts of the house. Once the foundation was cured, the wall structures were moved into place and nailed down, then the roof was lifted with a crane and lowered onto the walls. Finally, the interior and exterior were completed, the lawn was landscaped, the wiring and plumbing were installed, and the house was ready for a family to move in. All in two hours and 45 minutes! You can obtain a film about this feat by calling 619-450-1221.

> In 1983 a 2,000-square-foot house was built in 2 hours and 45 minutes to set a world record! It could be done only by using a really good schedule!

## SO HOW IS IT DONE?

Suppose you have made a to-do list for yourself. There are 10 fairly big tasks that you need to do before the end of the week. One approach is to do them in any order. Or perhaps one task must be done before you can do another. This would be called a *logical* dependency, with the second task depending on the completion of the first one.

> A logical dependency occurs when a task cannot start until a preceding one is completed.

It is also possible that your boss has said she wants a certain job completed by Monday afternoon, so you must do it before you do the other things. This establishes a *priority* relationship between the task your boss wants you to do and the other tasks on your list.

If there is no priority or logical sequence relating tasks to each other, then they could all be done at the same time—except that you only have two hands and happen not to be ambidextrous, so you can only do one at a time. This is called a *resource dependency* between the tasks. The nice thing about resource dependencies is that they can be resolved by getting someone to help you. This can't be done with logical dependencies—until the first task is done, you can't do the second. Of course, the first task might be done faster if someone helps, and this might be one way to speed up the project, as was done in building the house.

> A priority relationship exists when your boss wants one task done before something else, but no logical dependency exists.

If you wanted to know the absolutely minimum amount of time required to do a project, you would parallel all tasks that can be logically done that way, and logically sequence the others. So assume your to-do list containing 10 tasks had only two that are logically sequenced. You have estimated that one will take two days to complete and the other will take one day. In series, they will need three days to complete.

> A resource dependency exists when one task cannot be done before another one is completed by a certain individual.

If none of the remaining tasks will take more than three days, and they could all be done in parallel with the other two tasks, you would have the situation diagramed in Figure 7.1. In this arrangement, all 10 tasks would be finished by the end of three days.

The only problem is that you would need at least nine people to do all 10 tasks! Nevertheless, this is the quickest they could be done. When tasks that can be performed in

**F I G U R E  7.1**

To-Do List in Order

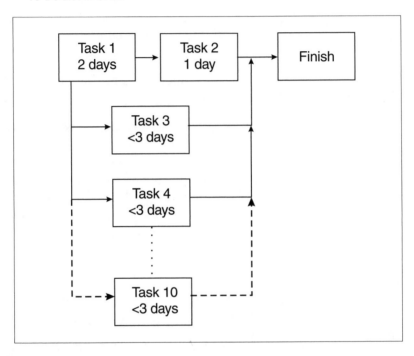

**F I G U R E  7.2**

The To-Do List in Series

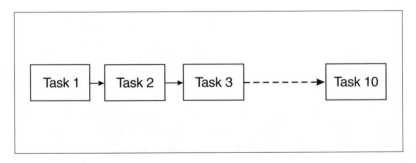

parallel are drawn in that way, regardless of whether the re-sources are available to do them, we say that you have cre-ated a schedule under the assumption of *unlimited resources.* Naturally, no organization has unlimited resources. So what would be the value of creating an unworkable schedule? Sim-ply that it tells you the fastest time in which the project can be accomplished.

If no one helps you, how long will it take to do every-thing on your to-do list? Well, the tasks will clearly have to be done one after the other, which leads to the result shown in Figure 7.2. With unlimited resources, you need three days to do the work, but with only one person working on all of it, you need five days.

The only thing anyone can question is your estimates of how long each task will take. The problem with all esti-mates is that the only way you ever know if they are "right" is to do the task and time it. Furthermore, if you do the task this week, it might take four hours and next week it might take four hours and 15 minutes. All activities vary in dura-tion from time to time and from person to person, as I pointed out in Chapter 6. This normal variation is a law of nature and must be accepted, meaning that the only way you can ever consider project dates to be precise is to vary the effort applied in order to finish each task in the specified calendar time. Project schedules are probabilistic and not deterministic!

## Overlapping Work

There is one special situation that must sometimes be man-aged. You don't always need to finish one task completely before you can begin another. You might have to do part of it, but not all. A good example of this is constructing a pipe-line that is several miles long. You start digging a trench, and after you get a sufficient amount done, you begin laying pipe. This is shown in Figure 7.3.

**F I G U R E  7.3**

Pipeline Construction

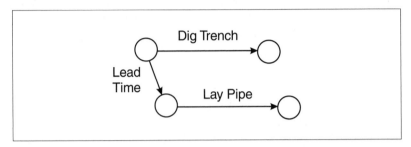

You also don't need to wait until all of the pipe is in the trench before you begin filling dirt back in, but you definitely want to get a certain amount of pipe laid, so again there will be a lead time that is needed for the pipe laying, at which time you can start the filling operation. This is shown in Figure 7.4.

Now consider the trench-digging operation. Imagine that the operator of the trenching machine gets finished. He looks back and in the distance he sees the pipe-laying crew. It will be

**F I G U R E  7.4**

Pipeline with Fill Operation Added

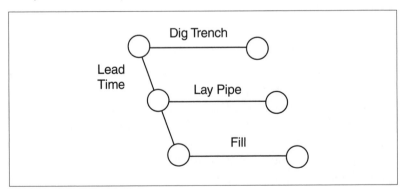

**F I G U R E  7.5**

Lags Shown for Pipe-Laying Job

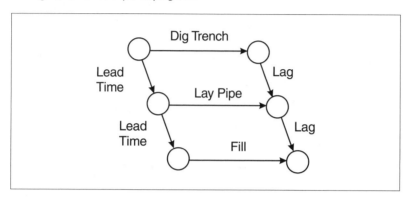

some time before they are finished, but he can leave this site and go on to another job. We say there is a lag from the completion of the trenching until the completion of the pipe laying. The same is true of the relationship between the pipe laying and the filling operation. This is shown in Figure 7.5.

This is called a ladder network, and some scheduling software won't let you do a full ladder. Note that the relationship at the beginning of trenching and pipe laying is a start-to-start, with a lead time of $x$ days, and the relationship at the end of each task is a finish-to-finish, with a lag of $y$ days. Microsoft Project™ will only allow you to do a start-to-start or a finish-to-finish, but not both. Generally, a start-to-start will suffice, but in some special situations, you may have to finagle to do what you want.

## Practical Suggestion

The easiest way to construct a schedule is to use a large white board and Post-it™ note sheets. These can be moved around until you achieve the logic you want, then connect the lines. Once everyone is satisfied that you have the logic you want, and that nothing is linked incorrectly, you can enter the diagram into your scheduling software. Trying to do this "from scratch" often leads to schedules that don't work, and at best requires that you print the network diagram many times to check it for accuracy. And, quite frankly, some scheduling programs don't do a very good job of printing the PERT diagram, so it is very cumbersome to check.

> The best way to construct a schedule is to use a large whiteboard and Post-it™ notes.

Another thing: If a task has no predecessors, it would have to be a beginning task. If it has no successors, it would have to be an ending task. It is possible that, while doing your diagram, you might forget to link a task to something else, yet it is neither a beginning nor ending task. We call this a "dangle"—a task that has been left hanging out "in the air," so to speak. Many software programs won't warn you about this, and you cannot see it on a bar chart unless you print links between tasks. It is, again, a good idea to construct the Post-it™ schedule first, as it is usually easier to spot dangles this way.

# 8

## CHAPTER

# Schedule Computations

As a working project manager, you need to know how to do scheduling computations only because you need to know what your scheduling software tells you. If you need an in-depth understanding of how to compute critical path, float, and so on, I highly recommend Moder, Phillips, and Davis (1983). Because the most common form of scheduling used today is Activity-on-Node notation, I will show how computations are done for (AON) networks only. The procedure is exactly the same for Activity-on-Arrow (AOA) networks, but the notation is different—refer to the Moder, et. al book cited above if you are interested in AOA networks.

### AN EXAMPLE

The network shown in Figure 8.1 illustrates the computation procedure. This is a small project to prepare a meal. However, this is not just a routine family meal; it is a dinner party.

Network Diagram for a Meal Project

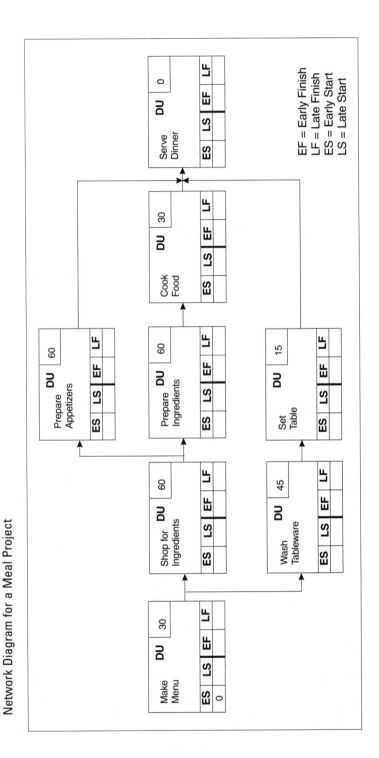

Your plan is to begin the project at 5:00 P.M., so that you can have the meal on the table by 7:00 P.M. This will give you enough time to eat a leisurely meal, followed by a five-minute drive to the theater, where you will attend a play that starts at 8:15 P.M.

In my experience, most projects are assigned with a due date. Furthermore, they are often constrained to start on a certain date because funding, specifications, or resources won't be available until then. This means that you must fit the work between two fixed dates. Inevitably, this leads to the *10 pounds of trash in a five-pound bag* problem. Put simply, the schedule just won't fit between those dates. It is too long, and you must try to compress it. That is the way it works most of the time, so that is how we will cover it in this chapter.

You might note several apparent discrepancies in the meal project network if you study it closely. First, why does "wash tableware" have to wait until the menu has been made? Because the menu will determine whether we need certain dishes. Next, why do we serve appetizers at the same time that we serve dinner? Simply to keep the network from being overly complicated. In reality, you would serve appetizers first and, after everyone has finished them, you would serve dinner.

You may also ask why the menu cannot be prepared the day before. It probably could. However, I am operating under the ground rule that the project has a constrained start time, to illustrate later on how the network will be compressed. So we might assume that some international guests are arriving around noon, and we will ask them what they would like for dinner this evening. That is why we can't make the menu a day ahead of time.

## Network Assumptions and Conventions

Under conventional network rules, once "make menu" has been completed, both "shop for ingredients" and "wash tableware" can begin. We assume that there is no handoff time, so

the early finish (EF) for "make menu" becomes the early start
(ES) for the two following tasks. We also assume that the estimated durations are fixed numbers, so that all tasks will take
as long as indicated, and this will yield the upper limit on project time. If anything takes less time than shown, then the project might finish early. On the critical path (which we have not
yet determined), if anything takes longer than the time shown,
then the end time for the project will slip.

## The Forward-Pass Computation

The first step is to do a forward pass through the network to
determine early start and early finish times for each task.
Note that scheduling software does exactly what we are going to do, but will drop nonworking times out of your schedule, and will show resulting calendar times. The software
provides a tremendous benefit, as calendar computations can
be very messy.

Because "make menu" has a duration of 30 minutes, if
we assume it starts at some time = zero (we can convert to
clock time later on), then it will finish 30 minutes into the
project. This means that "wash tableware" and "shop for ingredients" can start as early as 30 minutes into the project.

"Wash tableware" takes 45 minutes to complete, so it
will have an EF of 75 minutes into the job, while "shop for ingredients" takes 60 minutes, so it will have an EF of 90 minutes into the project. Proceeding in this manner, we finally
reach the box labeled "serve dinner," which will have an ES
of either 90, 150, or 180 minutes. Because the dinner cannot
be served until everything preceding it has been completed,
it will be 180 minutes into the project. The rule to follow is
that, when several tasks converge, the ES for the following
task must be the larger of the EF numbers from the preceding
tasks. (In terms of times, the ES must be the latest of the EF
times of the preceding tasks.)

We now have a special situation. "Serve dinner" has a
duration of zero, which means that it is not a task, but an

event or *milestone*. It is useful to put milestones at critical points in your projects, to force the software to print dates on which these will occur. I could have put a beginning milestone in this project, but because only one task started at time = zero, I chose not to do so. Had there been several tasks that could start at zero, it would have been useful to have a beginning milestone. Another use of milestones at critical points in projects is that reviews are usually conducted at these points. They will probably represent points at which significant phases of the project should be complete.

For the final milestone, the EF will be the same as the ES time, since the duration is zero. We now know the answer to our question: If we start the project at 5:00 P.M., can we serve dinner at 7:00 P.M.? No, we will be an hour late, and we now have to decide what to do. See Figure 8.2 for the solution to this point.

We know that we need to shorten the network if we are going to complete the project in two hours. But is that the only option? At this point we should consider it the only one, as we have received these dates by whomever gave us the project (speaking in terms of most real-world situations). Our job as project managers is not to try to have the times changed until we have first tried everything we can think of to meet them. So what might we do?

Well, the first thing to recognize is that we don't yet know which of the paths through the project is causing us to be late. To find this path, you have to do a *backward pass* through the network. This will be illustrated next.

## The Backward-Pass Computation

There are two ways to go about this. One would be to impose a late finish time (LF) of 120 minutes on the project. After all, that is the time by which the project needs to be finished. If this is done, you will find that you have negative float (or slack) on the longest path through the project. Float is calculated as shown:

Network with Forward Pass Completed

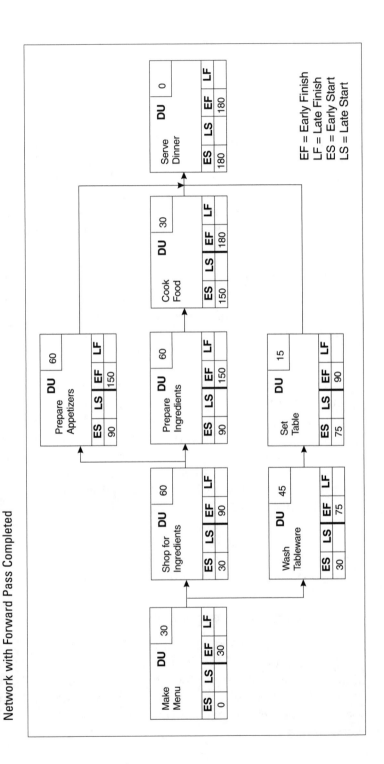

EF = Early Finish
LF = Late Finish
ES = Early Start
LS = Late Start

$$\text{Float} = \text{LF} - \text{EF}$$

or

$$\text{Float} = \text{LS} - \text{ES}$$

If we impose a late finish (LF) of 120 minutes on this project, we will have negative 60 minutes of float (120 − 180 = −60). When a path or activity has zero float, we call it the critical path, as I stated previously. However, when the float goes *negative*, we say the path is *supercritical*, and the amount of negative float is the amount of time by which the path needs to be compressed to meet the imposed completion time. We already knew this, so we do not gain much by knowing that we have a supercritical path, except that other paths might also have negative float, and this would suggest that they need to be shortened as well. I will show this solution later.

The second approach to the network is to let the LF time be the same as the EF time, or 120 minutes. This is the default condition that most software programs follow. The assumption is that the project won't finish any earlier than the EF time unless something is changed, and you don't want to stretch the job out unnecessarily, so the LF time should be the same as the EF time. Doing this will force one path to have zero float, and this will be the critical path. Once you know this path, you can then concentrate on trying to reduce durations of activities along the path. I will show this procedure first.

Because "serve dinner" has a zero duration, if it has an LF of 180 minutes it will have to start no later than 180 minutes. This 180 minutes will also be the LF for "prepare appetizers," "cook food," and "set table." This is because they must all finish by the LS time for "serve dinner."

"Prepare appetizers" has a duration of 60 minutes. If this task must finish no later than 180 minutes, it must start no later than 180 minus 60 or 120 minutes. The "cook food" task has a duration of 30 minutes, so it will have an LS of 180 minus 30 or 150 minutes. This 150-minute LS time becomes the LF time for "prepare ingredients," and because this task has a duration of 60 minutes, it will have an LS time of 150 minus 60 or 90 minutes. See Figure 8.3.

What should be the LF time for "shop for ingredients?" It must either be the 90-minute LS time for "prepare ingredients" or the 120-minute LS time for "prepare appetizers." If you study the network, you will see that it will have to be the smaller number. If you were to let "shop for ingredients" end at 120 minutes rather than 90, then it would slide the critical path out and the project would be even later than it already is. So the rule on a backward pass is that, at a junction, you let the LF for the preceding task be the smaller of the LS times on succeeding tasks. (In terms of time, the LF must be the earliest of the LS times on succeeding tasks.)

Continuing with the backward-pass calculations, we finally achieve the solution shown in Figure 8.4. The path through the middle is the critical path, and the paths through "prepare appetizers" and "wash tableware" have float. We now know the path that must be shortened by 60 minutes if we are to complete the project in 120 minutes.

## Reducing Activity Durations

If you are going to reduce durations of activities on the critical path, you will have to do one of the following:

1.  Add resources. You can do this by adding people or by working people you have more hours per day (this is called overtime).

2.  Reduce the scope of the task. In the case of the meal project, we could do this by buying ingredients that have already been cut up (frozen vegetables, for example).

3.  Reduce the quality of the work. This is not desirable, but if you put people under enough pressure to finish on time, it may be what they do.

Network with Partially Completed Backward Pass

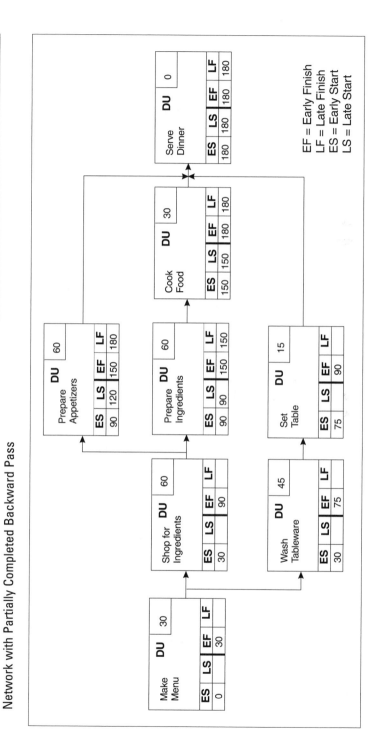

EF = Early Finish
LF = Late Finish
ES = Early Start
LS = Late Start

## F I G U R E 8.4

Network with Completed Backward Pass

**Make Menu** — DU 30

| ES | LS | EF | LF |
|----|----|----|----|
| 0  | 0  | 30 | 30 |

**Shop for Ingredients** — DU 60

| ES | LS | EF | LF |
|----|----|----|----|
| 30 | 30 | 90 | 90 |

**Wash Tableware** — DU 45

| ES | LS | EF | LF |
|----|-----|----|-----|
| 30 | 120 | 75 | 165 |

**Prepare Appetizers** — DU 60

| ES | LS  | EF  | LF  |
|----|-----|-----|-----|
| 90 | 120 | 150 | 180 |

**Prepare Ingredients** — DU 60

| ES | LS | EF  | LF  |
|----|----|-----|-----|
| 90 | 90 | 150 | 150 |

**Set Table** — DU 15

| ES | LS  | EF | LF  |
|----|-----|----|-----|
| 75 | 165 | 90 | 180 |

**Cook Food** — DU 30

| ES  | LS  | EF  | LF  |
|-----|-----|-----|-----|
| 150 | 150 | 180 | 180 |

**Serve Dinner** — DU 0

| ES  | LS  | EF  | LF  |
|-----|-----|-----|-----|
| 180 | 180 | 180 | 180 |

EF = Early Finish
LF = Late Finish
ES = Early Start
LS = Late Start

4. Change the process by which work is done. For the meal, this might mean microwaving the food instead of conventional cooking on a stove.

If none of these things works, then you may be able to change the way the network is drawn so that more tasks are done in parallel, or work is overlapped. The method of overlapping work will be shown later in this chapter.

One caution: It is tempting to tell everyone they will have to work overtime to meet the end date for a project. This is very bad practice. If you later encounter problems, you can't use overtime to "bail out" the project, which increases your chance of missing the end date. (You can't use overtime on the meal project, naturally.)

## Constrained Finish Computations

When the LF time is constrained to 120 minutes, you get the numbers shown in Figure 8.5. As you can see, there is a float of –60 minutes on the middle path (which we saw above is the standard critical path) and there is also –30 minutes of float on the "prepare appetizers" path. This suggests that we will have to take 30 minutes out of the appetizers path and 60 out of the critical path, unless we do something clever. It turns out that if we can reduce the "prepare ingredients" time to 30 minutes and "shop for ingredients" to 30 minutes, we will reduce the critical path time by the 60 minutes we need and also avoid having to reduce the time required to "prepare appetizers." This is shown in Figure 8.6.

## Overlapping Work

Another alternative might be to use the ladder network idea from the previous chapter. If your meal contains potatoes and broccoli, for example, you know that potatoes need considerably longer to cook than broccoli, so if you start cooking the potatoes first, you can then continue preparing broccoli

Finish Constrained to 120 Minutes

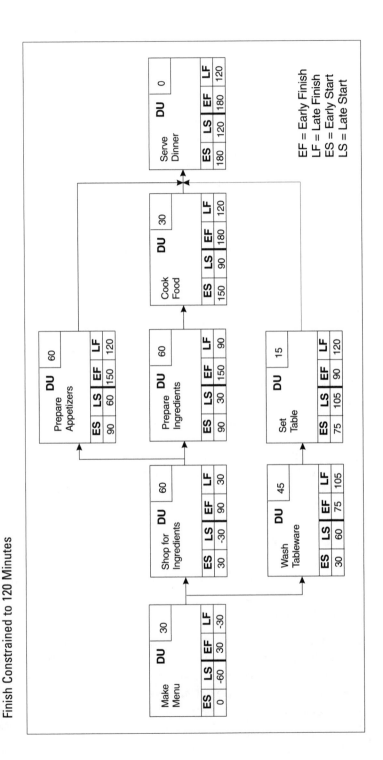

# F I G U R E 8.6

Network with Times Reduced for Shopping and Preparing Ingredients

| Make Menu | **DU** | 15 |
|---|---|---|
| **ES** | **LS** | **EF** | **LF** |
| 0 | 0 | 15 | 15 |

| Shop for Ingredients | **DU** | 45 |
|---|---|---|
| **ES** | **LS** | **EF** | **LF** |
| 15 | 15 | 60 | 60 |

| Wash Tableware | **DU** | 45 |
|---|---|---|
| **ES** | **LS** | **EF** | **LF** |
| 15 | 60 | 60 | 105 |

| Prepare Appetizers | **DU** | 60 |
|---|---|---|
| **ES** | **LS** | **EF** | **LF** |
| 60 | 60 | 120 | 120 |

| Prepare Ingredients | **DU** | 30 |
|---|---|---|
| **ES** | **LS** | **EF** | **LF** |
| 60 | 60 | 90 | 90 |

| Set Table | **DU** | 15 |
|---|---|---|
| **ES** | **LS** | **EF** | **LF** |
| 60 | 105 | 75 | 120 |

| Cook Food | **DU** | 30 |
|---|---|---|
| **ES** | **LS** | **EF** | **LF** |
| 90 | 90 | 120 | 120 |

| Serve Dinner | **DU** | 0 |
|---|---|---|
| **ES** | **LS** | **EF** | **LF** |
| 120 | 120 | 120 | 120 |

EF = Early Finish
LF = Late Finish
ES = Early Start
LS = Late Start

and other ingredients. Suppose you can start cooking the potatoes 30 minutes after you begin preparing ingredients. If you do this, you will have the solution shown in Figure 8.7.

This allows the project to finish 30 minutes earlier. If you were now to reduce the shopping time to 30 minutes, you would be able to complete the entire project in the 120 minutes required.

## The Effect of Nonworking Times on Schedules

Calendar time and working time will only be the same when a project is run 24 hours a day, seven days a week. In the case of the meal project, the two are equal because we are essentially conforming to this condition. When weekends are not worked, holidays intervene, or people are on vacation, then calendar time will always exceed working time.

In most scheduling software programs, you can enter into the global calendar holidays and other periods when no one works on the project. The software will then schedule

Calendar time and working time will be the same only when a project is run 24 hours a day, seven days a week.

**FIGURE 8.7**

Network with Overlap on Preparing Ingredients

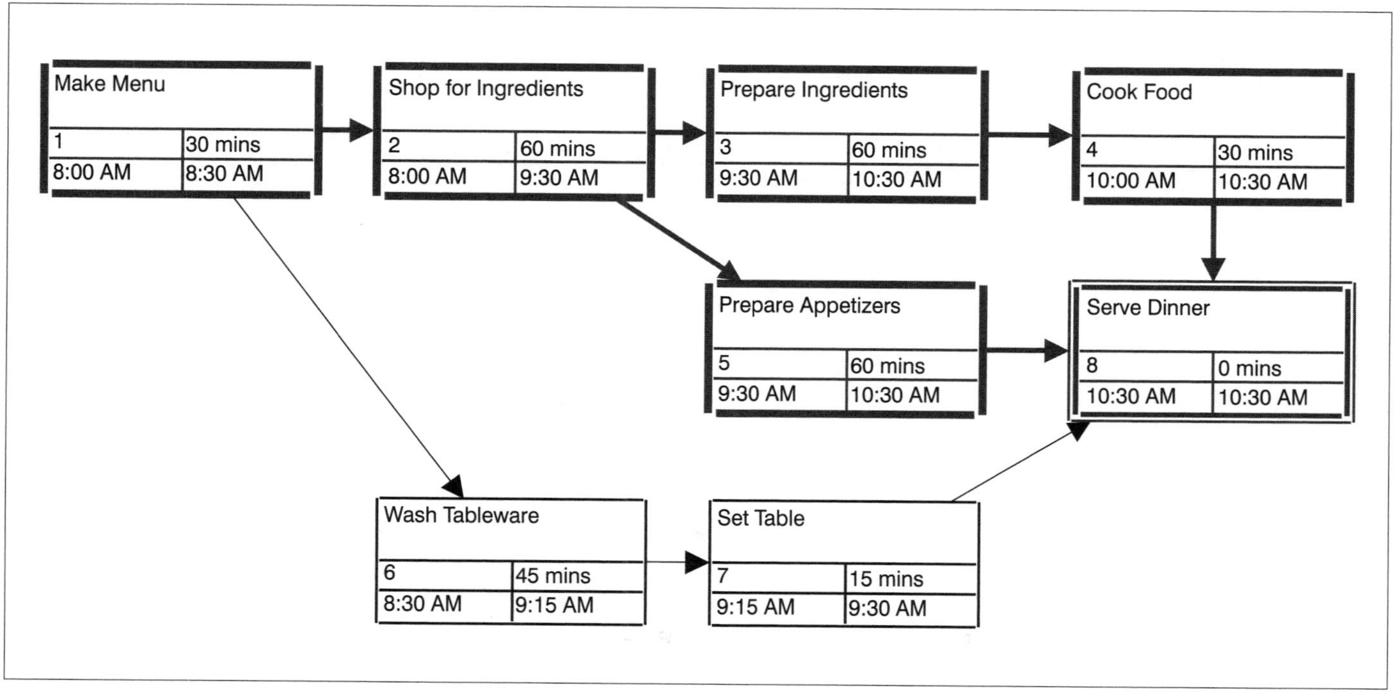

around these dates and tell you the actual date on which the project will end. You also can enter vacation days into a calendar for each resource, and the software will schedule around these. This feature is one of the most useful offered by current software.

## Network Diagrams and Bar Charts

Henry Gantt was the first to develop bar-chart schedules (called Gantt charts) for use in project scheduling. The beauty of bar charts is simplicity, and they should always be provided to team members because they are easy to read. However, it is absolutely essential to construct the schedule using network diagrams in order to find the critical path and float. Most software programs do this by specifying the predecessors or successors for each task. (You specify one or the other but not both.)

You can also tell the software that a task must start by a certain date or must end by a certain date. However, if you do too much of this, the software will simply regurgitate what you have input, and you will have lost the power of the tool, which is to tell you when tasks are going to end given the task durations you have specified. Then if these do not yield acceptable target dates, you need to massage the activity durations, revise the network, or negotiate a change in target dates.

# 9

## CHAPTER

# Scheduling with Resource Constraints

## THE ASSUMPTION OF UNLIMITED RESOURCES

All scheduling computations in the previous chapter assume that the activity durations were achievable. However, the time required to complete an activity depends on the resource(s) assigned to it, and if the level of required resources is not available, then the work cannot be completed as planned. We also said that if two tasks can be done in parallel, they should be drawn that way, but we added that this leads to the assumption that we have unlimited resources. Naturally that is not the case, even for the largest organizations.

Project scheduling cannot be successful unless the project manager can solve the resource-allocation problem. Every organization has a fixed amount of resources, which are shared among all projects. Also, while basic schedule computations can be made manually—even for fairly sizable networks—the resource-allocation problem quickly grows to such proportions that it can only be solved with a computer.

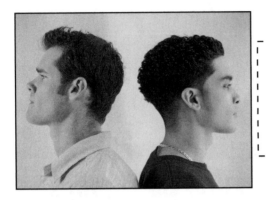

> A dispute should never become disruptive to a project.

Therefore, this chapter will illustrate how to develop a schedule that accounts for the availability of resources, using Microsoft Project™. Other PC software may handle the problem differently, but the approach illustrated here will give a general outline that will be representative of most of the software available today.

## The Effect of Limited Resources on Schedule Float

When resource limitations exist, the float identified by conventional critical-path analysis may have to be used to avoid overloading resources. To illustrate the resource-allocation approach, we will use the network shown in Figure 9.1, with resources assigned to each activity.

When a number of people can all do the same work, they are treated as a "pool" of resources. The initial analysis presented here will make use of pooled resources. That analysis will be followed by one in which specific individuals are assigned to the tasks.

In Chapter 6, on estimating, we said that we begin estimating an activity duration by assuming that a certain kind of resource will be applied. For example, a ten-year-old boy probably cannot mow grass with a push mower as fast as a 16-year-old. So if I am going to estimate how long it will take

PERT Diagram for Resource-Allocation Example

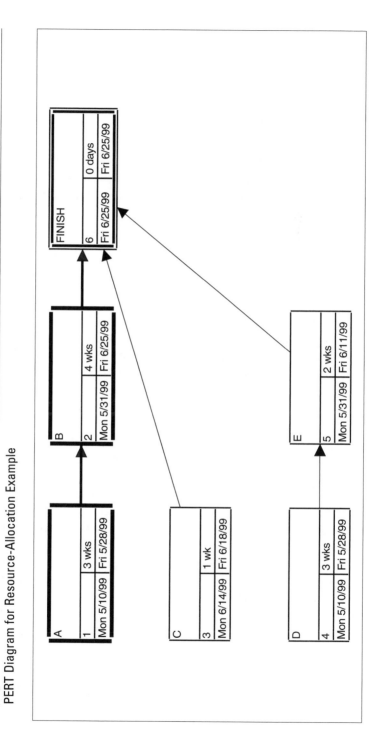

to cut the grass, I must begin by deciding who will do it. Then I will know how long it will take.

Using this approach involves another assumption: that the task has a fixed duration. This is the most usual way in which activity durations are handled, so I will illustrate that system first. However, if a task duration depends on how many resources are applied, we may be able to achieve a better schedule if we move resources around, changing activity durations. This is the *variable-duration* approach, and Microsoft Project defaults to treat resources as variable duration. If you want the task to have a fixed duration, you have to force Microsoft to treat it that way.

Another way to think of variable-duration tasks is to consider how many working hours the task will require, then ask what percent of time the person will work on it, and figure out the calendar time from that. For example, if a task will take 10 working hours to complete, but the person plans to work on it only 25 percent of her time, then it will take 40 calendar hours (or one working week) to complete the task. This is the Microsoft default. Providing significant detail on how to use the software is out of the scope of this book, but this chapter treats activities as fixed duration.

To allocate resources, the level of resources *available* to the project must be specified, together with the level *required* by each activity. The software then attempts to schedule work so that available resources are not overloaded.

The resource level available is measured by taking the number of people, multiplying by the total amount of time they will each work, and specifying the product as the availability. If two individuals are available for 40 hours per week, we say that 80 person-hours per week are available. If time is measured in days, then we say that for a five-day week, with two people, we have 10 person-days per week available. In Project 98, if you have three workers available, you tell the program that the resource called "Worker 1" is available 300 percent, which is the same as having three people available.

Note that holidays, vacations, and overtime will affect the amount of labor available during the period in which they occur, so that the schedule will reflect a total *elapsed* time that is different than that obtained if a constant level of labor were available. For the analysis that follows, no vacations or holidays have been entered.

The initial Gantt chart for the project is shown in Figure 9.2. Tasks A and E have two workers assigned (Worker 1 @ 200 percent), and tasks B, C, and D have one worker assigned. If you examine the first week of the project, you will notice that the project will require four workers if the work is to be done as scheduled, but we have only three available. This overload is confirmed by the resource-loading diagram shown in Figure 9.3.

## Time-Critical and Resource-Critical Leveling

After you have developed a schedule to meet a required end date, you don't want it to slip because of resource limitations. So, when resources are overloaded, you want the software to level them so that the end date can still be met. This is called *time-critical* leveling. In Microsoft Project , the dialog box asks if you want to level within the available slack. If you check this box, you get time-critical leveling.

Suppose you find that the overloads cannot be resolved with time-critical leveling. This will often be the case. Then you have to find additional resources, work your available people overtime, reduce scope, reduce quality, or extend the deadline. In many cases, the only options will be overtime or slipping the end date. The question is, how much will it slip? This can be answered by doing resource-critical leveling. To do this with Microsoft Project, (hereafter simply called Project) be sure the box asking if you want to level within the available slack is not checked.

## F I G U R E   9.2

Gantt Chart for Generic Resource Project

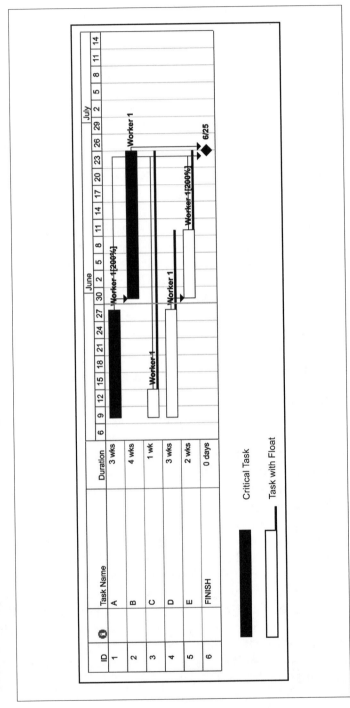

Resource-Loading Diagram for Project in Initial Form

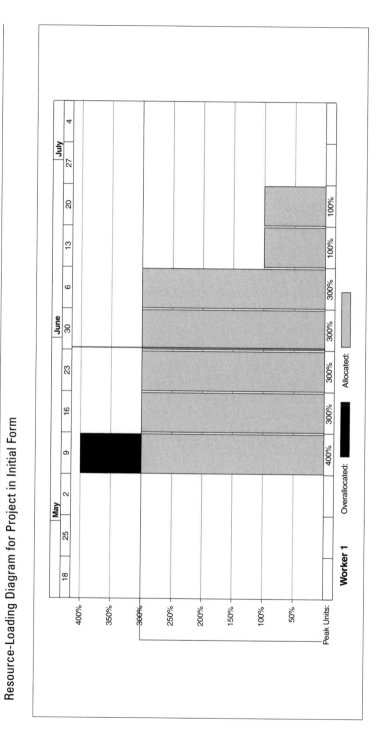

## Time-Critical Leveling of the Example

If you now tell Project to level resources, you get the solution shown in Figure 9.4. As you can see by a simple visual scan, no point in the project requires more than three workers. This is confirmed by the resource-loading diagram in Figure 9.5. Because the overloads can be resolved with time-critical leveling, you don't need to do resource-critical leveling for this project.

## Scheduling with Specific People

The previous example treated workers as a pool, which means they can all do the same work. This is the simplest possible situation. When this assumption cannot be applied, that is, workers are specialized, then you have to assign them by name. A project to illustrate this case is shown in Figure 9.6.

As you can see, Tom and Sue are double-scheduled in this project. Mary's tasks are in series, so she is okay. If you now tell Project to do time-critical leveling of resources, the overload for Tom can be resolved, but the one for Sue cannot. This is shown in Figure 9.7.

This is the best that can be done, unless another person can handle one of Sue's tasks. If this is not possible, then the project will slip. To find out what will happen, you level resources under resource-critical conditions. The solution under resource-critical conditions is shown in Figure 9.8.

As you can see, the end date has slipped. But what good is this schedule if you need to meet the earlier date?

Simple.

It gives you a bargaining chip. You can now show the project sponsor what is going to happen if you don't make tradeoffs. You can reduce the scope of work, reduce quality, work people overtime, or slip the end date. Those are the choices. Of course, you may be told to work faster or use a more productive person, but if this were possible, you

Schedule with Resources Leveled

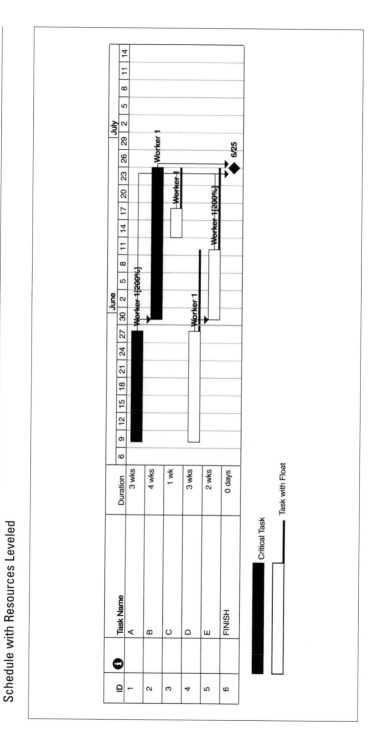

157

## F I G U R E 9.5

Resource-Loading Diagram with Resources Leveled

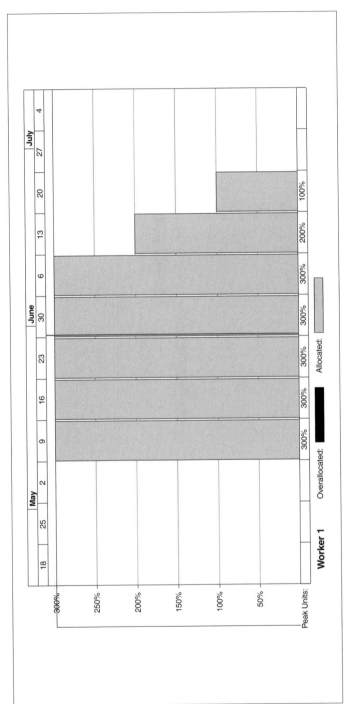

Bar Chart with Specific Individuals Assigned to Tasks

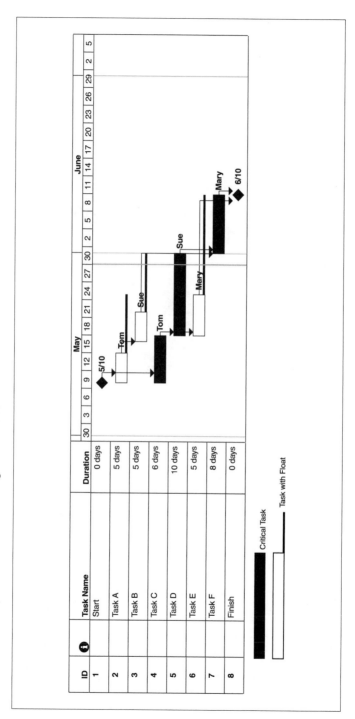

**F I G U R E  9.7**

Schedule with Tom's Overload Resolved

| ID | ⓘ | Task Name | Duration | May |  |  |  |  |  |  |  |  | June |  |  |  |  |  |  |  |  |  |
|----|---|-----------|----------|-----|---|---|----|----|----|----|----|----|------|----|----|----|----|----|----|----|---|---|
|    |   |           |          | 3 | 6 | 9 | 12 | 15 | 18 | 21 | 24 | 27 | 30 | 2 | 5 | 8 | 11 | 14 | 17 | 20 | 23 | 26 | 29 | 2 | 5 | 8 |
| 1 |  | Start | 0 days | ◆ 5/10 |
| 2 |  | Task A | 5 days | Tom |
| 3 |  | Task B | 5 days | Sue |
| 4 |  | Task C | 6 days | Tom |
| 5 |  | Task D | 10 days | Sue |
| 6 |  | Task E | 5 days | Mary |
| 7 |  | Task F | 8 days | Mary |
| 8 |  | Finish | 0 days | ◆ 6/10 |

Critical Task

Task with Float

Schedule Leveled Under Resource-Critical Conditions

| ID | ℹ | Task Name | Duration |
|---|---|---|---|
| 1 | | Start | 0 days |
| 2 | | Task A | 5 days |
| 3 | | Task B | 5 days |
| 4 | | Task C | 6 days |
| 5 | | Task D | 10 days |
| 6 | | Task E | 5 days |
| 7 | | Task F | 8 days |
| 8 | | Finish | 0 days |

Critical Task

Task with Float

wouldn't be having a conversation with the sponsor in the first place. This approach gives you an analytical way to deal with the project. If you had no computer solution, but simply *felt* that you needed more help, you would have no credibility with the sponsor at all. Remember: You are always making tradeoffs between the $P$, $C$, $T$, and $S$ variables in every project, and values for all four cannot be dictated. Three can be assigned, but the fourth must be allowed to float.

The subject of resource allocation has only been touched on in this chapter. To give a full treatment of the topic requires an entire book. If you need help dealing with specific aspects of resource allocation, you will have to consult the software manual to find out how the software handles the problem you are dealing with.

For example, some programs allow activity splitting and some do not. Activity splitting allows a person working on a 10-day task to work for two days, then shift to something else, then come back and finish the original task. This way, a higher priority task can be completed without being delayed. The only concern with activity splitting is the usual assumption that a split task will take the same time to complete as an un-split one. That is almost never the case. Once you have been away from a task for a few days, you need to rethink where you were, and this setup time will add to the total time needed to do the job. If this is not taken into account, your project schedule may not be correct. Naturally, if setup time is trivial, then it can be ignored.

# 10

# Scheduling with PERT

## PERT COMPARED WITH CPM

When a project consists of activities, most of which are similar to others that have been performed a large number of times, CPM scheduling is generally used. CPM bases estimates of activity durations on historical data, which are assumed to be the mean or average time that the activity has taken in the past.

However, when a project contains a majority of activities for which no experience exists—that is, no historical data is available—then the estimating difficulty becomes significant. When no experience is available to use as a guide, the only thing that can be done is make the best possible guess, based on *whatever* relevant experience one has.

It seems clear, however, that the more unique an activity is, the less certain the estimate of its duration, and therefore, the more *risky* the project will be in terms of control. A lot of projects (such as research and development) fall into this category, leading to the question as to whether some method could be employed to reduce estimating risk.

In response to this problem, the Navy and Booze, Allen, and Hamilton consulting firm jointly developed PERT around 1958 and applied it to the Polaris submarine project.

While estimates of activity durations for CPM projects are taken as averages based on history, once they are in place, they are often assumed to be more or less fixed, or to use the colloquial expression, they are "engraved in granite."

The PERT system, however, recognizes that estimates are uncertain, and therefore it makes sense to talk of *ranges* of durations, and the *probability* that an activity duration will fall into that range, rather than assuming that an activity will be completed in a fixed amount of time.

## EMPIRICAL FREQUENCY DISTRIBUTIONS

To understand the probability and statistics involved in PERT, consider an activity that has been performed in the past many times under essentially the same conditions. For the activity in question, duration times ranged from 7 to 17 days. Now suppose that you count the number of times the activity required seven days to perform, eight days to perform, etc., and you display the resulting information in the form of an empirical frequency distribution or histogram as shown in Figure 10.1.

As we know from statistics, if an infinite number of observations were made, the width of the intervals in this figure approach zero, and the distribution would merge into some smooth curve. This type of curve is the theoretical probability density of the random variable. The total area under such a curve is made to be exactly one, so that the area under the curve between any two values of $t$ is directly the probability that the random variable $r$ will fall in this interval. When this is done, the curve is called a *normal distribution curve*. It is also often called a bell-shaped curve. (For the benefit of my read-

**F I G U R E   10.1**

Empirical Frequency Distribution

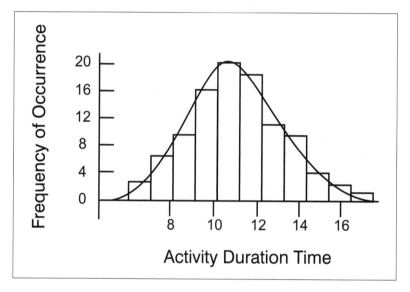

Activity Duration Time

ers who are well versed in statistics, please note that normal distributions were not assumed in developing the PERT system, but it is much easier to understand the intent of the system if normal curves are used. If you want a rigorous treatment of the statistics, consult Moder, Phillips and Davis [1983].)

Once the normal distribution curve exists for an activity, it is then a simple matter to extract the average-expected-activity duration from the curve and to use that time as the estimate for how long the work will take.

However, under those conditions when no such distribution exists, we could still say that the problem is to arrive at our *best approximation of what the average expected duration would be* if we *could* perform the work over and over to develop the normal distribution curve. The answer to this question forms the heart of the PERT system.

## PERT SYSTEM OF THREE TIME ESTIMATES

Even though a project may consist of activities for which little or no experience exists, most planners will have some relevant experience, so in most cases it is possible to make an educated "guess" of the *most likely* time the work will take. In addition, a project planner can estimate how long the work would take if things go better than expected and, conversely, if things go worse than expected. These are called the *optimistic* and *pessimistic* conditions, respectively.

They are not defined as best- and worst-case, however. See the definitions in Table 10.1 for the exact meanings of the terms *optimistic* and *pessimistic*.

These three estimates can be thought of as representing aspects of the normal distribution curve that could be developed if the work were performed a sufficient number of times. Another way to think of them is to say they represent *information* or data about the work in question. Taken together, you can perhaps compute the distribution *mean*.

### T A B L E   10.1

Terms Used in PERT Scheduling

| Term | Definition |
| --- | --- |
| *a* | Optimistic time: the time that would be improved only one time in 20, if the activity could be performed repeatedly under the same essential conditions. |
| *m* | Most likely time: the modal value of the distribution, or value that is most likely to occur more often than any other value. |
| *b* | Pessimistic time: the time that would be exceeded only one time in 20 if the activity could be performed repeatedly under the same essential conditions. |

This is the essence of the PERT system, although an admittedly simplified presentation. As mentioned above, interested readers should consult Moder, Phillips, and Davis (1983) for a more thorough treatment of the statistics involved. For our purposes, all that matters is the application of the method.

## PERT COMPUTATIONS

A formula based on principles from statistics combines the three estimates to calculate the expected mean duration for the activity. The following expression estimates average expected time to perform an activity:

$$t_e = \frac{a + 4m + b}{6}$$

where
  $t_e$ = expected time
  $a$ = optimistic time estimate
  $m$ = most likely time
  $b$ = pessimistic time

These values of $t_e$ are used as the durations of activities in a PERT network. Given those estimated durations, the network calculations are identical to those for CPM. A forward-pass computation yields earliest times for events and a backward-pass computation provides latest times.

## ESTIMATING PROBABILITY OF SCHEDULED COMPLETION

What is gained by PERT, compared to CPM, is the ability to compute a *confidence interval* for each activity and for the critical path, once it has been located. To do this, the standard deviation of each activity distribution must be known. PERT software automatically makes such a computation. However, if CPM software is used to do scheduling, the calculations can be made externally, perhaps using a spreadsheet (which is very simple to construct).

A suitable estimator of activity standard deviation is given by:

$$\hat{s} = \frac{b-a}{6}$$

where $s$ is the standard deviation of the expected time, $t_e$.

Once the critical path has been determined for the network, the standard deviation for the total critical path can be calculated by taking the square root of the sum of the variances of the activities on the critical path. Thus, in the case of only three activities on the critical path, the standard deviation would be given by:

$$\hat{S}_{cp} = \sqrt{S_1^2 + S_2^2 + \cdots + S_n^2}$$

From statistics, we know that there is a 68 percent probability of completing the project within plus-or-minus one standard deviation of the mean, 95 percent within two standard deviations, and 99.74 percent within three standard deviations. The normal curve is shown in Figure 10.2 for reference.

## An Example

To illustrate how PERT works, we will consider a single activity, for which two different planners made estimates. Each person's estimates appear in Table 10.2, together with the calculated values for $t_e$ and $s$.

Note that the standard deviation for the estimates made by person one is only half of a day, meaning that the spread on the normal distribution curve is quite small. For person two, the standard deviation is 1.8 days. For convenience, we will round this up to 2.0 days. The normal distribution curve, using these two different sets of numbers, is shown in Figure 10.3.

**F I G U R E   10.2**

Normal Distribution Curve

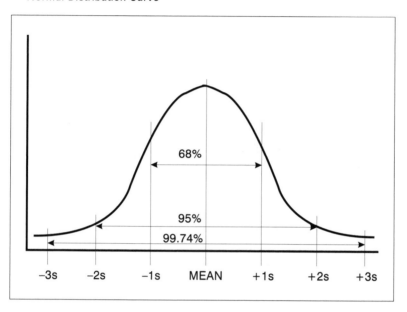

**T A B L E   10.2**

Estimates for an Activity Made by Two Individuals

| Description | Planner 1 | Planner 2 |
|---|---|---|
| $m$ = most likely | 10 days | 10 days |
| $a$ = optimistic | 9 days | 9 days |
| $b$ = pessimistic | 12 days | 20 days |
| PERT time | 10.166 days | 11.5 days |
| Standard deviation | 0.5 day | 1.8 days |

**F I G U R E  10.3**

Distribution with Confidence Intervals Shown

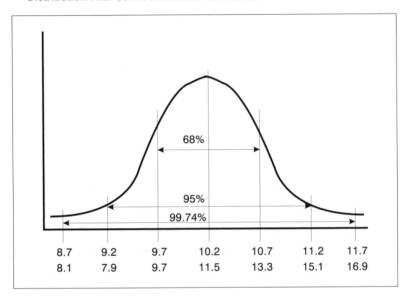

The impact on the activity estimate is that the *confidence interval* for person two is four times wider than that for person one for a *given probability* of completion of the task.

To illustrate, there is a 68 percent probability that the activity will be completed in the range of 9.7 to 11.7 days if the estimates made by person one were used, whereas the 68 percent confidence interval is 9.5 to 13.5 days if the estimates made by person two were used.

These statistics simply mean that person one has greater confidence or less *uncertainty* about his estimates than person two. Does that mean he is more correct? No. It is simply a reflection of the different experiences of the two individuals.

Perhaps because person two has had less experience with this particular activity than person one, he is not sure how long it will take. Therefore, the PERT system would tell

him to use an activity duration of 11.5 days as his best estimate of mean duration, whereas person one would only use
10.2 days. This can be thought of as automatically providing
some latitude for the person who has the least confidence in
his estimates.

## USING PERT

The fact that PERT requires planners to make three time estimates for each project activity—and that they plug these estimates into formulas to calculate a time estimate and standard
deviation—requires additional work compared with CPM.
For this reason, many planners do not consider PERT worth
the effort.

   Not only that, but some people question the validity of
the entire process. They argue that, if all three estimates are
guesses, why should the weighted composite of three
guesses be any better than just using the most likely estimate
in the first place? Indeed, there is merit to this argument. As

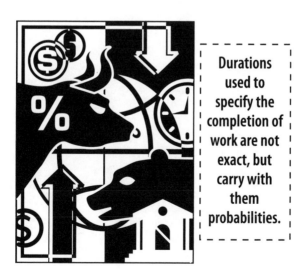

**Durations
used to
specify the
completion of
work are not
exact, but
carry with
them
probabilities.**

I see it, one principle advantage of PERT is that it makes everyone realize that durations used to specify the completion of work are not exact, but carry with them *probabilities*.

Should you choose to use PERT estimating with software that does not support it, you can download a spreadsheet from my Web site that will do the computations for you. The address is www.lewisinstitute.com. The downloads can be found in the company store, which was the most convenient place for me to place them. You will note that the price for each file is zero.

# PROJECT CONTROL
# AND EVALUATION

# 11

CHAPTER

# Principles of Project Control and Evaluation

## CONTROL AND EVALUATION PRINCIPLES

Proper project control and evaluation are necessary if project objectives are to be met. Therefore, the design of a project control system is very important, as is the practice of proper evaluation methods. Before such systems can be designed, it is essential to understand the basic concepts and principles of control and evaluation.

## PROJECT REVIEWS

There are three kinds of project reviews: status, design, and process. Each has a different purpose. A status review concentrates on whether the $P$, $C$, $T$, and $S$ targets are being met. Are we on schedule, on budget, is scope correct, and are performance requirements okay?

Predicting the future is easy. It's trying to figure out what's going on now that's hard.
~ Fritz Dressler

A design review only applies to those projects in which something is being designed, such as a product, service, or software. Some of the questions asked during such a review are: Does it meet specifications? Is it user friendly? Can we manufacture it? Is the market still looking for what we are developing? Are return on investment (ROI) and other product justifications still in line?

A process review (also called a lessons-learned review) focuses on *how* we are doing our work by asking two questions: What are we doing well? What do we want to improve?

During status and design reviews, a project may also be evaluated. An evaluation usually focuses on software or hardware development projects and tries to determine if the desired end result will be accomplished. Will the ROI target be met? Will the product be manufacturable? Can we sell it?

**T A B L E   11.1**

The Three Kinds of Project Reviews

| Type of Review | Purpose |
|---|---|
| Status | Are PCTS okay? |
| Design | Does it work? <br> Can we make it? |
| Process (also called lessons-learned reviews) | What have we done well so far? <br> What do we want to do better in the future? |

The answer to these questions determines whether the project will be continued or canceled. Table 11.1 summarizes the three project reviews.

Following are some of the general reasons for conducting periodic project reviews:

- ◆ Improve project performance together with the management of the project.

- ◆ Ensure that quality of project work does not take a back seat to schedule and cost concerns.

- ◆ Reveal developing problems early, so that action can be taken to deal with them.

- ◆ Identify areas where other projects (current or future) should be managed differently.

- ◆ Keep client(s) informed of project status. This can also help ensure that the completed project will meet the needs of the client.

- ◆ Reaffirm the organization's commitment to the project for the benefit of project team members.

> The purpose of a process review is to learn how to improve performance. If you go on a witch hunt, you will create witches where none existed before.

## PROCESS REVIEWS

The objective or purpose of a process review is to improve performance of the team. In reviewing performance, note that we do not ask, "What have we done wrong?" Asking that question simply raises defenses in team members who will then try to hide anything they think is wrong, because they assume they will be trashed for any mistakes that have been made. The purpose of a process review is to learn from experience, so that we can avoid those things that were not done so well and continue doing those things that have been done well. It is not a witch hunt. If you go about it in a "blame and punishment" way, people will hide their faults.

The other reason for not asking what has been done wrong is that the answer may be "nothing," and everyone may think this means a review is unnecessary. This is not true. The best-performing team must always attempt to get even better, as their competitors are not sitting idly by maintaining the status quo. They too are improving, and if you stand still for very long, they will pass you.

Also, the most dangerous place a team can be is successful. That may sound wrong, and maybe even a bit depressing, but it is true. A successful team can easily get complacent. Coaches of sports teams know this. When you have won every game of the season, your very next game is risky because you may get cocky and careless. For that reason, you can never be satisfied with the status quo.

It is very important to understand that process will always affect task outcomes! That is, the *way* you do something will always affect the results you get. As the old saying goes, "If you always do what you've always done, you'll always get what you always got." And the corollary is, "Insanity is continuing to do what you've always done and hoping for a different result." In terms of process, these statements mean, "If you aren't getting the results you want, change your process!"

> **Process will always affect task!**
> —Marvin Weisbord

In any project team, the processes we care about include those shown in the box. One of the most important of these is meetings. Projects cannot succeed without periodic meetings. However, as we all know, the large majority of meetings are badly run, leaving participants drained, frustrated, and wishing they would never have to attend another one. In his video, "Meetings, Bloody Meetings," John Cleese makes a profound comment about meetings. He says, "The essence of management is in how we run meetings."

Now if that doesn't make you depressed, you haven't thought about the implications. Meetings typically lose focus, have no clear direction to begin with, last ad nauseam, and don't accomplish anything. If you can't manage a meeting, how can you manage an organization?

One of the best meeting-management models I have seen was developed at Xerox and was described by Tom Kaiser in his book, *Mining Group Gold* (1995). The process is also illustrated in a video by the same name, distributed by CRM Films (see Chapter 32 for their 800 number). The essence of the model is that a pre-meeting agenda is published, with each agenda item time-limited. When the meeting starts, the agenda is reviewed to ensure that it is still valid. One member of the team serves the role of note-keeper (called the *scribe* by Kaiser). Note-taking is done on flip chart pages so that members of the group can see them throughout the meeting. Taking notes on standard paper does not permit constant viewing.

---

**Team Processes**

♦Leadership

♦Decision making

♦Problem solving

♦Communications

♦Meetings

♦Planning

♦Giving feedback to team members

♦Conflict management

---

Another member of the team serves as timekeeper, making sure the meeting stays on schedule. Finally, a person called facilitator has responsibility for controlling the meeting. All members are expected to be cofacilitators, however, so that if the meeting gets off track and the facilitator does not bring it back around, any member of the team can do so.

Another aspect of the model is that feelings must be processed before facts. If people get upset about something, they are asked to pause and reflect on why they are upset, then have an open discussion about their feelings. As Kaiser says, if you attempt to deal with facts while people are upset, you are just wasting your time.

This is a much more reasonable approach than telling people to keep feelings out of the meeting. Such a directive is totally unrealistic. People would not be people without feelings, so we must validate them and learn to deal effectively with them.

## The Process Review Report

When a project is reviewed, the lessons learned should be shared with other teams. By doing so, they can avoid the mistakes made by the team being reviewed and they can take advantage of the things they are doing well. The lessons-learned report should contain as a minimum the following:

1. **Current project status.** This is best shown using earned-value analysis, as presented in Chapter 12. However, when earned-value analysis is not used, status should still be reported with as much accuracy as possible.

2. **Future status.** This is a forecast of what you expect to happen in the project. Are significant deviations anticipated in schedule, cost, performance, or scope? If so, the nature of such changes should be specified.

3. **Status of critical tasks.** The status of critical tasks, particularly those on the critical path, should be reported. You should give special attention to tasks that have high levels of technical risk, as well as those outside vendors or subcontractors will perform, over which the project manager may have limited control.

4. **Risk assessment.** Have any risks been identified that highlight potential for monetary loss, project failure, or other liabilities?

5. **Information relevant to other projects.** What have you learned from this review that can/should be applied to other projects, whether presently in progress or about to start?

6. **Limitations of the review.** What factors might limit the validity of the review? Are any assumptions suspect? Is any data missing or suspected of contamination? Was anyone uncooperative in providing information for the review?

Generally, the simpler and more straightforward a project-review report, the better. The information should be organized so that planned versus actual results can be easily compared. Significant deviations should be highlighted and explained. Figure 11.1 presents a form you can use for a milestone-process review. For an end-of-project review, the form will be too small to capture all the data you have generated, so it should be used as a guide for what questions to ask. See also the project checklists in Chapter 30 for additional ideas.

## PROJECT EVALUATION

The dictionary defines the word "evaluate" as an attempt to determine if the overall status of work is acceptable—for our purposes, in terms of intended value to the client once the job is finished. Project evaluation compares the progress and perfor-

**evaluate:** to determine or judge the value or worth of.
—*Random House Dictionary*

mance of a job to the original plan. That evaluation provides the basis for management decisions as to how to proceed with the project. The evaluation must be credible in the eyes of ev-

Process Review Form

| Project Process Review |
|---|
| Project: |
| Prepared by:                          Date: |
| For the period from                   to: |
| Evaluate the following objectives:<br><br>Performance was on target ☐, below target ☐, above target ☐<br><br>Budget was on target ☐, overspent ☐, underspent ☐<br>Schedule was on target ☐, behind ☐, ahead ☐ |
| **Overall, was the project a success?** Yes ☐ No ☐ |
| If not, what factors contributed to a negative evaluation? |
| What was done really well? |
| What could have been done better? |
| What recommendations would you make for future project application? |
| What would you do differently if you could do it over? |
| What have you learned that can be applied to future projects? |

eryone affected, or decisions based on that evaluation will not be considered valid. The primary tool for project evaluation is the *project evaluation* or *audit*, which is usually conducted at major milestones throughout the life of the project.

The audit is actually a special combination of the status and design reviews. As was previously stated, it focuses on *P, C, T, S,* and whether the outcome of the project will meet all objectives.

One concern that I have is with the word *audit*. If you have ever been audited, you know that it was not a happy experience. People who audit you are usually out to get you. The word *evaluation* is a kinder, gentler word, to use the popular phrase. We are not out to get the project manager when we evaluate a project, even though it is true that the outcome may be to cancel the project. On the other hand, no one likes to cancel projects because of the sunk costs involved, so most project evaluations are really aimed at validating the project rather than canceling it. So I am going to use the term evaluation, rather than audit, throughout this chapter.

If an evaluation is to be effective, you must have an effective project control system. No evaluation can be successful unless proper control methods are first employed. The requirements for such a control system will be presented later in this chapter.

## Canceling Projects

One of the most traumatic things you can do is cancel a project. Anyone who thinks it is purely a "business" decision has probably not been there. People get upset, especially members of the project team. "It's a good project," they protest. "How can you cancel it?"

Managers are in equal agony. "I hate to cancel it and loose all that money we've spent." But sunk costs are sunk and can't be recovered in many cases.

> One of the most traumatic things you can do
> is cancel a project.

Marvin Patterson, former vice president of product development at Hewlett-Packard, wrote a book entitled *Accelerating Innovation* (Patterson, 1993), in which he discusses canceling product-development projects. He says that if you have never canceled a product-development project, then you have undoubtedly brought to market some products that should never have seen the light of day, because nobody is so good that they are 100 percent successful. On the other hand, if you cancel too many development projects, then there is something wrong with your project selection, product development, or project management processes. How many is too many? There is no way to give an exact answer, but in terms of normal distribution curves, you could expect that perhaps those out on the tail of the curve might fit. That might be a couple of percent.

Patterson offers a very simple way to address the issue of canceling projects, and I am unashamedly borrowing from him in the material that follows. There is no use re-inventing a wheel when someone has produced a perfect one!

The analysis is based on cash flow in development projects, as shown in Figure 11.2. When cash flow is negative, you are investing in development of the product (or software). When cash flow is positive, you are receiving money from sales. When money received (area B in the figure) equals total investment (area A), you have reached the break-even point, and revenues to the right of area B represent profits.

Now notice the points on the horizontal time line. On the far left is a point labeled $T_0$, which is the time when the *opportunity* for the product comes into being. Presumably, if we had the product at that time, customers would buy it if they could afford it. The problem is, we don't know the opportunity exists. Our marketing department has responsibility for finding out about these things, but they never have

**F I G U R E  11.2**

Cash Flow in a Product Development Project

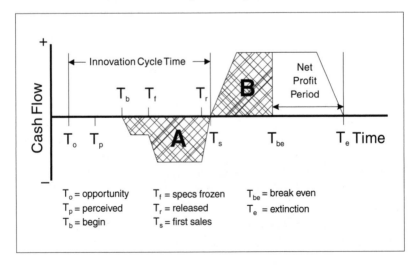

perfect environmental "radar," so there is a delay between $T_o$ and $T_p$, when the opportunity is finally *perceived*.

I'm sure you know that marketing people who find an opportunity to sell something will get very excited. (This is appropriate: they should be excited about doing their job.) Furthermore, they will try to see if they can justify developing the product. To do so, they look at whether there will be an acceptable ROI. This is the total revenue generated by lifetime sales of the product, divided by area A. Interestingly, marketers often do this without talking to anyone else. They estimate both sales and development costs, and if the ROI is acceptable, they try to get the project approved.

It is, of course, curious how they estimate development costs without talking to the development group, but I have figured that one out. They use a mathematical function I call *Tater's Transform*. I have named the function after a fellow from South Carolina named Mark Tate (whose friends call him "Tater") because he first made me realize how it works. Using Tater's Transform gives you an equation like this:

$$x \blacktriangleright\!\blacktriangleright y$$

The way you read this equation is, "X becomes Y." This means that whatever you put into the left-hand side becomes whatever you *want* it to be on the right-hand side. Furthermore, the equation is bilateral, so that you can also write:

$$y \blacktriangleright\!\blacktriangleright x$$

We have all known how to use Tater's Transform since infancy. I believe it is a genetic thing. It is wired in at birth. As evidence, consider the fellow who wants to buy a $5,000 hunting bow. His wife wants to know how he can justify spending so much money on a toy, and he assures her that the game and venison that he will bring home with his new bow will save them thousands in groceries over the years. He is using Tater's Transform.

So this is what the marketing folks do. But do you notice that even after they come in with their proposal there is a delay before we begin working on the product? Why is that? If it is such a great idea, why don't we get on it immediately?

Generically, this delay can be called *organizational inertia*, of which there are several possible sources. The first is the approval process itself. In some organizations, you need 27 signatures from people scattered all over the world before a project can get funding, and these 27 people all know intuitively that marketing people use Tater's Transform to justify their ideas. So it takes some time to convince everyone that the idea is valid. Secondly, there is the budget to consider. There is no money available to do the project, and if the marketing person happens to have the idea just after the close of next year's budget-approval cycle, the job might have to wait a year before being funded, by which time someone else already started working on the idea and they beat you to market.

The third reason that is pervasive in the U.S. today is downsizing. There are no extra resources sitting around waiting for something to do, so even if it is a great idea and we could fund it, there is no one to work on it.

In any case, the project is finally approved and work starts. At this point, called $T_b$, when work begins, cash flow goes negative, because the company is spending its own money—making an *investment* in the new product. Initially, the work done is an attempt to pin down the product specifications, so the point labeled $T_f$ is the time when the specs are frozen. This point, of course, is a myth. No product specifications are ever really frozen this early in the life cycle. The point they are really frozen is $T_e$, when the product becomes *extinct* in the marketplace. By default, they are frozen then. So we should really consider $T_f$ a tentative point.

Once the specs are tentatively frozen, development work begins in earnest, and the cycle proceeds to $T_r$, when the product is released to manufacturing. This point is quickly followed by $T_s$, which is supposedly when first sales occur, but everyone knows that the sales department would never wait until now to sell a product. No, they sold it way back at $T_p$, took orders for it, and promised deliveries, all without consulting the product-development group about whether the promised delivery date could be met. They also use Tater's Transform to arrive at the delivery date. So this point should really be when shipments occur.

Now cash flow turns positive, because the product is generating revenue, and this continues until $T_e$ is reached. At this time, the product is extinct in the marketplace. Point $T_{be}$ is the time when revenue generated equals total investment, so the company is at the break-even point, and all revenue to the right is net profit on the product. (This is *approximately* correct.)

This analysis would be fairly straightforward if $T_e$ were stable, but it is not. The extinction point can move around. If a competitor introduces a new product that is better, faster, or cheaper, your $T_e$ moves to the left. If a new market opportunity is found, $T_e$ is pushed to the right. Or when market saturation occurs, and everyone has all the product they need. Or if new regulations get passed, which prevent the product from meeting the requirements, so sales must be discontinued. Many such factors can cause extinction timing to move around. One of the best ways to push $T_e$ to the right is to develop a world-class product in the first place.

Now consider Figure 11.3. The company has just started really working on developing a product, and the marketing folks come in with gloom and doom written all over their faces. When asked what is wrong, they say, "We've just found that a competitor is going to beat us to market with their product, so that our product will be killed shortly after we release it." As the figure shows, this means that the investment will never be recovered, so if we continue with the program, we will just throw away a lot of money. This is a no-brainer—cancel the project and start a new one. That may mean redefining the product and going from there, or trying

**F I G U R E   11.3**

Extinction Time Moves Forward

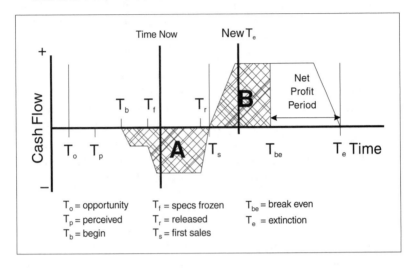

$T_o$ = opportunity     $T_f$ = specs frozen     $T_{be}$ = break even
$T_p$ = perceived       $T_r$ = released         $T_e$ = extinction
$T_b$ = begin           $T_s$ = first sales

to leapfrog the next generation, but you simply can't continue with the product as originally defined, unless you like to waste money.

As logical as this sounds, it is a very traumatic situation, and many organizations refuse to do the "obvious." They can't bear to throw away all of the money they have already spent (what we call sunk costs). Engineers get very emotional and complain that their project is a good one, and it is a shame to cancel it. Both arguments are fallacious. Sunk costs are sunk costs, and you may as well admit that they can't be recovered, short of a miracle, and there aren't enough miracles in business to be worth banking on. It may be a good product, but if it will never succeed in the marketplace, what value does it have, even to the engineer who is enamored with it? So the smart thing to do is kill the project and get on with something that promises a positive return on the investment.

The question is, if you are vulnerable to these kinds of market dynamics, what can you do to protect yourself? There are several things. First, you need to reduce the design cycle. This is shown in Figure 11.4. There are two ways to reduce design time. One is by using state-of-the-art design practices, such as rapid prototyping. The second is by doing very good project management. The ultimate objective would be to shorten the design cycle and to simultaneously reduce the cost of the cycle. This is shown in Figure 11.5. If we can reduce total investment (Area A), then we don't have to sell as much product to reach the break-even point, and become profitable. Good project management can help achieve this objective.

How? One way is by reducing rework through good planning. Estimates place rework at 30 percent of total product-development costs. This means that one of every three engineers or programmers assigned to development work is spending all of his time redoing what the other two did wrong in the first place. By eliminating the rework, you will improve your productivity by a corresponding amount.

## F I G U R E  11.4

Development Cycle Shortened

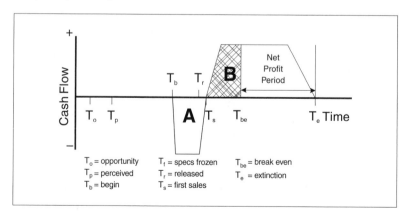

**F I G U R E  11.5**

Total Investment Reduced

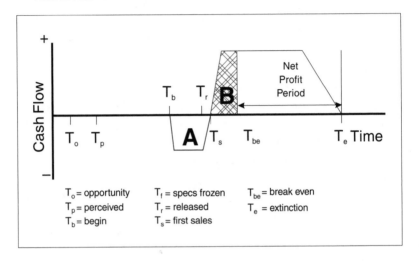

This is, incidentally, a good way to show that you are improving your management of projects. When you are new to formal project management, it is usually difficult to show that you are getting better, because you don't have good history on previous projects. But if you start measuring rework in projects, you should see that measure improve, and this is evidence that project management is paying good dividends.

Another way to protect yourself from competitive forces is to move $T_b$ leftward toward $T_p$. That is, reduce organizational inertia. Have some reserve capacity. Shorten the approval cycle.

You also want to move $T_p$ toward $T_o$, which requires the best market surveillance you can get. This requires living with your customers, watching your competitors, and forecasting trends.

Finally, you place $T_b$ to the left of $T_o$. This means that you develop the product before the opportunity comes into being. You are a market leader, rather than a follower. Examples include the automobile, telephone, Post-it™ note, SONY Walkman™, the personal computer, and many other products. As Jack Trout has said, it is a well-known fact that you cannot do market research on something not in the market (Trout and Rivkin, 1999), so market leaders must proceed on faith that what they are developing will ultimately sell.

## Project Control

The status review helps control a project. Control is an attempt on a day-to-day basis to keep project work on track. It consists of measuring the status of work performed, comparing that status with what was planned to be accomplished to date, then taking corrective action to get back on target if a deviation is discovered. The need for a good plan, against which progress can be compared, was emphasized in Chapter 3. In this chapter, the focus will be on attempting to assess or measure actual progress, which is not always such an easy task, as we shall see.

> **control:** comparing progress against plan so that corrective action can be taken when a deviation occurs.

One important distinction about control should be made. The word *control* often refers to power, authority, command, or domination. Another meaning, however, is that of guiding a course of action to meet a predefined objective. This is the meaning of control you should apply to project-control systems.

Based on these ideas, here are some premises of management-control systems.

- ◆ **Work is controlled—not workers.** The objective is to get the work done, not make workers "toe the line." Authoritarian management generally leads to

WORK is controlled—not workers! The objective is to get the work done.

resentment and an atmosphere that stifles creativity, which is just the opposite of what is needed. Control should be viewed as a *tool* that the worker can use to work more effectively and efficiently.

◆ **Control of complex work is based on motivation and self-control.** Control must be exercised by the person doing the work. Control by someone other than the worker creates a number of problems. Control is likely to degenerate into control of the worker, rather than the work. There is a need for communication between the worker and controller, but that communication may not take place properly. Finally, the controller probably does not know the work as well as the worker, and cannot establish reasonable checkpoints as required. The worker is in the best position to establish a course of action and monitor his or her own progress.

Self-control is part of the job of every knowledge worker. This should be clearly spelled out to those individuals. The best set of control procedures will not work unless the people involved are motivated to make it work.

◆ **Control is based on completed work.** To determine if the work process is achieving objectives, examine the product produced. In the case of a complex task, the work is subdivided (to the work package level, for example) and the smaller units are monitored. Each task must have a well-defined output (or deliverable), and there must be standards for evaluating the completed work.

◆ **Methods of obtaining control data must be built into the work process.** That is, the person doing the work must be able to tell where she/he is at any given time. When driving, we use road signs to tell us where we are, and we compare those to our map to see if we are on course. If a brick wall is being constructed, it is easy enough to count the bricks actually laid (or measure the height of the wall) so that figure can be compared to the plan. As I've pointed out previously, however, knowledge work is harder to measure and usually will be an estimate of progress.

As a further consideration, only data that is actually required for control should be collected. The control process should not be a burden.

◆ **Control data must go to the person who does the work.** Consider a pilot. Do you give information about the plane's position to the pilot's boss? Of course not. Yet this is often done in organizations, and results in a manager's receiving more control data than he can possibly use.

◆ **A control system is designed for the routine.** A thermostat turns a furnace on or off to control temperature. It cannot compensate for an empty fuel tank. A control system is designed to cope with the routine: exceptions must be given special handling. You must, then, decide what is routine and what is not.

◆ **Control of a complex process is achieved through levels of control.** That which is exceptional at one level may be routine at the next higher level. Only the most pressing problems should find their way to the top level of control.

## CHARACTERISTICS OF A PROJECT-CONTROL SYSTEM

There are four basic activities that must be performed to have a satisfactory control system:

1. Planning performance.
2. Observing actual performance.
3. Comparing actual and planned performance.
4. Adjusting as required.

Comparing performance against plan can be difficult when the work cannot be quantified. When work can be quantified, deviation from plan is called *variance*. For nonquantifiable work, performance must be judged subjectively. Usually such judgment is binary—that is, the work is either satisfactory or it is not.

Summary performance reports should be standardized for all projects. Data should also be presented in an effective way. There must be a balance between presenting too much and too little data.

### Objectives

The control system must focus on objectives. The designer of the control system should answer these questions:

◆ What is important to the organization?

◆ What are we attempting to do?

◆ Which aspects of the work are most important to track and control?

◆ What are the critical points in the process at which controls should be placed?

The important should be controlled. However, what is controlled tends to become important. Thus, if budgets and schedules are emphasized to the exclusion of quality, only those will be controlled. The project may well come in on time and within budget at the expense of quality.

To avoid that, the control system should factor in the following:

◆ **Response**. A control system should focus on response—if control data does not result in action, then the system is ineffective. That is, a control system must use deviation data to *initiate corrective action* or it is not really a control system but simply a monitoring system.

◆ **Timeliness**. The response to control data must be timely. If action occurs too late, it will be ineffective.

◆ **Human factors**. The system should be easy to use. In particular, the control system should be designed for the convenience of people, and not machines.

◆ **Flexibility**. One system is not likely to be correct for all projects. It may need to be scaled down for small projects and beefed up for large ones.

◆ **Simplicity**. The smallest control effort that achieves the desired result should be used. Any control data that is not essential should be eliminated. However, one common mistake is to try to control complex projects with systems that are *too simple!*

## Components of a Project Control System

In its simplest form, a project control system can be represented by a first-order feedback system, as shown in Figure
11.6. The system has *inputs, outputs,* and a *process* for transforming those inputs to outputs, together with a *feedback loop*
to ensure that the system continues processing inputs according to its design. The outputs are monitored, compared to
some preset standard, and if the outputs are not correct, that
information is fed back as an input to the system to correct
for the deviation.

This feedback system is a very simple one. It is not very
elegant, and has some serious limitations as a model on how
to achieve control in project management.

For readers unfamiliar with feedback systems, a good
analogy for the first-order system is the thermostat in one's
home. In the winter, the system provides heat and the desired room temperature is preset by adjusting the thermostat
to the proper level.

**F I G U R E   11.6**

First-Order Feedback System

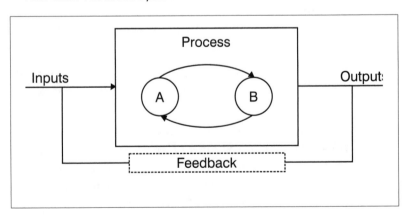

It should be clear that every system is designed to work properly only under certain conditions. For example, the home heating system might be designed to maintain the room at 70 degrees Fahrenheit as long as the outside temperature does not go below minus 30 degrees. When the outside temperature drops below that level, the heater will run continuously, but the room temperature will begin to drop below the preset level of 70 degrees.

To maintain the desired room temperature, the system would have to increase its heating capacity, but it cannot do this. Thus, it keeps running, without being able to adequately heat the house.

In a similar manner, a project may run into unexpected obstacles, which fall outside the boundaries for which the project control system was designed. Everyone is following the plan to the letter, but they are not getting the desired result. What is needed is to change the approach. However, a first-order control system does not have that capability. Something more flexible is needed. The third-order system shown in Figure 11.7 is the answer.

The system in Figure 11.7 has the same basic elements as the first-order system of Figure 11.6. There are inputs, processes, outputs, and feedback. However, the third-order system feeds information about the system outputs to a *comparator*, which weighs them against the original plan. If there is a discrepancy, that information is passed to an *adjust* element, which must decide if the discrepancy is caused by something wrong with the process, the inputs, or the plan itself.

Once that determination is made, the adjust element calls for a change in the plan, inputs, or the process itself. Note also that the adjust element has an arrow going back to the monitor. If a deviation is detected, the monitoring rate is increased until the deviation is corrected, then monitoring is decreased to its original level.

The real-world analogy is that if you were monitoring progress on a project weekly and a problem occurred, you

**F I G U R E  11.7**

Third-Order Feedback System

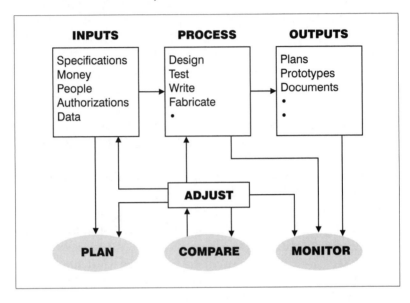

might begin to monitor daily. If the problem becomes serious enough, your monitoring rate might increase to several times each day. Once the problem has been solved, you would revert to your weekly monitoring.

Comparing performance against plan can be difficult when the work cannot be quantified. How do you know what percentage of a design is complete, for example? Or if you are doing a mechanical drawing of a part, is the drawing 75 percent complete when 75 percent of the area of the paper is covered? Probably not. Measuring progress in *knowledge work*, to use Peter Drucker's term, is very difficult.

This often leads to strange results. Suppose a member of the project team has agreed to design a new golf club, and has promised to finish it in 10 weeks. At the end of week one, she reports that the design work is 10 percent complete. At the end of week two, the work is 25 percent complete. In week three she hits a small snag and gets a little behind, but by week five she has gotten ahead again. Figure 11.8 shows a plot of her progress.

Everything goes pretty well until week eight, when she hits another snag. At the end of that week, she has made almost no progress at all. The same is true the following week, and the following, and the following.

What happened? For one thing, the 80/20 rule got her. In the case of knowledge work, it says that 80 percent of the work will be consumed by 20 percent of the problems encountered, and they will always happen near the end of the job.

The real issue, though, is how she measured progress in the first place. Chances are, at the end of the first week, she reasoned, "I'm at the end of the first week on a 10-week job. I must be 10 percent complete." And she would be in good company, because that is exactly what a lot of people do when *estimating* progress on knowledge work.

**F I G U R E   11.8**

Percent Complete Graph

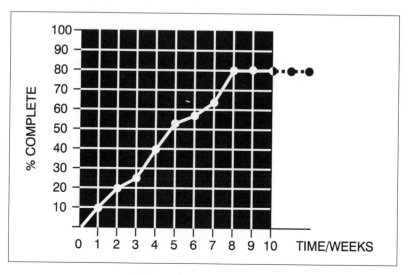

Note the word *estimate!* Assessing progress when work is not easily quantifiable is estimating, and subject to all the difficulties discussed in Chapter 6. This shows the limits of our ability to achieve control in management.

For this reason, two practices are advisable. First, work should be broken into small "chunks" that permit monitoring progress fairly frequently, perhaps in intervals no greater than two weeks. Second, tangible deliverables should be used as signposts to show progress. In design, a drawing is tangible evidence of progress. The same is true with software development. Printed code or written functional specs are evidence that work is complete. Having it "in one's head" is impossible to verify.

**12**

# Project Control Using Earned-Value Analysis

## USING VARIANCE OR EARNED VALUE ANALYSIS IN PROJECT CONTROL

Even though there are limits to assessing exactly how much work has been done on a project, there can be no control without some assessment. The most robust method of measuring project progress is through *variance* or *earned value* analysis. The method was originally developed to measure work accomplishment in manufacturing, and was later adopted as part of the cost/schedule control systems criteria (C/SCSC) for measuring progress in projects. If you have a knowledge of standard cost systems in manufacturing, you will be right at home with earned value analysis.

For a fuller explanation of the C/SCSC system, see Chapter 13 on progress payments. What follows in this chapter is an abbreviated approach that should be appropriate for application to most projects, not just large government jobs. For leaders who need a complete treatment of the C/SCSC system, see Fleming & Koppelman (1996).

First, we define variance as any deviation from plan. Variance analysis allows the project manager to determine "trouble spots" in the project and to take corrective action. As was mentioned previously, there are four areas of the project that the

**variance:** any deviation from plan.

project manager is expected to control. These are the performance, cost, time, and scope objectives.

In this set of variables, cost refers to labor costs. Material and capital equipment costs will be tracked, but they are not part of this set, because they do not directly relate to scope, time, and performance. Also, whether you talk about labor costs in terms of money or simply headcount, there is always a cost associated with the project. In some cases, when labor costs are not known, hours worked will be tracked. This is the easiest of the four variables to measure. The others are considerably more difficult in some situations.

Imagine, for example, that you are building a brick wall. The plan says the wall should be 10 feet high and one foot thick, and it should be vertical. You can inspect to see that the

Variance analysis allows the project manager to determine "trouble spots" in the project and to take corrective action.

---

### General Approach to Progress Monitoring

When progress is monitored, three questions should always be asked:

1. What is the actual status of the project?
2. What caused the deviation? (When there is one.)
3. What should be done about it?

In answering the third question, there are three responses that can be made:

1. Ignore the deviation.
2. Take corrective action to get back on target.
3. Revise the plan.

If the deviation is not significant, it can be ignored, but note the word *significant*. As pointed out in a previous chapter, what is meant by significant should be determined in the planning stage of a project. In general, a deviation should exceed 5 percent to be considered significant, as most control systems cannot maintain a tighter tolerance.

---

wall is vertical and that the mortar is clean—this is performance or quality of work done. You can also measure the height and thickness and you find that it is only eight feet high. In that case, you know that work on the wall is behind schedule. The workers have completed only about 80 percent of what was planned. The measure isn't perfect, but it is much better than measuring knowledge work projects.

As an example of the difficulty of measuring knowledge work projects, assume that a programmer is writing code. She estimates that she will have about 10,000 lines of code in the module, and she has written about 8,000 lines. Is she 80 percent complete? Probably not. For one thing, you can't tell if unfinished code will work when it is finished, so you have no idea about quality, and you don't have a good measure of percent complete by taking a ratio of lines written to lines estimated to be required. So if you don't know scope or quality, you can't know anything about progress on schedule. The only measure that is accurate is cost. You know how many hours she has worked on the code, but that is all.

This fact makes some people think that you shouldn't try to measure progress in programming, since it is so "iffy." One fellow I know likes to say that there is no value at all in unfinished code, so if you stopped work on it, there would be no salvage value, whereas the same is not true in making things. I don't agree with him. There is not much salvage value in an unfinished brick wall either. Yes, you could tear it down and reclaim the bricks, but nobody measures progress to determine the salvage value of the bricks. They do so solely to determine if the job is on schedule.

> In some organizations, project managers do not deal with costs, but rather with *labor hours.* Once standard variance analysis has been presented in terms of cost, a method of dealing with working hours will be presented.

In the chapter on scheduling, we said that engineering and programming work should be subdivided into one- to three-week increments, with markers that tell you if the increments have been completed. This means that at the end of the tracking period, the worker gets credit for doing the work if it is complete, and no credit if it is not complete. We don't try to estimate percentages, as this causes the problems described in Chapter 11.

If we begin by measuring scope and performance, we can then determine if there are schedule and cost variances. These are defined as follows:

◆ **Cost variance:** Compares deviations only from budget and provides no comparisons of work scheduled and work accomplished.

◆ **Schedule variance:** Compares planned versus actual work completed. This variance can be translated into the dollar value of the work, so that all variances can be specified in monetary terms.

Three measures can be used to assess cost and schedule variance. They are defined in the following paragraphs, together with examples of how they are calculated.

**Note:** the terms used in earned value analysis were changed a few years ago. I have retained the terms that have been in use for many years. However the new terms are as follows:

BCWS = PV, which stands for planned value

BCWP = EV, which stands for earned value

ACWP = AC, which means actual cost

If you plan to take the PMP® exam, it uses the two-letter nomenclature, so be sure you know the conversions. I have retained the four-letter codes because many of the older books on project management contain these terms, so I thought it would be useful for you to be able to "translate" them.

◆ **BCWS (PV):** (Budgeted Cost of Work Scheduled) is budgeted cost of work scheduled to be done in a given time period, or the level of effort budgeted to be performed in that period. This is the *target* toward which the project is headed. Another way to say it is that BCWS represents the *plan* that one is supposed to follow. It is basically the product of man-hours and the dollar labor rate that is paid during a given period of time, usually a day or week at a time. As an example, suppose that a project will employ two people working on the project for one week (40 hours) at the labor rate of $30 per hour each (loaded labor—with overhead included). In addition, a third person will work on the project for 30 hours during the same week, but at a loaded labor rate of $50 per hour. The budgeted-cost-of-work-scheduled for the week, then, is the sum of two products:

40 hours × $30/hour × 2          = $2,400
30 hours × $50/hour × 1          = $1,500
   Total BCWS = $2,400 + $1,500 = $3,900

♦ **BCWP (EV):** (Budgeted Cost of Work Performed) in a given period, also called *earned value,* measures how much work has been accomplished.

The BCWP figure is calculated as follows. For the example above, assume that the two employees who are assigned to work for a full 40 hours each do indeed put in that amount of effort. One worker actually completes her work, while the other only completes about 80 percent of the work he was supposed to do. The worker assigned to put in only 30 hours also completes his work as planned. We say that the earned value of the work completed, then, is as follows:

40 hours × $30/hour             = $1,200
0.8 × 40 hours × $30/hour        = $  960
30 hours × $50/hour             = $1,500
   BCWP TOTAL:                    $3,660

♦ **ACWP (AC):** (Actual Cost of Work Performed) represents the amount of money actually spent in completing work in a given period. This is the amount of money paid to workers (wages only—remember, none of these figures includes any material costs) to do the work that was completed during the time period in question.

Further, assume that the work completed has actually cost the organization $3,900. If this figure were compared with BCWS, we might think the project is in good shape. The scheduled work was supposed to cost $3,900, and that is what has been paid in labor. However, we also know that one person did not complete the work he was supposed to do. The value of his accomplishment is only $960, but was supposed to be $1,200. To see what this means for the project, the following formulas are employed:

Cost variance = BCWP − ACWP (or EV − AC)

Schedule variance = BCWP − BCWS (Dollar value) (or EV − PV)

Plugging numbers into these formulas, we have the following results:

Cost variance = $3,660 − $3,900 = −$240

In standard accounting practice, a negative variance is always unfavorable, so that a negative cost variance means that the project is spending more than was planned. Be careful with this term—a cost variance is not necessarily the same thing as budget variance.

Schedule variance = $3,660 − $3,900 = −$240

Again, a negative schedule variance is unfavorable, which means that the project is behind schedule.

Looking at these two figures together tells us that the project has gotten behind schedule in the amount of $240 worth of work, and because the cost variance is identical to the schedule variance, we know that the cost variance is due *only* to the schedule variance. That is, the work being done is costing what it was estimated to cost. If labor rates had escalated, then the cost variance would be greater than the schedule variance.

## VARIANCE ANALYSIS USING SPENDING CURVES

Variances are often plotted using spending curves. Figure
12.1 presents a BCWS curve for a project. It shows the *cumulative spending* planned for a project, and is sometimes called
a *baseline plan.* Such curves can often be plotted automatically by transferring spending data from a scheduling program (which calculates labor expenses on a daily or weekly
basis by multiplying labor rates times manpower expended)
to a graphics program using a DIF file or some other
file-transfer format.

In the event that software is not available to provide the
necessary data, Figure 12.2 shows how to generate data for
the curve. Consider a simple bar-chart schedule. Only three
tasks are involved. Task one involves 40 labor hours per

### F I G U R E   12.1

BCWS Curve

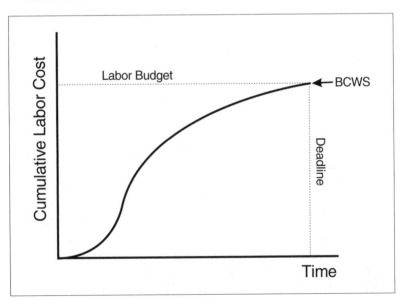

Cumulative Spending for Schedule

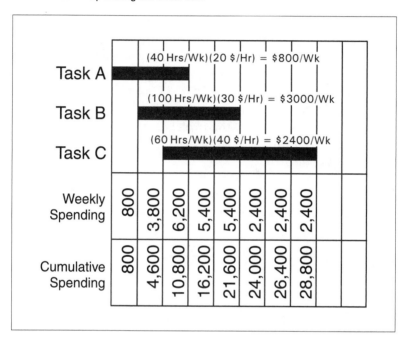

week at an average loaded labor rate of $20/hour, so that task costs $800/week. Task two involves 100 hours/week of labor at $30/hour, so it costs $3,000/week. Finally, task three spends $2,400/week, based on 60 hours/week of labor at $40/hour.

At the bottom of the chart we see that during the first week, $800 is spent for project labor; in the second week both tasks one and two are running, so the labor expenditure is $3,800. In the third week, all three tasks are running, so labor expenditure is the sum of the three, or $6,200. These are the *weekly* expenditures.

The *cumulative* expenditures are calculated by adding the cost for each subsequent week to the previous cumulative total. At the end of week one, $800 has been spent. At the end of week two, the figure is $4,600; at week three, it is $10,800, and so on.

These cumulative amounts are plotted in Figure 12.3. This is the spending curve for the project, and is called a BCWS curve. Because it is derived directly from the schedule, it represents *planned performance,* and therefore is called a *baseline plan.* Further, because control is exercised by comparing progress to plan, this curve can be used as the basis for such comparisons so that the project manager can tell the status of the program. Following are examples of how to make such assessments.

**F I G U R E   12.3**

Cumulative Spending Curve

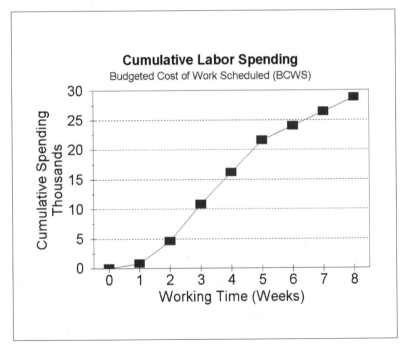

# EXAMPLES OF PROGRESS TRACKING USING SPENDING CURVES

Consider the curves in Figure 12.4. On a given date, the project is supposed to have accomplished $50,000 (50K) in labor (BCWS). The people working on the project were supposed to do 1,000 hours of work at a loaded labor rate of $50 per hour. Loaded labor means that the direct pay has added to it the overhead rates that are used to pay heat, water, lights, rent, and so on. Loaded labor is the actual cost to do project work, and should be used to calculate project costs.

When the project manager checks progress, he finds that the amount of work actually accomplished to date is 80 percent

**F I G U R E   12.4**

Curves Showing Project Behind Schedule and Overspent

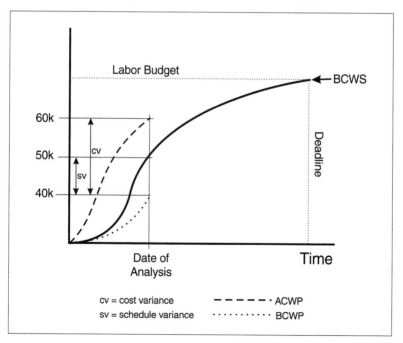

cv = cost variance          ─ ─ ─ ─ · ACWP
sv = schedule variance      ·········· BCWP

of what was supposed to be done. The value of this work to the organization is, then, 80 percent of the scheduled work (BCWS), or $40K. This is shown in Figure 12.4.

The actual cost of the work performed (ACWP) is $60K. This might be because the people doing work have put in 1,200 hours at $50 per hour, or they put in 1,000 hours of work but the labor rate was actually $60 per hour. Actual cost variance, then, is a composite variance. Either way it occurs, it means that labor is costing more than was originally planned. These figures are usually obtained from the accounting department, and are derived from all of the time cards that have reported labor applied to the project. Again, note that we do not include material or capital equipment costs in these figures. These are kept in a separate account.

The first question we ask is status. I always begin with schedule variance, which is BCWP – BCWS. If we take $40K minus $50K, we get –$10K. That is, the project is $10K worth of work behind schedule. You will note in Figure 12.4 that this variance can be obtained in dollars or time units. The project should have hit the $40K point earlier, so if you drop a perpendicular down to the time axis, you can see that the project is $x$ units behind schedule.

The cost variance is BCWP – ACWP. Think always of BCWP as what you got for the effort expended. We are then taking the difference between what we got for our money and what it cost us. In this case, we have $40K – $60K, or –$20K. In other words, if we spent $60K to accomplish $40K worth of work we are not getting enough benefit for our expense. Note that the $20K variance is the sum of two variances. You are $10K above the budget (BCWS) and $10K behind schedule, so the total cost or spending variance is the sum of the two.

So we are behind schedule and we have overspent. This is the worst situation a project can be in. It is bad enough to be behind schedule $or$ overspent, but to be both at the same time is really a problem. Unfortunately, it happens.

The second question we must answer is, "What caused it?" We generally don't know for certain. The estimates could be wrong. The work may have turned out to be harder than we expected, or there may have been unforeseen problems that caused the work to take longer and cost more than originally estimated. Or the people may have been unproductive. You don't know in many cases.

The third question that must be answered is, "What do we want to do about it?" There are a number of possibilities. In Figure 12.5, I have plotted trends for the BCWP and ACWP curves. If nothing changes, this appears to be where they are headed. Note that the BCWP curve must eventually hit the total labor figure of $x$, and if it continues as shown, the project will be late by $x$.

**F I G U R E   12.5**

Trends for the Project If Nothing Changes

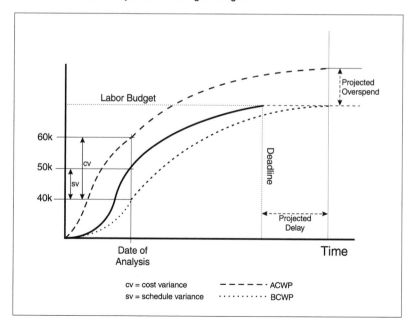

The ACWP curve must intersect the finish date, so at its present rate it will go up to approximately $x$ dollars, which means that the project will end up late and overspent by $x$ dollars.

But what if it is unacceptable to slip the end date? Can it still be met?

There are two possibilities. In Figure 12.5, note that if the scope were reduced to $x$ dollars, the project could be finished on time, even though it will be overspent by $x$ dollars, as shown. If this is acceptable to all stakeholders, then we could continue the project so that it would finish in this manner.

However, if it is not acceptable to be late *or* to reduce scope, then we are going to have to accelerate the work, making the BCWP curve turn upward, so that it will intersect the finish point on the required date. As shown, it is likely to cost us more money to do this, so the project will wind up spending $x$ dollars.

Now you may ask if it isn't somehow possible to finish on time without taking such a big hit on spending. The answer is, it is highly unlikely. Usually, if a project is in trouble just 15 percent of the way along the horizontal time line, it is going to stay in trouble. A study of more than 800 defense contract projects that were behind schedule or overspent at the 15 percent mark showed that not one ever recovered. The reason? Think about where the BCWS curve came from. It is based on all of our estimates of how long work will take. Another word for estimating is *forecasting*.

Now, with all due respect to weather forecasters, we know that if they can't tell us what will happen tomorrow, there is not much reason to believe that the long-term forecast will be accurate. The same is true for projects. If you can't forecast the near-term work accurately, why should you believe your end-of-project estimate will be right?

This is a good-news, bad-news story. The good news is that you can tell early in a project that it is likely to be a "bad" project, and you can take steps to cancel or make changes to the plan early. The bad news is that, if it is doing well at the 15 percent mark, it won't necessarily continue to do so.

Figure 12.6 illustrates another scenario. The BCWP and ACWP curves both fall at the same point, $60K. Beginning with the first question, "What is the status?" we see that the project is ahead of schedule, but spending correctly for the amount of work done. In other words, you have spent $60K and have accomplished $60K worth of work. However, the plan called for $50K worth of work, so the schedule variance (BCWP – BCWS) is positive $10K worth of work, meaning the job is ahead of schedule.

**F I G U R E   12.6**

Curves Showing the Project Ahead of Schedule, But Spending Okay

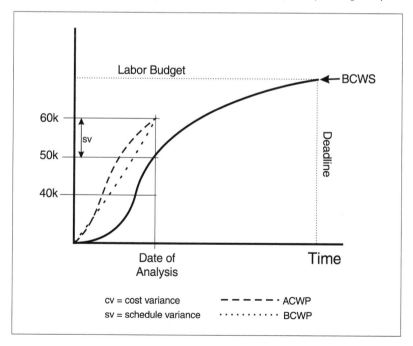

The second question we ask is, "What caused the deviation?" The most common cause of this situation is that extra resources were applied, but at the planned labor rate (since there is no spending variance). Then the question is, where did the project manager get the extra people? In a shared-resource environment there are two possibilities: either someone else had problems and couldn't use resources and gave them to you, or you diverted them to your project at someone else's expense. In construction projects this situation will occur because there were weather-delay days built into the schedule, and the weather has been good, so people have been able to do work they didn't think they would be able to do, but it is costing the correct amount.

The next question we ask is, "What should be done about this variance?" If you are like most people, your first thought is, "What does he mean, what should be done about it? I'm ahead of schedule and spending correctly, so I'm not going to do anything about it." I know, it sounds crazy to think you might need to slow down, but you might.

The reason is, ask yourself if being ahead of schedule could cause problems in the project, and you will see that it is possible. If you are producing something, your customer might not be able to use it if you finish early, and you have to pay to store it. Or you may reach a point in the project at which the people now have nothing to do, and you have simply delayed the inevitable.

Another consideration is cash flow. While the project is ahead of schedule, can it be funded at the rate being spent? If not, then the work would have to be decelerated. This might be true in construction projects, in which contractors want progress payments for the work they have done, and your controller can't pay the bills because money isn't coming in at the same rate as it is going out.

I know this is a little depressing. Just when you thought you were doing a good job, got ahead for the first time in your life, people start telling you to slow down. Naturally, it is a matter of degree. If you are a tiny bit ahead, no one is going to get excited. However, the variances I have shown in the figures are fairly large percentage deviations, and you may need to slow down in that case.

The next set of curves illustrates another situation. In Figure 12.7 the BCWP and ACWP curves are both at $40K. This means the project is behind schedule and underspent. The most likely cause? This project is probably starved for resources (perhaps the victim of another project manager being ahead). Labor is costing what it is supposed to cost, but not enough work is being done to stay on schedule. In asking

**F I G U R E   12.7**

Curves Showing Project Behind Schedule, But Spending Okay

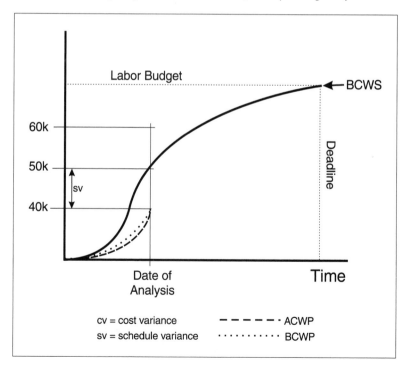

cv = cost variance            — — — — — · ACWP
sv = schedule variance        · · · · · · · · · · · BCWP

what you want to do, most of the time you want to get back on schedule. The problem for this project manager is that she will probably go over budget by trying to catch up, as premium labor will most likely be required.

Finally, Figure 12.8 looks like Figure 12.4, except the ACWP and BCWP curves have been reversed. Now the project is ahead of schedule and underspent. The accomplished work has an earned value of $60K, but the actual cost of that labor has been only $40K. At first glance, people think this is wonderful. But ask yourself how the variance happened.

**F I G U R E  12.8**

Project Is Ahead of Schedule and Underspent

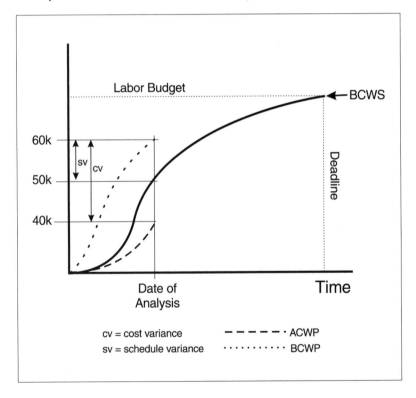

Three possibilities can explain how this project manager achieved the result shown:

1. Actual labor rates were considerably lower than expected, and/or the people were more efficient than anticipated.
2. The project team had a "lucky break." They expected to have to work really hard to solve a problem, but it turned out to be very easy.
3. The project manager "sandbagged" his estimates. He padded everything, playing it safe.

If you believe situation one, you will believe anything. It is very unlikely that both variances would happen at the same time.

Situation two happens occasionally. When all the planets are aligned—about once in a zillion years, you say. You bet!

Situation three is the most likely explanation. The project manager was playing it safe. And he would tell you that there is no problem. After all, if he continues along this course, the project will come in ahead of schedule and under budget, which means he will give money back to the company. No problem.

But is that true? First of all, I can almost guarantee that he won't give any money back. He will find a way to spend it, either by adding bells and whistles to the project, buying unplanned equipment or supplies, or throwing one huge party! No sane project manager wants to give the money back, because he knows that his next project budget will be cut.

However, suppose he did give back the money. Would that be okay? No. The reason is that the organization would have lost the opportunity to use that money to fund some other project. In fact, the first scenario we looked at was for a project that was behind schedule and overspent. The forecast showed that the project was going to be very late and over budget. It might well be that the project would be canceled, as it may no longer meet acceptable ROI ratios, or we simply say we can't fund it because no money is available.

But the money is available. It is tied up in the underbudget project. If that project were rescheduled and rebudgeted, the money would be available to keep the other project going, assuming that the ROI is still justified.

The question is, naturally, what is reasonable. We certainly cannot expect to have zero variances in a project. It all depends on the nature of your business. Well-defined construction projects can be held to very small tolerances—as small as plus-or-minus 3 to 5 percent. Research and development projects are likely to run higher tolerances, perhaps in the range of 15 to 25 percent. Each organization has to develop acceptable tolerances based on experience.

## Cross-Charging

There is another way to deal with the projects that are above and below on spending. You tell people working on the overspent project, "Don't charge any more time to this one. Charge your time to the underspent project." That way, both projects will come out right on target, and everyone will think you are doing a super job of managing.

This is called cross-charging. If you are doing defense contracting, you will be put in jail if they catch you doing it. Why? Because you are lying about what you have actually done. Progress payments (see Chapter 13) are made based on the BCWP that you report. If you cross-charge, you are reporting more work being accomplished on one job than you actually did, and less on the other.

But whether or not you are doing defense contracting, you are contaminating both project databases, and at the end of the jobs, you won't know how much either one really cost you. Does it matter? Of course. If it is new product development you are doing, part of the pricing formula is the cost to develop the product. One product is going to appear lower than it is and the other will be higher. The pricing of both will be wrong. Further, if a competitor enters the market, the sales people don't know for sure if they can lower the selling price and still make a profit. They also don't know when the break-even point is reached.

Worse yet, the status information on the project is used to decide whether to cancel the job if it is in trouble, and if you start charging time to other projects, you make it impossible for that decision to be made.

The proper way to deal with this situation is to do above-board transfers of money. You reduce the budget for the project that is doing well, and increase the budget for the other. That way, the databases are not contaminated.

The fear that project managers have is that once they give money back, they can't recover it should an unforeseen problem occur. Then they will come in over budget, which would not have happened if they had held on to the money.

It is a dilemma, and there is no easy answer. The question always is whether you expect to continue as you have already performed. If so, then give some of the money back. If not, keep it. However, the best predictor of future performance is past performance, and I would generally not expect that a project that has been doing really well would suddenly start getting in trouble, unless I knew that there were potential risks ahead.

Note that I said, give *part* of it back. It is proper risk-management practice to have a small contingency in a project to cover normal variances. All targets are estimates, and you can be sure that the variances won't be zero. As I pointed out previously, if you can hold tolerances of 5 percent, keep that much in reserve. If your tolerances are larger, keep a larger reserve account. No matter how you do it, this account should be aboveboard. It should be agreed to by everyone involved.

## REFINING THE ANALYSIS

The only problem with the analysis presented here is that it is an *aggregate* figure, and would not permit you to determine areas of the project in which a problem may exist, and may even hide a problem completely. For that reason, the variance analysis needs to be conducted on a task-by-task basis. This is usually done at whatever level in the work breakdown structure you have scheduled the work.

The importance of this was brought home to me by a client who reported that he had been using aggregate analysis to gauge project status for some time, and he discovered that a $100,000 overspend in one area of a project was being counterbalanced by a $100,000 underspend in another area. It looked like the project was in good shape, but such huge variances indicate a lack of control, and should be addressed.

The form in Figure 12.9 shows how to track individual tasks. The form has been filled in with some data to illustrate the various combinations of the numbers and their meanings.

The Project status report[1] shows the levels of project costs and work completed to date for each work package (or whatever level you wish to use to report progress). The report is configured as a QuatroPro® spreadsheet. The columns contain the following information:

◆ **Column 1:** The work package number.

◆ **Column 2:** BCWS (Budgeted Cost of Work Scheduled to date). Referring back to Figure 12.2, for task 1, at the end of the first week, the BCWS figure is $800. At the end of the second week, it is $1,600. Note that for task 2, nothing will be entered into this cell until week 2.

---

[1] This report can be downloaded free from my Web site: www.lewisinstitute.com.

**F I G U R E   12.9**

Earned-Value Tracking Report Form

**Earned Value Report**

Project No.:
Description:
Prepared by:

Date: 06-Jun-99          FILE:     PROJRPT2
Page _____ of _____
Signed:

| WBS # or Name | Cumulative-to-date | | | Variance | | At Completion | | | Critical Ratio | Action Required |
| | BCWS | BCWP | ACWP | Sched. | Cost | Budgeted (BAC) | Latest Est. (EAC) | Variance | | |
|---|---|---|---|---|---|---|---|---|---|---|
| | | | | 0 | 0 | | | 0 | NA | NA |
| | | | | 0 | 0 | | | 0 | NA | NA |
| | | | | 0 | 0 | | | 0 | NA | NA |
| | | | | 0 | 0 | | | 0 | NA | NA |
| | | | | 0 | 0 | | | 0 | NA | NA |
| | | | | 0 | 0 | | | 0 | NA | NA |
| | | | | 0 | 0 | | | 0 | NA | NA |
| | | | | 0 | 0 | | | 0 | NA | NA |
| | | | | 0 | 0 | | | 0 | NA | NA |
| | | | | 0 | 0 | | | 0 | NA | NA |
| | | | | 0 | 0 | | | 0 | NA | NA |
| | | | | 0 | 0 | | | 0 | NA | NA |
| TOTALS: | 0 | 0 | 0 | 0 | 0 | 0 | 0 | 0 | NA | NA |

NOTE: Negative variance is unfavorable || If critical ratio < 0.6, INFORM MANAGEMENT!     ( ) = NEGATIVE VALUES

225

◆ **Column 3:** BCWP (Budgeted Cost of Work Performed to date). This is the *earned value* figure defined previously.

◆ **Column 4:** ACWP (Actual Cost of Work Performed to-date). This is the actual cost of labor to date, as previously defined.

◆ **Column 5:** Schedule variance—the difference between BCWS and BCWP—calculated by the spreadsheet.

◆ **Column 6:** Budget variance—the difference between ACWP and BCWP—calculated by the spreadsheet.

◆ **Column 7:** The at-completion target cost for the work. For task 1, the at-completion cost for labor will be $2,400 (three weeks at $800/week). For task 3, the at-completion cost will be $14,400 (six weeks at $2,400/week). Naturally, labor spending will not always be uniform. This example uses uniform spending for simplicity.

◆ **Column 8:** The latest estimate of what the work will cost when complete. If we find on task 1 that we actually have to spend $22 per hour for labor rather than the $20 that was originally budgeted, but we expect the work to be completed in the same number of working hours that we originally estimated, then the budgeted-at-completion (BAC) will be $22 × 40 × 3 or $2,640, rather than the originally budgeted $2,400, or an overspend of $240. It is also possible that the BAC can differ from original estimate because more or less labor hours will be needed, but labor costs will be what were originally planned. The BAC figure is extremely important when decisions are being made as to whether to continue or terminate a project.

◆ **Column 9:** The at-completion budget variance expected—the difference between columns 7 and 8, calculated by the spreadsheet.

- ◆ **Column 10:** The critical ratio—calculated as described below.

- ◆ **Column 11:** Action required—determined by the spreadsheet using an "F-formula." These rules are explained below.

## The Critical Ratio

Part of the C/SCSC system involves calculation of two ratios that indicate how well the project is doing. One of these is called a *cost performance index* (CPI) and the other is called a *schedule performance index* (SPI). The CPI is the ratio of BCWP and ACWP (BCWP/ACWP). The SPI is the ratio of BCWP and BCWS (BCWP/BCWS). Meredith & Mantel (1985) describe a control-charting method that can be used to analyze progress in projects. They calculate a *critical ratio*, which is the product of the CPI and SPI, using the following formula:

$$CR = SPI \bullet CPI$$

or

$$CR = \frac{BCWP}{BCWS} \bullet \frac{BCWP}{ACWP} \text{ or } \frac{EV}{PV} \bullet \frac{EV}{AC}$$

As is true for control charts used to monitor manufacturing processes, rules can be devised for responding to the critical ratio. Meredith and Mantel (1985) suggest limits and actions as shown in the diagram in Figure 12.10. These limits are only suggestions, and the project manager will have to devise limits that are appropriate for his/her own programs.

Using a spreadsheet allows you to automate the process of interpretation. The progress report in Figure 12.9 includes an "IF" formula in the final column. This formula looks at the critical ratio calculated in the previous column and subjects it to tests. Based on those tests, the formula returns the words

**F I G U R E   12.10**

A Control Chart for Tracking the Critical Ratio

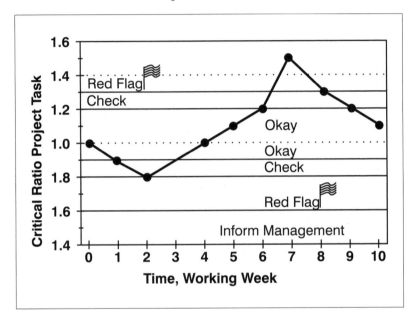

"OK," "CHECK," "RED FLAG," or "NA," meaning no critical ratio has yet been calculated in the cell being tested. The tests are simple:

Print "OK" if the critical ratio (CR) is between the values 0.9 and 1.2

Print "CHECK" if the CR is between 0.8 to 0.9 or 1.2 to 1.3

Print "RED FLAG" if the CR is above 1.3 or below 0.8

In addition, if the ratio falls below 0.6, company management should be informed, as progress is so much better than expected that some changes probably should be made to the project plan.

Following is the IF-formula for a spreadsheet with the critical ratio in cell K10 and the IF-formula in cell L10.

@IF(K10>1.3#OR#K10<0.8,"RED FLAG",

@IF(K10>1.2#AND#K10<1.3#OR#K10>0.8#AND#K10<0.9,

"CHECK","O.K."))

Note that the example is set up so that the bottom-line summary for the project looks very good. The critical ratio for the overall project is 0.96, indicating that everything is fine. However, there are three work packages with RED FLAGS and two with CHECKS indicated, which means that some parts of the project are in trouble. If this were my project, I would be concerned.

However, a complete assessment of the project cannot be done using just this report. We also need to know exactly where in the project these work packages fall. Are any of the ones with problems on the critical path? If so, we know we have a more serious problem than indicated by the summary analysis. Even if none are critical, are any of them behind far enough to be running out of float? If so, then they will soon be critical. (See, for example, work packages numbered 504 and 510. These are far enough behind that they could be in real trouble.)

## THE NEED FOR ALL THREE MEASURES

Occasionally project managers fall into the trap of trying to track their projects using only BCWS and ACWP. As long as they see no difference between what they had planned to spend and what has actually been spent, they think the project is running smoothly. However, we saw from the above examples that this may not be true, and the manager would not spot a problem until it had perhaps gotten serious.

In fact, a controller from one organization told me that he constantly sees this happen in his company. For a long time the project goes along being underspent or right on target. Then the project manager realizes that the work is not getting done as required, and a big effort is applied to catch

**F I G U R E 12.11**

Overshoot Curve

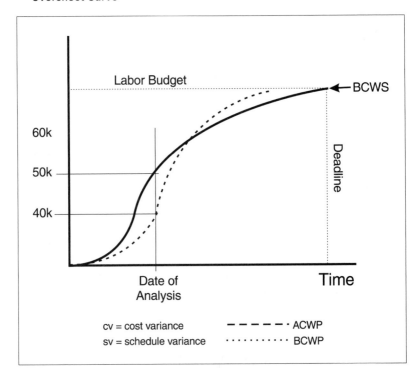

cv = cost variance     – – – – – · ACWP
sv = schedule variance   · · · · · · · · · · · BCWP

up. The usual result is that spending overshoots the planned target. This is illustrated by the curves in Figure 12.11.

## Variance Analysis Using Hours Only

In some organizations, project managers are not held accountable for costs, but only for the hours actually worked on the project and for the work actually accomplished. The argument used to justify this way of working is that project managers usually have no control over labor rates. This is because an individual may be assigned to the project by his functional manager simply because he was the only person available who could do the job, but his rate is 25 percent higher than what the project manager expected to pay when original estimating was done.

The other cause of problems is that the accounting department may change burden allocation rates (for valid reasons), which causes total labor costs to go above original estimates. This naturally creates a cost variance in the project, but one over which the project manager had no control, and so the argument is that he should not be held accountable.

In this case, the same analysis can be conducted by stripping the dollars off the figures. This results in the following:

BCWS becomes total planned (or scheduled) hours

BCWP becomes earned hours (scheduled hours × percent of work accomplished)

ACWP becomes actual hours worked

Using the new numbers, it is possible to compute the following variances:

$$\text{Schedule variance} = \text{BCWP} - \text{BCWS} =$$
$$\text{Earned hours} - \text{Planned Hours}$$

$$\text{Labor variance} = \text{BCWP} - \text{ACWP} =$$
$$\text{Earned hours} - \text{Actual hours worked}$$

# 13
## CHAPTER

# Progress Payments and Earned-Value Analysis

*This chapter is a composite of Chapters 1 and 5 of* Subcontract Project Management and Control: Progress Payments, *by Quentin W. Fleming and Quentin J. Fleming (Chicago: Probus, 1992). Used by permission of the authors.*

## SOME BACKGROUND ON PROGRESS PAYMENTS

One of the major challenges facing all prime contractors is managing the risks of contract performance: the cost, schedule, and technical risks. With the progressively larger share of contract dollars now going outside of prime contractors down to their subcontracting base, many prime contractors are looking outward at their suppliers to share some of the "glory" of the risks of contract performance.

There are a multitude of ways to minimize the risks associated with prime contractor performance. One of the more obvious is by preparing high-quality specifications for a program—system, performance, process, development, and procurement, to mention just a few. Another key factor in risk management is the ability to define an airtight statement of work, both for internal budget performance and most particularly for subcontracted (external) supplier performance.

However, many times it is not possible to precisely define either a tight specification or even an adequate statement of work. In these cases the prime contractor may attempt to transfer some of its own risks to subcontractors by selecting an appropriate contract type for the occasion—choosing from the two broad families of contract types, either a fixed-price or a cost-reimbursable contract.

The importance of selecting the appropriate type of contractual arrangement for a given subcontract is a critical one for all procurements. The type of contract selected depends on many factors. Perhaps none is more important to both parties than the amount of "cost risk" that the buyer (the prime contractor) wishes to transfer to the seller (the subcontractor) and, conversely, how much of the cost risk the seller is willing to assume.

If the prime contractor is willing to retain the risks of cost growth, for whatever reason, then it will likely choose a cost-reimbursable contract. If, however, it is the buyer's intent to transfer the maximum potential cost risk to the subcontractor, then some type of fixed-price contract would be used, likely a firm fixed-price (FFP) subcontract.

Under an FFP subcontract, a supplier is obligated to assume the complete risk of any resulting cost growth and losses. This is the normal arrangement, but there is one very important condition, almost an exception, that should be understood. When the subcontract includes a "progress payment" clause, there is some likelihood that the cost risk factor *may* have remained with the prime contractor and did not transfer to the supplier. And, although not a widely publicized fact, there is a history of—shall we say—"unfortunate cost experiences" (called losses) in the industry as a direct result of the poor management of progress payments. For example, one of the more obvious ways for a prime contractor to lose money is to make progress payments in advance of the supplier's physical performance, and then have the supplier close its doors.

Proper management of progress payments begins before the subcontract is awarded, and must continue throughout the life of the subcontract. A prime contractor that uses progress payments is particularly vulnerable if its buyers fail to understand the importance of doing the right things both prior to and after the subcontract is awarded.

Today progress payments are commonplace in the government contracting business, and prime contractors are "encouraged" by the government to flow these financial arrangements downward to all their subcontracting team members. Thus, the subject of progress payments and the associated risks must be clearly understood in order to best protect the interests of prime contractors and, of course, the U.S. government.

## JUST WHAT ARE PROGRESS PAYMENTS?

In their simplest form, progress payments may be viewed as a temporary interest-free loan from a buyer (the prime contractor) to a seller (the subcontractor). They are based on costs incurred by the supplier in the performance of a specific order and are paid directly to the supplier as a stipulated and agreed-to percentage of the total costs incurred, as defined in the federal acquisition regulation (FAR). The supplier promises to "pay back" the temporary progress payment loan by (1) making contractual deliveries or completing contractual line items, and (2) allocating some portion of the proceeds of the delivered unit price or completed line-item values to liquidate the loan, based on the established subcontract unit price of the articles or services delivered.

Note that there is an important distinction to be made between the "loan" value (the progress payment rate) and the repayment of the loan (the "liquidation" rate for the progress payments). Progress payments are paid as a percentage of *costs* incurred by a supplier—for example, 80 percent of the

In their simplest form, progress payments may be viewed as a loan from the buyer to the seller.

costs incurred. By contrast, the liquidation of the loan is based on a percentage of the unit *price* of article or service deliveries, which includes the supplier's fee. As such, the loan liquidations will include both the supplier's costs and the supplier's profit (i.e., the full subcontract unit values of the delivered articles).

Thus, the delivery of contract units and the completion of line items once started will result in a dramatic reduction of the outstanding progress payment loan. However, contract deliveries must first happen, and subcontractors must make physical progress in order to liquidate or repay the loan. This sometimes is the very heart of progress payment difficulties.

Progress payments are a form of contract financing to be used on *fixed-price* contracts. The payments cover the period from when a supplier begins to incur costs against an authorized order to when the supplier is making unit deliveries or completing contractual tasks. This results in a supplier getting paid on the basis of established unit or line-item task prices. The intent of progress payments is to prevent an "impairment" of the working capital of industrial suppliers doing business under U.S. government contracts.

With this introduction in mind, we now turn to how the earned-value approach is used to control progress payments. For a complete treatment of progress payments, the interested reader is referred to the book by Fleming and Fleming, from which the material for this chapter was taken. (See the end-of-chapter notes for a complete citation.)

## PROGRESS PAYMENTS AND THE EARNED-VALUE (C/SCSC) CONCEPT[1]

On January 7, 1991, Secretary of Defense Richard B. Cheney canceled the A-12 Avenger program. Because of this single action—reportedly the largest contract ever terminated by the Department of Defense (DOD)—upward of 9,000 employees immediately lost their jobs.

Without debating the rightness or wrongness of the Cheney decision, we may consider its value in understanding the link between progress payments and the earned-value concept. To those of us who are interested in management control systems for government programs, particularly major programs, the A-12 Avenger cancellation provides a case study that will likely be discussed for years. To those of us who are specifically interested in the subset elements of "progress payments" and "earned value" performance management, the A-12 incident provides a lessons-learned opportunity of major importance.

The exact circumstances surrounding the A-12 cancellation will not be available to the general public for several years. It was what is called a secret SAR (special access required) program, which kept it out of the main monitoring

---

[1] The material that follows is taken from Chapter 5 of *Subcontract Project Management and Control: Progress Payments*, by Quentin W. Fleming and Quentin J. Fleming (Chicago: Probus, 1991).

processes of the DOD and certainly the general public. Nevertheless, enough public information has surfaced for us to draw certain conclusions.

The prime contracts were awarded on January 13, 1988, under a fixed-price incentive contractual arrangement that contained a target price of $4.379 billion, a target cost of $3.981 billion, and a ceiling price of $4.777 billion.[2] Full compliance with the cost/schedule control systems criteria (C/SCSC) and periodic cost performance reports (CPRs) were required from the two prime contractors: McDonnell Douglas, St. Louis, and General Dynamics, Fort Worth.[3] Progress payments were included in the fixed-price contractual arrangement.

Reliable DOD sources have acknowledged that the C/SCSC management control systems were implemented properly, and were functioning well at both the principal contractors.[4] But as early as April 10, 1991 (some 90 days after cancellation), it was reported that the government was demanding a return of $1.35 billion in "overpayments" made to the prime contractors.[5] And by June 8, 1991 (five months after cancellation), the two contractors had filed a 78-page lawsuit against the government, arguing that they were entitled to keep the questioned overpayment of funds.[6] Stay tuned—this saga will be continued.

---

[2] Chester Paul Beach, Jr., Inquiry Officer, in a memorandum for the Secretary of the Navy, "A-12 Administrative Inquiry," November, 28, 1990, p. 2.

[3] Ibid., pp. 3 and 4.

[4] Wayne Abba, Office of Acquisition Policy and Program Integration, Office of the Secretary of Defense, in public remarks made on the A-12 program to the management systems subcommittee of the National Security Industrial Association, Costa Mesa, CA, January 16, 1991.

[5] Eleanor Spector, Director of Defense Procurement, Office of the Secretary of Defense, in Congressional testimony, April 9, 1991.

[6] Los Angeles Times, from Reuters, June 8, 1991.

Final settlement of this "major difference of opinion" between the U.S. government and two of its largest contractors will likely take years in the courts. However, if it is generally acknowledged that (1) the C/SCSC management control systems were working well with both of the prime contractors and (2) there was an overpayment of one-third of the total program's target costs only part way through the contractual period, then one can only conclude that the C/SCSC administrators appear not to have been communicating well with the progress payment administrators! Thus, contractor progress payments would appear not to have been linked with earned-value (C/SCSC) performance measurement. Time will tell.

This chapter will not focus on the A-12 program cancellation. The A-12 merely provides us with a case study, a role model, of what can go wrong, and perhaps some examples of future practices we will want to do differently ourselves, if at all possible.

Rather, in this chapter we will address four basic subjects in a generic sense, attempting to "link" the activities of progress payments with the earned-value performance measurement concept:

1. A brief overview of the earned-value (C/SCSC) performance measurement concept.

2. Relating progress payment data to earned-value performance measurement data when full C/SCSC *is* formally imposed on the subcontractor.

3. Relating progress payment data to performance on firm fixed-price (FFP) subcontracts when *no* formal C/SCSC is imposed on the supplier.

4. Methods (the formula) used by earned-value (C/SCSC) practitioners to forecast an independent estimate of costs at completion (EAC), based on the actual cost and schedule performance of the subcontractor.

## The Earned-Value (C/SCSC) Concept in a Nutshell

In spite of the heading, the earned-value performance measurement concept is a complex subject that is difficult to present in a "nutshell." One of the best introductions to the theory of the earned-value concept comes from one of its founders, in an article he wrote after retirement from the government:

> Since 1967, the DOD has employed the cost/schedule control systems criteria (C/SCSC) as a means to ensure that major contractors' internal management systems are sound and can provide government program managers with reliable, objective cost performance information for use in management decision making. The "criteria approach" allows contractors to adopt the systems and controls of their own choosing, provided those systems can satisfy the criteria. Compliance is determined by government teams which review the systems in operation after contract award.
>
> The C/SCSC require that a contractor establish an integrated cost and schedule baseline plan against which actual performance on the contract can be compared. Performance must be measured as objectively as possible based on positive indicators of physical accomplishment rather than on subjective estimates or amounts of money spent. Budget values are assigned to scheduled increments of work to form the performance measurement baseline (PMB).
>
> In order to measure contract performance, budgets for all work on the contract must sum to the contract target cost (CTC) so that each increment of work is assigned a value (budget) that is relational to the contract value. When an increment of work is done, its value is earned; hence the term earned value. By maintaining the budgetary relationship to contract target cost, variances from the budget baseline reflect ongoing contract cost performance.[7]

---

[7]  Robert R. Kemps, Humphreys & Associates, Inc., formerly with the Department of Defense and later the Department of Energy, in "Solving the Baseline Dilemma," an article he wrote for the Performance Management Association's newsletter, Autumn 1990.

To properly put the earned-value performance measurement concept into historical perspective, we must go back in time some three decades and trace the evolution of cost/schedule control systems criteria from its two ancestors: PERT/time and PERT/cost.

The program evaluation and review technique (PERT) was introduced by the U.S. Navy in 1957 to support the development of its Polaris missile program. PERT attempted to simulate the necessary work to develop the Polaris missile by creating a logic network of dependent sequential events. Its purpose was threefold: to plan the required effort, to schedule the work, and to predict the likelihood of accomplishing the objectives of the program within a given time frame. The initial focus of PERT was on the management of time and predicting the probability of program success.

There was great excitement surrounding the new PERT program management concept. Unfortunately, the technique's successes fell far short of its proponents' expectations. Part (perhaps most) of the difficulty with PERT was not with the concept itself, but rather with the computers at the time. Both computer hardware and software were not up to the required challenges in the late 1950s. Computers were scarce, and PERT network processing had to compete with the processing of the company's payroll; somehow the company payroll always won. Also, the software programs, evolving initially out of simple linear network concepts, just could not provide the needed flexibility to support the program management requirements at the time.

Although the PERT planning, scheduling, and probability forecasting concepts have survived to this day, PERT's intended use as a program management tool initially "suffocated" a few short years after its introduction. The technique was too rigid for practical applications with the computer hardware and software available at the time. There was also the problem of the overzealous government mandate to use PERT. Industry management rightfully resented being told what tools to use in the management of their contracts.

Then, before PERT was accepted by program management in industry, the U.S. Air Force came up with an extension of PERT by adding resource estimates to the logic networks. PERT/cost was thus born in 1962, and just plain PERT was thereafter known as PERT/time. Needless to say that if PERT/time as a management technique was too rigid for practical applications at the time, PERT/cost with the added dimension of resources only exacerbated the problem. PERT/cost as a management control tool had a lifetime of perhaps two years.

What was significant about PERT/cost, however, was not the technique itself, but rather what evolved from it. The earned-value measurement concept was introduced to industry in March 1963 when the government issued its *Supplement No. 1 to DOD and NASA Guide, PERT/Cost Output Reports*, which provided industry with a simple definition of the earned-value concept:

> VALUE (work performed to date): The total planned cost for work completed within the summary item.[8]

Thus, instead of relating cost plans to cost actuals, which historically had been the custom, PERT/cost related the *value* of work performed against the cost actuals, to determine the utility/benefits from the funds spent. What was **physically accomplished** for what was **actually spent** was a simple but fundamentally important new concept in program management. Hence, the earned-value concept was introduced in 1963, but had to wait until the issuance of the formal C/SCSC to have its full and lasting impact on American industry.

For various reasons the U.S. Air Force gave up on the PERT/cost technique in the mid-1960s, but correctly held on to the earned-value concept. When the Department of Defense formally issued its C/SCSC in 1967, the earned-value concept was

---

[8] Russell D. Archibald and Richard L. Villoria, *Network-Based Management Systems (PERT/CPM)* (New York: John Wiley & Sons, 1967), p. 475.

solidly contained therein. With the subsequent adoption of these same criteria by the Department of Energy in 1975, and the reaffirmation of the criteria by the Department of Defense in its major 1991 defense acquisition policy statement, the earned-value concept of cost and schedule management was firmly established in the U.S. government acquisition process.[9]

A detailed discussion of the 35 specific criteria contained in the C/SCSC is beyond the limited scope of this book. There are full textbooks, week-long seminars, and practitioners/consultants available to cover these matters. Here we will merely attempt to summarize some of the more significant features in order to relate the earned-value concept to our primary subject: progress payments to fixed-price subcontractors.[10]

The C/SCSC are divided into five logical groupings, which contain the 35 criteria:

1. **Organization** *(5 criteria)*: To define the required contractual effort with use of a work breakdown structure (WBS), to assign the responsibilities for performance of the work to specific organizational components (i.e., the organizational breakdown structure [OBS]), and to manage the work with use of a single "integrated" contractor management control system.

2. **Planning and Budgeting** *(11 criteria)*: To establish and maintain a performance measurement baseline (PMB) for the planning and control of the authorized contractual work.

3. **Accounting** *(7 criteria)*: To accumulate the actual costs of work performed (ACWP) and materials

[9] Department of Defense Directive 5000.1, dated February 23, 1991, "Defense Acquisition"; Department of Defense Instruction 5000.2, same date, "Defense Acquisition Management Policies and Procedures."

[10] See Fleming, *The C/SCSC System*.

consumed in a manner that allows for comparison with the actual performance measurement (BCWP).

4. **Analysis** *(6 criteria)*: To determine the earned value, to analyze both cost variances (CV) and schedule variances (SV), and to develop reliable estimates of the total costs at completion (EAC).

5. **Revisions and Access to Data** *(6 criteria)*: To incorporate changes to the controlled performance measurement baseline (PMB) as required, and to allow appropriate government representatives to have access to contract data for determining C/SCSC compliance.

We will briefly discuss some of the critical elements of these five criteria groupings to provide a quick overview of the earned-value concept. Each of the acronyms used above will be defined in the discussion that follows.

## Criteria Group 1

The five criteria required by the **organization** section can best be illustrated by a review of the diagram in Figure 13.1. The first criterion (1a) requires the use of a work breakdown structure (WBS) to define the required effort, whether it be a contract, a subcontract, a company-funded internal project, or other undertaking. The WBS approach allows program management to comprehensively define and then perform a given contract within the maze of a company's functional organization. The use of a WBS to define the program is illustrated in Figure 13.1, at the extreme left side.

The second criterion in group 1 (1b) requires assignment of the defined WBS work tasks to the organizational breakdown structure (OBS) for performance. This concept is illustrated in the upper portion of Figure 13.1. Internal functional organizations (OBS) will perform the contract tasks as defined by the WBS.

The third criterion (1c) requires integration among the contractor's management control functions as well as their in-

**F I G U R E   13.1**

Work Breakdown and Organizational Breakdown Structures

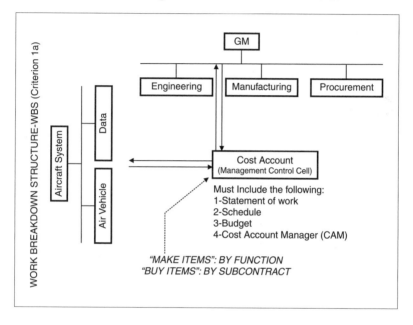

tegration with the defined WBS and OBS elements. This re-quirement is achieved by the creation of "management control cells," which are referred to in the C/SCSC as cost ac-counts, and are displayed in Figure 13.1. Tasks that are "make items" (work to be performed internally by the con-tractor) must be identifiable to both the WBS and the OBS. Likewise, "subcontracts" must be identifiable to both. Thus the hundreds (or more) of these self-contained management control cells (cost accounts) in the C/SCSC must all be relat-able either by the WBS to comply with the precise language of the prime contract's statement of work or by the OBS to satisfy the requirements of internal functional management within a given company.

Each management control cell (cost account) must have four elements to maintain the integrity of the management control unit and to carry out the performance measurement of data contained therein: (1) a statement of work for the cell, (2) a time frame or schedule for the cell, (3) a budget of financial resources, and (4) a responsible manager, typically referred to as the cost account manager (CAM). The cost account concept or management control cell is fundamental to the C/SCSC and is displayed in the lower-right corner of Figure 13.1.

## Criteria Group 2

The 11 criteria contained in the **planning and budgeting** section require the formation of a baseline against which the supplier's performance may be measured. This requirement can be illustrated by a review of Figure 13.2. There are 12 specific components of what is called the C/SCSC performance measurement baseline (PMB). To follow the discussion, we need some understanding of what is meant by each of the elements contained in the baseline. Therefore, these 12 PMB elements are defined below, relatable by number to the elements displayed in Figure 13.2.

1. **Contract (or subcontract) target price (CTP)**: The negotiated estimated cost plus profit or fee for the contract or subcontract.

2. **Fee/margin/profit**: The excess in the amount realized from the sale of goods, minus the cost of goods.

3. **Contract (or subcontract) budget base (CBB)**: The negotiated contract cost plus the contractor's (or subcontractor's) estimated cost of authorized but unpriced work.

4. **Contract (or subcontract) target cost (CTC)**: The negotiated cost for the original definitized contract and all contractual changes that have been definitized, but excluding the estimated cost of any authorized, unpriced changes.

5. **Authorized unpriced work**: The effort for which definitized contract costs have not been agreed to,

**F I G U R E  13.2**

The Performance Measurement Baseline

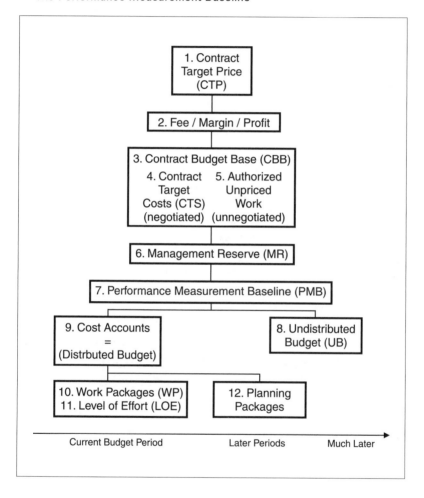

1. Contract Target Price (CTP)

2. Fee / Margin / Profit

3. Contract Budget Base (CBB)

4. Contract Target Costs (CTS) (negotiated)   5. Authorized Unpriced Work (unnegotiated)

6. Management Reserve (MR)

7. Performance Measurement Baseline (PMB)

9. Cost Accounts = (Distrbuted Budget)

8. Undistributed Budget (UB)

10. Work Packages (WP)
11. Level of Effort (LOE)

12. Planning Packages

Current Budget Period          Later Periods          Much Later

but for which written authorization has been received by the contractor or subcontractor.

6. **Management reserve (MR)**: A portion of the contract budget base (CBB) that is held for management control purposes by a contractor to cover the

expense of "unanticipated" program requirements. MR is not initially a part of the performance measurement baseline (PMB), but is expected to be consumed as PMB prior to completing a contract. Any MR not consumed at program completion becomes pure profit (item 2 above) and some portion may be returned to the buying customer under an incentive-type arrangement.

7. **Performance measurement baseline (PMB)**: The time-phased budget plan against which project performance is measured. It is formed by the summation of budgets assigned to scheduled cost accounts and their applicable indirect budgets. For future effort that is not currently planned to the cost account level, the performance measurement baseline also includes those budgets assigned to higher-level WBS elements. The PMB normally equals the contract budget base less management reserve.

8. **Undistributed budget (UB)**: The budget applicable to contract effort that has not yet been identified to WBS elements at or below the lowest level of reporting to the government or prime contractor.

9. **Cost account (CA)**: A natural intersection point between the work breakdown structure (WBS) and the organizational breakdown structure (OBS), at which functional management responsibility for the work is assigned, and actual direct labor, material, and other direct costs are compared with earned value for management control purposes. Cost accounts are the focal point of cost/schedule control.

10. **Work package (WP)**: A detailed short-span job or material item, identified by the contractor for accomplishing work required to complete a contract. Work packages are discrete tasks that have specific end products or end results.

11. **Level of effort (LOE)**: Work that does not result in a final product (e.g., liaison, coordination, follow-up, and other support activities) and that cannot be effectively associated with a definable end product process result. It is measured only in terms of resources actually consumed within a given time period.

12. **Planning package**: A logical aggregation of far-term work within a cost account that can be identified and budgeted but that is not yet defined into work packages. Planning packages are identified during the initial baseline planning to establish the time phasing of the major activities within a cost account and the quantity of the resources required for their performance. Planning packages are placed into work packages consistent with the "rolling wave" scheduling concept prior to the performance of the work.

It may come as a surprise to some that the C/SCSC performance measurement baseline (PMB) represents a value less than the total contract or subcontract amount. However, this fact is true only for the initial PMB. Profit or fee is not intended to be used in the performance of the contract, or else the result will be zero profit to the contractor or subcontractor. By contrast, management reserve (MR) is expected to be consumed during contractual performance, and when it is needed, MR is shifted into the PMB. Any management reserve remaining at the end of the contract is used to offset unfavorable variances, or may represent contract underrun and/or profit.

## Criteria Group 3

The seven criteria in the **accounting** group require that both cost actuals and schedule performance be relatable in the same time period with the earned-value achievement, or what PERT/cost called simply "value." Important point: By definition in the C/SCSC, a cost variance (CV) is the difference

F I G U R E   13.3

Conventional Cost Control

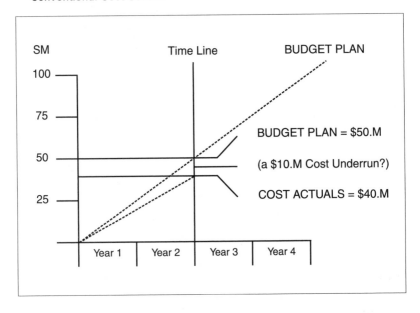

between the earned value achieved and the cost actuals for the same period. A schedule variance (SV) is the difference between the value of the scheduled work for the period and the earned value achieved in the same period. Let us discuss this simple but fundamental concept with a review of the data displayed in Figures 13.3 and 13.4.

Figure 13.3 presents an imaginary four-year, $100 million contract, using the "conventional" cost control method. The plan calls for the expenditure of exactly $25 million each year for the four years. At the end of exactly two years of performance we find we have spent $40 million, compared with our plan, which called for the expenditure of $50 million. How are we doing? Truthful answer: We really do not know, using the "conventional" planned costs versus actual costs method.

## F I G U R E  13.4

Earned-Value Performance Measurement

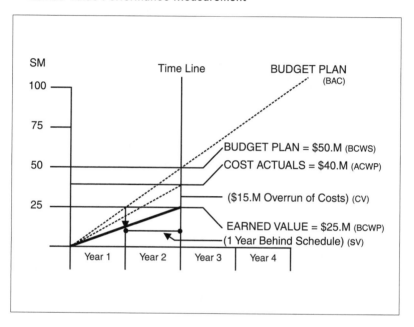

An optimist might look at the data in Figure 13.3 and say we have accomplished $50 million dollars of work with only $40 million in actual costs; therefore, we have underrun our costs to date by some $10 million. And remember, most program managers and senior executives and CEOs are optimists by their very nature!

A pessimist might look at this same chart and conclude that we have completed $40 million of our planned work and have exactly $40 million in actual costs; therefore, we are the equivalent of $10 million of work behind our schedule. On the other hand, our cost performance is just fine!

In reality, we cannot tell how well or poorly we are doing by simply using the "conventional" cost control method of comparing planned cost expenditures with actual cost expenditures. Our conclusions can, and will likely, be most deceiving. Under the traditional methods of cost management, we cannot tell if we have overrun or underrun our costs, or are ahead of or behind our schedule. And being optimists, pessimists, or realists will not improve the process. We need to know what physical work we have accomplished against our physical work plan, for the actual dollars we have spent in a given time frame. We need earned-value performance measurement to be able to make an objective assessment of our program accomplishments.

Figure 13.4 has added the critical third dimension of earned-value performance measurement. The results are shocking. We have accomplished only $25 million in physical work. Therefore, since we have spent $40 million, we are in fact $15 million overrun in costs. To add to our distress, of the $50 million in work we had planned to accomplish in the initial two years, only $25 million has been accomplished. We are thus $25 million in equivalent work behind schedule; stated another way, we are one year behind schedule!

By equating our cost dollars spent to our earned value, we know (sometimes painfully) exactly how well or poorly we are doing in our cost performance. By equating the planned schedule with earned value, we know (sometimes painfully) how much of the authorized contract work we have accomplished against our own schedule. Earned-value performance measurement is "objective" measurement. It takes the guesswork out of the cost and schedule management of contracts or subcontracts. Perhaps of greatest importance, the supplier's actual cost and schedule performance can be used to intelligently forecast (1) the final estimate of costs to complete the effort and (2) the necessary time to complete the effort.

To follow the discussion covered in the final section of this chapter—on using C/SCSC performance data to predict the final outcome—we will need to master some of the C/SCSC jargon. However, if we look at these very specific terms here and immediately relate them to the data in Figure 13.4, perhaps we can minimize the pain. Nine definitions of specific C/SCSC terms are needed:

- **Budgeted cost for work scheduled (BCWS):** The sum of the budgets for all work packages scheduled to be accomplished (including in-process work packages) plus the amount of level of effort scheduled to be accomplished within a given time period.

The BCWS is nothing more than the "plan" against which contractor performance will be measured. In Figure 13.4 the plan or BCWS through year 2 was $50 million.

- **Budgeted cost for work performed (BCWP):** The sum of the budgets for completed work packages and completed portions of open work packages, plus the appropriate portion of the budgets for level of effort. Also known as earned value.

The BCWP is the earned value, the physical value of the work done at a given point in time. In Figure 13.4 the BCWP or earned value at year 2 was $25 million.

- **Actual cost of work performed (ACWP):** The costs actually incurred and recorded in accomplishing the work performed within a given time period.

The ACWP is the actual cost for a given period. The ACWP through year 2 was $40 million.

- **Cost variance (CV):** The numerical difference between earned value (BCWP) and actual cost (ACWP).

The CV is the earned value () less the actual cost (ACWP). In Figure 13.4 the BCWP is $25 million, less the ACWP of $40 million, for a CV of –$15 million. Note the important difference in C/SCSC performance measurement: There is no comparison of the plan (BCWS) with the actual cost (ACWP), as there is with the "conventional cost" method.

◆ **Schedule variance (SV)**: The numerical difference between the earned value (BCWP) and the budget plan (BCWS).

The SV is the difference between what was scheduled to be done (BCWS) and what was accomplished, or the earned value (BCWP). In Figure 13.4 the BCWP is $25 million, less the BCWS of $50 million, for an SV of –$25 million.

◆ **Budget at completion (BAC)**: The sum of all budgets (BCWS) allocated to the contract. It is synonymous with the performance measurement baseline (PMB).

The BAC is important as a comparison with the estimate at completion, which will take place during the period of performance. In Figure 13.4 the BAC is $100 million at the end of four years, synonymous with the BCWS in this case.

◆ **Estimate at completion (EAC)**: A value periodically developed to represent a realistic appraisal of the final cost to complete an effort. It is the sum of direct and indirect costs to date, plus the estimate of costs for all authorized work remaining.

EAC = ACWP + Estimate at Completion

Thus, whenever we apply sound business practices to ourselves, or with progress payment administration, or with C/SCSC performance measurement, periodically we will want to make an estimate of what it will take to complete a given job. In Figure 13.4 no EAC is forecasted by the supplier. However, with a CV of –$15 million and an SV of –$25 million only halfway through the contract period, a realistic EAC is definitely in order.

◆ **Cost performance index (CPI)**: The cost efficiency factor achieved by relating earned value (BCWP) performance to the actual dollars spent (ACWP).

The CPI is the critical indicator of program performance under the earned-value technique. The CPI is derived by dividing the earned value (BCWP = $25M) performance by the dollars actually spent (ACWP = $40M), which provides the cost efficiency factor for work accomplished after two years. The result of $25 million divided by $40 million provides an efficiency factor of .625 percent. Stated another way, for every dollar spent to date, this program achieved a benefit of only .625 cents on the dollar!

+ **Schedule performance index (SPI):** The schedule efficiency factor achieved by relating earned value (BCWP) against scheduled work (BCWS).

The SPI is a critical corollary index to the CPI, and is often used in conjunction with the CPI to forecast the final outcome. The SPI is derived by dividing the earned value (BCWP – $25M) performance by the scheduled work (BCWS – $50M), which provides the schedule efficiency factor for work after two years. The result of $25 million divided by $50 million equates to a factor of only 50 percent. Stated another way, for every dollar of equivalent work planned, this contract accomplished only one-half of it.

Thus, we must conclude that the work initially scheduled to be done in years 1 and 2 will now be performed in an extended contract period into years 5 or even 6. And we all know the simple truth that work done in later periods likely will cost more to accomplish, thanks to inflation.

With these nine definitions, related back to the data contained in Figure 13.4, we will be in a position to better understand the forecasting techniques in the final EAC section below.

## Criteria Group 4

The **analysis** section contains six criteria that require the contractor or subcontractor to make an assessment of what has occurred with its cost and schedule performance to date.

Most important, however, this criteria group requires the supplier to analyze the cost and schedule performance to date, and then to estimate the cost and schedule requirements necessary to complete the effort, to forecast the EAC. Estimates at completion will be covered thoroughly later in this chapter.

## Criteria Group 5

The **revisions and access to data** section contains six criteria that require the supplier to maintain the performance measurement baseline (PMB) throughout the life of the contract by incorporating all new work into the PMB in a timely manner. Obviously, the maintenance of the baseline is vital to the integrity of any performance measurement system. Also, this group requires the contractor to give the customer's representatives access to performance data so they can verify strict compliance with the criteria.

Since the Defense Department issued the C/SCSC in 1967, the application of the concept has been intentionally limited to those contracts in which the customer (the buyer) has retained the risks of cost growth (i.e., on cost or incentive-type contracts and subcontracts). The dollar thresholds for formal C/SCSC implementation vary from period to period and are set by the buying customer. Currently they are generally imposed at $50 million on prime contracts ($25 million for subcontracts) for developmental work, and $160 million ($60 million for subcontracts) for production efforts. Any full application of C/SCSC calls for a periodic report (typically monthly) called the "cost performance report" (CPR).

For smaller contracts, the lesser cost/schedule status report (C/SSR) or cost performance report/no criteria (CPR/NC) is now generally set at $5 million in contract value and a minimum of 12 months in program duration. However, program and subcontract management should weigh the risk factors involved in a given effort and decide the earned-value applications on a case-by-case basis.

This overview was out of necessity a very limited discussion of a very large subject. One last question needs to be addressed: Does the earned-value (C/SCSC) performance measurement concept really work, or is it just another government requirement? To best answer this question, we should review the results of an impressive Department of Defense study.

Covering the period 1977–1990, more than 400 DOD contracts in which formal C/SCSC was implemented were studied. The results of the analysis are most impressive, and without exception the findings are consistent for all 400-plus contracts monitored.

Once the C/SCSC performance measurement baseline (PMB) is in place and at least 15 percent of the planned work has been performed, the following conclusions can be drawn on the future performance of a given program:

- The overrun at completion will not be less than the overrun to date.

- The percent overrun at completion will be greater than the percent overrun to date.

- The conclusion: You can't recover.

- Who says?: More than 400 major DOD contracts since 1977.

- Why?: If you underestimated the near term, there is no hope that you will do better on planning in the far term.[11]

Before closing this section on the basics of the earned-value concept, we should consider the objectives sought to be gained through the performance measurement

---

[11] Gary E. Christle, Deputy Director for Cost Management, Office of the Undersecretary of Defense for Acquisitions, in a paper entitled "Contractor Performance Measurement—Projecting Estimates at Completion," Atlanta, GA, October 26, 1987. Data updated from 200 to 400 contracts from the Beach report, November 28, 1990, p. 6.

concept to monitor and manage contractors and subcontractors. Once again, let us call upon one of the originators of the concept who did so much to implement the technique during his tenure with the DOD and later with the DOE. Robert Kemps summarizes the four objectives we can obtain from employing the earned-value (C/SCSC) performance measurement concept on our programs:

◆ Sound contractor systems
◆ Reliable, auditable data
◆ Objective performance measurement
◆ No surprises[12]

Four simple programmatic objectives, not always easy to obtain.

## Comparing Progress Payment Data with C/SCSC Cost Performance Report (CPR) Data

The reporting of differences from a contractor or subcontractor will likely be the norm, not the exception, when we compare the cost data contained on progress payment invoices with the cost data contained in the formal C/SCSC cost performance report (CPR) or the lesser C/SSR or CPR/NC. Two issues require a reconciliation when differences exist:

1. Comparison of the *cost actuals* (ACWP) reported to date—between those contained in the progress payment invoice and the cost actuals reflected on the CPR.

2. Comparison of the *estimates at completion* (EAC), the effort—between those forecasted on the progress payment invoice and those forecasted on the CPR.

---

[12] Robert R. Kemps, Director of the Office of Project and Facilities Management for the Department of Energy (DOE), in "Cost/Schedule Control Systems Criteria (C/SCSC) for Contract Performance Measurement," a paper delivered at the Performance Management Association Conference in San Diego, CA, April 1989.

For purposes of this discussion we will consider the three distinct C/SCSC cost and schedule performance reports (CPR, C/SSR, and CPR/NC) as being identical for the purpose of reviewing the data contained therein. Any generic differences in these three reports deal with other matters, not the actual cost (ACWP) or the estimate at completion (EAC) contained in the report.

We would expect that some direct relationship exists, or should exist, between what a contractor or subcontractor reports as its cost actuals position on a progress payment invoice and what it reports reflect on other cost summaries (e.g., a CPR). After all, the cost data do come from the same supplier, reporting its cost status from a single accounting system.

However, in practice, it is not unusual to receive multiple cost reports from a supplier reflecting different financial actuals for the same reporting period. Any time this happens, it is incumbent on the buyer to request a reconciliation from the subcontractor, requiring an explanation of any differences in the cost reports.

Such discrepancies can be attributed to several factors that make the data contained in any of these cost reports unique. These factors are:

1. Different cutoff dates for the reports, or the data contained or reported therein. In some cases the date on the report reflects a specific accounting closure date, but at other times it reflects the date of report submittal. Not infrequently, the progress payment closure date will have a different cutoff from the general ledger closure date.

2. Cost data only (which exclude fee or profit) versus "price" data, which include some estimate of earned fee or profit on lower-tier subcontracts. Often there are distinct professional differences of opinion between a buyer and seller as to how much profit or fee a given supplier will likely have earned on the effort at a given point in time.

3. Progress payments to lower-tier suppliers. These may be included or excluded in the cost actuals being reported.

4. Negotiated statement of work versus unnegotiated statement of work—that is, changes. Unnegotiated work will often be placed into several categories, such as (1) authorized, priced, and proposed; (2) authorized, unpriced, and unproposed; and (3) unauthorized and still under discussion. Not infrequently, there are legitimate differences of opinion between buyer and seller as to the correct value of the "yet to be negotiated" work.

5. The projected estimated supplier costs at completion, in absolute overrun or underrun terms, with the cost-sharing impact on a supplier's earned profits under an incentive-type contractual arrangement.

6. Termination liability projections at any given point in time, which will include either a supplier's open commitments or its expenditures only. Remember, small businesses may include accounting accruals as cost actuals for purposes of requesting progress payments. Large businesses must actually pay the bills in order for the payments to qualify as actual expenditures.

7. Materials purchased (e.g., raw stock, nuts, bolts, chemicals), received, and placed directly into inventory, but not yet charged to work in process. The costs of these materials may or may not be incorporated into the cost actuals reported.

There are doubtless additional factors, all legitimate reasons, which may cause differences in the reported data between the progress payment request (SF1443) and the C/SCSC cost performance report (CPR). These seven items are not intended to be all-inclusive.

What all this means to the buyer and the seller is that they should insist that those who prepare such cost reports invest them with a few choice narrative words that clarify any assumptions they may have made when the data were submitted. This is particularly true when multiple cost reports rely on similar financial terms that can have different meanings to the practitioners. However, any time different values are reported, the buyer has a programmatic responsibility to understand the reasons for these discrepancies prior to authorizing funds for the progress payment invoice.

## Comparing Progress Payment Data without the Formal C/SCSC on Firm Fixed-Price (FFP) Subcontracts

How do you get earned-value performance measurement on subcontracts that do not have formal C/SCSC requirements imposed? One approach is to impose full C/SCSC requirements on all contracts and subcontracts that are funded by the U.S. government. One government official, William Hill, has suggested exactly that in his timely article on managing contractor progress payments. Note that in the following excerpt, "flexible" refers to cost or incentive-type contracts and "inflexible" refers to firm fixed-price (FFP) contracts:

> The DOD would be well advised to insist validated cost/schedule procedures be implemented on all large dollar contracts—flexible and inflexible, prime and subcontracts—that require payments reviews by the government. Validated cost/schedule reporting will ensure proper program controls and provide the government with a more effective and efficient method of conducting government payment reviews.[13]

Hill makes the point that since hundreds of contractors have fully validated C/SCSC systems, and since it is important

---

[13] William J. Hill, "Toward More Effective Management and Control of Contractor Payments," in Defense Systems Management College's *Program Manager* magazine, January–February 1991, p. 21.

to connect the approval of progress payments with the physical performance of a contractor, why not extend C/SCSC to all programs that are funded by the government? This is certainly a valid point, but it is not recommended for a number of reasons.

In the first place, although there are currently more than 200 actively validated C/SCSC management control systems in the United States, that number represents only a small fraction of all the contracts and subcontracts covered by government progress payments. Most of the firm fixed-price (FFP) contracts and subcontracts would not be affected by such an edict, because most suppliers do *not* possess a validated C/SCSC management control system. Two hundred approved management systems out of several thousand suppliers is but a small percentage of the total.

Of greater significance, extending full C/SCSC to all programs that have progress payments would simply increase the costs of the government's procurement of major systems. The formal C/SCSC, with their 35 specific criteria, have too much "non-value-added" requirements to be universally and indiscriminately applied to all programs that have progress payments. Full C/SCSC applications should be limited to cost or incentive-type contracts, with their inherent cost risks, which can benefit from having an early-warning monitoring system.

In 1967, when C/SCSC was introduced, there was some confusion as to the types of contracts or subcontracts that should be governed by the criteria. It was decided at that time to limit the formal application of C/SCSC to those efforts in which the risk of cost growth was on the buyer (i.e., to cost or incentive-type contracts). That principle is still valid today. There are better, less costly ways to achieve the same goal of linking progress payment approvals to the physical performance of the supplier requesting payment.

When a supplier requests progress payments and the buyer is prudent enough to require the creation and monthly submittal of a Gantt chart, the prime contractor (buyer) has all that is needed to employ at least a modified version of the earned-value concept. Even a modified earned-value approach can be significant for monitoring fixed-price suppliers, who traditionally have refused to allow any performance monitoring by prime contractors.

It is important to have the subcontractor prepare a Gantt chart for a project. The subcontractor should list all the planned tasks necessary to perform the purchase order. Each of the listed tasks must receive a weighted value, the sum of which must be 100 percent of the purchase order price. The Gantt chart with weighted values provides, in effect, a simple form of an earned-value plan, which in the C/SCSC vernacular is the budgeted costs for work scheduled (BCWS). With the supplier's own plan, we can quantify each task with its value into a time frame to form a cumulative percentage curve. Figure 13.5 illustrates the approach with data that would be supplied by a subcontractor to quantify its own performance plan and its own BCWS, monthly and cumulative.

Each month, as the supplier reports actual performance against the Gantt schedule, it must report a percentage completion against the plan. Suppose that previously the supplier had reported 28 percent complete as of October 1991, and then 34 percent as of January 1992. This analysis compares unfavorably with our assessment of the data in Figure 13.5. To best illustrate what this supplier is reporting to us in its schedule performance, we should lay out the data as in Table 13.1.

Figure 13.5 shows what the subcontractor originally planned to do. We can immediately see that with the passage of time, this supplier is getting progressively behind in accomplishing the work set out in the original plan. And by measuring the schedule position with earned-value performance indices, we can quantify precisely how well or poorly the supplier is doing. Its schedule performance index (SPI) went down from 76 percent of accomplishing planned work in October 1991 to 74 percent 90 days later.

# F I G U R E  13.5

## Establishing the BCWS

### Hypothetical Engines, Inc.

| Item# | Task | % | J | F | M | A | M | J | J | A | S | O | N | D | J | F | M | A | M | J | J | A | S | O | N | D | J | F | M | A | M | J |
|---|---|---|---|---|---|---|---|---|---|---|---|---|---|---|---|---|---|---|---|---|---|---|---|---|---|---|---|---|---|---|---|---|
| 1 | Des.Mod. | 5 | 1 | 2 | 2 | | | | | | | | | | | | | | | | | | | | | | | | | | | |
| 3 | Qual.Test | 5 | | | | 5 | | | | | | | | | | | | | | | | | | | | | | | | | | |
| 5 | Pur.Mat. | 20 | | | | 4 | 4 | 4 | 4 | 4 | | | | | | | | | | | | | | | | | | | | | | |
| 7 | Fab.Parts | 10 | | | | | | | | 2 | 2 | 2 | 2 | 1 | 1 | | | | | | | | | | | | | | | | | |
| 9 | Comm.Assy | 12 | | | | | | | | | | 1 | 2 | 2 | 1 | 1 | 2 | 1 | 2 | | | | | | | | | | | | | |
| 11 | #1 | 4 | | | | | | | | | | | | | | | | | | 2 | 2 | | | | | | | | | | | |
| 12 | #2 | 4 | | | | | | | | | | | | | | | | | | | 2 | 2 | | | | | | | | | | |
| 13 | #3 | 4 | | | | | | | | | | | | | | | | | | | | 2 | 2 | | | | | | | | | |
| 14 | #4 | 4 | | | | | | | | | | | | | | | | | | | | | 2 | 2 | | | | | | | | |
| 15 | #5 | 4 | | | | | | | | | | | | | | | | | | | | | | 2 | 2 | | | | | | | |
| 16 | #6 | 4 | | | | | | | | | | | | | | | | | | | | | | | 2 | 2 | | | | | | |
| 17 | #7 | 4 | | | | | | | | | | | | | | | | | | | | | | | | 2 | 2 | | | | | |
| 18 | #8 | 4 | | | | | | | | | | | | | | | | | | | | | | | | | 2 | 2 | | | | |
| 19 | #9 | 4 | | | | | | | | | | | | | | | | | | | | | | | | | | 2 | 2 | | | |
| 20 | #10 | 4 | | | | | | | | | | | | | | | | | | | | | | | | | | | 2 | 2 | | |
| 21 | #11 | 4 | | | | | | | | | | | | | | | | | | | | | | | | | | | | 2 | 2 | |
| 22 | #12 | 4 | | | | | | | | | | | | | | | | | | | | | | | | | | | | | 2 | 2 |
| BCWS | Month% | 100 | 1 | 2 | 2 | 9 | 4 | 4 | 4 | 6 | 2 | 3 | 4 | 3 | 2 | 1 | 2 | 1 | 2 | 2 | 4 | 4 | 4 | 4 | 4 | 4 | 4 | 4 | 4 | 4 | 4 | 2 |
| BCWS | Cum.% | | 1 | 3 | 5 | 14 | 18 | 22 | 26 | 32 | 34 | 37 | 41 | 44 | 46 | 47 | 49 | 50 | 52 | 54 | 58 | 62 | 66 | 70 | 74 | 78 | 82 | 86 | 90 | 94 | 98 | 100 |

**T A B L E   13.1**

Layout of Supplier's Performance Plan

|  | October 1991 | January 1992 |
|---|---|---|
| BCWS plan (from Figure 13.5) | 37% | 46% |
| BCWP performance (from previous reports) | 28% | 34% |
| Schedule variance position | −9% | −12% |
| SPI (BCWP divided by BCWS) | 76% | 74% |

What this percent-complete estimate provides is a sort of modified earned value, or BCWP (budgeted costs for work performed) in the C/SCSC terminology. The difference between the planned BCWS versus what was accomplished in the BCWP provides the schedule performance (SV) position for a subcontractor. It tells the prime contractor whether the supplier is accomplishing the work it had set out to do, and in a timely fashion. The performance of Hypothetical Engines is not going well, 12 months into a 30-month effort.

Now let us relate the earned value (percent complete) to the costs this supplier is experiencing. Each month as the supplier submits a request for progress payments, it must complete an SF1443 invoice form. Line 12a of the SF1443 contains the supplier's total actual costs incurred, cumulative to date. The amount listed on line 12a is equivalent to the actual cost values in C/SCSC, or what is called the ACWP (actual costs for work performed). When we relate the ACWP to the earned value (BCWP), we have the cost variance (CV) for performance by a supplier. With this information we can deduce the cost performance efficiency factor for the supplier (BCWP divided by ACWP) to determine how much a supplier has earned for every dollar it has spent. If the supplier spends $1.00 but accomplishes only $.85 in earned value, the subcontractor should be watched closely. It could be heading for a loss, which will require the application of the loss ratio to all progress payments made once the total "projected" cost penetrates the subcontract price value.

Thus, by requiring that a subcontractor put in place a few elementary cost and schedule plans prior to a subcontract award, a buyer can employ a simple but effective earned-value performance measurement concept. With this, the performance of even firm fixed-price suppliers may be monitored during the life of their subcontracts to provide a linkage between progress payment approvals and earned-value measurement.

## Using C/SCSC Performance Indices to Predict the EAC

The best estimate at completion (EAC) forecast for a given program is typically referred to as a "bottoms-up" or "grassroots" EAC. Here, each of the remaining tasks to be worked is examined by the very functions that will perform the tasks, and a detailed estimate at completion all the work is prepared. However, to accomplish a legitimate bottoms-up EAC takes a lot of program resources—the very same resources that are trying to complete the job in a timely manner. Therefore, grassroots EACs can be accommodated only once or twice each year per program in order for such exercises not to interfere with the primary mission of completing the contractual effort. At the upper extreme, a grassroots EAC may be done quarterly, but that frequency may well overtax the limited resources of any program and have an adverse impact on successful contractual performance.

However, and this is the good news, the cost and schedule performance data generated by the earned-value C/SCSC activities provide an effective way of complementing the periodic (annual, semiannual, or quarterly) grassroots EACs done by the functional organizations. Without disrupting personnel in the performing organizations, and with the help of computer software programs in place today, a monthly (or even weekly) full range of EAC forecasts may be efficiently provided, based upon the actual C/SCSC performance data.

In addition, work being performed by all subcontractors should be submitted to monthly EAC analysis, independent of what the supplier may be "officially" forecasting. Periodic subcontractor EACs should be verified independently by the responsible cost account manager (CAM). One of the best ways to accomplish this is by examination of the supplier's earned-value performance. Another benefit of the analysis—should the CAM be the same individual who approves all progress payment invoices—is to establish a critical linkage between the two management processes. Finally, the preparation of an independent EAC forecast for subcontractors provides better assurance to the government that a "loss ratio adjustment" will be invoked at the appropriate time to preclude any overpayment of government funds.

In 1991, when the Department of Defense made its long-awaited changes to the C/SCSC requirements documentation and incorporated them directly into a new acquisition policy statement in DODD 5000.1 and DODI 5000.2, there were no changes to the C/SCSC. There were, however, two important changes in the analysis of the C/SCSC data, particularly as related to providing the estimates at completion on a given program.

The first change requires a "range of EAC estimates" to be provided by the military service program manager who is responsible for the management of a given acquisition system. The service program manager must, from the cost/schedule performance data:

(1) Enter the range of estimates at completion, reflecting best and worst cases.[14]

_____

[14] DOD 5000.2-M, p. 16-H-6.

The second DOD change to the C/SCSC requires a justification, again from the military service program manager, whenever an estimate of costs at completion forecasts a final value that is *less* than an amount forecast by the cumulative cost performance index (CPI):

> (2) Provide the estimate at completion reflecting the best professional judgement of the servicing cost analysis organization. If the contract is at least 15 percent complete and the estimate is lower than that calculated using the cumulative cost performance index, provide an explanation.[15]

The "15 percent" threshold relates to the DOD empirical study, covered earlier, of more than 400 contractors that performed under the C/SCSC.[17] What a contractor has achieved after performing 15 percent of a contract is likely to be the *lower-end* value of what it will do by the end of the contract.

With the added emphasis on using earned-value performance data to forecast the final cost/schedule outcomes of contracts, we would be wise to make sure that we fully understand some of the formulas available to forecast a "range of estimates." Although C/SCSC practitioners utilize a multitude of EAC formulas, we will address only the basic three, since these constitute the more accepted methods in use:

1. The *low-end* estimate at completion (mathematical EAC).
2. (a) The *middle-range* estimate at completion (CPI EAC).
   (b) What CPI performance factor it will take "to complete" an effort, called the to-complete performance index (TCPI), in order to achieve the CPI EAC forecast.
3. The *high-range* estimate at completion (CPI × SPI EAC).

---

[15] DOD 5000.2-M, p. 16-H-6.

We will examine each of these mathematical forecasting methods individually, building on the definitions of C/SCSC terms covered earlier in this chapter. To follow this discussion, we need to return to the C/SCSC jargon covering the display of data in Figure 13.4—particularly, the cost performance index (CPI) and the schedule performance index (SPI). A perfect CPI is 1.0, which means that for each dollar actually spent, one dollar of physical work was performed. A perfect SPI is also 1.0, which means that for each dollar of work planned to be accomplished, one dollar of physical work was accomplished.

If a contractor achieves what it sets out to achieve in its cost and schedule baseline plans (PMB), that is considered acceptable or even "perfect" efficiency in a performance measurement environment. This concept is illustrated in Figure 13.6.

## F I G U R E  13.6

Gantt Chart to Support Progress Payment Evaluations

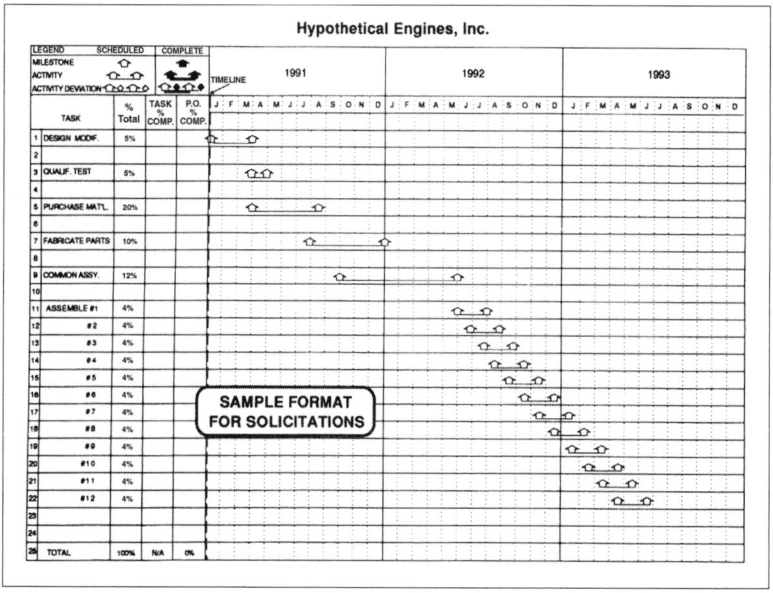

If after establishing the performance measurement baseline (PMB) the contractor achieves a cost performance factor
of 1.0, this is considered an excellent result. For every dollar
spent, the contractor has one dollar in physical earned-value
accomplishments. Anything less than 1.0 is considered negative performance. Anything greater than 1.0 is considered
positive or even exceptional efficiency.

How might a contractor actually achieve a greater
than 1.0 performance? On occasion, a contractor may perform slightly under 1.0 in the first part of a contractual period, then exceed 1.0 in the final stage. This may be the
result of conservative planning of the performance baseline, where the final 100 percent achievement of various
tasks is restrained in order to stimulate exemplary performance by program personnel.

However, if a contractor claims achievement "significantly" greater than 1.0, perhaps 1.5, then someone might want
to pay the supplier a visit and find out how such "miracles"
have occurred. Often, but not always, a performance attainment
much greater than 1.0 is the result of an improper original performance measurement plan. And sometimes, exceptional performance is just plain "gamesmanship" by those who are
preparing and/or approving the cost/schedule reports.

Likewise, schedule performance of 1.0 is considered as
good as it can get, under normal circumstances. For every
one dollar of work planned to be accomplished, one dollar of
performance was achieved.

Now let's look at the range of EAC possibilities. The
low-end EAC forecast is called the mathematical EAC, as displayed in Figure 13.7. Some people refer to the mathematical
EAC formula as being useless, or unrealistic, or even optimistic. Yet many firms in the industry have been using this EAC
method since the C/SCSC were issued in 1967. The formula
for the mathematical EAC is budget at completion (BAC),
less the cumulative earned value (BCWP), plus the cumulative actual costs to date (ACWP). What this EAC does in effect is to "buy out" any poor performance to date, but

F I G U R E   13.7

Monitoring Earned-Value Performance

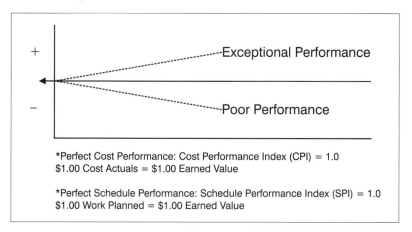

*Perfect Cost Performance: Cost Performance Index (CPI) = 1.0
$1.00 Cost Actuals = $1.00 Earned Value

*Perfect Schedule Performance: Schedule Performance Index (SPI) = 1.0
$1.00 Work Planned = $1.00 Earned Value

assumes that starting tomorrow, all remaining work will be performed at perfect or 1.0 efficiency (on the average).

Although the mathematical EAC is not an accurate device for forecasting what a program will likely cost at the end, it does provide a "floor" EAC, that value which represents the absolute minimum cost for the program. Such revelations sometime come as a shock to management, and do provide the lower-end range of EAC possibilities.

The middle-range EAC forecast is called the cumulative CPI EAC, as displayed in Figure 13.8. The formula is the budget at completion (BAC) divided by the cumulative cost performance index (CPI). There are a number of variations for this midrange EAC, but none offers value to us in this limited discussion of the subject. Some people use only the last three or six months of the CPI to reflect a recent trend or change in the direction of the CPI. For our purposes we need only understand that the total budget available is divided by the cumulative performance efficiency factor. If that efficiency factor is less that 1.0, then the estimate at completion the job will grow from the original allocated budget.

**F I G U R E   13.8**

"Mathematical" Estimate at Completion (EAC)

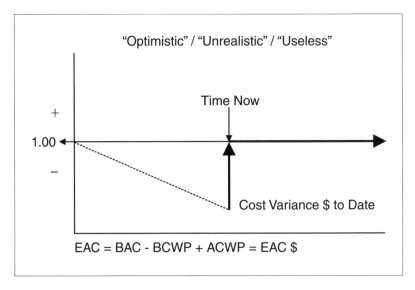

The CPI EAC is the most common and accepted EAC method. Some people consider this method to reflect the "most likely" EAC forecast, while other, more conservative individuals feel it reflects only the "minimum" EAC. Whatever. In the recent acquisition policy statement DODD 5000.2-M, as quoted earlier, the military service program manager must now "provide an explanation" for any EAC forecasts that predict a final performance value that is less than that using the cumulative CPI EAC method.

One of the most important tools in C/SCSC forecasting does not deal with how much it will cost, or how long it will take to complete the job. Rather, the to-complete performance index (TCPI) has its utility in determining what performance efficiency factor it will take to do what you say you will do. Simply put, if you complete half a job with a CPI of .95 percent, then in order to complete the job within the approved budget for the remaining work, you must achieve a CPI of 1.05 percent for the balance of the effort. This concept is illustrated in Figure 13.9, along with the formula to calculate the TCPI.

The value of the TCPI formula is that it can be used to answer a number of questions, all related to achieving some future objective. For example, what efficiency factor will it take (1) to stay within the budget at completion (BAC), (2) to stay within the latest estimate at completion (EAC), (3) to stay within the latest over-the-target budget (OTB), or (4) to stay within the fixed-price incentive (FPI) ceiling? The TCPI is used to "puncture" blind optimism, which sometimes affflicts company management, particularly more senior management.

The high-end EAC forecast is called the CPI x SPI EAC forecast. It adds the dimension of scheduled but unfinished work—work that was in the original plan, but has not been completed. This concept is illustrated in Figure 13.10. The

**F I G U R E  13.9**

"Cumulative CPI" Estimate at Completion

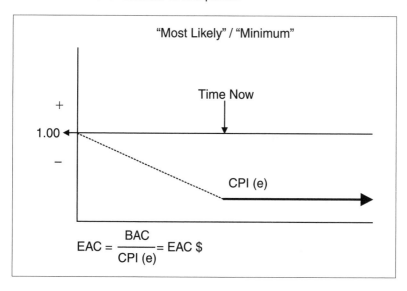

**F I G U R E  13.10**

Performance Index TCPI

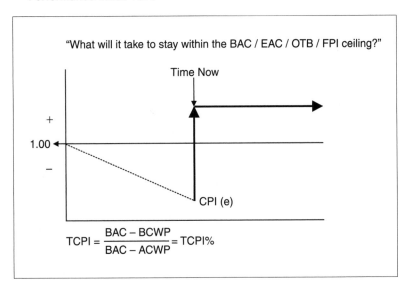

"What will it take to stay within the BAC / EAC / OTB / FPI ceiling?"

$$TCPI = \frac{BAC - BCWP}{BAC - ACWP} = TCPI\%$$

formula is the work remaining to be performed (BAC less BCWP), divided by the product of the cost performance index (CPI) times the schedule performance index (SPI), plus the ACWP. Obviously, if you performed under 1.0 in both the CPI and SPI, the resulting estimate at completion will be substantial.

This EAC method can get to be quite emotional to those involved in managing programs. Some consider this technique to represent the "most likely" EAC, while others call it the "worst-case scenario." Some program managers, attempting to keep their costs under control, refer to this technique irreverently as a "self-fulfilling prophecy."

This method is generally considered to be the high-end EAC method, and was used by the DOD cost analysts on the A-12 program to forecast its total estimate at completion. It is a most valuable high-end EAC forecasting technique.

Now, what do all these EAC methods do for us when we attempt to forecast the final costs of a given program? If we take each of the formulas as displayed in Figures 13.7 to 13.10 and relate them to the data provided from the performance in Figure 13.4, perhaps we can discern the value in employing these EAC techniques.

Starting from the low-end EAC method, we can line up a range of EAC forecasts:

## The Mathematical EAC

$$BAC - BCWP + ACWP = EAC\$$$
$$\$100M - \$25M + \$40M = EAC\ \textbf{\$115M}$$

## The CPI EAC

$$BAC\ /\ CPI = EAC\$$$
$$\$100M\ /.625\% = EAC\ \textbf{\$160M}$$

## The TCPI

$$(BAC - BCWP)\ /\ (BAC - ACWP) = TCPI\%$$
$$(\$100M - \$25M)\ /\ (\$100M - \$40M) = \$75M\ /\ \$60M = TCPI\ \textbf{1.25\%}$$

## The CPI × SPI EAC

$$(BAC - BCWP)\ /\ (CPI \times SPI) + ACWP = EAC\$$$
$$(\$100M - \$25M)\ /\ (.625\% \times .500\%) + \$40M = EAC\ \textbf{\$280M}$$

The low-end EAC method (mathematical EAC) tells us we will spend $115 million, the minimum floor. The midrange EAC (CPI EAC) forecasts a total cost requirement of $160 million, and if anyone predicts a lesser amount, a military program manager will have to justify the lesser amount in order to comply with the new DODD5000.2-M. The high-end EAC (CPI × SPI EAC) tells us we will need $280 million to complete the job—quite an increase over our budget of $100 million! With these formulas we can provide a full range of EAC estimates.

What is also significant is the fact that in order to stay within the original approved budget of $100 million, we must achieve a CPI performance efficiency factor of 1.25 percent for all our remaining effort. A very ambitious goal for any mortal person or group to achieve.

The various EAC forecasting tools available to us when earned-value methods are employed can be most beneficial in the management of our contracts or subcontracts, and provide a complementary adjunct in the effective administration of contractor progress payments.

## IN SUMMARY

There is no universal acceptance of the concept that a linkage should or must exist between the progress payments being made to suppliers and the physical performance they are achieving on such work. Nonetheless, the A-12 program experience will likely require such relationships in the future. This important linkage will likely improve both management processes: progress payments and cost/schedule performance measurement.

By linking physical performance measurement to the approval of progress payments, the prime contractor should avoid the potential cost risks of making overpayments to the supplier. Also, the federal acquisition regulations covering progress payments specifically require that there be some monitoring of the supplier's performance in order to know when it might be necessary to adjust the repayment rate, or to suspend further progress payments, or to invoke the loss ratio, among other things.

By linking progress payments with C/SCSC performance measurement, the buyer will have a better understanding of what the suppliers are actually achieving in satisfying their statement of work. To exclude progress payment data from the actuals being reported in the cost performance report (CPR) does nothing but distort the desired earned-value measurements. And with the subcontracted portions (the buy content) becoming such a major part of most prime contractor dollars (upward of 80 percent in some cases), the exclusion of progress payment data in performance measurement can reflect major distortions in the data being reported. A better approach, it is felt, is to measure the physical performance of all suppliers involved in progress payments, including firm fixed-price suppliers, and to incorporate these actual dollars into all CPRs.

We touched on a couple of issues rather hurriedly in the discussion above, and it might be beneficial here to re-emphasize these points. It is important that the buyer—the individual who has delegated procurement authority to issue the subcontract—be given the responsibility for the review and approval of each and every progress payment invoice before any such payments are made. This is a fundamental issue. Also important, it is believed, is the concept that this same buyer be held responsible for the total management of his or her subcontract, including that of functioning in the role of cost account manager for the performance measurement of the supplier.

If a prime contractor thus places the responsibility for (1) the full administration of progress payments, including the approval or disapproval of all payment invoices, and (2) the management of a subcontract earned-value cost account in a single individual, then the prime contractor will have achieved a "linkage" of both activities. This critical coupling should prevent any future overpayment of suppliers, in advance of their actual physical work accomplishments and improve the overall subcontract management processes.

We hope we have made the case for employing this approach.

# 14 CHAPTER

# Project Change Control

## THE NEED FOR CHANGE CONTROL

One of the fallacies of project management is that, once a project plan has been assembled, the world will stand still while the plan is executed. This was probably not true in the past, and it certainly is not true today. Any project that lasts longer than a few months is almost certain to be affected by some change in the environment, and the project manager must respond to that change. The objective is to deal with the change in such a way that all stakeholders know what is going on and approve of the response.

As an example, consider the situation in which someone is having a house built. Midway through the construction project, the customer says to the builder, "I've been thinking that it would be nice to pave the driveway to the house, rather than just putting in a gravel drive like we originally intended."

"No problem," says the builder. "I can do that for you."

---
**One of the fallacies of project management
is that, once a project plan has been
assembled, the world will stand still.**

---

"Can you still be finished on time?" asks the customer. "I have a lease on my apartment and don't want to have to renew it, so it's important that we be able to move into the house as originally scheduled."

"No problem," says the builder.

"Okay," the customer continues, "that sounds fine. But how about construction quality? That won't be affected, will it?"

"Oh no," the builder says with confidence. "No problem with quality."

"Well, then, I just have one more question," the customer replies. "How much will it cost?"

"Oh, it won't be much," the builder says casually.

You know, of course, that if the customer leaves it at that, there is bound to be a problem later. The builder knows that, as driveways go, this is not an expensive driveway. It will be around $10,000. The customer, who knows nothing about the cost of driveways, is thinking about $2,500. When he sees a bill for $10,000, he is bound to have heart failure.

Here, the builder has an obligation to the customer to specify the impact on the project for this change in scope. That way, the customer can make an informed decision about what to do. He may say, "That's more than I want to pay, so just forget it," or he may say, "Well, it's a lot more than I expected, but go ahead." Either way, there are no surprises at the end of the job.

Note also that by specifying the impact of the change, the builder is protecting herself from the repercussions that will occur if the customer is hit with an unexpected high driveway cost at the end of the job. You might say that the project manager (the builder in this case) has an obligation both to the customer and to herself, to protect both.

Now, does this mean that every time someone asks for a small change to a project, the manager should say, "It will cost you!"? I don't think so. Behaving that way will get you a reputation for being a nit-picker. It is best to absorb a few changes.

However, small changes add up to a big impact, and at some point, you may have to say, "I've absorbed all of the changes I can, so I'll have to charge you now." This is, of course, the way that *scope creep* works—small changes are made repeatedly, until the final project is much larger than it started out to be.

## THE CHANGE CONTROL PROCESS

Every organization should have a formal project-change control process or procedure. I believe very strongly in the KISS principle (Keep It Simple Stupid), so the procedure should be no more burdensome on the organization than is necessary to protect against even worse long-term effects of changes. Here are some factors to consider when a change is requested:

- ◆ Will the change affect scope, cost, performance, or schedule?
- ◆ Will tooling or capital equipment be affected?
- ◆ How about inventory levels of parts or finished goods?
- ◆ In product development projects, will the change affect form, fit, or function of the product?
- ◆ Will the change make the product more or less desirable in the marketplace?
- ◆ Will it affect return on investment or net present value? If so, can the project still be justified at this level of ROI or NPV?
- ◆ How is the change justified? Needed for competitive advantage? Mandated by some regulation? What is the business need?
- ◆ Is the change required to get the project back on track? Or is the project so far off its original target that the change is simply documenting where we are now and will serve as a baseline against which to track future progress?

Some guidelines for change control are:

- ◆ Changes should be made only when required by stakeholder input, or when significant deviations from the original plan require the change. Note that the level representing *significant* should be defined at the beginning of the project. For example, if you can only maintain a plus-or-minus 10 percent tolerance around your schedule or budget, and you are off 20 percent and see no way of recovering, then the plan should be changed. The 10 percent boundary should have been established at the beginning.
- ◆ Causes of all changes should be documented in a factual way for future history. The objective is not to

**F I G U R E   14.1**

Project Change Approval Form

---

## Project Change Approval

| Project Name: | Project Number: | Date: May 19, 1999 |
|---|---|---|
| Project Manager:<br>Requested By: | Department: | Change in:<br>■ Scope  ■ Schedule<br>■ Budget  ■ Performance |

### Deviation Information

Description of change being requested:

Reason for change:

Effect on schedule:

Effect on cost (budget):

Effect on performance (quality):

Effect on scope:

Justification:

| Class | Distribution of Estimated<br>Cost  Deviation | The Requested Change Is: | |
|---|---|---|---|
| Capital | | ■ Absolutely necessary to<br>achieve desired results | ■ Scope reduction that will<br>not impact original targets |
| Noncapital | | ■ Discretionary—provides<br>benefits beyond the<br>original target | ■ Scope reduction that will<br>impact original targets |

### Required Approvals ■

| ■ Project Leader/Manager (type name) | Sign: | Date: |
|---|---|---|
| ■ General Manager (type name) | Sign: | Date: |
| ■ Concerned Dept. Manager (type name) | Sign: | Date: |
| ■ Controller (type name) | Sign: | Date: |
| ■ Concerned Vice President (type name) | Sign: | Date: |
| ■ President (type name) | Sign: | Date: |
| ■ Other (type name) | Sign: | Date: |

place blame or administer punishment, but to learn from history to enable improved performance in future projects.

◆ Who should approve the change? One guideline that I find very practical is that only those stakeholders affected by the change need to approve it. By following this guideline, you avoid slowing down the approval process by having too many signatures. The change-approval form shown in Figure 14.1 allows flexibility by having a check placed by the individuals who must sign the form. In this way, if a given individual is not affected by this specific change, then he/she does not have to sign it.

# CAUSES OF PROJECT SUCCESS AND FAILURE

# 15

# Defining Project Success and Failure

Under ordinary circumstances, I'm sure that no one sets out to fail in managing a project. We all want our projects to be successful. However, it is not at all clear what is meant by success or failure. What is needed is an operational definition of these terms. An operational definition is one that has criteria that all parties involved can agree to use to define the outcome.

> When you don't meet a target that was just pulled out of the air, should that be called a failure?

The most frequently used definition is that a project is a failure when it does not meet its cost, performance, time, or scope ($C, P, T, S$) targets. However, there are a couple of things wrong with this definition. First, where did the targets come from? When they are just "pulled out of the air," and are therefore unrealistic, should failing to meet those targets be considered a failure? Second, even if you meet all these targets, does the project solve the problem it was intended to solve? Does the customer use it? If not, was it really a success? As you can see, these are not trivial questions.

Schutz, Sleven, and Pinto (1987) have identified four errors that can be made in solving problems. As we have said, project management is problem solving on a large scale, so their concept applies equally well in this area. These are:

1. Type I error: Not taking an action when one should be taken.
2. Type II error: Taking an action when none should be taken.
3. Type III error: Taking the wrong action (solving the wrong problem).
4. Type IV error: Addressing the right problem, but the solution is not used.

Using their definitions, we can say that a project that meets its C, P, T, and S targets but is not used is either a Type III or Type IV error. In some cases, the fact that a Type III error has been made will ultimately cause the project to be a Type IV error. That is, we have solved the wrong problem, so no one uses the project. This happens on internal software projects sometimes when we talk to department managers about their requirements and implement the system based on their comments, but their people won't use the system because it does not really meet their needs.

## OTHER PERSPECTIVES

In their book *Learning from Failure: The Systems Approach,* Fortune and Peters (1995) say, "A simple definition of failure is something that has gone wrong, or not lived up to expectations. Moving a little way beyond this simple statement, various types or categories of failure can be identified" (p. 21).

> A simple
> definition of
> failure is that
> something has
> gone wrong or
> has not lived up
> to expectations.

They go on to establish four types of failures, much like Schutz, et. al. These are shown in Table 15.1. Type 1 failures are those that we encounter every day. Examples are software that never worked properly or a new product that won't sell.

Type 2 failures meet the original objectives, but create undesirable consequences or side effects. In step 4 of my model of project management (see Chapter 2), we choose strategy by subjecting the candidate strategy to a number of tests, one of

**T A B L E  15.1**

Types of Failures

|        | Failures |
| ------ | -------- |
| Type 1 | Objectives not met |
| Type 2 | Undesirable side effects |
| Type 3 | Designed failures |
| Type 4 | Inappropriate objectives |

which is "Are consequences acceptable?" This question is designed to help project managers avoid Type 2 errors.

Most of today's environmental problems are the consequences of solutions to problems we had yesterday. Fortune and Peters cite the drug thalidomide as an example of a product that seemed beneficial but caused numerous birth defects. More recently, we have breast implants, and the outcome nearly destroyed Dow-Corning. So we are surrounded by many Type 2 errors.

The next category of failure is one that is intentional, and therefore is not considered bad. For example, a fuse that is designed to blow (fail) when an appliance exceeds a certain current level. Sprinkler systems fail to hold water in pipes when a fire breaks out. These are called Type 3 failures.

The fourth category of failure is similar to Schutz, et. al Type III, solving the wrong problem. Examples include installing a conveyor to reduce breakage of manufactured goods that does not solve the breakage problem, but moves goods around the factory just fine; products that work fine but don't meet the needs of the market; and the Apple III computer, which was probably technically superior to the IBM-PC at the time, but was not accepted in the marketplace because of IBM's superior name and because no software was available to run business applications. We might say the same about Beta format in video players. The format was technically superior to VHS, but because Sony tried to keep it proprietary, most manufacturers adopted VHS, and Beta eventually died in the home-entertainment market. (Most studio-quality recorders still use Beta format.)

> ☞ It is extremely important that major stakeholders agree upon criteria for success before projects are started.

As Fortune and Peters go on to say, almost all judgments about failure are subjective; they are colored by personal perception, circumstances, and expectations. I have a client company in which people lament that the actual person with whom they work in a customer organization will regard their work as successful, while that person's boss will call it a failure. No doubt this is often true where multiple stakeholders are involved, and it illustrates how important it is to develop criteria that are mutually agreed upon as definitions of success before such projects are started.

## DELIVERABLES, RESULTS, AND EXPECTATIONS

We need to consider three outcomes of a project that affect the judgment of success of failure. These are: project *deliverables;* the *results* achieved; and whether *expectations* of stakeholders were met. Consider the combinations shown in Figure 15.1.

We can say that outcome one is a totally successful project. Deliverables and results are as promised, and stakeholder expectations have been met. Outcome two, however, is one that suffers from political fallout. Deliverables and results are as promised, but stakeholder expectations have not been met. This might happen if a stakeholder changes midway through a project and he has different expectations than those of the original person. This highlights the need for project managers to monitor changing expectations, rather than considering them to be engraved in granite from the very beginning.

As an example of changing expectations, consider computer technology. In the days of the first personal computers, most users were in awe of how fast a spreadsheet would recalculate rows and columns. A few years later, they were complaining about how slow many computers were. The reason? Expectations for performance grew. Jeremy Rifkin actually wrote a book entitled *Time Wars* (1989), in which he argued that perceptions of speed have changed over the years. At one time we were satisfied with mail delivery that required a month for a letter to cross the country. Then along came Federal Express, and next-day delivery was born. Now we have

All Combinations of Deliverables, Results, and Expectations

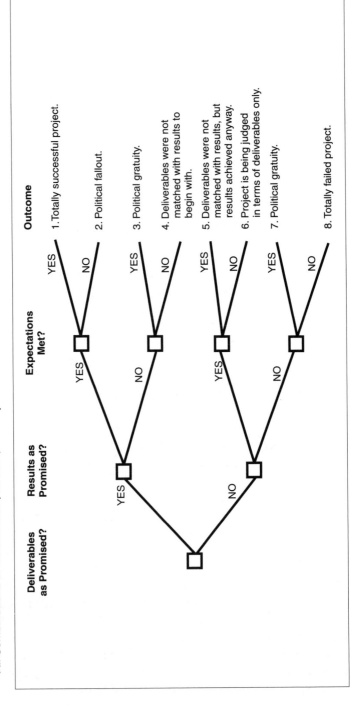

fax machines and e-mail, both of which speed the process so that it is almost instantaneous. What a great time for those of us who like to procrastinate! We can now wait until a few milliseconds before the deadline and send it electronically!

Outcome three is interesting. Deliverables were as promised, yet did not get results, but expectations were met. First, we need to consider that deliverables were not matched with results. That is, we thought that what we delivered would get results, but we were wrong. If expectations were met, it either means that the stakeholder is very forgiving, or that everyone had decided ahead of time that results would not be forthcoming.

Outcome four is similar to three, except the stakeholder is not forgiving in this case.

Outcome five is strange. Deliverables were not as promised, yet results were achieved and expectations met. This could mean that people realized partway through the project that original deliverables should be changed if results were to be achieved.

For outcome six, deliverables are not correct, yet results are okay, but expectations are not met. This would seem to be a stakeholder who is holding the project manager to original promises for deliverables, and ignoring that desired results were achieved in spite of the disconnect.

In outcome seven, we have a truly forgiving stakeholder. This is probably a project run by one of the stakeholder's relatives.

Finally, in outcome eight, we have a totally failed project, and it should well be considered as such.

## RESEARCH FINDINGS

In 1974, Murphy, Baker, and Fisher reported the results of a study of more than 650 projects to determine the factors that affect project success. This study is summarized in Cleland and King's *Project Management Handbook*. They asked the question, "Why are some projects perceived as failures when they met the *P, C, T,* and *S* targets?" And "Why are others considered successes even when they are late and over budget?" Based on their study, they decided that success must be defined as follows:

> If the project meets the technical performance specifications and /or mission to be performed, and if there is a high level of satisfaction concerning the project outcome among key people in the parent organization, key people in the client organization, key people on the project team, and key users or clientele of the project effort, the project is considered an overall success (Baker, et. al, 1974).

The important concept here is *perceptions.* If the right people perceive that the project was a success, then it was, for all practical purposes. Note that the definition does not include schedule and cost performance as criteria for success. The authors go on to say that one reason for this is that the research was conducted on completed projects. No doubt those not yet finished are under pressure to meet cost and schedule targets, but once a job is complete, if it satisfies a lot

If the right people consider a project a success, it is, for all practical purposes.

of key people in terms of satisfying their need, the missed cost and schedule targets become less important. The study identified a number of variables that are important for perceived project success and a number that contribute to perceived project failure. An important finding was that for a project to be perceived as successful, many, if not most, of the variables associated with success must be present. Similarly, most, if not all, of the variables associated with failure must be absent.

They also confirmed something that contradicts what many managers seem to believe about project management: it is not just scheduling! PERT/CPM do contribute to project success, but the importance of scheduling is far outweighed by other factors, including use of tools known as system-management concepts. These include work breakdown structures, life-cycle planning, systems engineering, configuration management, and status reports. In fact, the overuse of PERT-CPM was found to hamper success! The reason is that the project manager spends so much time updating the schedule that day-to-day managing suffers.

Baker, et. al report that seven broad factors contribute to project success. This is based on a regression analysis of data. Taken together, these seven factors explain 91 percent of the variance in perceived project success, which is strongly compelling. These are listed in Table 15.2. They are all statistically significant to a probability of less than 0.001. The table shows the standardized regression coefficient, together with the cumulative $R^2$ for each variable.

Note that a negative regression coefficient means that the direction of the effect is reversed. In other words, while increased coordination causes an increase in project success, an increase in competitive pressure will cause a *decrease* in project success.

Because coordination and relations alone account for 77 percent of the variance in perceived project success, it is instructive to take a closer look at just what this means. Table

T A B L E  15.2

Seven Factors of Project Success

| Determining Factor | Regression Coefficient | Cumulative $R^2$ |
|---|---|---|
| Coordination and relations | +.347 | .773 |
| Adequacy of project structure and control | +.187 | .830 |
| Project uniqueness, importance, public exposure | +.145 | .877 |
| Success criteria salience and consensus | +.254 | .886 |
| Competitive and budgetary pressure | −.153 | .897 |
| Initial overoptimism, conceptual difficulty | −.215 | .905 |
| Internal capabilities buildup | +.084 | .911 |

15.3 contains a summary listing of the factors that make up the overall variable.

Because a number of factors cause people to perceive a project as a failure, and because these must be avoided, I have listed these in Table 15.4. Note again that you must *perform* those things that cause perceived project success and *avoid* doing those that cause perceived failure.

One final note about the study: Project managers are sometimes inclined to complain about their situation and say that they could not succeed because of its adverse nature. The authors concluded that project managers actually can achieve high levels of perceived project success, even under adverse circumstances, if they properly attend to the factors listed in the tables.

> Project managers can achieve high levels of perceived success, even under adverse circumstances.

**T A B L E   15.3**

Coordination and Relations Factor

---

- ◆ Unity between project manager and functional managers
- ◆ Project team spirit, sense of mission, goal commitment, and capability
- ◆ Unity between project manager and public officials, client contact, and his superior
- ◆ Project manager's human and administrative skills
- ◆ Realistic progress reports
- ◆ Supportive informal relations of team members
- ◆ Authority of project manager
- ◆ Adequacy of change procedures
- ◆ Job security of project team
- ◆ Project team participation in decision making and major problem solving
- ◆ Parent enthusiasm
- ◆ Availability of backup strategies

## TARGETS AND VARIATION

I mentioned at the beginning of this chapter that failure is often defined as not meeting the C, P, T, or S targets, but I question whether it is failure to meet targets that have been set based upon wishful thinking. Unless targets are realistic to begin with, everyone associated with a project is getting set

**T A B L E  15.4**

Characteristics That Affect Perceived Project Failure

◆Insufficient use of progress/status reports

◆Use of superficial status reports

◆Inadequate project manager administrative, human, and technical skills

◆Insufficient project manager influence and authority

◆Poor coordination with client

◆Lack of rapport with client and parent organization

◆Client disinterest in budget criteria

◆Lack of project team participation in decision making and problem solving

◆Excessive structuring within the project team

◆Job insecurity within the project team

◆Lack of team spirit and sense of mission within the project team

◆Parent organization stable, nondynamic, lacking strategic change

◆Poor coordination with parent organization

◆New "type" of project

◆Project more complex than parent has handled previously

◆Initial underfunding

◆Inability to freeze design early

◆Inability to close out the effort

◆Unrealistic project schedules

◆Inadequate change procedures

up. If I, as a project manager, agree to meet targets that I am pretty sure are unrealistic, because my manager puts pressure on me to do so, then we are both being set up. Eventually, when I can't meet the unrealistic target, my manager is going to be in trouble as well. So I have an obligation to insist on committing only to targets that I believe to be realistic.

How do you know if a target is realistic? You only know if it is based on some history. Until you make estimates at a level in a work breakdown structure where tasks are somewhat repeatable, and you have some history on similar tasks, you are guessing. And even then, there are tolerances on all estimates. We should understand that working times for *all* activities are probabilistic, not deterministic. Yet we assign durations to activities based on best guesses, then link them together, and do deterministic calculations to find critical paths, float, and so on.

If you think about it, there is reason to wonder how any project is ever successful, as defined by coming in on schedule. I believe the only way this ever happens is that we vary the effort applied to meet the times. However, if you were to

**T A B L E  15.5**

Some Sources of Variation in Project Work

| Source | Example |
|---|---|
| Estimate of task duration is based on a small sample (it has been done only a few times before). | People are robbed from the project to put out fires on other projects. |
| The person for whom the original estimate was made is not available to do the work when the time comes. | Long stretches of overtime cause fatigue, which causes errors, which leads to more overtime, which leads to . . . |
| Sharing resources on multiple projects causes increased setup time, with a corresponding decrease in work efficiency. | Work has to be done over because mistakes are made as a result of poor planning, communication errors, and so on. |
| Unexpected technical problems cause tasks to take longer than expected. | Illness, serious personal problems, child care, and jury duty lead to delays. |

track both schedule performance and actual hours worked against original estimated hours, I think you would find that the price paid is in large variances of actual compared to estimated working hours. Consider the many causes of variation in Table 15.5.

Here, too, there are unrealistic expectations about what magnitude of variance is likely in project work. Many managers who have experience with department budgeting think that project budgets should be held to the same tight tolerances that are possible with departments. But projects aren't budgeted the same way as departments. In a department, you budget for next year by looking at forecasted headcount. You tally up the salary increases you plan to give, add in the cost of rubber bands, paper clips, computers, and other supplies, and away you go. Such budgets can often be held to a few percent.

A project, on the other hand, is based on how much work has to be done, and that exact quantity is not well known at the outset, so labor costs cannot be accurately determined. There is a saying that the ultimate certainty of project costs increases the closer you get to the end. This is shown in Figure 15.2.

The one thing that we must all do is accept variability. It is a part of any process. You can reduce it over time, but you can never eliminate it. An injunction sometimes heard in organizations states: you cannot go over budget—but neither can you come in under budget. Such an injunction demands that people violate a law of nature. If they do it—that is, come in right on target—it is always through fancy footwork or pure accident. It is not because they were actually able to control work to achieve the result.

**F I G U R E   15.2**

Ultimate Certainty of Project Cost

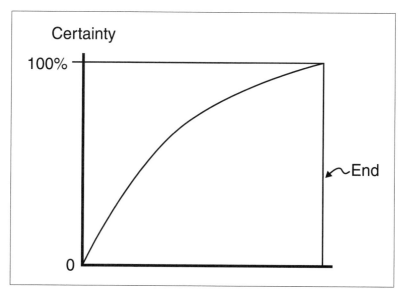

# 16

CHAPTER

# Causes of Project Failure

## THE HIGH COST OF PROJECT FAILURE

According to some estimates, nearly half of the work done in some organizations is of a project nature. That means, clearly, that if many projects are failures, the organization as a whole is on its way to disaster.

And fail they do.

The Standish Group surveys information-systems projects yearly, and finds that only 17 percent meet their original targets, 50 percent need to change the targets, and the remaining 33 percent are canceled. The cost to U.S. companies is around 80 billion dollars a year.

What causes so many failures?

There are 13 fairly common causes. Those who understand these causes presumably can take some steps to avoid them. At least that is the intention of this chapter: to alert the project manager to the typical causes of failure with prevention as the objective.

> It has been estimated that nearly half the work
> done in some organizations is of a project nature.

## Causes and Recommendations for Solution

**1. Failure to properly define the problem.** This was commented on in an earlier chapter. As Juran says, a project is a problem scheduled for solution. If the problem is not well understood, then we may make the classic error of developing the right solution to the wrong problem. This can be avoided by attempting to understand the *real* reason for doing the job, then writing a problem statement to reflect that objective.

For example, a group is given the assignment to relocate an office to another part of the building. They may see their job as just moving furniture and partitions. But what is the real intention of moving the office? Perhaps it is to achieve better coordination between the people being moved and those nearby the new location. Is there an optimum layout that will make the move more effective? Only by understanding the real purpose of the move can this question be answered or addressed.

**2. Planning was based on insufficient data.**   For example, an engineering project is planned that will involve significant use of a test facility. What the team doesn't know is that the test facility is scheduled to be relocated just when their testing is scheduled to start.

Another fairly common problem occurs with system-development projects. The client has an "itch" that needs scratching. Unfortunately, the client knows very little about the capability of software, and the programmers know very little about the user's operation. As they get into the project, they both begin learning, and the scope of the job begins to grow.

**3. Planning was performed by a planning group.**   Although this is necessary in some environments, it can lead to disasters. Elsewhere in this handbook, I have described a project manager who forgot the site preparation work on a construction job, which resulted in a $600,000 overspend on a job originally estimated at around $2 million. The cause: he planned it by himself, thus violating the rule that *the people who must do a job should participate in planning it.*

**4. No one is in charge.**   This happens sometimes in organizations in which the project manager's role is not well defined or accepted by everyone in the organization. This can mean that no one person is really responsible for the project, so that things "fall through the cracks." When the project manager's role is weak, she/he may be given no approval authority over expenditures, thus resulting in a "blank check" for people in the organization. Managing a project by committee can also be a problem, especially if the members of the committee lack the skills to reach consensus, etc.

**5. Project estimates are best guesses, made without consulting historical data.**   Sometimes there *is no historical data!* In many companies, good records of what actually happened in projects do not exist, so there is nothing to refer to for planning the next project. Or the reporting of labor hours was contaminated because salaried people do not report overtime (because they are not paid for it) and the current project was planned using the labor figures on the books.

**6. Resource planning was inadequate.** For example, no one bothered to check and see if a person with certain specialized skills would be available when needed in the project. Or a functional group is expected to do work for several projects, but no one noticed that the composite workload would require 300 percent more man-hours than were actually available in the department. Poor resource planning may very well be the most frequent cause of project failures.

**7. People don't see themselves as working on one team.** When work is divided up into different functional areas, individuals sometimes lose sight of the fact that the ultimate result requires the combining of all of the parts. They build walls around themselves, don't talk to or coordinate their efforts with members of other subgroups, and the result is chaos. A project manager has to work on team building to avoid this.

**8. People are constantly pulled off the project or reassigned with no regard for impact.** This often happens because functional managers have no concern for projects. They are "rewarded" for making their functional departments run smoothly, not for achieving project objectives. Again, this is because people in organizations do not see the importance of project work or the project manager. Rewards must be consistent with what the organization wants to happen, since it is a psychological premise that *what is rewarded gets done.*

**9. The project plan lacks detail.** When a project is planned with too little detail, it is difficult to anticipate what kind of problems may develop. Further, it is hard to manage resources adequately, do proper estimates of time or costs, and develop workable schedules. Invariably this "broad-brush" approach to planning results in numerous conflicts and frequent changes, and creates interference with other projects being executed at the time. One caution, however: the opposite approach is not desirable either. A basic rule is that no project should be planned in more detail than can be managed. Clearly, a balance is required.

**10. The project is not tracked against the plan.**   This seems inconceivable, but it happens. There are two general reasons. One is that the plan was a broad-brush plan, which had too little detail, so is not worth following, but then the team winds up having no control, because control can only be exercised by following a plan. The second problem is that a detailed plan is developed, but a problem develops during execution and people go into the panic mode and forget the plan. Again, they lose control. Planning should not be done just to satisfy some requirement that it exist. A plan that is not followed is useless.

Another thing that happens is that people take the attitude that the plan keeps changing, so they may as well abandon it. This is like saying, since we have encountered several detours on our drive across the United States, we may as well throw out the map and just "wing it." This is clearly nonsense, unless you don't care where you are at any given time, or where you end up.

**11. People lose sight of the original goal.**   Engineers involved with product development sometimes do this. They become so enamored of the technology that they forget they were supposed to be developing a product. Or they become perfectionists and waste time trying to make it better than the specification calls for. Project managers must continuously monitor project activities and, if necessary, remind contributors of the purpose of their work.

**12. Senior managers refuse to accept reality.** Sometimes senior managers have an idea of what should be required to do a job based on knowledge of a previous job or some other factor. When a project manager turns in an estimate that is out of line with what the manager thinks it should be (with the estimate being higher, of course), the manager insists that it be reduced. If the project manager is coerced into agreeing to targets in this manner, the project will probably fail.

In line with this is the tendency to dictate performance, cost, schedule, and scope targets simultaneously, thus violating the rule that only three of the four can be pinned down—the fourth must be allowed to be what it is, as the four are interdependent.

**13. Ballpark estimates become official targets.** Sometimes a project manager is asked for a ballpark estimate, which is to be used for a "go/no-go" decision. When people are only at the thinking stage, details are sketchy. The estimate is made

> Ballpark estimates sometimes become "official targets."

based on that sketchy information. A decision is then made to do the job, but now more detail is available, and it turns out that the ballpark figure was way too low. At this point, however, the manager cannot go back to higher-ups and tell them that the job will cost more, as they were originally told a lower figure and have come to think of that figure as *the* correct figure. So the ballpark becomes the target. To avoid this, the estimator needs to document all assumptions, make clear *in writing* that the estimate is a ballpark, with tolerances of plus-or-minus $x$ percent, so that it is clear from the beginning that the figures are subject to revision. (Of course, the ballpark may still become the target, but at least you have documented your original position.)

# 17

CHAPTER

# Managing Project Risks

**P**erhaps the most famous law of all is Murphy's Law, which is usually stated as, "Whatever can go wrong, *will!*" Given that this seems to be true in the experience of most people, it seems reasonable to ask how one should deal with Murphy's Law.

> **Principle:**
> We are all inclined to overestimate our ability and underestimate difficulties. As someone has said, "Even Murphy was an optimist!"

It seems clear that, when something goes wrong, we have *the possibility of suffering harm or loss,* which is defined as *risk.* I therefore define risk as anything that can go wrong in a project, which would impact project targets, and because impacted targets are of concern, I then need to ask how we can *manage* risks in projects.

> **risk:** anything that can go wrong in a project that will affect project targets.

In my experience, this is a neglected area in managing projects. It is sometimes caused by an overzealous "can-do" approach to managing.

A lot of managers subscribe to this attitude. Anyone who voices any concerns about being able to meet targets is immediately labeled a whiner or worse. They are told that if they can't get the job done, management will find someone who can. This is the macho attitude captured by the quote "Damn the torpedoes! Full speed ahead!"

There are certainly times when such an approach is justified, but there are many more when it is not. There is a difference between being foolhardy and taking a reasoned approach to real risks.

> It is an unhappy fact of life that there are usually more things that can go wrong with a project than can unexpectedly go right.
> —John R. Schuyler (1995)

I am certainly not advocating that people take an "Ain't it awful" attitude to projects, in which identified risks lead to paralysis. I am advocating that identified risks be *managed.* I would also say that adopting a can-do approach that ignores risks is project *mis*management.

One reason for doing risk management is that, when things go wrong unexpectedly, they throw you off balance and cause major crises for your projects. Trying to deal with a problem that has hit you without warning is always more difficult than planning ahead before the problem has occurred.

As an example, I have seen design engineers put all of their effort into a design that they couldn't make work. They never even *considered* the possibility! It may be that to consider that they might not be able to make the design work would be to admit their fallibility, and that might be too much for some perfectionist types to do. Whatever the reason, engineers who encounter design problems are often thrown into the panic mode, and may have to start over, since they have put "all of their eggs into one basket." Naturally, such a setback can have a serious impact on the project.

Another example was related to me by a participant in one of my seminars. A woman told me that her husband was managing a project to install a new manufacturing line in a plant. The equipment was being made in Italy. A few days before the ship date, Air Italia went on strike. He had a terrible time finding an alternative carrier, as the strike shifted all of Air Italia's cargo to other carriers. Whether he could have anticipated this risk is doubtful, but suppose he had. What might he have done? Arranged for an alternative carrier? Advanced the ship date so the machine could be sent over by marine transport rather than by air? Both are possibilities.

If you refer to my project methodology (the flow chart), you will see that there are two places in which risk management needs to be done. The first is in planning project strategy. The second is in implementation planning.

In planning strategy, you are trying to develop an approach for managing the project that may involve the choice of technology as well as an execution method. I have called these *project strategy* and *technical strategy* in Chapter 5. Both strategies have risks in most cases. When employing proven technology, the risks of failure are usually low. However, if cutting-edge technology is being applied, then the risks are much higher. Further, some project strategies have higher risks than others. For example, a "farm-out" project strategy might be more risky that one in which all work is done internally.

Either way, the first step in doing risk analysis is to identify what might go wrong. (This is true at both Step 4 and Step 6 of the flow chart.) When I do this with a team, I have them brainstorm a list of these and record them on a flip chart without discussion or evaluation. To help them identify risks, I simply ask, "What could go wrong that could impact schedule, cost, performance, or scope in the project?"

## THREATS VERSUS RISKS

You will notice in step 4 of the flow chart that you are supposed to test a strategy against risks and SWOT analysis. (SWOT stands for strengths, weaknesses, opportunities, and threats.) Unless you can manage risks, offset weaknesses, and contend with threats, your project strategy is likely to fail. The question is, what is the difference between threats and risks?

If you adopt a purist definition, risks are things that can happen without having any deliberate intention to cause harm behind them. Examples of risks might be accidents; acts of nature such as earthquakes, weather, and so on; losing key members of the team; fires; escalating labor rates or inflation; changes in the exchange rate for international projects; political instability, and so on. A threat is something that is done by a competitor or adversary to offset whatever you have done. For example, when an airline tries to capture a route by offering a very low fare, they are usually unsuccessful because the competition just matches their fare and nobody gains any more market share. While threats and risks are technically different, for the purposes of managing projects, they can be lumped together in the same analysis.

## It Is Best to Avoid Risk

It seems reasonable to say that it is always better to avoid risk than it is to manage it (Levine, 1995, p. 30). This should be done through better planning, not by avoiding a good opportunity. As I said above, you begin by identifying what can go wrong that might affect time, cost, performance, or scope in your project. Then you ask what might be done to avoid these effects. If it is not possible to avoid the effect, can you reduce the impact?

As an example, weather can hold up projects, and cannot be avoided. The solution is to examine the weather history for the area and time of year and to build into the schedule a reasonable amount of delay. If the weather is better than usual, you will get ahead of schedule, and conversely.

On the other hand, I would rather avoid the risk of putting an inexperienced project manager on a highly important project than to try to manage the risk once I have done so. Prevention is always less expensive than failure.

> It seems reasonable to say that it is always better to avoid risk than it is to manage it.
> ~ Harvey Levine

## QUANTIFYING RISKS AND THREATS

It is helpful to have some measure of the impact a risk or threat might have on a project. Naturally most of these cannot be quantified in any objective way, but a subjective method seems to work fairly well. The approach was first devised by engineers to identify where product designs might fail, and is therefore called failure mode effects analysis or FMEA. For any of you who are math challenged, this is a foreboding-sounding term, but don't be intimidated by it. The approach is very simple and requires nothing more difficult than multiplication.

I am going to call the approach Project Risk Analysis and Management, because I want to emphasize that it is not

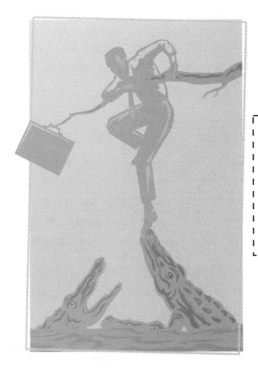

It is not enough to just identify and quantify risks. Risks should be managed!

enough to simply *identify* risks—you have to manage them as well. Furthermore, I am lumping risks and threats together, so I don't have to keep saying "risks and threats" every time. From now on, you will understand that *risks* refers to both.

## Assessing Probability

Once we have brainstormed a list of risks, we have to estimate the probability that they might occur. To do so, we use Table 17.1. In the FMEA terminology, something that goes wrong is referred to as a failure. I have changed that word to *occurrence,* since the word failure does not always apply. For example, political unrest in a country that might affect an international project is not a failure but an occurrence or event. You will note that the probability scale is a logarithmic scale, whereas the remaining scales are linear.

**T A B L E   17.1**

Probability of Occurrence

| Probability of Occurrence | Possible Occurrence Rate | Rank |
|---|---|---|
| Very high: occurrence is almost certain | ≥ 1 in 2 | 10 |
|  | 1 in 3 | 9 |
| High: repeated occurrences possible | 1 in 8 | 8 |
|  | 1 in 20 | 7 |
| Moderate: occasional occurrences | 1 in 80 | 6 |
|  | 1 in 400 | 5 |
|  | 1 in 2,000 | 4 |
| Low: relatively few occurrences | 1 in 15,000 | 3 |
|  | 1 in 150,000 | 2 |
| Remote: occurrence is unlikely | ≤ 1 in 1,500,000 | 1 |

## Estimating Severity

The next thing that we need to consider is how severe the effect of the event or occurrence is on the project. An event that has a high probability of happening but a low impact on the project is of little concern, whereas an event that has low probability but severe impact is of great concern. In Table 17.2, you will note the word *customer* being used several times. For this analysis, customer can mean an actual customer for the project or your company management, whichever is appropriate.

**T A B L E  17.2**

Severity of the Effect

| Effect | Criteria: Severity of Effect | Rank |
|---|---|---|
| Hazardous— without warning | Project severely impacted, possible cancellation, with no warning. | 10 |
| Hazardous— with warning | Project severely impacted, possible cancellation, with warning. | 9 |
| Very high | Major impact on project schedule, budget, or performance; may cause severe delays, overruns, or degradation of performance. | 8 |
| High | Project schedule, budget, or performance impacted significantly; job can be completed, but customer will be very dissatisfied. | 7 |
| Moderate | Project schedule, budget, or performance impacted some; customer will be dissatisfied. | 6 |
| Low | Project schedule, budget, or performance impacted slightly; customer will be mildly dissatisfied. | 5 |
| Very low | Some impact to project; customer will be aware of impact. | 4 |
| Minor | Small impact to project; average customer will be aware of impact. | 3 |
| Very minor | Impact so small that it would be noticed only by a very discriminating customer. | 2 |
| None | No effect. | 1 |

## Can It Be Detected?

In conventional FMEA analysis, detection capability has to do with whether a fault can be detected before a design is completed or a product is shipped. Using that meaning in assessing project risks leads to a 1 for the detection value most of the time, making this component useless. This is because you almost always know after the fact that a problem has occurred. However, if you change the meaning of detection to mean that a problem can be detected *before* it occurs, then you have a more useful definition.

As an example, if the oil runs out of your car while you are driving it, the effect will be severe. If you have an oil gauge, you should be able to see that the oil pressure is getting low and take action before the situation becomes serious. If you have a broken oil gauge or an indicator light that comes on at some threshold level, it is not as easy to detect the problem beforehand.

In projects, things like bad weather can be predicted with some accuracy, so that steps can be taken to compensate. Accidents, however, tend to happen without warning, so they are harder to deal with. Table 17.3 is used to measure

**T A B L E  17.3**

Detection Capability

| Detection | Rank |
|---|---|
| Absolute uncertainty | 10 |
| Very remote | 9 |
| Remote | 8 |
| Very low | 7 |
| Low | 6 |
| Moderate | 5 |
| Moderately high | 4 |
| High | 3 |
| Very high | 2 |
| Almost certain | 1 |

the detection capability of a risk in a project. Note that this scale is reversed. That is, the more certain it is that you can detect a hazard, the lower the number.

## THE RISK PROBABILITY NUMBER

For each risk that you have identified, you now have three measures—a probability level (P), severity measure (S), and detection capability index (D). These three numbers are multiplied to obtain a risk probability number (RPN). The higher that number, the more serious the risk. To see how this works, consider the three risks in Table 17.4.

The general approach to dealing with high RPNs is to ask whether any of the three individual components can be reduced. That is, can risk or severity be lowered, and/or can detection be increased (which will lower its number). As an example, we can reduce the probability of a weather delay in a project by doing it during a calendar period that historically has good weather. We can reduce severity of weather delays by padding the schedule, and we can increase our ability to detect forthcoming bad weather by paying close attention to weather forecasts.

For the examples in our table, the RPN for bad weather is so small that it can be ignored. However, the other two

**T A B L E  17.4**

Risk Analysis for a Project

| Identified Risk | P | S | D | RPN |
|---|---|---|---|---|
| Bad weather | 3 | 2 | 4 | 24 |
| Loss of key team member | 2 | 8 | 8 | 128 |
| Technology won't work | 6 | 10 | 8 | 480 |

risks have significant RPNs, and we should consider what to do. First, let's examine loss of a key team member. While it has a probability of only 2, it has a high severity and high detection. As a general rule, whenever severity is high, regardless of the RPN, special attention should be given to this particular risk.

A possible example of this is the *Challenger* disaster. It was believed by some members of the team that the probability of O-ring failure at the low launch temperature was quite low. However, the severity of failure was a 10, because the astronauts on board would be killed. Because of this fact alone, greater caution should have been exercised. It has been my experience that when people think the probability of something is low, they throw caution to the wind. Perhaps an example is that some people think the probability that they will have an automobile accident is very low, so they take chances with their driving—and get killed or seriously injured.

The severity of losing a key team member can be reduced if we have someone available to cover for her. This is what live theatrical productions do. They have an understudy who can play the part of a regular performer in the event of illness or accident. We might not be able to reduce detection in this case, but reducing severity alone might be enough.

The third risk in Table 17.4 is that technology won't work. There are a couple of possibilities in this case. First, the probability of failure is shown as 6 points, which is moderate. This might not give us too much cause for concern. However, if probability of technology failure were higher, say around 8 or 9 points, then I would suggest that a feasibility study be conducted before any kind of application of that technology be attempted. A basic premise is that discovery and development should be separated, if you are to have control over project schedules.

Even if we have low probability, the severity of a technology failure can be very high. One way to deal with this is to be ready with an alternate. In some very high-risk projects, where it was not possible to do feasibility studies, I have known some companies that have launched parallel development paths. The first technology that could be made to work was the one they continued with. This obviously costs a lot of money, and would only be done where time is more important than costs, which is true in some situations.

Finally, can we detect failure of technology with any ease? Perhaps not. However, it might be prudent to establish some decision criteria about how many failures will be tolerated before an approach is abandoned in favor of one that is more certain. This can be a blow to the ego of a professional, but in business, we must do what is prudent, rather than what is self-serving. An exception might be an attempt to develop a vaccine for a disease such as AIDS. However, even here, we must ask if repeated failures at a particular approach might not dictate adopting an alternative strategy.

## DEVELOPING CONTINGENCY PLANS

As I stated earlier, it is not enough to identify and quantify risks. The idea is to manage them. This might be done in three ways:

1. Risk avoidance.
2. Mitigation (reduction, such as using air bags).
3. Transfer (such as in loss prevention through insurance).

### Risk Avoidance

In the case of risk aversion or avoidance, we want to avoid the risk altogether. In case of the *Challenger*, the decision to delay the launch until the temperature warmed up would be an example of risk avoidance.

Japanese manufacturing has for many years employed "foolproofing" as a risk-avoidance strategy. The idea is to set up the assembly process so that it cannot be done incorrectly.

For example, they occasionally would start to install a gas tank in a car, only to find that one of the four mounting brackets had not been welded onto the tank. The solution was to set up a fixture to hold the tank while the brackets were welded onto it. Feelers were attached to detect the presence of the brackets. If all four brackets were not in place, the welding machine would not weld any of them.

In construction projects, we pad the schedule with rain-delay days, based on weather history for the area and time of year. This way, we avoid the risk that we will be delayed by bad weather. In engineering design, I mentioned using parallel design strategies to avoid the possibility that the deadline might be missed because one strategy proves difficult to implement. In any project, risk aversion or avoidance might be the most preferable strategy to follow.

## Mitigation or Risk Reduction

If we can think of contingencies in the event that a risk takes place, we can mitigate the effect. Placing air bags in cars is an attempt to reduce the severity of an accident, should one occur. Stafford Beer (1981) has argued that seat belts and air bags in cars actually give drivers a false sense of security. We have defined the problem as protecting the driver from being harmed if he is in an accident. Beer argues that it would perhaps be better to redefine the problem as how to keep a driver from having an accident in the first place (risk avoidance). He suggests that if we lined the dash board of the car with spikes, making it very clear that an accident has serious consequences, we might give drivers incentive to be more careful. His suggestion is not without merit.

In projects that involve procurement, sole-sourcing is a risk to consider. The alternative is to second-source all procured parts or equipment. That way, if a supplier can't deliver on time or at the specified price, the second supplier might be able to. This can be thought of as either risk avoidance or mitigation.

> Temporary
> workers are
> used as
> backups for
> critical
> personnel who
> become ill or
> are injured.

Temporary workers are used as backups for critical personnel who become ill or are injured. Overtime is used as a contingency when tasks take longer than estimated. This is one reason why overtime should not be planned into a project to meet original targets, if possible. Rather, it should be kept in reserve as a contingency.

Another possible contingency is to reduce scope to permit the team to meet the original target date, then come back later and incorporate deferred work to finish the job.

Having a fire evacuation plan in a building can be thought of as a contingency and also a loss-prevention plan.

## Loss Prevention

Insurance is one way of protecting against loss in the event that a risk manifests. Having alternative sites available into which a group can move in the event of a disaster is a loss-prevention strategy. Backup personnel can also be thought of as loss avoidance. If someone else can do the work, then when a key person is ill, there will be no loss to the project. Of course, this is difficult to do with highly skilled personnel.

## Cost Contingency

Cost contingency is also called "management reserve." Unfortunately, it is misunderstood. Too often it is believed that management reserve is there to cover poor performance. This is incorrect. Management reserve is a fund that is part of a project budget to cover the cost of unidentified work. All projects should have a work budget, to cover the cost of identified work, and a management reserve to cover work not yet identified. In addition, on projects that are paid for by a customer, there will be a component of the total job cost called *margin.* This is the intended profit for the job. Poor performance eats into margin, not management reserve.

The management reserve account is not touched unless we identify new work to be done. This is a change in scope, of course. At that point, money is transferred from the management reserve account into the work budget, and performance is subsequently tracked against the revised budget. A log should be maintained of all scope changes and their effect on the work budget, management reserve, and margin (if the change has such an effect). In customer-funded projects, the customer may be required to pay for scope changes, so that there is no impact to the management reserve account.

Schuyler (1995) has developed a list of possible ways to mitigate or avoid risks. These are listed in Table 17.5.

## PROJECT MANAGEMENT APPROACH AS A FUNCTION OF RISK

As Jean Couillard (1995) has written, much of the literature on managing projects proposes a uniform set of tools and methods to manage all kinds of projects. A study by Couillard confirms a suggestion by McFarlan (1981) that the

**T A B L E   17.5**

Schuyler's Ways of Mitigating or Avoiding Risks

| | |
|---|---|
| **Portfolio Risks** | **Operational Risks** |
| Share risks by having partners | Hire contractors under turnkey |
| Spread risks over time | contracts |
| Participate in many ventures | Tailor risk-sharing contract clauses |
| Group complementary risks into | Use safety margins; overbuild and |
| portfolios | overspecify designs |
| Seek lower-risk ventures | Have backup and redundant |
| Specialize and concentrate in a | equipment |
| single, well-known area | Increase training |
| Increase the company's | Operate with redirect and bailout |
| capitalization | options |
| | Conduct tests, pilot programs, and |
| **Commodity Prices** | trials |
| Hedge or fix-in the futures markets | |
| Use long- or short-term sales (price | **Analysis Risks (Reducing** |
| and volume) contracts | **Evaluation Error)** |
| Tailor contracts for risk sharing | Use better techniques (i.e., decision |
| | analysis) |
| **Interest Rate and Exchange Rate** | Seek additional information |
| Use swaps, floors, ceilings, collars, | Monitor key and indicator variables |
| and other hedging instruments | Validate models |
| Restructure the balance sheet | Include evaluation practices along |
| Denominate or index certain | with project postreviews |
| transactions in a foreign | Develop redundant models with |
| currency | alternative approaches and |
| | people |
| **Environmental Hazards** | Involve multiple disciplines and |
| Buy insurance | communicate across disciplines |
| Increase safety margins | Provide better training and tools |
| Develop and test an incident- | |
| response program | |

nature of the project should dictate the proper tools and methods. Risk, in particular, is a characteristic that should determine the best management approach.

Couillard found that, if project risk is not considered, standard PERT/CPM techniques, project monitoring, and control do not have a significant influence on project success. However, in high-risk projects, these techniques *do* have a significant influence on success. In high-risk projects, using PERT/CPM, which increases the frequency of project monitoring and control, does improve the likelihood of project success. He concludes that high-risk projects should be more closely planned, monitored, and controlled than low-risk projects.

The study also showed that when technical risk is high, pure-project organization structure (see Chapter 18) has a significant *negative influence* on project success. It turns out that matrix structure is better for such projects, presumably because technical expertise can be more easily drawn from a matrix structure than the pure-project (or stand-alone) structure.

> When technical risk is high, matrix is better than pure-project organization.

To measure success, Couillard employed the factors shown in Table 17.6 based on the findings of Baker, et al. (1974). His measures seem to be appropriate, as the point is that project success should be called *perceived* success, because the quantitative measures alone (cost, performance, time, scope) do not always correlate with whether a project is judged successful or not. As you can see, Couillard is explicit in calling the measures *subjective*.

Altogether, Couillard used 17 factors to indicate aspects of project management. These are shown in Table 17.7.

Using regression analysis, Couillard concluded that communication patterns and project goal understanding significantly influence all six measures of project success. This supports the frequent suggestion in the literature that you must have a clear, shared understanding of the project

**T A B L E   17.6**

## Project Success Measures

| Measure | Description |
|---------|-------------|
| Tech1 | The subjective measure of technical success relative to the initial requirement |
| Tech2 | The subjective measure of technical success compared with other projects |
| Cost | The subjective measure of budget overrun or underrun |
| Time | The subjective measure of schedule overrun or underrun |
| Overall | The subjective measure of overall project success |

Source: Adapted from Couillard (1995). Used with permission.

**T A B L E   17.7**

## Management Factors

| Project Manager Experience | Project Management Method | Project Management Tools and Techniques |
|---------|-------------|-------------|
| Number of projects managed | Understanding of project goals | WBS utilization |
| Responsibility index | Level of project manager authority and responsibility | PERT/CPM utilization |
| | Level of project director authority and responsibility | C/SCSC utilization |
| | Organizational structure | Periodic technical reports |
| | Senior management involvement | Periodic cost reports |
| | Communication patterns | Periodic schedule reports |
| | Problem handling | Frequency of project monitoring |
| | Project team support | |

Source: Adapted from Couillard (1995). Used with permission.

mission to be successful. Good communication within the team is also essential.

The authority given to the project manager to make decisions at the project level was also a factor, as were support received from the project team and problem handling by the team. This offers some support to the complaint by project mangers that they have a lot of responsibility and no authority. Based on this finding, senior managers should be sure to give the project manager the needed authority to deal with project issues directly.

Project managers in the study were also asked to assess project risk with regard to three objectives: technical performance, schedule, and cost. He used a three-point scale in which risk was rated as low, medium, and high. It was found that more experienced project managers are generally assigned to the high-risk projects. Also, PERT/CPM, C/SCSC, and periodic technical reports are more frequently used in high-risk projects.

## Technical Risk

When technical risk is high, project success is influenced by project manager authority, communication, team support, and problem handling. As previously mentioned, pure-project structure is also negatively correlated with success when technical risk is high.

## Cost Risk

When cost risk is high, project success is influenced by understanding of project goals by the team, project manager authority, team support, and communication.

## Schedule Risk

If schedule risk is high, two factors are important: the project manager's experience and the frequency of monitoring progress.

## CONCLUSION

Many success factors in projects center around human relationships, which says that project managers must master these skills no matter the project risk. High-risk projects need more careful planning, monitoring, and controlling than do low-risk projects. In general, if you have any one or a combination of technical, cost, or schedule risks, it seems prudent to follow these guidelines:

1. Emphasize team support.
2. Give the project manager appropriate authority.
3. Improve problem handling and communication.
4. Avoid the pure-project structure.
5. Increase the frequency of project monitoring.
6. Use the WBS, PERT/CPM, and C/SCSC.
7. Establish clear project goals for the team.
8. Select an experienced project manager.

SECTION

# OTHER ISSUES IN
# PROJECT MANAGEMENT

# 18

## CHAPTER

# Sociotechnical Systems and Project Organization

*I wish to acknowledge the contribution of Michael C. Thomas, Ph.D., to my thinking in writing this chapter.*

## TRADITIONAL PROJECT ORGANIZATION

Over the years a number of structures have been tried for organizing projects. Some of these are illustrated in Figure 18.1. At present, only two of the structures are widely used, those being pure hierarchy (sometimes called pure-project form) and matrix. In fact, a number of writers almost consider matrix to be synonymous with project organization, although in practice this is by no means true. Many projects are still organized in hierarchical form when speed is of the essence in product development. Some of these are called *skunk works* projects.

Both forms of organization have strengths and weaknesses. I describe these in another chapter, so they will not be repeated here. Rather, this chapter examines project organization in the light of sociotechnical systems design principles,

# F I G U R E   18.1

## Project Organization Structures

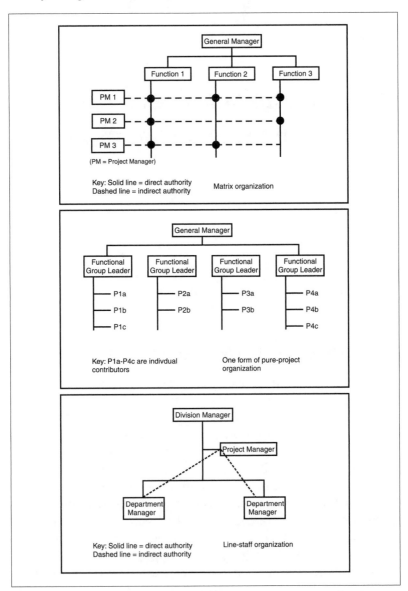

and offers some observations and recommendations for organizing large projects based on those principles.

The recommendations offered are not the cookbook type, however. That is, we do not have a step-by-step, how-to-do-it approach worked out. What we recommend is more in the nature of experiment, experiment, experiment!

That is not very comforting to those who want nice, tidy prescriptions, but it is the best we can do, given the state of the art today in organization design. Our primary purpose in offering this chapter is to make readers think about the issues, to at least increase *awareness* of the complexity of the problem. We used to call this *consciousness-raising*. It is our belief that, by being aware of the issues involved, project managers will be able to at least avoid some of the problems of traditional forms of organization and perhaps invent some solutions.

## What Is a Sociotechnical System?

The phrase *sociotechnical system* was coined by Eric Trist (Weisbord, 1987) to identify systems that are combinations of human and technical components. A system is characterized by four basic elements, as shown in Figure 18.2. It has *inputs, outputs,* a *process* that converts those inputs to outputs, and a *feedback* mechanism to regulate the transformation process.

We also have the term *open system,* which means that the system is open to interaction with its external environment, which of course suggests that the external environment affects the system performance. A closed system, on the other hand, will not experience such effects.

In a sociotechnical system, the process, inputs, output, and feedback elements are all combinations of people and technical "things" such as computers, manufacturing equipment, telephones, and so on. The basic gist of sociotechnical systems design is that there must be a joint optimization of the social and technical elements for the system to function at

F I G U R E  18.2

A Feedback System

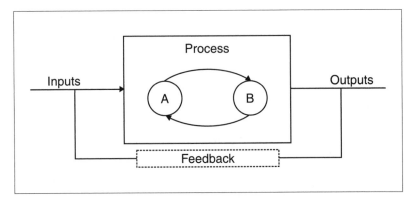

optimum levels. If only the technical components are optimized, then the social component may suffer.

John Naisbett has referred to our society as a "high-tech, low-touch" system, because technology has become so dominant that human interaction at the "touch" level has been reduced. We interact by phone or computer, often not dealing with people face to face, which is causing some grief to individuals who need that human interaction.

A third component that is actually a part of the social and technical systems, and which every organization contains, is its *reward* system. This component is a major influence on organization performance. As shown in Figure 18.3, the three interact, so that changes in one may affect the other two. For example, a change in technology will affect both the social and reward components. Introduction of computers changes the way people interact, which affects both the social system and the reward system, at least for those individuals who derive significant rewards from interacting with other people. In addition, some individuals will find working with the new computers to be rewarding, while others find it boring or threatening—in short, *un*-rewarding.

**F I G U R E  18.3**

Reward, Technical, and Social System

A change in the reward system may affect the social system as well as the way in which the technical system is employed. If people are rewarded for making better use of the new technology, then it should affect that utilization.

In short, there must be a joint optimization of all three components if an organization is to operate optimally. That is the thrust of sociotechnical systems design.

## WORKING PREMISES OF THIS CHAPTER

This chapter is based on a number of premises that may be argued. However, we base them on the current body of evidence from studies and real-world organization events.

### Need for Continuous Improvement

The quality movement of the 80s seems to have convinced most people of the need to improve organizations continuously. As Dr. Edwards Deming, one of the most widely respected gurus of quality has said, there are two kinds of organizations—those that are improving and those that are dying. An organization that is standing still is dying—it is just that no one knows it yet. The reason is simple: the world is dynamic, and one's competitors are certainly improving their performance, so if you stand still for long, pretty soon your competition will leave you behind.

Interestingly, many people do not have a good understanding of their competition and what they are doing, and so become complacent. I asked some fellows from the sanitation department of a county government once if they had any competition.

"Nope," was the positive answer.

"You better wake up," someone in the audience told them. "If a private garbage collection agency bids a lower price to the county than you guys cost them, you'll be out on the street."

I agree completely with that position.

We also know of numerous organizations that have failed to see the impact of critical events on themselves until it was too late. Some have only one customer—in most cases, the military—and when that customer quits buying, they are in trouble. Others fail to realize how a major development in new technology will affect them, again, until it is too late.

The American auto industry has had to make major changes as a result of Japanese competition. At one time it required as much as a week or more to change over a production line to begin manufacturing a new model car. The Japanese got it down to hours, and American industry was forced to do the same.

Likewise, it used to take six to eight years to develop a completely new automobile design. The Japanese got it down to three years. You can't compete with someone who brings out a new model in three years when it takes you six years.

In fact, speed is almost the name of the game today. Tom Peters has emphasized this in a film that he titled *Speed Is Life*, in which he features companies that managed to shorten their development times considerably through the use of cross-functional teams and other approaches.

Another factor that enters into the equation is the current labor shortage. When I first wrote this chapter in 1991, demographic forecasts for the United States were that by the year 2000 our population would grow by 12 million, while 14 million new jobs would be created. The prediction was that we would have a shortfall of some 565,000 engineers. Those figures are coming very close to the mark. And one thing is certain: growth of jobs will eventually outpace the growth of population, so that every organization must find ways to *do more with less*. Thus the need for improvement of processes.

During the past decade, much of the effort to improve organizations has been aimed at manufacturing. Only in the past few years have people begun to realize the importance of improving organizations *across the board*. In fact, we seem to have reached a point in which reducing labor costs through improvements in human productivity may not be all that useful. Peter Drucker has argued that we now need to focus on the application of capital, as the largest portion of product costs are now in that area.

However, we still have a lot to gain through the improvement of performance in administration, support, engineering, and project teams. The costs to develop new products have reached staggering dimensions, with labor costs being in the range of $40 to $100 per hour. Because of those high costs, companies must either charge high prices for products or sell large quantities of them just to recover their investment, which has made the development of some products too expensive, and those markets have gone to companies that have lower hourly costs for development.

## The Impact of Management on Projects

Whatever happens or doesn't happen in a project is because management either wants it to happen or *permits* it to happen. The first part of the premise will be accepted by most people. The second, that management permits (undesirable) things to happen in a project, may raise some defensiveness. Nevertheless, with the exception of acts of nature, it is management's responsibility to monitor project work closely enough to anticipate and address effects that might have a negative impact on a project. Failure to do so is to permit the impact through neglect.

## Project Organization Is a Sociotechnical System

Based on the description of sociotechnical systems at the beginning of this chapter, it is clear that all project organizations are sociotechnical systems. They employ technology and people, and have a reward component, all of which must be jointly optimized for the organization to function optimally. Sociotechnical systems-design methods therefore should be applied to projects.

To date, the most visible applications of sociotechnical systems design have been in self-directed work teams and other job designs. As I mentioned earlier, this has restricted the application largely to manufacturing, but I believe the application can be just as readily made to project organization.

This chapter, then, examines what sociotechnical systems-design principles have to offer in the organization of projects—especially product development projects, though it is believed that the principles can be applied to any kind of project team.

## SOCIOTECHNICAL SYSTEMS DESIGN OF PROJECT ORGANIZATIONS

### Involvement of All Members of the Organization

One of the tenets of the quality movement is that the person closest to a job is likely to be the most competent person to improve it. Whether this principle comes from sociotechnical systems theory or not, many organizations find that employees who are closest to the operational processes must be involved in the organizational design process. When this is not done, the consequences are low employee commitment to the job, incorrect estimates of time, cost, and other factors, omissions of work, and other errors. This happens when the design process involves only technical specialists and senior managers. It is seen most frequently in projects as planning of the project being done by people *other* than those who actually have to carry out the work, and this has been discussed in Chapter 4 on project planning.

Managers often complain that people in their organizations resist change. I don't believe this is true. In my view, people don't resist change, but they *resist being changed.* That is a significant difference. If we make people a part of the change process, then we do not get such resistance.

Another part of this is that *people don't argue with their own data.* If you make people part of the change process, then they get data first-hand that validates the need for change, so they don't argue with it. Further, the fact that they develop the change process means they do not resist it. These are important facts for managers trying to bring about improvements in organizational performance.

## Assessment of Strengths and Weaknesses of the Organization

One of the practices of project planning that is recommended in Chapter 6 is for the team to conduct a SWOT analysis. The acronym stands for strengths, weaknesses, opportunities, and threats, with threats and risks being more or less synonymous. The SWOT analysis should always be conducted through a review of objective data whenever possible. When the analysis depends only on individual perceptions and general ideas, it is suspect, partly because managers often are too optimistic at the beginning of a project, tend to minimize weaknesses and threats, and do not take risks seriously enough. Further, their optimism sometimes causes them to underestimate the number of resources or time required to do the work.

There is, in fact, a *macho* notion prevalent among some managers, that one should never admit any weakness—whether organizational or personal. Clearly, failure to admit weakness means that such weakness is not accessible to correction. Chris Argyris (1990) has discussed the processes that prevent organizations from learning from SWOT analyses and post-mortems of previous projects. There are two key processes that prevent learning: defensive routines and fancy footwork.

Defensive routines are attempts by members of the organization to avoid embarrassing anyone, so they hide *from* the truth as well as hide the truth from other members of the organization, preventing using the truth to signal the need for change.

Fancy footwork often involves reinterpretation of the data so that it has a favorable meaning. An example of this was the October 1992 release of unemployment statistics. The unemployment rate dropped by 0.1 percent in September of that year, and appears to be in part because some people just gave up looking for jobs, so were dropped from the list of unemployed. This would mean, of course, that the situation really is not improved at all. Nevertheless, President Bush appeared on television saying that it was a very positive sign, especially because it was the third consecutive month in which a drop had occurred.

## The Need For Joint-Optimization

As has been stated previously, optimum performance of any organization can only be achieved through joint-optimization of the social and technical systems. In the past, we have seen organizations falter because they came under the influence of someone who optimized only the social component. These individuals may have been heavily influenced by the human relations movement of the 50s and 60s. Their bias was that what was important in organizations was promoting job satisfaction, good relations, promoting low levels of interpersonal conflict, and so on. In other words, they tried to create a

> Optimum performance of any organization can only be achieved through joint-optimization of the social and technical systems.

"country club" environment in the workplace. Unfortunately, making people happy does not always correlate with good organizational performance such as quality, productivity, and profitability, and such country-club companies soon found themselves in trouble.

At the opposite extreme are organizations that try to optimize only the technical component. They invest in state-of-the-art equipment, streamline the work processes, employ statistical process-control methodology, and ignore the social system except for the bare minimum requirements. People are allowed to atrophy through lack of training and development. Rewards are dispensed only in the form of money. Conflicts are allowed to reach the boiling level before any attempt is made to resolve them, and then the resolution may take the form of warning the parties involved that it will not be tolerated, rather than trying to get at the root cause and eliminate the conflict.

Unfortunately, joint-optimization is much more difficult to achieve than it is to prescribe. Part of the difficulty is in the fact that the systems are not independent. We talk about them separately for convenience, but they are in most cases inter-related and therefore, as stated above, if a change is made in one, it affects the others. In fact, it may well be the *interaction* effects that are more important than the *first-order* effects.

For example, giving Tom a computer is a first-order effect in the technical component of the system. Whereas Tom previously had to do his calculations manually, he now has new technology, making it possible for him to make the calculations considerably faster than before.

However, he now finds that he is not as free to talk with Charlie as he used to be. Before the computer came along, he and Charlie often met together to work up weekly reports, helping each other with the calculations. Now each has a computer and is expected to perform the calculations individually. This is an *interaction* effect. The change to the technical system has caused a change in the social system, and this change may have more severe consequences than the first-order effect. The reason: Tom and Charlie both miss their social interaction so much that their morale declines. They begin complaining to their co-workers that the organization is becoming too cold and impersonal for their tastes, and they do so much "rabble-rousing" that soon there is a spread of low morale.

Their manager notices their rabble-rousing and warns them that it must stop. This further confirms that the organization (represented by their boss) has become cold and uncaring about them as human beings. They protest more. The boss finally dismisses them because he cannot live with their *attitudes!*

Another example comes from a client organization that had a piece of equipment they planned to eliminate because it was considered obsolete. The word got out that this was their plan. Unfortunately, the fellow who had operated the equipment for years saw the handwriting on the wall. If there was no need for his machine, what would happen to him?

He became despondent, believing that he would go out the door with the machine. His performance declined. His boss thought he was trying to retire on the job, and became concerned. Ultimately the employee was forced out of the company—his belief about the company's intentions became a *self-fulfilling prophecy.*

The sad thing is, the company fully intended to move him to another position when they disposed of his machine. He was always considered a valuable employee. Yet no one took the time to tell him what was going on (thereby attending to the social system component). Unfortunately, this is not an isolated incident.

### Reactive versus Proactive Management

Much has been written about the tendency of American management to focus on the short term rather than the long term, and to be reactive rather than proactive. This same problem typifies project management in many cases. The project manager becomes so involved in solving today's problems that she/he fails to look ahead, or to interpret the problems as symptoms of a greater "illness" which afflicts the project. This is understandable, when one realizes that we generally respond most strongly to that which is most salient in our experience, and *immediate problems* clearly are most salient. Tomorrow is "out there" somewhere in never-never land. It is not tangible.

It takes real discipline and the ability to back away from today and look at the "big picture" to get out of this short-term focus. It may even require an outside auditor to help, which is why periodic project audits are recommended as a safeguard against this tendency. (See Chapter 12 on audits.)

## Goal Selection and Orientation

Organizations tend to make choices of goals in an either/or manner. *Either* we can have quality *or* we can have it finished on time, but we can't have both! This sometimes leads to our seeing the customer as the enemy.

I got into a cab at O'Hare airport once and told the driver where I wanted to go. It was in the outskirts of Chicago. As he started to drive away, he said aloud, "The other cabs get to go downtown. Me, I get to go to (my destination)."

I said to him, "Look, if you don't want to take me there, let me out, and I'll get another cab."

"No, it's too late," he said. What he meant was that he had lost his place in the queue and would lose even more if he had to start over.

I must admit to being more than a little steamed. Finally I said to him, "It seems to me you have forgotten who pays your salary. Your customers are not the enemy. If you don't want to take them wherever they want to go, then you should hang a sign on your window saying 'downtown only.'"

He didn't say anything, but I know that he was only thinking about profits. If he went downtown, he had a good chance of picking up someone at a hotel who wanted to go back to the airport. Taking me to a suburban hotel meant that he would probably have to return to the airport empty, thus losing money.

I understand his concern, but for him to dump on me, the customer, was inappropriate.

As has been stated on project missions, it is necessary that a project team understand its primary reason for existence, which is *to satisfy the needs of its customers.* Failure to keep that in mind is certain to lead to failure overall.

As I have said in a previous chapter, the prime *motive* of a business is to make a profit, but its mission must be customer satisfaction. But this is not an either/or choice. They both must be achieved simultaneously. The same is true for a project team.

## Limits of the "Old Standbys"

The two categories of project organization, hierarchical and matrix, are the old standbys with which everyone is familiar. The problem is, when they are viewed as the only choices, they limit our ability to achieve more optimum solutions. Often we limit ourselves by working from a constraint orientation that emphasizes what cannot be changed, rather than from an innovative orientation which looks for what *can* be changed.

We must constantly search for organization forms that solve some of the problems of matrix and hierarchical structure. The most recent trend is cross-functional management, which is neither matrix nor hierarchical. This form of organization is described by Dimancescu (1992). Boeing assembled design-build teams to design the 777 aircraft. Nearly 215 teams, of as many as 15 members each, were assembled. Many were co-located to avoid the problems typically encountered with matrix, in which members are spread out physically so that communication occurs haphazardly, if at all.

This form of organization created a unique situation. Matrix results in a one-person-two-bosses form, which has long been deplored, yet deemed necessary to get complex jobs done. The Boeing organization created a situation of two-bosses-one-hat.

Cross-functional management is probably here to stay for the foreseeable future. Multidisciplinary teams are essential to deal with complex engineering projects, and the old matrix structure has proven to have numerous problems. No doubt cross-functional management will as well.

## Regarding the Organization Design as "Finished"

To expect that the design of an organization is finished "once-and-for-all," is to limit new possibilities and freeze our response capability in the face of changes that make the old design obsolete. It is better to regard design work as a part of regular operations and not a separate front-end activity. This requires setting goals for people development so that appropriate skills and flexibility are developed as needed to respond to the changing environment.

## A FINAL CAUTION

While this chapter has suggested that principles from sociotechnical systems design might be applied to project organization, a word of caution is in order. Most applications of sociotechnical systems principles have been applied to manufacturing environments, where jobs tend to be simplified, boring, and nonchallenging. In those cases, cross-training of workers tends to enlarge and enrich their jobs, making them more motivated.

To apply the same ideas to knowledge workers can be risky. For example, the idea to cross-train engineers in project teams was suggested by one practitioner of the art. My response was that this is like trying to teach a brain surgeon to do heart surgery, and vice versa. You wind up with two surgeons who are no good at either profession. The reason is simple—it is very nearly impossible to keep up with one's profession now, much less try to learn the skills of another!

Marvin Weisbord (1987), who is regarded by his colleagues as one of the nation's foremost practitioners of organization development, says:

> Anyone who tries to clone this procedure for project management, product development, or planning, quickly discovers that knowledge work happens differently from repetitive production work (a continuing source of irritation between scientists and cost accountants). The flow chart spills out in all directions. People already have multiskilled jobs, with considerable decision latitude (p. 324).

In my opinion, improving project team performance requires applying the ideas of cross-functional management, as discussed above. To that approach, we might apply sociotechnical systems-design principles and come up with the project organization of the twenty-first-century.

# 19

CHAPTER

# Profiling the World-Class Project Management Organization

## By Robert K. Wysocki

*For a more expansive treatment of the material presented in this chapter, see Robert K. Wysocki and James P. Lewis,* The World-Class Project Manager: A Career Development Guide, *(Reading, MA: Perseus Publications, 2000).*

## CHAPTER SUMMARY

First, let us understand that there are very few world-class project management organizations. After surveying more than 200 organizations, Harold Kerzner concluded that the number that could claim such honors were very few. In his book, *In Search of Excellence in Project Management,* he concludes, "Unfortunately, there are not many companies that have actually achieved excellence." In fact, from among those surveyed, he only includes 29 companies as having achieved excellence or being on the right track. They are:

Armstrong World Industries    Kinetico, Inc.

Battelle                      Lincoln Electric

Bellcore                      MCI

BellSouth                     Mason & Hanger Corporation

BTR Sealing                   Motorola

Centerior Energy              National City Corporation

ChoiceCare                    Nortel

Ericsson                      OEC Medical Systems

General Electric              Radian International

General Motors                Roadway Express

B. F. Goodrich                Sprint

Hewlett-Packard               Standard Products

ISK Biosciences               United Technologies

Johnson Controls                  Automotive

Key Services Corporation      USAA

While several others would undoubtedly like to achieve world-class status, they have not. The first question such organizations should ask is, "How are we doing with respect to becoming a world-class project management organization?" The answer to that question can be determined by taking the one-minute survey later in this chapter.

Assuming the one-minute survey shows that the organization is not a world-class project management organization, the next question should be, "Is our organization ready to move towards world-class project management?" Wanting to be world class is certainly a necessary condition, but desire is not enough. Can they become world class? This is an equally important question. The organizational readiness assessment presented in this chapter will help senior management make this determination.

Another part of the investigation of an organization's readiness for project management is an assessment of the competencies and skills of those who are or would like to function as project managers. Some will have the required experience and skills to be *full-time project managers*, others will be *occasional project managers* with some training and experience, others will be *accidental project managers* with no training or preparation, while others are *wanna-be project managers* who are simply drawn to the profession. Below we discuss the competencies and skills needed for all types of project managers.

For our purposes we classify projects based on their technical and business characteristics. Because all projects are inherently different, one would expect that they would require different skills of those who manage them. That is in fact the case and so we associate a project manager type with each project type. The project types have a natural ordering from least complex to most complex, and the project manager types associated with each project will also have a natural ordering. Using this construct we will then have defined a career path for project managers. Movement along that career path will be equivalent to acquiring the skills needed to manage projects of increasing complexity.

In this chapter we will present a profile of project managers in terms of the skills they need to manage successfully the project type to which they are assigned. Using these profiles as a reference point, any individual can compare her skills with those required to manage projects of a given type. The difference between the skills she possesses and the skills required is defined as her "skill gap." The greater the gap between the competencies and skills needed and the actual competencies and skills possessed provides some measure of the challenge the organization faces. Knowing their skill gap, individuals can begin to address that gap and prepare themselves to manage projects of increasing complexity.

# WHAT IS A WORLD-CLASS PROJECT MANAGEMENT ORGANIZATION?

A quick way to assess your organization's position relative to being a world-class project management organization is through the one-minute survey in Figure 19.1

Take a minute to answer the seven questions and compute your organization's score. How close are you to world-class status? Were you surprised at the results?

## Organizational Readiness

Given that the results indicate that world-class status is still a goal to be attained, the next question is, "Are we ready to become a world-class project management organization?" To answer that question we can use a readiness-assessment tool developed by Enterprise Information Insights, Inc., a project management consulting organization headquartered in Worcester, Massachusetts. Their assessment tool measures an organization's readiness for adopting an enterprisewide project management process.

Through a survey consisting of 66 questions (see Figure 19.2 for a sample of the survey questions), the assessment tool produces a report (Figure 19.3) that measures 20 dimensions that portray organizational readiness for an enterprisewide project management methodology, assesses the current management of the organization's project portfolio, the extent to which the professional staff are aware of and have implemented effective project management practices, and the relationship of project managers and teams to their customers[1]. Figure 19.4 interprets the data summary graphic used in Figure 19.3 Several conclusions can be drawn from the report. These are listed in Figure 19.5.

---

[1] Enterprise Information Insights, Inc. offers a Web-enabled version of the Organizational Readiness Assessment. For more information or to arrange for an assessment of your organization, contact EII, Inc. at 508-791-2062 or email them at rkw@eiiinc.com

F I G U R E   **19.1**

One-Minute Survey

## ✓ Take This One-Minute Survey

|  | YES | MAYBE | NO |
|---|---|---|---|
| Our organization successfully completes more than 70 percent of its projects. | ❑ | ❑ | ❑ |
| Our project portfolio is always aligned with our business goals and objectives. | ❑ | ❑ | ❑ |
| Our senior managers know the business value and status of all active projects. | ❑ | ❑ | ❑ |
| Our managers visibly support our enterprise-wide project management process. | ❑ | ❑ | ❑ |
| Our managers have the skills to deliver business value from projects. | ❑ | ❑ | ❑ |
| Our project managers are achieving their professional development goals. | ❑ | ❑ | ❑ |
| Our managers proactively address the training needs of their project teams. | ❑ | ❑ | ❑ |

To compute your score count
the number of checked boxes

☑ Yes   x 5 = _____
☑ Maybe x 3 = _____
☑ No     x 1 = _____
TOTAL SCORE = _____

## How did you do?

Score  What does it mean?

31-35  Your project management environment is world class!
22-30  Performance is acceptable. There is room for improvement.
13-21  Corrective action is required. Get a team to work at once.
7-12   Immediate action is required. Outside help will be needed.

**F I G U R E   19.2**

A Sample of Organizational Readiness Questions

## A Sample of Questions from the Organizational Readiness Assessment Survey

 SA (Strongly Agree)    A  (Agree)    N (Neutral)
D (Disagree)    SD (Strongly Disagree)
If you have no experience or observation that pertains to the question, respond with an "N", the neutral response.
Try to answer as many questions as possible with a non-neutral response.
Circle the correct response to each question.

1. I know when the project manager understands what I have requested.    SA  A  N  D  SD

2. My staff feels like they are really part of the project team.    SA  A  N  D  SD

3. Executives have communicated the importance of project management.    SA  A  N  D  SD

4. I often participate in problem resolution for projects in my area.    SA  A  N  D  SD

5. Project managers are handling scope changes in a professional manner.    SA  A  N  D  SD

6. We have a formal change management process.    SA  A  N  D  SD

7. Turnover on project teams is comparable to turnover in other departments.    SA  A  N  D  SD

8. We do a good job managing resources that are allocated to projects.    SA  A  N  D  SD

9. Project managers are genuinely concerned about customer satisfaction.    SA  A  N  D  SD

10. Project managers display a positive "can do" attitude.    SA  A  N  D  SD

11. I understand why certain project priority decisions have been made.    SA  A  N  D  SD

12. Project managers read project management publications.    SA  A  N  D  SD

**F I G U R E   19.3**

Typical Project Management Organizational Readiness Assessment

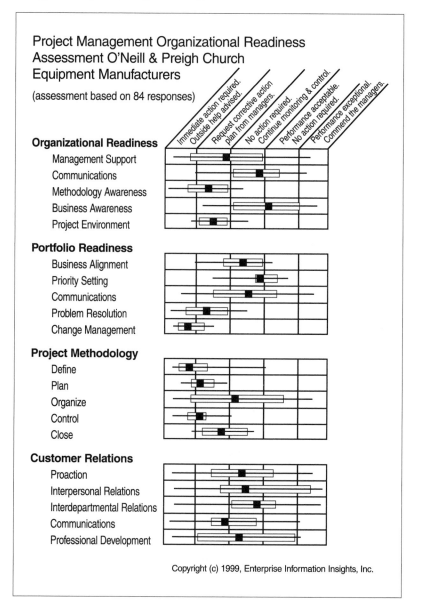

Project Management Organizational Readiness
Assessment O'Neill & Preigh Church
Equipment Manufacturers

(assessment based on 84 responses)

**Organizational Readiness**
Management Support
Communications
Methodology Awareness
Business Awareness
Project Environment

**Portfolio Readiness**
Business Alignment
Priority Setting
Communications
Problem Resolution
Change Management

**Project Methodology**
Define
Plan
Organize
Control
Close

**Customer Relations**
Proaction
Interpersonal Relations
Interdepartmental Relations
Communications
Professional Development

Copyright (c) 1999, Enterprise Information Insights, Inc.

## F I G U R E  19.4

How to Interpret the Data Summary Graphic

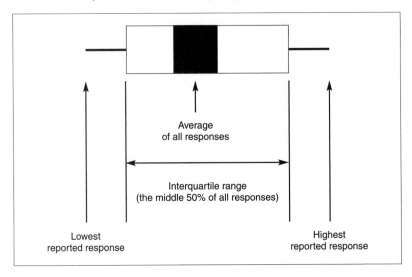

## F I G U R E  19.5

Conclusions from the O'Neill & Preigh Organizational
Readiness Assessment

❑ Management support for an enterprisewide management
methodology varies widely.

❑ The current project management methodology is not widely
understood nor is the corporate environment supportive of current
project management practices.

❑ Problem resolution and change management processes are not
meeting management expectations.

❑ Overall the lack of understanding of project management practices
has resulted in poor practices, especially in the definition, planning,
control, and closing phases of projects.

❑ Customer relations vary widely, which indicates that some business
units' expectations are being met while others are not. This may be
indicative of varying business awareness on the part of project
managers and team members, as evidenced by the wide range of
responses in the business awareness dimension.

The analysis of the organization's readiness data will help them formulate a plan for attaining world-class project management status. We are assuming that the data supports that effort. The organization should develop a strategy for addressing the areas needing improvement before they commission the project to design, develop, and implement an enterprisewide project management methodology. For example, the conclusions given in Figure 19.5 suggest the following corrective action as a prerequisite to any further steps toward achieving world-class project management status:

1. Determine the reasons for some managers' reluctance to support an enterprisewide methodology and put a program in place to address their concerns.
2. Address the lack of understanding of current project management practices through simple documentation, communications, and training initiatives.
3. Charge task forces with developing and implementing problem resolution and change management processes.
4. Use training to address a widespread and consistent lack of project management knowledge, which has resulted in poor practices.
5. Develop interpersonal skills, which are generally lacking. This problem is not consistent across the organization, as evidenced by the large variance among the responses. There are probably areas where the relationship is good and others where it has sadly deteriorated. Investigate the reason for these differing relationships.

## A TAXONOMY OF PROJECTS

We could use various criteria to classify projects: by total budget, project duration, risk, business value, team size, or some combination of them. For the purpose of matching project manager and team members with the type of project team they are qualified to join, we will use a classification based on the technical and business environments that characterize the project. Figure 19.6, adapted from the Project Complexity Assessment Matrix developed by the Center for Project Management, graphically displays our classification scheme.

Given a project, the complexity assessment process—that the Center for Project Management has developed and uses in its consulting engagements—measures as many as 40 characteristics of the project to map it into two dimensions: business environment and technical environment. At least conceptually, a typical project can then be plotted as a data point on the project complexity assessment matrix. The data point will fall into one of four regions on the matrix. Starting from the simplest situation, a Type IV project has low business value and

**F I G U R E   19.6**

Project Complexity Assessment Matrix

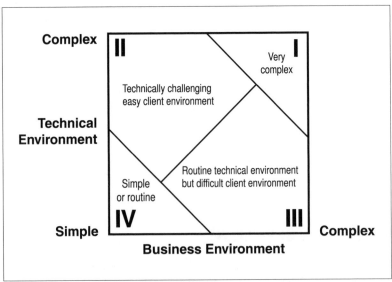

Source: Adapted from the Project Complexity Assessment Matrix developed by the Center for Project Management.

uses well-established technology. In fact, it is a project that may have repeated itself several times and has become rather routine. Type II projects, on the other hand, may be using new or complex technologies and while business value may be low or moderate, it can be distinguished from Type IV projects. Type III projects are characterized by their high business value even though they may have low or moderate technical complexity. These projects are therefore distinguished from the other two by their high business content. Type I projects bear all of the characteristics of Type II and III projects in that they use complex technologies and have high business value. They are the most demanding of the four types and are often mission critical as well.

## A CLASSIFICATION OF PROJECT MANAGERS

Just as projects come in several flavors, so do project managers. The more seasoned project managers are qualified to manage the most complex and mission critical projects (Type I projects). On the other hand, those who have just been anointed project managers might be limited to less complex and noncritical projects (Type IV projects) and require additional training that may eventually lead to promotions and the opportunity to work on more complex projects

We can relate project manager classifications to project classifications. We define four classes of project manager: Team Leader, Project Manager, Senior Project Manager, and Program Manager. They relate to the project complexity assessment grid in the following way. Type IV projects can be managed by anyone of the four classes of project manager, but will most frequently be managed by those who have demonstrated Team Leader qualifications. By choosing the appropriate Type IV project, the project manager and project team can learn and practice new skills. Type II and III projects can be managed by anyone who has demonstrated Project Manager or above qualifications but will most likely be managed by someone who has reached Project Manager status. Depending on the mix of technical and business skills they possess, they will be assigned to either Type II or Type III projects. Type I projects are the domain of the Program Manager or Senior Project Manager classes. The most critical of the large Type I projects may be treated as programs and be staffed by a Program Manager and several Senior Project Managers or Project Managers. Later in this chapter we will profile each type of project manager based on the competencies and skills needed to be effective at that class.

To each of the four types we will assign types of project managers, as shown in Figure 19.7.

This matching of project manager type to project classification will facilitate our discussion of skill profiles of project managers as a function of the type of project they are assigned to manage. That discussion follows later in this chapter. In preparation for that discussion, let us first look at the functions and tasks that any one of our four project manager types may be called upon to perform.

**F I G U R E   19.7**

Project Manager Type by Project Classification

| Project Complexity | Team Leader | Project Manager | Senior Project Manager | Program Manager |
|:---:|:---:|:---:|:---:|:---:|
| I | | | X | X |
| II | | X | X | X |
| III | | X | X | X |
| IV | X | X | X | X |

## JOB FUNCTIONS AND TASKS FOR PROJECT MANAGEMENT

Project managers are called upon to perform a variety of functions and tasks. Many might seem to be removed from the direct management of the project. We will set the stage for our discussion of competencies and skills by providing the following list, which was first developed by the Boston University Corporate Education Center in partnership with several of their clients and is used with permission here.

I.  **Project Planning (strategic and tactical)**
    a.  Develops preliminary study with project team, identifying business problem, requirements, project scope, and benefits.
    b.  Identifies key project results and milestones.
    c.  Develops project plan and work breakdown structure and communicates to team and client.
    d.  Determines needed resources, including client involvement.
    e.  Estimates time lines and phases.
    f.  Influences selection of project team members.
    g.  Assigns project responsibilities based on assessment of individual skills and development needs.
    h.  Defines clear individual roles and performance expectations.
    i.  Establishes acceptance criteria.
    j.  Determines appropriate technological approach.

II. **Managing the Project**
    a.  Continually reviews project status.
    b.  Reviews work against key results criteria.
    c.  Uses systematic method for logging project status—checking against schedule.
    d.  Uses change management/request procedure.
    e.  Uses project meetings to measure progress against plan, communicate changes and issues.

    f.  Assesses skill-needed documentation of meetings, work, conversations, and decisions.

    g.  Measures quality through testing against requirements.

    h.  Conducts project reviews and walk-throughs (with appropriate client involvement).

### III. Lead Project Team

    a.  Involves team in planning.

    b.  Uses both formal and informal methods to track project status.

    c.  Recognizes individual and team accomplishments or results.

    d.  Manages performance issues in a timely manner.

    e.  Delegates tasks effectively based on understanding individual strengths and weaknesses.

    f.  Maintains open door for staff ideas and concerns.

    g.  Sets performance and development objectives for staff.

    h.  Schedules and holds regular team meetings.

### IV. Building Client Partnerships

    a.  Involves working jointly with client in defining project goals and key results.

    b.  Works with client to assure alignment of project to overall business goals.

    c.  Listens and responds actively, documents client needs, changes, and demands.

    d.  Implements procedures for controlling and handling change.

    e.  Develops client understanding of the system and trains in systems use.

    f.  Presents and reports periodically to client.

    g.  Establishes lines of responsibility and accountability to client.

### V. Targeting to the Business

    a.  Manages in accordance with visions and values.

    b.  Links overall architecture principles.

Negotiation skills are "necessary" skills.

c. Interfaces effectively with business systems and processes.
d. Plans for impacts on related systems/departments to achieve maximum efficiency.
e. Understands business needs, time, and cost pressures.
f. Keeps current with competitors' business and technology developments.
g. Aligns project with corporate and business priorities and direction.

## Competencies and Skills of the World-Class Project Manager

If anyone has a foolproof method of identifying a professional who will make a competent project manager, please contact one of the authors. We can show you how to make a lot of money. In fact, it is very difficult to identify someone with the requisite competencies. Figure 19.8 demonstrates the reason why it is so difficult. There are two levels of characteristics that determine success or failure as a project manager. At the visible level are skills, whose degree of mastery can be measured and that a person can acquire through training. That is the easy part. More difficult are those traits (competencies) that lie below the surface. We can see them in practice but we cannot

**F I G U R E  19.8**

Project Manager Competencies and Skills

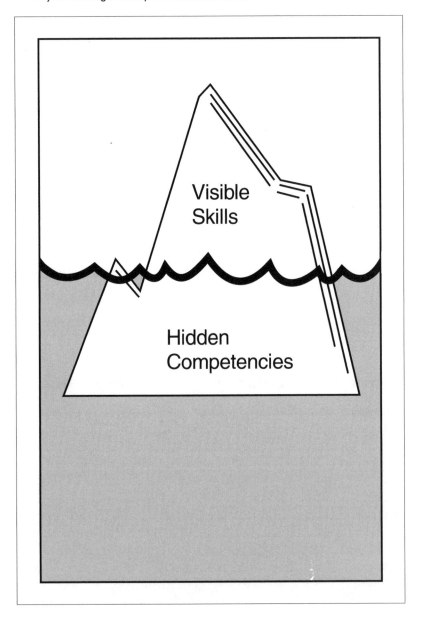

directly measure them in the sense of determining whether or not a particular person has them and, if so, to what degree. They are also the traits that are more difficult to develop through training. Some of them may, in fact, be hereditary.

Enterprise Information Insights uses an assessment tool to measure competency in 18 different areas based on a set of observable behaviors related to the competencies. To establish competency level, we recommend an individual take a self-assessment and that several of his co-workers also assess the individual. These co-workers might be the individual's manager, peer professionals, subordinates, and customers. Using this approach, the individual's self-assessment can be compared with his co-workers' assessments. While this approach is simplistic, it is practical and has surfaced rather insightful conclusions regarding individual performance.

For competency assessment we define business, personal, interpersonal, and management categories. Skill assessment adds project management skills as a fifth category. Effective project managers require competencies and skills that are specific to the discipline in which they manage, and they require a set of non-discipline-specific skills that fall into one of the five categories described below.

1. **Business.** These competencies and skills relate to the business and business processes in general and do not involve specific business function knowledge.
2. **Personal.** Competencies and skills in this category relate to the individual. The skills do not involve another party to be practiced.
3. **Interpersonal.** Competencies and skills in this category relate to the individual. The skills involve at least two people, neither one of whom manages the other.
4. **Management.** These competencies and skills relate to all aspects of management, whether people management or work management. They also include skills related to the performance of strategic and tactical management functions not specific to any individual.

5. **Project Management.** Project management skills span the five phases of project management: initiation, planning, organizing, controlling, and closing.

## COMPETENCY PROFILE OF THE WORLD-CLASS PROJECT MANAGER

This section discusses the competencies common to all levels of project manager. It is meant to give you a general sense of what is required to be an effective project manager and to match your current competencies against those required of world-class project managers. This examination will highlight the gap between your competencies and those you will need to add to your profile as you move through the ranks of increasing project management responsibility. This assessment will form the core of your personal learning contract.

Figures 19.9 through 19.12 provide a capsule description of the business, personal, interpersonal, and management competencies required to be an effective project manager. As we begin, it would be a good exercise to review this list and personally assess how your competencies measure up. The list was originally developed by the Corporate Education Center of Boston University in cooperation with several of their major corporate accounts. It has since been revised through experience with several other clients and has been adapted here with permission.

This survey format allows you to evaluate the extent to which you practice each competency. The rating scale is 5 = Strongly Agree, 4 = Agree, 3 = Neutral, 2 = Disagree, and 1 = Strongly Disagree. Evaluate yourself on each of the competencies and follow the summary instructions at the end.

Add the score value for each of the 19 competency areas. The resulting scores are interpreted as follows:

**F I G U R E   19.9**

Business Competencies

## Business Competencies

**Business Awareness**
Ensures that the project is linked to the organization's
business plan and satisfies a business objective
by solving a business problem.                              5  4  3  2  1

Evaluates the impact of industry and
technology developments.                                    5  4  3  2  1

Balances ideal technical approaches and project
scope against business deadlines and priorities
to find the best compromise.                                5  4  3  2  1

Quickly adapts to changing business conditions.   5  4  3  2  1

              TOTAL BUSINESS AWARENESS SCORE  [          ]

**Business Partnership**
Follows up with business partners, throughout
the cycle of the project, to ensure full understanding
of the business partners' needs and concerns.     5  4  3  2  1

Seeks meaningful business area participation
during the design process.                                  5  4  3  2  1

Conducts business-oriented walkthroughs.          5  4  3  2  1

Structures the activities of the project team, so that
systems staff work closely with a business partner.  5  4  3  2  1

              TOTAL BUSINESS PARTNERSHIP SCORE  [          ]

**Commitment to Quality**
Pushes for more efficient ways to do things.      5  4  3  2  1

Sets and enforces high standards of quality
for self and others.                                        5  4  3  2  1

Develops a quality plan coordinated with
the project plan.                                           5  4  3  2  1

Monitors performance against quality plan
and objectives.                                             5  4  3  2  1

              TOTAL COMMITMENT TO QUALITY SCORE  [          ]

**F I G U R E   19.10**

Personal Competencies

## Personal Competencies

**Initiative**

Develops innovative and creative approaches to
problems when faced with obstacles or limitations.      5  4  3  2  1

Takes calculated risks.      5  4  3  2  1

Takes persistent action to overcome obstacles
and achieve solutions.      5  4  3  2  1

Puts in whatever effort is needed to get job done.      5  4  3  2  1

**TOTAL INITIATIVE SCORE** [ ]

**Information Gathering**

Actively solicits input from all groups that may
be affected by the project.      5  4  3  2  1

Seeks information or data from various
sources to clarify a problem.      5  4  3  2  1

Identifies and consults individuals and groups
that can expedite project activities or provide
assistance.      5  4  3  2  1

Gets enough information to support design and
implementation decisions.      5  4  3  2  1

**TOTAL INFORMATION GATHERING SCORE** [ ]

**Analytic Thinking**

Develops an overall project plan including
resources, budget, and time.      5  4  3  2  1

Translates business goals into project goals
and project goals into detailed work breakdown
structures.      5  4  3  2  1

Uses project management software to develop
plans and track status.      5  4  3  2  1

Generates and presents logical, clearly
reasoned alternatives.      5  4  3  2  1

**TOTAL ANALYTIC THINKING SCORE** [ ]

Personal Competencies

## Personal Competencies (continued)

**Conceptual Thinking**

Considers the project within the context of a broader view of how the business and technology will be changing over the next several years.   5 4 3 2 1

Uses understanding of business and technical objectives to prioritize effectively (for example: project tasks, test cases, issues to be resolved).   5 4 3 2 1

Anticipates and plans for the impact of the project on other systems.   5 4 3 2 1

Develops a clear vision or conceptual model of the deliverables.   5 4 3 2 1

**TOTAL CONCEPTUAL THINKING SCORE** [ ]

**Self-Confidence**

Presents a confident and positive attitude to set the tone for the team.   5 4 3 2 1

Confronts problems with others quickly and directly.   5 4 3 2 1

Controls own feelings and behavior in stressful situations.   5 4 3 2 1

Works effectively under pressure.   5 4 3 2 1

**TOTAL SELF-CONFIDENCE SCORE** [ ]

**Concern for Credibility**

Maintains credibility by consistently delivering what has been promised.   5 4 3 2 1

Stays on top of the details of the project effort, to be able to answer questions authoritatively and maintain credibility.   5 4 3 2 1

Answers questions honestly, even if awkward to do so.   5 4 3 2 1

Promptly informs management and the customer about any difficulties.   5 4 3 2 1

**TOTAL CONCERN FOR CREDIBILITY SCORE** [ ]

**Flexibility**

Adjusts readily to changes in the work environment.   5 4 3 2 1

Adjusts own managerial style, depending on the people and situation.   5 4 3 2 1

Uses or shares resources to best accomplish organizational goals.   5 4 3 2 1

Delegates tasks and activities to others.   5 4 3 2 1

**TOTAL FLEXIBILITY SCORE** [ ]

Interpersonal Competencies

## Interpersonal Competencies

**Interpersonal Awareness**

Tries to know team members, to understand
what motivates them.                                             5  4  3  2  1

Understands the issues and concerns of other
individuals and groups.                                          5  4  3  2  1

Notices and interprets nonverbal behavior.                      5  4  3  2  1

Is objective when mediating conflicting positions of
team members.                                                   5  4  3  2  1

**TOTAL INTERPERSONAL AWARENESS SCORE** ☐

**Organizational Awareness**

Identifies and seeks the support of key stakeholders.           5  4  3  2  1

Proactively engages groups and individuals with
technical and/or financial overseeing responsibilities.         5  4  3  2  1

Takes the time to understand and consider the political
dynamics among groups involved in the project.                  5  4  3  2  1

Uses relationships with people from other units within the
organization to resolve issues or provide assistance.           5  4  3  2  1

**TOTAL ORGANIZATIONAL AWARENESS SCORE** ☐

**Anticipation of Impact**

Adapts style or approach to achieve a particular impact.        5  4  3  2  1

Manages expectations by ensuring that what is
promised can be delivered.                                      5  4  3  2  1

Arranges for a senior manager to attend the initial project
meeting and explain the project's mission and objectives.       5  4  3  2  1

Considers the short- and long-term implications of
project decisions.                                              5  4  3  2  1

**TOTAL ANTICIPATION OF IMPACT SCORE** ☐

**Resourceful use of Influence**

Develops strategies that address other people's
most important concerns.                                        5  4  3  2  1

Enlists the support of his/her management to
influence other managers.                                       5  4  3  2  1

Enlists cooperation by appealing to people's unique expertise.  5  4  3  2  1

Involves project team members in the detail planning
of the project, so they will have ownership of the plan.        5  4  3  2  1

**TOTAL RESOURCEFUL USE OF INFLUENCE SCORE** ☐

**F I G U R E  19.12**

Management Competencies

## Management Competencies

### Motivating Others

Ensures that team members understand the
project's goals and purpose.                              5  4  3  2  1

Provides rewards and recognition to people
as milestones are reached.                               5  4  3  2  1

Initiates informal events to promote teamwork.           5  4  3  2  1

Takes appropriate action to assist and counsel
marginal performers.                                     5  4  3  2  1

**TOTAL MOTIVATING OTHERS SCORE** [          ]

### Communications

Organizes and meets regularly with a management
team composed of representatives from all areas
affected by the project.                                 5  4  3  2  1

Plans and holds regular, frequent meetings with the
project team to discuss status, resolve issues and
share information.                                       5  4  3  2  1

Ensures that presentations are well organized.           5  4  3  2  1

Tailors his/her language to the level of the audience.   5  4  3  2  1

**TOTAL COMMUNICATIONS SCORE** [          ]

### Developing Others

Gives team members assignments or training to
provide opportunities for growth and development.        5  4  3  2  1

Provides direct, specific, constructive feedback and
guidance to others regarding their performance.          5  4  3  2  1

Empowers team members to create challenge
and stretch their abilities.                             5  4  3  2  1

Provides closer supervision for inexperienced
people.                                                  5  4  3  2  1

**TOTAL DEVELOPING OTHERS SCORE** [          ]

*Continued*

F I G U R E　19.12 (Concluded)

Management Competencies

## Management Competencies (continued)

### Planning

Develops and maintains a detailed master plan that shows resource needs, budget, time schedules, and work to be done.　　　5　4　3　2　1

Assesses project design and implementation approach often to ensure that the project properly addresses the business problem to be solved.　　　5　4　3　2　1

Ensures a common understanding and agreement on the project scope and objectives and on any subsequent changes.　　　5　4　3　2　1

Maintains control of accepted changes to the project plan and ensures that any changes are communicated to all team members.　　　5　4　3　2　1

**TOTAL PLANNING SCORE** [＿＿＿＿＿]

### Monitoring and Controlling

Regularly obtains status information from each project team member on their assigned tasks, monitors resource usage and schedule variances, and keeps the project on schedule.　　　5　4　3　2　1

Identifies the economic and schedule consequences of requested and/or mandated scope changes and communicates these to management.　　　5　4　3　2　1

Accepts responsibility for resolving project issues, especially scope changes, focusing on solutions, recommendations, and actions.　　　5　4　3　2　1

Conducts a post-project review to identify what went well, what should have been done differently and what lessons were learned.　　　5　4　3　2　1

**TOTAL MONITORING AND CONTROLLING SCORE** [＿＿＿＿＿]

| Score Range | Project Manager Competency Level |
|---|---|
| 4–7 | Does not meet minimum competency level |
| 8–10 | Meets team leader minimum competency level |
| 11– 15 | Meets project manager minimum competency level |
| 16–18 | Meets senior project manager minimum competency level |
| 19–20 | Meets program manager minimum competency level |

Knowing your scores on each of the competencies will give you a rough guide as to where you should concentrate your development activities. You might want to ask your co-workers to assess your competencies and compare their responses to yours. You will discover that others do not perceive you as you perceive yourself. Their perceptions are reality regardless of how closely they agree with reality as you see it. Figure 19.13 is a typical competency assessment report.[2] The narrow, filled rectangle is the individual's self-assessment; otherwise the rest of the graphic is interpreted as defined in Figure 19.4 above.

## SKILL PROFILE OF THE WORLD-CLASS PROJECT MANAGER

In this section we turn our attention to skills of the project manager. Unlike competencies, skills are visible and can be assessed. We use Bloom's Taxonomy of Educational Objectives—Cognitive Domain to measure skill levels. Bloom's Taxonomy is a six-level taxonomy that measures cognitive abilities as described in the following. It is based on observable and verifiable events as they relate to each of the skills,

---

[2] Enterprise Information Insights, Inc. offers a Web-enabled version of the Individual Competency Assessment. To get more information or to arrange to have the assessment conducted at your organization, contact them at 508-791-2062 or email them at rkw@eiiinc.com.

## F I G U R E  19.13

Competency Assessment Report

O'Neill & Preigh Church
Equipment Manufacturers
(assessment based on 8 responses)
Competency Assessment Report
for Sy Yonra

**Business Competencies**

Business Awareness
Business Partnership
Commitment to Quality

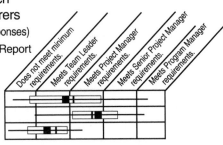

**Personal Competencies**

Initiative
Information Gathering
Conceptual Thinking
Self-Confidence
Concern for Credibility
Flexibility

**Interpersonal
Competencies**

Interpersonal Awareness
Organizational Awareness
Anticipation of Impact
Resourceful Use of Influence

**Management
Competencies**

Motivating Others
Communication Skills
Developing Others
Planning
Monitoring & Controlling

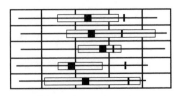

as they, in turn, relate to competencies. Listed below is a definition of each of the six levels of that taxonomy.

## 1.0   Knowledge (I can define it)

Knowledge, as defined here, involves *the remembering or recalling* of ideas, materials, or phenomena. For measurement purposes, the recall situations involve little more than bringing to mind the appropriate material. Although some alteration of the material may be required, this is a relatively minor part of the task.

## 2.0   Comprehension (I can explain how it works)

Comprehension involves those objectives, behaviors, or responses that represent an understanding of the literal message contained in a communication. In reaching such understanding, the "student" may change the communication in his mind or in his overt responses to some parallel form more meaningful to him. There may also be responses that represent simple extensions beyond what is given in the communication itself.

## 3.0   Application (I have limited experience using it in simple situations)

This skill level involves the use of abstractions in particular and concrete situations. The abstractions may be in the form of general ideas, rules of procedures, or generalized methods. The abstractions may also be technical principles, ideas, and theories, which must be remembered and applied.

For example, the individual will use an abstraction correctly, given an appropriate situation in which no mode of solution is specified. She will apply generalizations and conclusions to real-life problems and apply scientific principles, postulates, theorems, or other abstractions to new situations.

## 4.0    Analysis (I have extensive experience using it in complex situations)

This involves breaking down a communication into its con-stituent elements or parts such that the relative hierarchy of ideas is made clear and/or the relations between the ideas expressed are made explicit. Such analyses are intended to clarify the communication, to indicate how the communica-tion is organized and the way in which it manages to convey its effects, as well as its basis and arrangement. Analysis deals with both the content and form of material.

## 5.0    Synthesis (I can adapt it to other uses)

This requires putting together elements and parts so as to form a whole. It involves the process of working with pieces, parts, elements, etc., and arranging and combining them in such a way as to constitute a pattern or structure not clearly there before.

## 6.0    Evaluation (I am recognized as an expert by my peers)

Here, the individual can make judgments about the value of material and methods for given purposes. Specifically, it in-volves quantitative and qualitative judgments about the ex-tent to which material and methods satisfy criteria, and use of a standard appraisal. The criteria may be those determined by the individual or those which are given to him.

### Application of Bloom's Taxonomy

Envision a matrix of skills (the rows of the matrix) by project manager class (the columns of the matrix). At the intersection of a row (skill) with a column (project manager class) a value from 1 to 6 indicates the skill level that is required for a pro-ject manager of that class. Figure 19.14 through Figure 19.18 gives the skill levels for project management, management, business, personal, and interpersonal as a function of project

**F I G U R E   19.14**

Project Management Skills of Project Managers

| PROJECT MANAGEMENT SKILLS | IV | III | II | I |
|---|---|---|---|---|
| Charter Development | 3 | 4 | 4 | 4 |
| Complexity Assessment | - | 3 | 3 | 4 |
| Cost Estimating | 3 | 4 | 4 | 5 |
| Cost Management | 3 | 4 | 4 | 5 |
| Critical Path Management | 3 | 4 | 4 | 4 |
| Detailed Estimating | 3 | 4 | 4 | 5 |
| Project Planning (WBS, network, PERT, etc.) | 3 | 4 | 4 | 4 |
| Project Closeout | 3 | 4 | 4 | 5 |
| Project Management Software Expertise | 4 | 4 | 4 | 4 |
| Project Notebook Construction & Maintenance | 3 | 4 | 4 | 4 |
| Project Organization | - | 3 | 3 | 5 |
| Project Progress Assessment | 2 | 3 | 3 | 4 |
| Resource Acquisition | 2 | 4 | 4 | 5 |
| Resource Levelling | 2 | 4 | 4 | 5 |
| Resource Requirements | 2 | 4 | 4 | 5 |
| Schedule Development | 3 | 3 | 3 | 4 |
| Scope Management | 3 | 4 | 4 | 5 |
| Size Estimating | 3 | 4 | 4 | 5 |

Management Competencies of Project Managers

| MANAGEMENT SKILLS | IV | III | II | I |
|---|---|---|---|---|
| Delegation | 3 | 4 | 4 | 5 |
| Leadership | - | - | - | 4 |
| Managing Change | - | 4 | 4 | 4 |
| Managing Multiple Priorities | 3 | 4 | 4 | 5 |
| Meeting Management | 3 | 4 | 4 | 5 |
| Performance Management | - | 3 | 3 | 4 |
| Quality Management | 3 | 3 | 3 | 4 |
| Staff and Career Development | - | - | - | 4 |
| Staffing, Hiring, Selection | - | 4 | 4 | 4 |

Business Competencies of Project Managers

| BUSINESS SKILLS | IV | III | II | I |
|---|---|---|---|---|
| Budgeting | - | 3 | 3 | 4 |
| Business Assessment | - | 4 | 4 | 4 |
| Business Case Justification | - | - | - | 4 |
| Business Functions | 3 | 3 | 3 | 4 |
| Business Process Design | - | 3 | 3 | 3 |
| Company Products/Services | - | 3 | 3 | 3 |
| Core Application Systems | 3 | 3 | 3 | 3 |
| Customer Service | - | - | - | 3 |
| Implementation | 4 | 5 | 5 | 5 |
| Planning: Strategic and Tactical | - | 3 | 3 | 3 |
| Product/Vendor Evaluation | - | - | - | 4 |
| Standards, Procedures, Policies | 3 | 4 | 4 | 4 |
| Systems and Technology Integration | - | 4 | 4 | 4 |
| Testing | 4 | 4 | 4 | 4 |

**F I G U R E  19.17**

Interpersonal Competencies of Project Managers

| INTERPERSONAL SKILLS | IV | III | II | I |
|---|---|---|---|---|
| Conflict Management | 3 | 4 | 4 | 4 |
| Flexibility | 3 | 4 | 4 | 4 |
| Influencing | - | 3 | 3 | 4 |
| Interpersonal Relations | 3 | 4 | 4 | 4 |
| Negotiating | - | 3 | 3 | 4 |
| Relationship Management | - | 4 | 4 | 5 |
| Team Management/Building | 3 | 4 | 4 | 4 |

Copyright (c) 1999, Enterprise Information Insights, Inc.

manager class. Note how skill levels change for each class of project manager. Project managers can identify skills development needs as they consider progression through the ranks of project management.[3]

---

[3] Enterprise Information Insights, Inc. offers a Web-enabled service to assess skills and skill gaps of individuals and groups using self-assessments and user-defined 360 assessments. For more information or to arrange to have a skill assessment for your staff contact us at 508-791-2062 or email at rkw@eiiinc.com.

F I G U R E   **19.18**

Personal Competencies of Project Managers

| PERSONAL SKILLS | IV | III | II | I |
|---|---|---|---|---|
| Creativity | 3 | 4 | 4 | 5 |
| Decision Making/Critical Thinking | - | 4 | 4 | 5 |
| Presentations | - | 4 | 4 | 4 |
| Problem Solving/Trouble Shooting | 4 | 4 | 4 | 5 |
| Verbal Communications | 3 | 4 | 4 | 4 |
| Written Communications | 3 | 3 | 3 | 4 |

Copyright (c) 1999, Enterprise Information Insights, Inc.

# 20

## CHAPTER

# Improving Your Communication Skills

It is a fact of life that when you survey organizations, you always find that people say there are communication problems. This is probably the most widespread problem in organizations. In spite of all the talk about information overload, people are hungry for information, and if they don't get the information they need, they make things up. This is sometimes the source of the rumor mill.

There is, of course, a lot of talking going on in most organizations. There just isn't much communication taking place. The problem exists on both sides of the fence—the talker isn't being effective and the listener isn't practicing good listening skills.

Communicating is not just talking—it is both talking and listening, and to teach a person good talking skills without also dealing with listening is to deal with only part of the problem. Project managers (in fact, most managers) have problems with both aspects of communicating. They don't

> Communication
> is not just
> talking—it is
> both talking
> and listening.

listen well when team members talk, and they don't talk in ways that their team members understand. Add to this that team members also don't communicate well and you have a standard formula for miscommunication.

The question is, can you solve the problem yourself? If others don't listen well, can you do anything about it? Perhaps not completely, but you can improve the "hit rate" by improving your own speaking and listening skills.

There are five factors that affect whether a person is a good or poor communicator. These factors are *self-concept, listening, clarity of expression, coping with angry feelings,* and *self-disclosure* (Bienvenu, 1969).

## SELF-CONCEPT

The most important factor affecting a person's communications with others is his self-concept. This is how a person sees himself. Every person has many concepts about himself: who he is, what he stands for, what he does and does not do, what he values, what he believes, and so on. Most of us are very clear on some of these concepts, while other parts are vague or fuzzy. The Johari window illustrates this in Figure 20.1.

The Johari window shows that there are things that we know about ourselves, that others know about us. This is called our *public self.* There are also things about ourselves that we know, but that no one else knows. This is called our *private self.* Then there is the *unknown* self—those aspects of ourselves that neither we or anyone else know about. And finally, there is the part that we don't know but that everyone else knows. We are *blind* to this part of ourselves.

**F I G U R E  20.1**

The Johari Window

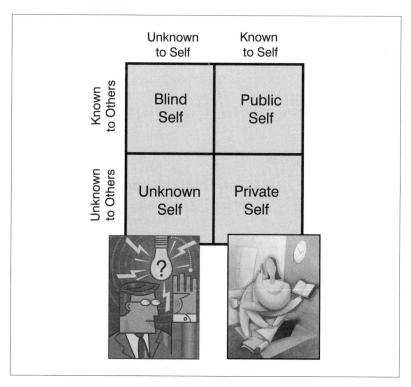

The core of a person's self-concept is formed early in child-hood and is based on what family members tell him about him-self. The "telling" is not necessarily verbal, of course. The child receives messages about who he is that are both verbal and nonverbal. There is evidence that just the amount of holding, nurturing, and "baby talk" that parents give an infant will affect his self-concept and chances of survival.

If the messages received by a child say that he is okay, that he is loved and cared for, that he can do whatever he sets out to do, then he will develop a positive self-concept. How-ever, children told that they are *not* okay, that they are not loved and wanted, and that they can't do a lot of things, tend to develop low self-esteem.

Although the core self-concept develops very early, one's self-image continues to develop throughout life. One way in which this is done is through a process called *social comparison*. We compare ourselves to others throughout our lives to see how we stack up. If we seem about the same or better than most people, then we have a positive self-image, and conversely. Self-concept can change as we gain new life experience. So a person who begins with low self-esteem can gain new confidence through successful life experiences.

## EFFECTIVE LISTENING

As I have said previously, much of communications skills training focuses on talking. There is not nearly enough em-phasis on listening, and we find that the cause of many of our communication problems are caused by poor listening habits. An effective listener listens not only to the words but to the *meaning* of the words. This includes understanding what the speaker is *feeling*. Not attending to the speaker's feelings can cause that person to feel unappreciated and misunderstood.

For this reason, we should practice *active* listening, as opposed to *passive* listening. Passive listening occurs when a person responds to the speaker by saying "Uh-huh," nodding affirmatively, or saying, "I understand." The speaker has no way of knowing whether the listener really understands, or whether she simply thinks she understands.

In active listening, the listener repeats back to the speaker what she has heard, but she rephrases it so that it is in her own words. If she simply parrots exactly the same words used by the speaker, it might seem that she understands what the speaker intends to say, even when she doesn't.

> An effective listener listens not only to the words but to the *meaning* of the words.

For example, suppose the speaker says, "There is a problem with this schedule. I don't think you have enough resources to do the work as you are showing."

The listener could say, "You don't think I have enough resources to do the work?"

Speaker: "Right."

Now this might seem almost trivial, and if you do it with every comment the speaker makes, you will be accused of being deaf or playing games. But it is a useful way to check your understanding when an issue is difficult—especially if it is emotional.

When people are upset with each other, they almost always feel that the other person does not understand them and their position on an issue. Active listening is a way of assuring the other person that you have heard and understood.

Consider this exchange:

John: "I don't think you appreciate how hard I have been working to get this job finished on time. All you want is more, more, more!"

Tom: "You don't think I appreciate your hard work, John? Is that true?"

John: "You bet!"

Now John may still be upset with Tom, but at least he knows that Tom is listening to understand his viewpoint.

With that, it is possible for them to resolve their conflict. Otherwise, they will arrive at an impasse.

Listening actively when you are presented with data or factual information is a very useful approach to understanding a situation. Problem solving involves understanding the problem, and unless you are careful to listen for the proper data, you might define the problem incorrectly

There are two main reasons that cause people not to listen effectively. One is that they simply don't care what the speaker is saying. The other is that they are trying to think of a response to what the speaker just said, so they miss what the speaker is currently saying. Another reason for not listening effectively is that the listener is distracted by noises, activities nearby, or previous concerns. When it is important to listen, these causes should be eliminated. Get away from the noise or nearby activity, if possible. If preoccupations with previous concerns are keeping you from listening, then ask the speaker to meet with you later, after you have had a chance to deal with your concerns.

## SPEAKING CLEARLY

Some people seem oblivious to the fact that others do not understand them. They seem to think that, because what they are saying is clear to themselves, that it must be clear to the other person. I have seen instructors respond to a question from a student by going back through the original explanation in the very same words that they used the first time. It makes me want to say to them, "If those words had been any good, the person wouldn't have had a question. Change the way you say it this time!"

To communicate effectively, follow these rules:

1. Know what *outcome* you want. Are you trying to inform? Get information? Give advice? Get the person to do something, change his behavior, or stop doing something? Are you trying to punish him verbally

or shame him? Unless you are clear on your desired outcome, you may not communicate effectively.

2. Decide to *whom* you need to communicate. Is it the entire group? One person? It has always been a pet peeve of mine to see managers respond to some undesirable behavior of one team member by writing a memo (or develop a written policy) to all group members telling them not do what the offender did. In the first place, they probably had no intention of doing so, and in the second place, the memo to the group probably won't affect the behavior of the offender if she decides to misbehave again. The memo or policy is just a cop-out to avoid dealing face-to-face with the offender, and a manager who is afraid to confront employees who behave inappropriately should rethink his role.

3. What is the best *mode* in which to communicate? Written, verbal, both? We know that putting things in writing can lead to future problems. This is especially true when you get angry about something and blast someone in writing. However, if you want to be sure that someone has clear instructions about something, then you might want to write them out.

4. Have *sensory awareness* to notice when you get the response that you want. I have seen teachers who seemed completely unaware that people in their classes were totally lost. I have often thought that it would make no difference to them if the room were empty—they would give their lecture, pack up, and go home. Clearly, you need to pay attention to the listener(s) when you talk, and try to determine from their nonverbal responses if they are with you or not.

5. Acquire *flexibility*. Be able to vary your communication until you manage to get through to the other person. If you continue to repeat yourself, using the same words, you are deadlocked.

## DEALING WITH ANGER

Sometimes we deal with our anger inappropriately and thus block communication with the other person. When I first entered the workforce, I heard a manager tell someone to leave his feelings outside when he came to work. Yet he wanted the person to be motivated. It never occurred to him that motivation and emotion have the same root—that is, feelings and motivation are both emotions. What he really wanted was for the person to leave his anger outside, because he felt uncomfortable dealing with it.

The result of such a rule is that some people learn to suppress their anger, for fear that others will think their behavior is inappropriate. The problem is, this is saving up brown stamps, to use a term from transactional analysis, and eventually you "fill up your book" and "cash them in." Of course, the way you cash them in is to have an explosion. It may be an emotional explosion or it might be a physical explosion, in which your body literally explodes into a serious illness. Neither outcome is desirable.

Being able to express feelings appropriately is necessary if we are going to have healthy relationships with others. Bienvenu offers the following suggestions for dealing with your emotions:

1. Be *aware* of your feelings. When we are afraid of our emotions, we sometimes create a blind spot that keeps us from even knowing that we are feeling anything. If you have done this, it may take some time for you to regain your awareness.

2. Admit that you have feelings—especially those considered "bad" or undesirable. We all have negative feelings sometimes. It is not human to be feelingless, or to have only positive feelings. We aren't robots.

3. Accept responsibility for what you do with your emotions. If you lash out at someone when you are angry, you must accept the consequences of that behavior.

4. Tell people how you are feeling. Congruent communication requires that there be an accurate match between what you are experiencing and what you are saying.

5. Learn from understanding your emotions. Ask yourself what caused you to feel as you did. Do this even with positive emotions.

## SELF-DISCLOSURE

If you want to have really good relationships and good communications with others, you must be willing to disclose things about yourself that help the other person get to know you. This must be a mutual process, of course. If the other person is closed off, it will be hard to get to know him. The more we know about each other, the more effective our communications can be. Referring to the Johari window, this means that you are disclosing more of your private self to your associates.

> **SELF-DISCLOSURE**
> The more we know about each other, the more effective our communications can be.

It is virtually impossible to know and relate to people who never let you know anything about themselves except that which is superficial. Unfortunately, in some companies there is such a climate of suspicion and fear that some employees do not want you to know them, and any attempt to do so is met with resentment. These individuals see your attempt to get to know them as a way of taking advantage of them.

As an example, a human resources manager told me about a manager in his company who wanted to enroll his children in a private school. Someone told him that a woman on the assembly line had her children in a school that interested him, so he went to talk to her. When he asked if it were true that she had her children in that school, her reaction shocked him. "It's none of your business," she said angrily, so he backed off. The next thing he knew, she went to HR and complained about this invasion of her privacy. In such settings, it is nearly impossible to get to know members of your teams.

## CONTENT AND RELATIONSHIP

Every communication carries two components—a message or content aspect and a definition of relationship with the person or group you are addressing. For example, suppose I say to someone, "Close the door." The content is clear. I want the door closed. The definition of relationship being expressed is one in which I feel it is okay to tell the person to do something, and can expect her to do it.

Contrast this with, "Please close the door." The content is the same, but the definition of relationship is different. We would say that in the first instance the relationship is one of unequal status, whereas the second suggests a more equal relationship. If the relationship is seen by both parties the same way (either equal or unequal), then the definition offered will be accepted. However, if the other person sees the relationship as equal and you define it as unequal, then your definition will most likely be rejected.

All of us constantly have to deal with this definition of relationship issue, whether we are conscious of it or not. Furthermore, it is impossible to communicate without offering a definition of relationship. To see why this is true, have you ever been on a plane or bus and the person sitting beside you stared out the window and never spoke to you?

> Every communication carries two components—a message or content aspect and a definition of relationship with the person or group you are addressing.

What did their silence convey to you about the way they viewed the relationship with you? Clearly, they did not want to engage you at all. They saw the relationship as nonexistent. So even silence communicates.

The technical terms for relationships are *complementary* and *symmetrical*. A complementary relationship is one of unequal status, whereas a symmetrical one is equal status. It is interesting to note that symmetrical relationships can be stable over the long term (on average, we might say), but they are unstable on a minute-to-minute basis. For example, my relationship with my wife might be symmetrical on average, but at any given moment, she may "call the shots" and at another time I might do so. When she is calling the shots, the relationship is momentarily complementary—unequal status— and when I call the shots the same is true, but now in reverse.

## METACOMMUNICATION

Not only do we define relationships when we communicate, but we also communicate the true meaning of a remark through the *manner* in which we do it. This is called metacommunication. It is communication *about* the communication. As an example, suppose someone comes into my office and I say, "Get out of my office," in an obviously joking way. The person knows not to take me seriously. This is the meta-aspect. The fact that I have jokingly told her to get out of my office also defines our relationship as one in which we are very comfortable with each other, and like to kid around.

Suppose, however, that I say, "Get out of my office" in a way that sounds serious, and therefore really means that the words are to be understood at face value. The person turns around to leave. If I really mean for the person to leave, then the communication and meta-communication are congruent. However, if I really didn't mean for her to leave, then the meta-communication was incongruent, and she will be totally confused.

It is also possible that I was joking but she thought I was serious. The other person always has to interpret the true meaning of a communication, and this is where difficulty enters the picture. If she misinterprets my meaning and gets angry, then I am going to have to repair the damage to our relationship, and this can sometimes be almost impossible, because she is convinced that she understood my meaning, and that I was serious.

## PUNCTUATION OF COMMUNICATION

We often see our behavior as a response to that of someone else. In an ongoing exchange between individuals, this is called punctuation of the communication. Consider the following exchange that might take place when I try to talk to my friend, who thinks I have thrown her out of my office.

"Celia, I need to talk to you. When you came into my office earlier I was just joking when I told you to get out."

"Sure you were. You were serious, and you know it. I've never been so insulted in my life!"

"Come on, Celia, you know I was just joking. I would never throw you out of my office. You're welcome any time."

"Well, you sure sounded serious to me, and I think you're just trying to get out of it now."

"You're being silly, Celia. You know very well I wasn't serious."

"Well! Now you're calling me silly! I guess you don't want silly people in your office!"

"Well, if that's how you see it, I sure don't!"

"Fine!"

"Fine!"

Now note what happened. If you asked Celia why she behaved as she did, she would tell you that she was only responding to my behavior. If you asked me why I behaved as I did, I would tell you that I was only responding to Celia's behavior. After all, she's the one who misunderstood and overreacted, I would tell you.

Thus, I see my behavior as a response to Celia's behavior, and she sees her behavior as a response to me. In fact, there is a sense in which I see her behavior as *causing* mine, and she will say the same, that my behavior caused her to behave as she did.

The exchange can be diagramed as shown in Figure 20.2. I see the exchange as going 1-2-3, whereas Celia sees it

**F I G U R E  20.2**

Punctuation of Communication

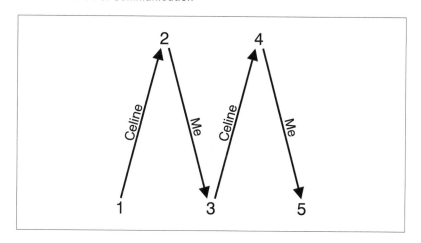

as 2-3-4. Not only that, once this exchange starts, it is very difficult to extinguish. It becomes what is called a *game without end*, but naturally we don't mean fun and games. This is the essence of many conflicts, and explains why they are so hard to resolve: each side sees their behavior as a response to the other, and they will tell you, "I wouldn't have done what I did if *he* hadn't done what he did!"

## CONDITIONS REQUIRED FOR EFFECTIVE COMMUNICATION

Communication depends on having:

♦ **A common culture.** When communicating with nontechnical people, we do not share a common culture. Using jargon and failing to explain technical points will result in failed communication. The engineering manager serves a translation role between nontechnical personnel and the engineering staff.

♦ **Common expectations.** When expectations differ, communication suffers.

♦ **Motivation to communicate.** You will have a hard time getting through to someone who has decided he doesn't want to hear what you have to say.

## SENSORY PREFERENCES AND COMMUNICATIONS

We gain knowledge about the world in which we live through the five senses. Most of us, in fact, prefer one of the five senses over the others, and find that we gain knowledge and understanding most easily through that sense. In our society, the preferences tend to be for visual, then auditory, and finally kinesthetic (feelings).

Our language reflects the use of the sensory systems, as shown by the following examples:

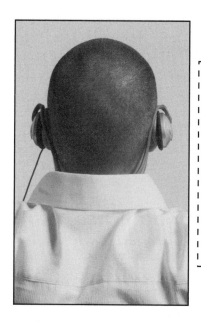

> You will have a hard time "getting through" to people who have decided they don't want to hear what you have to say.

1. VISUAL: I don't *see* how you got such a distorted *picture* of things.
2. AUDITORY: I *hear* what you are saying, but it still doesn't *sound* right.
3. KINESTHETIC: That doesn't *feel* right to me! I still can't get a *handle* on it.
4. SMELL: This proposal *smells* fishy to me!
5. TASTE: The whole affair left a bad *taste* in my mouth!

Note that, although smell and taste are seldom primary systems for individuals, smell is a powerful memory jogger. When you smell a certain fragrance, you may be reminded of a former flame.

Following are some of the more common expressions used in visual, auditory, and kinesthetic modalities.

**T A B L E  20.1**

Primary Representational Systems

| Meaning | Kinesthetic | Visual | Auditory |
|---|---|---|---|
| *I (don't) understand you.* | What you are saying feels (doesn't feel) right to me. | I see (don't see) what you mean. | I hear (don't hear) what you are saying. |
| *I want to communicate something.* | I want to put you in touch with something. | I want to show you something. | I want to tell you something. |
| *What do you mean?* | I can't get a handle on that. | I don't see what you are saying. | What are you saying? |
| *Do you understand me?* | Does that feel okay to you? | Do you see what I mean? | Do you hear what I'm saying? |

## THE IMPORTANCE OF THE REPRESENTATIONAL SYSTEMS

Because individuals most efficiently process information when it is presented in the sensory system they prefer, you will find it helpful to notice which system they use and communicate accordingly. Auditory people, for example, don't prefer to read long reports. A quick verbal summary is adequate. Visual people, on the other hand, want pictures, diagrams, and so on, to most efficiently process information. And kinesthetic individuals want to *experience* it first-hand. They like "walkthroughs" and other experiential ways of dealing with information. They prefer a "hands-on" approach.

21

# Managing Business-to-Business Marketing and Communication Projects Successfully

**By Julian Stubbs**

*Julian Stubbs has worked in advertising and marketing his whole career, on both the consultancy side and the client side. Today he is the CEO of DOWELL//STUBBS, a specialist Brand Communications company based in Stockholm, Sweden.*

## INTRODUCTION

This chapter focuses on how to manage business-to-business marketing and communications projects successfully from a client's perspective. It is written for people who are new to the area and need a little help understanding what marketing-campaign planning is all about. Typical projects covered under this would be the creation of campaigns involving areas such as advertising, literature, direct mail, public relations, graphic design, etc.

Often you will be working with third-party suppliers such as advertising agencies, public-relations consultants, or designers. The chapter will also give you some insight into what they will expect from you as a client.

The chapter does not go into the actual mechanics of setting up a project flow-chart, as this is well covered in the other sections of this book. It focuses much more on the major topics and phases that you will encounter while running such projects.

We have developed over a number of years a well-proven marketing-management tool called The BASE-UP™ approach,[1] designed to help set out the main tasks of any marketing project, and to help you move through the various phases of such a project.

> **BASE-UP:** A structured approach to handling marketing and communications projects.

The composition and handling of the project team is obviously a vital consideration of any project and some thoughts about this appear later in this chapter.

## THE BASE-UP SYSTEM

At DOWELL//STUBBS we have developed a five-step program to help us manage a client's project successfully. This program, called BASE-UP, stands for **B**rief, **A**udit, **S**trategy, **E**xecution and follow-**UP**. This very much fits the Lewis model presented in Chapter 2.

---

[1.] BASE-UP is a trademark of Dowell//Stubbs.

We will describe in detail each of these steps and how we should approach each task we need to consider within those steps.

A number of years ago, while working with a large London-based advertising agency, I noticed how unstructured the majority of marketing-communication projects were on both the client side and the agency. Disorganization seemed to breed disorganization. It wasn't that things didn't get done—they did. And they were highly creative. But the waste, subsequent cost, and chaos caused en route were immense, to say nothing of the stress levels inherent in this business anyway.

I promised myself from that moment that should I ever be in a position to work in a more organized way, I would.

A number of years later I moved to Sweden, where structure and orderliness are inbred as a matter of course to most Swedes. It is the ultimate "planned" society. In fact, the entire society is managed as one large project. Amazingly, most people generally stick to the goals and rules of the project!

In working with a number of large Swedish clients, I realized quickly that I still needed to be capable of delivering creative excellence, but in a structured way.

The result of this was the BASE-UP program, a structured approach to managing creative marketing communications effectively, in a well-managed fashion. A general diagram for BASE-UP appears in Figure 21.1.

## STEP ONE: THE BRIEF

The starting point for managing any marketing-communications project successfully has to be the brief. This is the method of detailing all of the relevant information regarding the marketing task you are undertaking. If working for an outside vendor, the brief will give them the right information they need to create the right results for you. The

**F I G U R E  21.1**

The Base-Up System

**B**

> **STEP ONE – BRIEF** The correct parameters are defined with the client to help build the brief. This important document will be the benchmark against which all elements of the work will be judged.

**A**

> **STEP TWO – AUDIT** At this stage, existing research is studied or new research, internal or external as required, is carried out. Dowell//Stubbs gets intimately involved in the research and analysis phase to provide the right context for the brief to be truly evaluated.

**S**

> **STEP THREE – STRATEGY** Based on the brief and using the research as a foundation, Dowell//Stubbs will give a playback strategy brief to the client detailing the strategy to be undertaken, its execution plan, and timing.

**E**
**.**
**.**
**.**
**.**

> **STEP FOUR – EXECUTION** Dowell//Stubbs will then work alongside existing advertising or PR agencies if required, or can work with another partner company in the Matrix network. Dowell//Stubbs stays with the project at this vital stage ensuring that the strategic goals are being met in the actual execution of the work. An important point to note here is that we specialize in working with clients' overseas partners or subsidiary companies, ensuring they are fully part of the implementation, planning, and execution process.

**U**
**P**

> **STEP FIVE – FOLLOW-UP** The project is not finished until a full follow-up and evaluation is performed. This is all documented and presented back to the client for final sign-off and discussion of any subsequent actions that are needed.

brief is without doubt the single most important step in any marketing and communications project. Simply put, if the brief is correct, the work and creative approach will also be correct 9 times out of 10. (Note that the brief is equivalent to step 2 of the Lewis model presented in Chapter 2, and as that chapter pointed out, this is where projects often fail.)

Too often, however, the brief is poorly managed with too little time spent on it and, in the enthusiasm to get to the "fun bit" (working on the creative execution), the brief is ill defined.

Agencies and outside vendors can sometimes be guilty themselves of letting a junior person handle the briefing stage and then hoping "the creatives" will produce stunning ideas to put right a flimsy brief.

Even worse, in some instances, the clients do not really have a clear idea of the goal or objective of what they need to produce, so they wait until the creative work is presented as visuals or scamps[2] before deciding what they really want to say with their communication! "The client loved the advertisements but thinks they are wrong" is a comment heard too often in any agency and does not count as any type of success. This is not only a little frustrating for the poor creative, but very wasteful of time and money.

In the next section, I will present a typical example of an advertising brief form used by an agency, which you could use to produce most marketing-communications material. It shows the main headings and by working through it you will start to understand the main function of the brief. It will show you what the agency or consultant wants from you to produce the right creative solution.

---

[2.] "Scamp" is the name given to outline visual ideas presented by an agency or consultant.

## Function of the Brief

The main function of the brief is to give direction to the work and most important, to answer the question, what do we want to achieve? The brief is the opportunity for you to write down all the relevant facts as you see them. Any existing research data should be handed over at the same time to help support the brief. It could well be that additional research is needed and will be carried out to help substantiate the whole campaign (see Step Two: Audit). The sample brief below is based on one used by one of Europe's leading business-to-business advertising and communications companies, MMC International, based in London and Stockholm. All work in agencies would normally begin with such a brief. Although the format can vary a little, most good briefs cover the same ground.

## The Typical Briefing Form, Explained

### 1. Background Information

The first step is to give all relevant background information that you can that will give insight to the agency or consultant. It's a good idea to give a general overview of information you might cover later in more detail in the brief as a synopsis. This should be the main goal of the campaign and could go on to cover such items as product information, pricing details, other linked promotional activities, salesforce information, etc.; whatever is relevant and will help everyone understand the campaign or marketing project goals.

If the brief relates to a specific product, describe how the product will be used, describe the alternative, and detail the specific benefits the user will derive.

### 2. Market Information

Describe the conditions of the marketplace in which you are or will be competing. Is it growing, declining, or segmenting?

Maybe give some of the history of the market and describe the major forces within it. Which are the main market drivers: technology, price, or delivery systems? Try to be as specific and straightforward as you can. It also helps to express things "as simply" as possible so people outside of your business area can understand the information.

### 3. Competitor Information

What is the competition up to? What products do they have that compete in this sector? How are their products positioned against yours? Be as realistic here as you can be. Be honest about the reasons why customers buy the competitors' products. They must be doing something right, and understanding them will help you create an approach that will hopefully work successfully for you against them.

### 4. Target Audience

Who are we trying to reach with our campaign? Is it just the user of the product? Is it more than one group? Are senior management as well as purchasing agents important in the decision as well? Describe them as best you can and give a real profile of the people you will be targeting with the campaign.

### 5. Campaign Goal

Put simply, what result do you want from your target audience? Do you want them to pick up the phone and call you? Are you expecting them to buy a product or service off the page? Do you want to alter their opinions about your product or service and make them start to see it in a different way? Do you want them to see your company as a younger company and more dynamic than they had thought before seeing this particular promotion? Be specific. And remember, goals involving the changing of attitudes and opinions will normally take a good while to achieve, so don't expect miracles from one advertisement. The cumulative effect over a period of time will produce the desired result.

## 6. Essential Message

Now we come to the heart of the brief. The essential message is the single most important part of the briefing process for the creative people working on the marketing-communications project. Keep the essential message very realistic and don't waffle. The shorter the better. One way to view the essential message is to pretend you had a customer in front of you and you had to tell him, in just 15 words, the one thing about your product/service/company that would make the difference between him buying your product or a competitor's.

## 7. Support to the Essential Message

If the essential message is the most important part of a brief, then the support is probably the second most important part. This provides the hard evidence and proof that your claim in the essential message is fact and not fiction. If you have market research data, customer studies, and independent assessments, these can all help support the claim made in the essential message.

It's unfortunate that too often clients make claims about their products that are not justified. The biggest problem with this is that it is just kidding yourself and will probably not produce the most effective promotion.

As an example, if the competitor really has the quickest gizmo on the market, don't just make a claim that your gizmo is as quick as his. The customers will know the truth if this is not a substantiated claim. Look instead to reposition the competitor by perhaps showing (if it is supportable with facts) that your product is much easier to use, and that this gives a much higher overall speed of use over $x$ number of operations.

The message is: *don't try to copy but look to reposition.*

## 8. Mandatory Details

This section should include all details and mandatory items. Instruction regarding use of trade names, corporate identity comments, typeface specifications, length of body copy, pictures or graphics to be used, etc.

## 9. Timing

Finally, when does all this have to happen? What happens when? In the case of advertisements, deadlines are normally very fixed as you will have booked media space and they will be waiting for your copy. Otherwise you will be paying for a large piece of white space with nothing in it! In the case of an overall campaign brief, when do we want the various elements in the campaign to appear?

Again, be realistic with the timing. These things can be done extremely quickly under abnormal time constraints, but this is no way to organize things on a regular basis. It will cost you more in stress and mistakes and much more in vendor costs as everything will be on a rush charge.

## STEP TWO: THE AUDIT

The audit stage presents the chance to validate a lot of information contained within the brief. If the supporting information or analysis is in the brief itself, all the better. This is not always the case, however. A common pitfall of many briefs is that the client will claim their own product is faster/more economic/more recognized/more advanced than their competitors. They will also tell you, with authority, that their customers love them and are quite happy paying more for their products!

The audit stage is there to provide the proof and evidence that the brief stage might still need. Many a brief has been amended in light of some research facts that the client omitted from the original briefing.

And finally, the audit stage can provide excellent benchmarks against which you can judge the future success of any marketing campaign.

## Secondary or Primary Research and Data?

Information that is already available to you is called "secondary research data" and is based on accessing and digesting research that has already been carried out. Primary research is carried out in a new study, often specifically for adding new information that will help you better understand a client's situation.

### Secondary Research—Internal Sources

Usually vital information can be found quite simply by accessing a company's existing records. The company's operating records can often throw a huge amount of light on a marketing situation. Records may show customer groups and segments, geographic sales, advertising costs and returns, distribution costs, customer complaints, sales reports, etc.

And normally within the company there will be an archive of commissioned or purchased external research reports that can be accessed for additional reference.

### Secondary Research—External Sources

We now turn to the potentially enormous area of "accessing" secondary research via external sources.

Often there will be a large amount of "officially" published government statistics available on many markets. To this you can add the large amount of information published by banks, stockbrokers, trade and professional associations, media organizations, etc.

Finally, secondary data can be purchased through any of the many research companies that exist, often with distinct specialist areas.

## Primary Research

Conducting primary or original research can involve many different areas of focus.

In the consumer area, highly professional and targeted research is often critical in helping determine the correct approach for a marketing or advertising campaign. Sophisticated techniques, developed over many years, have been well proven and the analysis can provide valuable information.

In the business-to-business or industrial market, research is used far less and there are additional complications of which you should be aware. Who makes the purchase decision, for example? In industrial marketing, a number of different individuals can influence the purchase decision, and all these views should be taken into consideration at the audit stage.

In general, research can be divided between *qualitative* and *quantitative.*

Qualitative research provides an in-depth view on a subject, often via focus groups, personal interviews and one-on-one phone interviews. This form of interviewing can be costly.

What we are seeking here is quality, in-depth information on the research subject. This is without doubt one of the most demanding areas of research to conduct, as it contains so many variable factors. The form of questioning, the moderator's ability, and the analysis of the research are all important considerations that can dramatically influence the result.

In industrial markets, it is naïve to ask questions such as "Are you influenced by advertising?" or "Do you read direct mail?" Having sat through many hundreds of hours of research, I can tell you the answers already. Most people claim never to have been influenced by advertising, and they have never read a piece of direct mail! Unfortunately, this is not the truth. The art of conducting good qualitative research requires eliciting the information you need without asking for it directly.

A final point on qualitative research: too many industrial marketing managers assume that the answer to all of their marketing problems is to conduct research and ask their customers what they want. What would you like to see in an advertisement? What color should our product be? When would you like us to send you direct mail?

This approach is not only supremely naïve, it is also a total delegation of the responsibility of any manager. If the customer knows the answer better than you do, he would be doing your job!

If qualitative research gives us an in-depth view, then quantitative research gives us some numbers and scale.

Quantitative research is really focused on producing reliable statistics to support a proposition. The sample size should be sufficiently large enough to allow us to draw conclusions about how many and what sort of customers behave and think about products and services in a given way.

Typical techniques employed in the quantitative research area would include mass teleresearch, mail questionnaires, increasingly Internet-based research and short, one-on-one questionnaire surveys conducted with a *statistically significant and representative* sample size.

Finally, when the two are employed together they can be very insightful. First conduct qualitative research to reveal in-depth views and attitudes, then use quantitative research to add some scale and support.

## STEP THREE: STRATEGY

The brief has been taken and examined. The audit has hopefully brought further relevant facts to the brief to inform our thinking and add substance and benchmarking possibilities.

> Never let strategy get in the way of tactics.

We then move to the strategy stage, where all the thinking and evaluation come together in a plan of action to meet our goals.

### Making the Strategy Work

We believe at DOWELL//STUBBS that devising strategies that actually work is very much a mix of art and science. Many analogies have been made between business strategies and military strategies, which have some validity. Two principle reasons make the analogy worthy.

First, far too many strategies are set in stone and are not adjusted for any reason. The managers insist the strategy must be carried out as planned! This approach will result in missing the many very real possibilities and opportunities that usually present themselves en route to achieving most strategic goals.

And at the end of the day, achieving the goal *is* the objective, not just playing out the strategy for its own sake.

In the military analogy, if two opposing armies were to meet on the field of battle, you would expect both opposing generals to have strategic plans ready for the battle. What happens, however, when the day of battle arrives and predicted good weather turns into a downpour, turning a solid field into a quagmire? The winning general will be the one who can amend his strategy to take account of very real tactical considerations and conditions. Business strategies are exactly like this. Things happen that are not always foreseen. A competitor brings out a new product line. Another competitor radically lowers his price. On the positive side, maybe a competitor pulls out of a market segment you had both been fighting over. The lesson is: never let the strategy get in the way of tactics.

The second reason military and business strategies are similar is that they must be dosed with a good measure of reality-based thinking. They must take into account the reality of the organization through which the planned strategy must be executed.

The general in his bunker, putting forward grand plans and sophisticated ideas and strategies, will not succeed if his troops are not in tune with his thinking and if they are not capable of carrying out the plan of action. Specifically, his immediate commanders must be the champions of the plan and make that plan a reality. They must also be the ones to inject a good dose of realism into any strategy.

Like any big organization, an army can fall prey to what we call "the inertia effect" of large organizations, which can badly slow down or possibly derail plans.

A marketing and communications plan can fail at this vital step.

So the simple messages are:

◆ Keep the strategy flexible; and

◆ Take a big reality check and find champions.

## Project Planning and the Strategy Stage

So, how do we apply this knowledge to the process of managing a project at the vital strategic stage? We should keep in mind some immediate rules:

1. Let everyone in the project group know at the outset that the objective is to achieve the project goal, not just to rigidly carry out the strategy.

2. Should the strategy have to change due to tactical considerations and opportunities, make sure as soon as possible everyone in the project group is aware of the change and why.

3. This change is bound to affect critical original objectives and criteria such as timing, costs, and execution steps. Make sure all of these are amended and all affected parties are aware of the implications to the project.

4. The project team itself, on any marketing and communications based project, is often the critical factor in solving any organizational problems you might face. The project team must become the immediate project champions. Otherwise the inertia effect sets in. Should you be aware of certain parts of an organization that will be most affected by a project or is against a specific project, the wise approach is to make the most critical individuals project members themselves. Even if you cannot always win them over to the project completely, having them on the inside is probably safer than having them on the outside.

## STEP FOUR: EXECUTION

One simple rule applies to the execution phase. The devil is in the detail. Staying on top of that detail is *everything* in a marketing project. I have seen wonderful concepts and ideas turn into very average campaigns through lack of attention to detail.

As we said in the strategy stage, one must also never lose sight of tactical considerations and opportunities when executing a marketing project.

> The devil is in the detail.

Such opportunities will occur and can often add enormous value when fully taken.

## The Marketing Project Team

Making sure the project team is set up correctly at the beginning of the project is always a vital consideration. There are some points worth noting with project teams:

1. One person alone should be appointed as *project sponsor*. This is the person who, at the end of the day, should take responsibility for the success or failure of the project. This person, when called upon to make big decisions, should be capable of doing so. The role of adjudicator also falls to the project sponsor.

2. there should then be a separate *Project Manager* to take care of the hands-on management of the project. This person is responsible for running the project, meeting time schedules and budgets, and keeping all group members fully informed as to what is happening as the project progresses.

3. *Project group members.* I have always believed that having good representation from all interested parties in the project group is vital to any marketing project. Not only does it give a wider spread of experience to the project, but having all parties adequately represented, even those who might not

fundamentally agree with the overall marketing project goals, is better than excluding them from the
project altogether. By working with them in the project you might well be able to win them over. And
at worst, at least they cannot say they did not know
what was going on!

4. *Consultants.* There will often be the need to employ
consultants in a marketing project; indeed, for a typical campaign you might end up using several different consultants. Coordination is the key here and this
should fall to the project manager to perform. All
consultants should, when any action is performed or
meeting attended, typically confirm what happened
in the form of a written contact report (see below).

5. Contact reports are vital. At Dowell//Stubbs we
send a contact report after every main contact with
the client confirming what was said or what happened. The contact report is a simple means of confirming actions and understanding. All marketing
projects should employ them.

Following are some helpful hints to remember during
the execution stage of a marketing project.

## Visuals or Roughs

Often in a marketing project you will be working with consultants or agencies that will need to present visual ideas to
you at an early stage. These are most often called "visuals"
but can also be known as "roughs" or sometimes "scamps."

The visual is an artistic interpretation of what the final
piece will look like. Often the text, called copy, has been filled
in with dummy text to represent where the copy will be
placed and how much copy there will be.

Remember the visual is just that. Don't be intimated by
the consultants' or agency's presentation of this work of art!

It is, after all, just a working document that will need enhancements and changes, but it should (provided the brief has been well written) provide you with a good starting point as to what the finished piece will end up looking like.

## Photography

You might well need to commission photography in your marketing project. A very simple rule applies here: hire the best photographer you can afford. A picture does speak a thousand words. Whenever I have saved a bit of money by hiring a cheaper photographer I have always regretted it.

> Hire the best photographer you can afford.

Get the best you can afford.

## Signing Off

As a project progresses, text or copy will have to be approved, visuals amended, and graphics worked on. The client tries to make the consultants' job easier by coordinating the sign-off process. If you are the project manager on a marketing project, have the consultant send you the piece of work needing approval only. Make your own comments and changes, then pass it around to other involved members of the project team for their approval or amendments and comments. This way the consultant or agency is dealing with just one set of changes or comments and the process will work a lot more smoothly, to say nothing of being cheaper!

## Strong Creative Work

Rarely, if ever, have I seen a good promotional campaign that everybody in a company agrees with or endorses. We all have different opinions about style, approach, writing style, etc. So remember you cannot please everyone and you are bound to ruffle a few feathers if the creative work on a campaign is strong and stands out. If you are using an agency or consultancy to produce the work, remember you are not paying them to produce wallpaper. The first rule of a promotional piece is that it has to stand out from the crowd (the second rule is that it must be a relevant proposition to what is unique about your product).

So, be brave and don't water down great creative work.

## STEP FIVE: FOLLOW-UP

Of all of the neglected areas in marketing, I would rate the follow-up area as the most important step that almost everybody forgets. This step is called "lessons learned" in the Lewis model. So much can be learned at this stage and applied to future planning, campaigns, and promotions. The dreaded topic of failures is also one people in marketing are sensitive about. There is a value even in failures though, of learning *what went wrong* and being able to apply that knowledge to future campaign plans.

But many people fail to take this final step.

## Marketing Project Scorecard

At DOWELL//STUBBS we like to conduct a formal project sign-off where we can go through with the client a marketing project scorecard of how successful a particular project has been. This is simply a way of reviewing and recording the facts of the project.

You can use a generic project scorecard, such as the one shown in Figure 21.2, as a basic guide. You could certainly make a more specific scorecard for your own project.

## F I G U R E  21.2

### Marketing Project Scorecard

Where asked to, weight your answer, 1 through 5; 5 denotes that the project met expectations completely and 1 denotes the result was far from expectations. Circle the number that best reflects the outcome.

1.    How closely did the project meet the original objectives?

1    2    3    4    5

Please give some commentary.

_____

_____

_____

_____

2.    If the project objectives were changed en route, how closely did the project meet the new objectives?

1    2    3    4    5

Please give some commentary.

_____

_____

_____

_____

3.    Did the project meet the original time plan objectives?

1    2    3    4    5

Please give some commentary.

_____

_____

_____

_____

## Marketing Project Scorecard

4.  Were the budgetary and financial costs of the project met?

    1   2   3   4   5

    Please give some commentary.

    _____

    _____

    _____

    _____

5.  Were the budgetary and financial sales/income objectives of the project met?

    1   2   3   4   5

    Please give some commentary.

    _____

    _____

    _____

    _____

6.  If the project goals were not short-term sales or financially driven, were these other objectives measurably met?

    1   2   3   4   5

    Please give some commentary.

    _____

    _____

    _____

    _____

*Continued*

**F I G U R E  21.2 (Concluded)**

Marketing Project Scorecard

7.    Give a review of how well the project team worked.

_____

_____

_____

_____

_____

8.    What worked best about this project?

_____

_____

_____

_____

9.    What did not work well in the project and what would you change
      next time?

_____

_____

_____

_____

10.   Finally, any thoughts about what we could do better next time?

_____

_____

_____

_____

Public relations consultancy Makovsky & Company in New York, have really set standards in the whole area of client quality control and follow-up programs. *Inc.* magazine and the *PR Strategist* both ran stories on their approach. Similar to the marketing project scorecard above, Makovsky clients get to complete an assessment form rating how well the consultancy is doing on projects. Their assessment goes pretty deep, even probing details of examining the consultancy's sensitivity to their client company's culture.

Too few PR companies or advertising agencies take enough time on the follow-up aspect, in my opinion.

Finally, and this is probably the most difficult thing of all, how do you make your marketing campaign convince, persuade, or influence the mind-set of those with whom you are communicating?

Remember this: telling people something is not the same as them understanding it. Advertisements that shout at the reader "We are the best" will probably only elicit the response, "Well, they would say that, wouldn't they."

> Don't shout. But whisper loudly.

The secret is that well-executed campaigns have the reader do some thinking. Once they themselves understand a clever proposition they can judge for themselves whether to believe you or not.

So don't shout. But whisper loudly.

# 22

## CHAPTER

# Project Management in a Creative Environment

### By Heather Maxwell Chandler

*Heather Maxwell Chandler is a multimedia producer with more than 10 years of entertainment-software-industry experience. Her company, Media Sunshine Inc., provides consulting services for game developers. She is also the author of* The Game Localization Handbook, The Game Production Handbook, *and numerous articles on game development. Heather graduated with honors from Vanderbilt University and earned an M.A. from the USC School of Cinema-Television. For more information, please visit www.mediasunshine.com.*

## INTRODUCTION

Imagine being a project manager who can't even complete the "definition phase" in the Lewis Method<sup>SM</sup> of Project Management. This makes it difficult to complete the other steps as well, which ultimately means you will be working on a project without a plan, and if you have no plan you have no control.

However, as an experienced producer of entertainment software, I am accustomed to managing chaotic projects with ill-defined concepts, shifting schedules, increasing scope, and variable resources. On top of this, the development team is filled with creative people—artists, designers, and engineers—who are reluctant to concretely define anything about the project, for fear of stifling any creative energy or losing the ability to change major project features at the last minute.

It goes without saying that chaotic projects like this are difficult, but not impossible, to manage. If you are persistent, you can establish control over the project, while still giving creative leeway to the team members. The key is to be flexible, both in managing the project and the people. This chapter presents some issues to be aware of when working on a chaotic project with a creative group of people.

## WORKING WITH CREATIVE PEOPLE

First, I'd like to share some insights about working with creative people, based on my experiences working with game developers. But these insights are likely valid for creative people on other types of teams. However, it is worth noting that the average member of a game-development team is young (under 30), has limited professional work experience (they are either self-taught or right out of college), and is highly creative and passionate (playing games is both a hobby and a career). These factors may influence some of these insights more heavily than others, but overall, creative attitudes are a part of any project team.

### Creative teams contain both artistic and technical types.

All creative teams contain artistic and technical types, but both types must be considered as creative contributors. The artistic ones traditionally come up with the creative ideas and the technical types normally determine the best way to im-

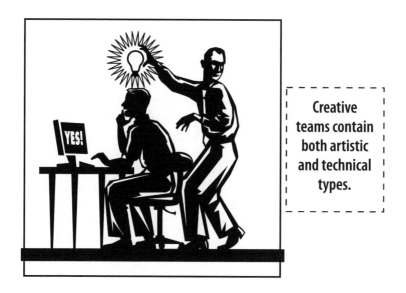

Creative teams contain both artistic and technical types.

plement these ideas. For example, if an artist wants to show a character aging throughout the game, an engineer must consider the technical ramifications and determine if the idea can be implemented. This requires the engineer to figure out different solutions, many of which involve making creative decisions about how this feature can viably work in the game. Conversely, an engineer may come up with creative suggestions for the story or characters, and it is up to the designer to consider these ideas when making design decisions. Therefore, don't assume that because someone is a "techie" that they don't have a desire to make creative contributions or that they completely lack creative talent. Everyone's creativity must be considered to have a strong team that works well with each other.

### Creative people prefer unimpeded creative control.

Creative people are averse to committing to deadlines and requirements, for fear of losing creative control or limiting their creative ideas to a predefined set of parameters. In their minds, these situations impede their creativity and they cannot do their best work. For example, a game designer wants to include as many features in the game as possible, and will be hardpressed to let you know which features are the most important ones. In his mind, all of the features are important and eliminating any directly impacts his creative vision of the game. The same goes for artists and engineers as well—each person has a unique creative vision he wants to include in the game, and this vision will not be realized if they have to limit their creativity in order to remain within the boundaries set by the schedule and scope of the project.

They are reluctant to acknowledge they are working on a project that must have one centralized vision, which means not every single idea fits within this vision, and that the project must be finished and released by a specific deadline in order to be profitable. These are inherent limitations to any consumer product and the creative team needs to recognize and understand the purpose of these constraints, and realize that this doesn't mean their creativity is impeded. In fact, limitations often bring out the best creative work, as people must be creative in overcoming them.

### Creative people thrive on chaos (or think they do).

Creative people claim they do their best work when things are in chaos—when deadlines are looming, the technology is not working, and resources are dwindling—because it fuels their creative energy and inspires them to come up with ingenious solutions for all the problems. This is just not the case. In my experience, the reason people think they enjoy chaos is because it absolves them of any concrete responsibilities. If a chaotic project is late, low quality, or overbudget there are numerous excuses people can give as to how this wasn't their fault—"You didn't listen to my ideas," "I told you the technology wouldn't work that way," "You didn't start testing soon enough," "Your schedule was completely unrealistic," etc. Notice that the person blamed in all these excuses, is you, the project manager.

Another reason people are used to chaos as a "preferred" working environment is because they don't feel the pressure to plan their tasks and work at an even pace throughout the project. Instead, they put things off until the last possible minute, and then think they can work overtime to get all the work completed that was supposed to be done over the course of six months. Unfortunately, if working on a poorly managed project in which everyone does this, things will go downhill fast. As a result, the team as a whole will put in many hours of overtime at the end of the project to make up for the work that didn't get done at the beginning, which usually means the quality of work is lower and scope must reduced, because there is not enough time to finish everything that was originally planned.

Creative people also have a tendency to think that chaos equals creative freedom. If nothing on the project is set in stone and things are constantly changing, there is always the chance for them to squeeze in one more feature or completely redesign something during the last few months on the project. What they don't realize or refuse to accept is that organization actually gives them more freedom. If the project is well managed, the scope is defined, and resources are allocated correctly, everyone will spend their time being productive instead of wasting time putting out fires. For example, game artists and designers will have more freedom and time to tweak and polish their work after it is in the game, and possibly make changes. This also enables the team to assess the currently status of the project accurately and make an educated determination of whether a new feature can be added or redesigned. This process also keeps everyone on the team informed of what's going on with the project, instead of having several individuals add features that no one even knows are there.

## Creative people are very passionate about their work.

Creative people are motivated more by passion for the work than for the money they make doing it. In many cases, creative people (especially in the game industry) work for less pay than they would receive working in a more professional environment. They believe strongly in the work they are doing and often take their work home with them, or are constantly thinking about work, even while eating dinner. In the game industry especially, people will work on games all day and then go home and play games in the evening to relax and check out the competition.

## Creative people are suspicious of "suits."

In general, creative people don't trust management types who have authority to make changes on the project, especially creative ones. Creative people assume that management is not knowledgeable enough of the ins and outs of the project to make effective creative decisions. In addition, there is little respect for management's creative abilities. Certainly, managers have been known to come in and make ridiculous requests: "Hey, this would be a more mature and scary horror game if all monsters looked like cuddly stuffed animals." But this does not mean their requests shouldn't be seriously considered; after all, they usually control the purse strings on the project.

Additionally, creative people fear that management will come in and ruin a great idea, turn it into something completely different, or dictate the vision of the project and expect the team to fulfill it. This does sometimes happen, but can be minimized if the team is open to listening to management and finding ways either to implement management feedback, demonstrate why the particular mandate will not work, or provide an alternate solution. It is important to remind people that management and the team both want to complete a successful product that makes money.

## Creative people are NOT difficult to work with.

Because of their passion, creative people have a tendency to take criticism and feedback personally, even if they are open to receiving it. While many creative stereotypes, such as movie directors, are portrayed as being difficult to work with, mainly because they see feedback as a personal attack, in reality this is not always the case. Many creative people are open to hearing critiques of their ideas and will seriously consider any feedback, even though they still have a high personal stake in their proposed ideas.

This is not to say that there aren't creative people who are difficult to work with; I've certainly encountered a few in my career. In cases when someone completely shuts down or lashes out at criticism of his or her ideas, there are usually extenuating factors that cause this undesired behavior. For instance, the person may be feeling quite overwhelmed by his creative responsibilities on the project and is afraid to admit this, for fear of being replaced. In other cases, the person may not have a highly developed ability to separate his personal feelings from his professional responsibilities, and therefore does not understand how to respond to criticism. Of course, it is entirely possible the person is a jerk who enjoys making people feel uncomfortable when they question his decisions. Whatever the reason, the project manager must find out the best way to manage this person and get him to respond professionally to feedback.

## MANAGING CREATIVE PEOPLE

As discussed above, creative people don't have to be difficult to work with. If you can figure out ways to manage them effectively, they are a lot of fun to work with and the project is an enjoyable experience for everyone involved. Anyone who has spent a lot of time managing creative people has invented some unique techniques to manage them effectively,

> The most important thing for you to do as a project manager is to *listen.*

mainly because each individual requires a different type of management style. However, you should be aware of some commonalities that will help you get the most out of a creative team.

### Listen to and consider everyone's ideas.

The most important thing for you to do as a project manager is to *listen* to everyone's ideas. When working on a creative project, everyone from the low man on the totem pole to senior management will have feedback, suggestions, and ideas for the project. Don't discount any of these. The quickest way to have a disgruntled group of employees is to disregard their thoughts and feelings. People will have suggestions about how the art looks, what the characters say, and what technologies to use, and the decision makers must seriously consider all of this feedback. If possible, set up a central location, either on a team Web site or in the project notebook, to track and respond to all the feedback.

Additionally, be sensitive to everyone's ideas. If someone tells you an idea for a new game play feature that you find completely ridiculous and undoable, don't cut her off before she finishes telling you about it, and don't just absent-mindedly dismiss it. Track it with all the feedback you receive—you may find that some aspect of this idea can be used elsewhere or even on a future project. Also, if someone has a negative experience while presenting their idea, they will become unhappy and possibly become a source of negativity that infects the entire project team. If this happens, you will have a huge morale problem on your hands.

Most people understand that not every idea can be included, but they at least like to know their ideas were considered. Be sure to inform people why their ideas cannot be used. Be specific about the reasons, such as: it did not fit with the overall vision of the project, it will cost to much to implement, or we don't have time to add or make changes. Never tell someone the reason is because people didn't like the idea, as this gives them no concrete feedback on why the suggestion is not useable. In cases like this, the person may continue to make suggestions that never get used since he has no understanding of what types of ideas are useful and doable on the project.

## Don't give yourself all the creative decision-making power.

A big complaint I've heard from creative teams is that management—the "suits"—really have all the decision-making power and just dictate the creative mandates to the team. This doesn't encourage a healthy working environment and causes people to feel like they are just cogs in the wheel and that they have no direct influence over their own work. As stated earlier, creative people are very passionate about their work and are motivated by the thought that their ideas can make a difference; if this motivation is removed, they may just as well be working some mindless corporate job in a cube farm.

Therefore, establishing how creative decisions are handled on the team is extremely important. As the project manager, it is fine for you to have creative input, but do not put yourself in the position of making all the final creative decisions on a project. There are a couple reasons for this. First, you were probably appointed to head up a given project based on your project-management expertise, not your creative skills. This is not to say you can't have creative input, but don't consider it more valid then anyone else's input, especially the input of the creative experts on the team, such as an art director. This is the quickest way to alienate the team and turn them into disgruntled employees with low morale.

Second, the team feels more secure and is more productive if its members know everyone is fulfilling his or her assigned role on the project. This means the project manager is managing the team, schedule, and resources; and the art director, creative director, and so on are focusing on making the best the creative decisions for the team and project. Of course, this doesn't prevent the "suits" from dictating creative decisions, but it does maintain what little creative freedom is still available at the team level.

## Tailor your management style to the individual.

The most effective way to manage people, especially creative ones, is to tailor your management style to each individual. Everyone has a preferred way of working, and if you can cater to these preferences you will get the most out of your team. For example, some people prefer to receive a task, go off to do the work, and then come back when it is finished. Other people may have a lot of questions and need more guidance on a given task. Still others cannot yet be trusted to work on their own and need to have an assigned mentor who can check with them on a daily basis. Whatever management style is effective is the one to use.

Don't be concerned about not treating everyone equally on the project, as this is not a question of equal treatment, especially in a creative environment. There are certainly common policies that everyone is expected to obey—wear shoes in the office, put in eight hours a day, be respectful to your peers—but this does not mean that everyone must sit down on a daily basis and review their work with a manager, or that everyone is expected to be completely autonomous in their work.

Keep in mind that some creative people who are perceived as difficult are usually just poorly managed. For instance, a demanding art director who doesn't listen to anyone's ideas or just can't be pleased may actually be very frustrated about the lack of control on the project. His manager may not be checking with him on a regular basis, so to feel like things are under control, the art director acts out against his colleagues. Other difficult people may not even be aware that people find them unpleasant to work with, because their manager never told them. People can't be expected to change their behavior if they don't even know there is a problem with how they are acting.

### Educate people on how project management can help them.

Because creative people are suspicious of "suits," it is natural for them to be suspicious of any policies or procedures the "suits" want to impose on them. The more paperwork there is to fill out before a decision can be approved, the less creative people are going to be—they don't want to deal with the hassle of going through the red tape to make an improvement or suggestion for a new feature. However, this does not mean that they won't respond positively to project-management practices that will improve their workflow. It does mean they will initially be suspicious of anything the project manager says will help them be more productive.

In my experience, team members who are reluctant to impose any order or control on a project normally have little understanding of project management and how it can help them. They assume it is just more paperwork to make their lives difficult. They've also had negative experiences in the past with out-of-control schedules and increasing scope that caused the last few months of the project to be a blur of 80-hour work weeks, and it seems impossible that situations like this can be managed better. I've found that taking time at the beginning of the project to explain briefly basic principles of project management gets the team excited about the possibilities of spending less time working and enthusiastic about trying something that will help them do this.

Remember that most people resist change, especially if they don't understand why the change is being made. Change needs to be introduced gradually so that people feel comfortable and have a chance to get used to new things. You can't expect to implement fully the Lewis Method of Project Management all at once. This is likely to upset your team and decrease its productivity.

## MANAGING CREATIVE PROJECTS

When implementing basic project-management techniques on a creative team, make sure people are open to new ways of doing things. Get them actively involved, as they will have a bigger stake in making the changes work. Create an open environment that is conducive for people to discuss why they work the way they do and how their working conditions can be improved. For example, a programmer may prefer to work late into the night because he is constantly peppered with questions during the day and is most productive after everyone has gone home. In reality, his workload is probably normal, but he can't use his time wisely during the day because others are constantly interrupting him. Once the reason for his overtime is defined, discuss with the team alternative ways for people to receive technical information. It is likely they will come up with some new processes that will improve the workflow of the programmer in question and also others on the team.

It is ideal to educate the team on new project-management practices before beginning any work. However, it is rare, particularly in my line of work, for the same project manager to be in charge of a team from beginning to end. In game development, the projects don't start with a project manager; instead, the creative team is put in place to determine ideas and concepts. By the time a project manager comes into the picture, several bad project-management habits are already established—no schedule, no plan, and no defined scope, just a lot of great ideas and enthusiasm for the game. Therefore, you will likely find yourself in the position of imposing organization on something that already has a life of its own, and it is difficult to introduce new ways of doing things in these situations. There are a few basic techniques that can help in situations like this, and I've used them successfully with several game-development teams.

## Use weekly meetings as a forum for change.

Weekly team meetings are a great way to introduce project-management changes, especially when the project is already in full swing and starting to get out of control. First, the team meetings are an established forum for distributing information and answering questions about the project. Second, everyone is in the same room at once, making it easy to discuss new ideas and receive feedback. Third, this guarantees that at least once a week, everyone is thinking about the project as a whole and the impact their work has on other people.

Be sure to establish an agenda for each team meeting and decide in advance which project-management change you will discuss. A great first topic is norms and guidelines, especially as these pertain to meetings. If people understand the guidelines for the behavior that is expected in team meetings, they can make better contributions to the discussions.

Norms are a great way for people to throw out their ideas about how things are handled in a given situation. For example, at one team meeting members discussed a miscommunication between art and engineering. From this discussion, the team decided to establish communication norms for the team as a whole. They really enjoyed contributing their thoughts on how to improve communication, and this was a great way for me to see where the worst communication problems were. Even the lighthearted suggestions, such as "Don't be a low talker," were treated seriously, as this is often a problem with shyer members of the team.

### Focus on basic project-management techniques that have the biggest impact on the project.

As stated earlier, it is unlikely you can revamp the entire project-management process overnight, so you have to be selective about which aspects will help the team the most. One thing I change immediately on any new project is the way meetings are run. Everyone has spent time in seemingly pointless meetings where nothing is accomplished. This certainly is a huge problem in a creative environment—you have a lot of creative people bursting with ideas, who have a lot of experience initiating concepts, but have little experience with choosing a single concept and implementing it in a timely fashion. Meetings are microcosms of this. Everyone sits around the table discussing where there are problems, but they don't have any idea or inclination to determine a course of action for fixing these issues. Changing the way meetings are run usually fixes this, and people are very surprised at how useful meetings suddenly become. As discussed in Chapter 11 of this book, it is important to establish an agenda, take notes, and determine action items (and follow up on them) for every meeting. It only takes a few extra minutes and is well worth the overall working time saved on a project.

Because of the chaotic work environment of game development, I've also found that techniques that focus on project definition are also easily implemented, with excellent results.

For example, work breakdown structures (WBS) are especially useful when you are trying to educate the team on how each individual's tasks affects the work of others. An artist might not realize how being two days late in completing a character model will severely impact a QA tester's workload, or an engineer may not understand why delivering the new lighting tool one week late creates a bottleneck with the art department's workflow. To use WBS effectively, select a large task, collect everyone who contributes work to this task, and create the WBS structure together—this exercise will demonstrate very concretely to everyone how their work can delay or stop someone else's work. Post the WBS in a public area and use it as a teaching tool in the next team meeting.

A role-definition exercise also proves to be very useful in creative working environments. If people truly understand what their responsibilities are on the project, they can tailor their expectations accordingly. In addition, if people on the team clearly understand everyone's roles and responsibilities on the project, productivity and morale are likely to increase. This is because people will know exactly to whom to go for different types of information and they will also feel secure knowing that they are fulfilling the defined expectations of their role on the team.

### Present the information in entertaining ways.

It goes without saying that people like to have fun. They don't like the idea of dragging themselves into work every morning to face another pointless and uninspiring eight hours of work. You want people to show up for work every day with enthusiasm and excitement about the work ahead, otherwise they will not generate new or inspired ideas. So when you are discussing ways to improve the team's productivity, be sure to present the information in entertaining ways that involve the team—don't just dictate the changes to them and expect them to happy to oblige.

For example, I post a hard copy of the detailed project schedule in the team rooms and color in the tasks with a highlighter as tasks are accomplished. The team enjoys seeing the completed tasks highlighted, as this a strong visual indicator of how much progress the project has made. Another enjoyable thing is to have different team members talk for a few minutes at each team meeting about their work on the project. This provides more reinforcement that everyone depends on each other.

If you can maintain a relaxed atmosphere and attitude when gaining control of your project, the team will have a positive experience and will adapt more quickly to the changes. Once they realize that adding processes doesn't create more work for them, and in fact can be fun, they will probably have more suggestions on ways to improve the project's workflow.

### Show the team how project management has improved the working conditions.

As you get project-management processes implemented, let the team know the positive impact these changes are having. If feedback was not centrally tracked in the past, but there is now a feedback process in place, remind the team that the quality of feedback has improved and everyone's ideas are being seriously considered. Also, point out that people are spending less time in meetings and that the meeting time is more productive overall. It is especially important to remind the team of these improvements if they start complaining about the new way of doing things. This doesn't mean they don't have a right to complain, but it is good to remind them how far things have progressed since changing to these new processes—they are likely to have a better appreciation and understanding of why things were changed to begin with.

## CONCLUSION

Managing creative people and projects can be frustrating if you take a passive approach to dealing with the problems you encounter on a daily basis, especially if the creative people on your team resist any process they assume stifles their creativity. The problems only get worse the longer you ignore the issues, and eventually the team becomes nonproductive and demoralized.

Convincing creative people that project management can help them is not difficult when you educate them on the basic principles and involve them in any changes made on the project. Remember that the ideas presented in this chapter are not magic bullets that make all your problems go away—there will still be chaotic schedules, scope changes, and varying resources. However, these problems can be minimized if the team works together as whole on making small changes in the process that will bring order to some of this project uncertainty.

# 23

## CHAPTER

# The Need for Systems Thinking in Project Management

### LINEAR VERSUS SYSTEMS THINKING

Unless you are very young or in some way exceptional, you almost undoubtedly learned to think in linear causal terms. I say this because a few schools are beginning to teach systems thinking, some at the urging of Dr. Jay Forrester, one of the pioneers of the discipline.

For most of us, however, the proposition that cause-effect relationships can be described as "A causes B" seems reasonable, and perhaps irrefutable. This has been so often our experience of the world that we seldom stop to think that things do not always operate in this manner. When an accident happens, we ask, "What caused it?" If two children get into a fight, we ask, "Who started it?" Interestingly, if the children are asked, they may both point at each other, adamantly claiming "He did!"

Adults tend to get frustrated at that response. When I was a child and my sister and I would have an altercation,

my father would ask, "Who started it?" We would both ac-
cuse the other. He would get annoyed at this response and
threaten to punish
both of us if the
*guilty party* didn't
confess. In his
mind, A causes B.
It could not be pos-

> In human interaction, A causes B causes A.

sible that A causes B causes A, but that is exactly how it
works in systems terms.

You might say that, at the microsecond level, one party
made the first move.

However, there is communication at both the verbal and
nonverbal levels, and the nonverbal channel is operating continuously in both directions. Because some, if not most, of the
influence between humans is a function of the nonverbal
channel, that influence is operating simultaneously, so again,
it does not operate linearly, but circularly.

In systems thinking, you must abandon linear causality
and talk in terms of circular causal effects. This is because
systems involve *feedback*, which introduces circularity. This is
shown in Figure 23.1. When you are heating your home in
the winter, the thermostat senses the room temperature and
tells the furnace to turn on when the temperature drops below the level at which the thermostat is set. As the heat
causes the room to warm up, the thermostat sends another
signal to the furnace, telling it to shut down.

We can say, then, that as the temperature drops the furnace comes on and causes the temperature to rise, which
causes the furnace to stop. That causes the temperature to
drop, and so on, in a limitless number of cycles. Notice how
convoluted our language becomes when we try to describe
circularity. Our language itself is inherently linear. Notice:

Johnny hit the ball.

Johnny is the subject. The action is that he *hit*, and the
object is the ball. Johnny is A in the equation A causes B, and

Heating System

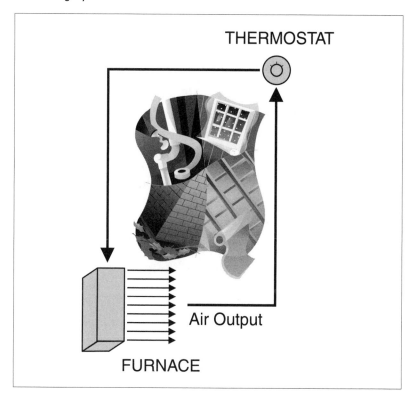

THERMOSTAT

Air Output

FURNACE

the ball is B. The causal link is *hit*. Notice that the verb hit can be replaced with all kinds of action descriptors: stole, dropped, held, threw, saw, accepted, liked, and so on.

It would be just as accurate to say that the ball hit Johnny's bat, as the bat swung through an arc, and rebounded at almost the same velocity at which it hit the bat. It would be just as accurate. But it would take forever to say anything.

Consider this sentence:

Johnny cried until his mother gave him some cake and then he smiled.

It is a linear flow, but it does involve a reciprocal action. The action goes from A to B and back to A. Johnny's crying causes his mother to give him some cake, which causes him to smile. A causes B causes A.

## THE LANGUAGE OF MANAGING

This same linear causal thinking carries over into managing. Managers are supposed to "make things happen." One common definition of managing is that "A manager gets work done through other people." This suggests that she is a causal agent and that she does no work herself. A causes B.

Now suppose the employee does not do what the manager has directed him to do. Then the manager will respond. She may give the directive again, probably in more forceful terms. If there is still no response, she may take disciplinary action. How do we understand this exchange in systems terms? The manager is A and the employee is B. A causes B causes A causes B causes A. The employee's response to the first directive causes the manager to give another directive, which elicits another response from the employee, which causes another directive (or discipline) from the manager, and so on.

Causality in human relations, then, is circular, and must be drawn as shown in Figure 23.2.

There are times when the action of one person causes the other person to do more of what he was doing and other times when the action causes him to do less. For example, behavioral-reinforcement theory suggests that rewarding a person for performing well on the job will usually make him try to perform even better in the future. Thus, positive reinforcement (sometimes called positive "strokes") increases desired performance. This is shown as a graph in Figure 23.3.

Conversely, negative reinforcement should cause a behavior to diminish. If the behavior being displayed is undesired, then negative reinforcement should extinguish it. Unfortunately, there are times when desired behavior is also extinguished because it is negatively reinforced. See Figure 23.4.

## F I G U R E   23.2

Circularity in Human Relations

## F I G U R E   23.3

Positive Reinforcement Increases Desired Behavior

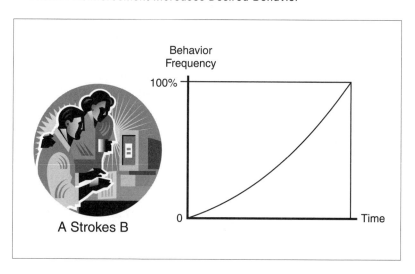

### F I G U R E  23.4

Negative Reinforcement Extinguishes Behavior

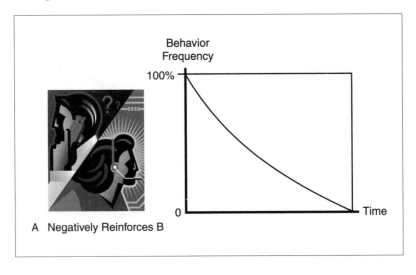

It is interesting to consider the interaction between a manager and employee in terms of behavioral reinforcement. If a manager strokes an employee for good performance and the employee performs even better in the future, what effect does this have on the manager? She is rewarded for stroking the employee. What does she do? She strokes him even more. His performance improves. She is rewarded. She strokes the employee again, and so on. (Who is controlling whom?) This is called a positive feedback loop, in which each action is followed by a reaction of increasing strength. Can this go on forever? No.

Eventually the employee becomes satiated with strokes or the manager becomes fatigued from so much stroking. There are always limits to growth in any system. Note that as a person becomes satiated with strokes, each additional stroke loses some value. Thus, there is nonlinearity in the system. This is shown in Figure 23.5.

The Value of Strokes Diminishes as the Quantity Increases

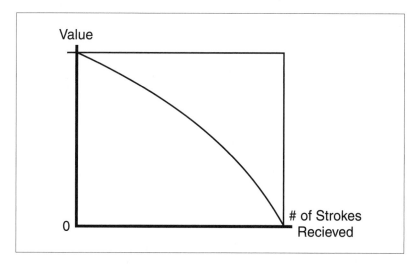

The opposite effect is also possible. An employee suffering from stroke deficit disorder, a term I have borrowed from organization development specialist Lee Kleese (1996), values strokes much more highly than someone who is in stroke overload. People tend to suffer from stroke deficit disorder at the left side of the curve in Figure 23.5 and to suffer stroke overload on the right side of the curve.

## CONTROL IN RELATIONSHIPS

In all human relations there is a constant struggle to define the relationship. There are basically two kinds of relationships, as defined by status. These are either symmetrical, meaning equal-status, or they are complementary, which is unequal-status. Every communication between two individuals carries a proposed definition of the relationship, as defined by status. Note that the communication can be verbal or nonverbal. If you have forgotten, nonverbal aspects of a communication include body gestures and/or posture, tone of voice, inflections, phrasing, and so on. Verbal communication is strictly words.

Consider the following question:

"Can you *solve* the problem?"

By stressing the word *solve* the meaning is something like, "Is it possible for the problem to be solved at all, or is it likely that it will come back again?"

Now suppose the stress is changed:

"Can *you* solve the problem?"

The meaning is very different. There seems to be doubt that this particular individual can solve the problem. Perhaps someone else can, but not this person. The meaning of the words has changed just by changing the stress on one word in the sentence.

Now suppose a supervisor says to an employee:

"Have your report to me by 3 o'clock tomorrow."

This communication suggests that the supervisor sees the relation with this employee as very complementary (unequal status). Compare this to:

"Would you please get your report to me by 3 o'clock tomorrow?"

In both cases, the message is the same: the supervisor wants the report by 3 o'clock tomorrow. However, in the second case, the relationship definition offered by the supervisor is more equal-status, or symmetrical.

Does it matter?

Sometimes it does. In American culture, we recognize that there are status differentials between supervisors and employees, but we do not like them to be emphasized too strongly. If the employee feels that the supervisor is coming on too strong, then he may get angry. This can result in a conflict, in which the two try to define the relationship in mutually acceptable terms.

It is bad enough for us to have to interpret relationship definitions from the nonverbal component of a communication. It is even worse when a person offers a definition opposite the one he really wants.

## Let's Go Out for Dinner

Lee Kleese, whom I cited previously, has a wonderful example of this. You come home from work dead tired. Your significant other says, "Dear, I've had a really hard day and obviously you have too, so why don't we go out for dinner."

"That's a great idea," you say. "Where would you like to go?"

"I don't care. Where would you like to go?"

Now you say, "I don't care," but inside you're thinking, "If you loved me as much as I love you, you'd say steak."

"Well, if it really doesn't matter, I'd like to try that new Chinese restaurant. Everyone says it's really good."

There may be a momentary flash of disappointment on your face, but this quickly changes to a forced smile and you say, "Okay. Let's go."

Inside you're thinking, "Chinese! That doesn't have *anything* to do with steak. I'll go, but you owe me one."

Some time goes by. You come home from work again, dead tired, and your significant other says, "Dear, I'm really tired, and you seem to be also. Why don't we go out to dinner."

"Great idea," you say. "Where would you like to go?"

"I don't care."

"Me either." But the little voice inside is saying, "If you loved me as much as I love you, you'd say *steak*."

"Well, if you really don't care, I'd like to try that Italian place on Vine Avenue. Margie says it's really good."

"Italian!" the little voice screams. "That doesn't have anything to do with steak."

This time, the little voice wins. "I don't want to eat Italian," you say. "I want to eat steak."

"Well, why didn't you say so?" says your significant other politely. "Let's go."

So you go eat steak.

Do you think you're going to enjoy it?

Not a chance!

Now the problem here is that you have offered a definition of your relationship with your significant other that is symmetrical. What you really would like to do, of course, is call the shots and choose steak. When your significant other chooses something else, you get upset. It would be much clearer if you had said, "Well, I'd like to have a steak. Maybe we can have steak this time and Italian the next (or vice versa)." When you agree that one person chooses this time and the other chooses the next, that says the relationship is symmetrical over the long run but complementary for the specific choice. When both parties agree to this, there is no problem.

You notice that, in systems terms, the system is trying to adjust itself for stability. It turns out, though, that the most

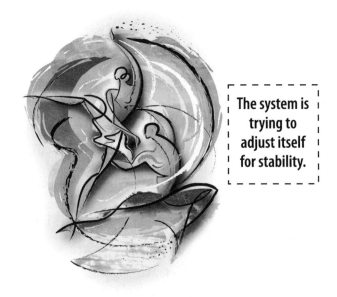

The system is trying to adjust itself for stability.

unstable system is one that is symmetrical. A tiny shift causes it to become complementary. A system that is inherently complementary, however, can experience shifts in either direction and will remain stable. This is why people who are highly concerned that they be treated as equal-status with everyone else are always frustrated. They are constantly seeing signs that the relationship is unequal, and they attempt to restore balance. That attempt may be met with a counter-response aimed at keeping the system unbalanced, and thus a conflict develops.

This is not to suggest that all relationships would be better if they were unequal-status. It is important that we recognize that no relationship can ever be totally equal all the time for every situation. The only thing we can achieve is equal status on the average.

## CONFLICT IN MANAGEMENT

Inevitably there are conflicts in human relations. Conflict occurs when one person frustrates the concerns of another person. Those concerns include goals, values, self-interests, status, and control. This is one area in which systems thinking is essential if we are to understand and deal with such situations.

Remember the example of two children having an altercation? When asked who started it, each blamed the other. This is because *each sees his own behavior as a response to the behavior of the other child!* The way this works is shown in Figure 23.6.

Person A behaves. This is the arrow 1-2. Person B responds, as sequence 2-3. Person A responds to that behavior as 3-4. This goes on as a long series of interactions that we can call *move-countermove, move-countermove.* Now, as I have said previously, if you ask each person why she behaved as she did, she will tell you that she was only responding to the other person's behavior. Person A sees the exchange as sequence 2-3-4, while person B sees it as 1-2-3. This is called

**F I G U R E** 23.6

Punctuation in Human Relationships

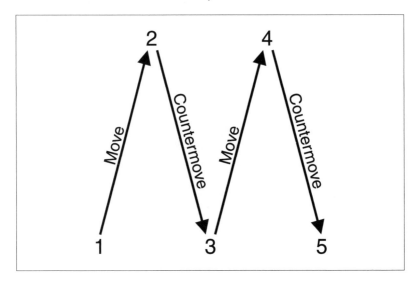

punctuation in communication (Watzlawick, Beavin, and Jackson, 1974), and was discussed in Chapter 20.

In some cases, once such an interaction begins, it becomes almost impossible to stop. Each side sees her behavior as a response to that of the other. Such a sequence is called a game without end, and naturally, we don't mean game in the fun sense. Examples of such games without end are the Middle East conflict and the religious conflict that has gone on in Northern Ireland for so long. There have been many attempts to resolve those conflicts, and they have been only temporarily successful. The conflict breaks out all over again when one side makes a move that is seen by the other as similar to previous moves.

There is only one way to end a game without end, and that is to break the pattern. This was done by President Gorbachev in the arms race. In this game, the United States increased its weapons and the Soviet Union countered by doing the same. Over time, each country stockpiled massive quantities of weapons—by most estimates, enough to destroy all life on earth several times over. The cost to each country was enormous, and the money spent on weapons could not be used for improving the lives of the citizens of either country.

Finally Gorbachev realized that the Soviet Union could not continue this race indefinitely. They had limited resources (as does the U.S.). So he told President Reagan, "I am going to deprive you of an enemy." He did this by beginning to disarm the Soviet Union, without waiting for the U.S. to follow suit. This broke the move-countermove pattern. His countermove was exactly the opposite of what it had always been: instead of increasing armaments, he decreased them, thus breaking the pattern.

In systems terminology, the exchange had been a reinforcing loop. Each move on one side caused a corresponding increasing move on the other. Gorbachev's action changed the system to a balancing loop initially. Later on, it became a reinforcing loop again, but this time in the opposite direction. As he decreased Soviet arms, we did the same. Of course, neither side is willing to decrease their arms to zero, as each has the potential to be attacked by someone other than their original foe.

This is an important lesson for project managers. When conflicts break out in our teams, it is often unproductive to try to get at causes. Each party will just blame the other. When this happens, it is more productive to find some way to break the pattern. This means you have to get at least one party to the conflict to abandon the normal behavioral response and do the opposite of what he has been doing. Here I am suggesting what you would do if you were mediating a conflict between two members of your team. If it is conflict between yourself as project manager and someone else, and you want to resolve it, then you will have to break the pattern by behaving differently than you have been doing.

## THINKING IN SYSTEMS TERMS

The previous examples show that we must abandon linear thinking if we are to understand the dynamics of much of what happens in human affairs. This is especially true in project teams. In the next chapter, we will expand our understanding of systems thinking and introduce some tools that will help us understand how certain actions on our part can make our projects better and how some can actually make them worse.

# 24
## CHAPTER

# Understanding
# Systems Thinking

For several hundred years scientists have tried to understand the world through reductionist thinking. They initially believed that you could understand a thing by taking it apart and studying the components individually. After all, they reasoned, a machine is the sum of its parts, and Newtonian physics had led them to believe that the universe is a big clockwork mechanism.

> A house is not the same as a pile of building materials.

At first glance, this sounds okay, until you begin to realize that a house is not the same as a pile of building materials. Further, you cannot understand the qualities of a house by analyzing a single brick or an individual board that goes into the house. This is even more true of more complex aggregates of parts, such as biological organisms and complex machines.

## WHAT IS A SYSTEM?

Even after you put all of the parts together, you still don't have a system. There is no active quality to a house. It just sits there. It may be cozy, comfortable, and great to live in, but it doesn't do anything! A system, on the other hand, is active. It does do something. In fact, a system is defined as follows:

A system is a collection of parts that interact with each other to function as a whole.

The parts of a system, taken separately, are often useless. To be of value they must be present and arranged correctly. If the arrangement and interaction of parts does not matter, then we are not dealing with a system but with a "heap." Further, the definition of a system leads to an interesting conclusion: a system is actually *greater* than the sum of its parts. This has been called synergy and is one of the things that differentiates systems from nonsystems.

The human body is a large system, and it in turn contains a number of subsystems. The nervous system is a subsystem of the body. So is the circulation system. When a system is part of a larger system, it is called a subsystem. Likewise, the earth is a part of the solar system, which is a part of a galaxy, and our galaxy is part of the collection of galaxies known as the universe.

Returning to human beings for a moment, note that a person is a complex system in her own right. Put her with a number of other individuals, and have them work together to achieve a certain result, and you have a larger system called a team. You can study each member of the team individually and you can describe their personalities, motivations, neuroses, and other characteristics. However, this understanding will not tell you a great deal about how the individual will function in the team, nor will it tell you a lot about the team as a system. Notice that I am not saying you will know nothing about the team; I am just saying that understanding will be limited.

The reason is in part because we are different persons in different settings. The attributes of a gear might not change when you assemble it into a clock. The attributes of human beings, however, are not so stable. I am a different person when teaching a seminar than when I am interacting with my family. Naturally, some characteristics are constant, but the differences make it hard to predict group behavior by observing individual behavior. I am also not the same in all teams. It is a very context-sensitive thing.

The importance of this for a project manager is that you have to be careful making predictions about what kind of project team you will have by looking only at individual team member qualities. As a simple example, you like Jane. You have worked with her before and found her to be reliable, hard-working, intelligent, cheerful, and resilient. You also like working with Bob. He is also very intelligent, extremely knowledgeable about a certain technology that you intend to employ, and he has very desirable work habits. You are certain that if you put these two on your team, you will have a dynamite combination!

The only thing is, Jane and Bob take an immediate dislike to each other. There is an intense jealousy that manifests as sniping, competitiveness, and other acts of sabotage. Individually, they may be great. They may even be great for *you* to work with. It is just that the two of them can't work together.

> The key to understanding systems is in the word *interact.*

Again, the key to understanding systems is in that word *interact.* Jane and Bob interact with each other in a dysfunctional way. Naturally, for a team to be a good team, the members must interact in a harmonious, cooperative manner. So Jane and Bob together turn out to be a bad combination for your team.

Now consider a simple interaction that most of us experience every day. You are driving a car. This forms a simple human-machine system. As you drive along, you approach a hill that you must climb. The car begins to slow down, so you press down on the accelerator, and the car speeds up. When you have regained your original speed, you relax the pressure a bit and the car resumes a constant speed. When it reaches the top of the hill, you have to back off on the accelerator even more, or else the car will begin to speed up. This interaction between yourself and the car is a process called "negative feedback." It is called negative because the feedback negates the change in system behavior. As the car slows down, your pressing the accelerator negates the change in speed. As the car speeds up, letting up on the pedal negates the change in speed again. This can be diagramed as shown in Figure 24.1.

Note that negative feedback does not have the colloquial meaning in this case. It is customary for people in organizations to talk about giving each other positive and negative feedback. By this they mean that they are either giving each other compliments (positive feedback) or criticism (negative feedback).

**F I G U R E  24.1**

Simple Feedback System for Driving a Car

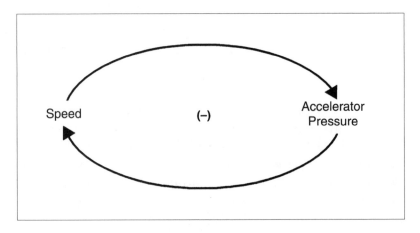

Returning to our example of driving a car, some people are able to maintain very good speed control going up and down hills. Others seem not to notice the feedback that tells them their speed is varying, so they speed up and slow down (even on level ground). When there is a lot of variation in a system, we say it is a *loose* system. Note that a self-stabilizing system does not prevent change; it just responds to change to try to minimize its effect on the system. The thermostat that turns your furnace on and off does this. It too has a certain amount of looseness. The room temperature may vary several degrees. The typical home thermostat only costs a few dollars. A system that would maintain temperature to a degree would cost many times more, and probably wouldn't be worth the cost to most people. It is important to know the limits of a system.

Another characteristic of systems is reaction time. This is the amount of time it takes a signal to go around the loop. If it is too slow, the system can be damaged. An example is that if you touch a hot surface and don't feel it instantly, you can be seriously burned. This is, in fact, the problem with sunburn. It takes so long for you to realize that you are being burned that by that time, it is too late. The damage is done. This is analogous to placing a frog in a pot of water and slowly heating it up. The frog doesn't react. He just feels warmer, until the temperature is too hot. He lets himself be boiled. If you were to drop the frog into very hot water, however, he would jump out.

## ANTICIPATION

What if you can't afford the delay of even a fast-response system? For example, it is best not to get burned in the first place, rather than to react to being burned. Systems cope with this problem by reacting to *warnings*. Avoiding a growling dog is better than taking a chance that he might bite. Countries that wait until they are attacked to arm themselves may never get the chance. It is more prudent to pay attention to intelligence reports that indicate imminent danger and

**F I G U R E   24.2**

Avoiding Danger versus Simply Responding to It

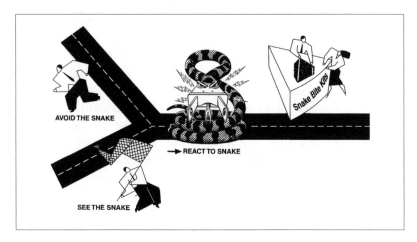

arm in advance. Figure 24.2 shows the difference between avoiding danger and simply responding to it.

When systems only respond to problems, rather than anticipating them, it may be too late to deal with the problem, and the system is destroyed. The lesson for managers is that we should try to anticipate problems and deal with them ahead of time, rather than simply reacting to them. This is the difference between reactive and proactive management. This is also called risk management, and is covered in Chapter 17.

## POSITIVE FEEDBACK

So far we have discussed systems that contain negative feedback loops. Negative feedback loops keep systems stable. They *resist* change. We often encounter such feedback systems when we try to change organizations. The French have a saying about such systems, which, roughly translated, is, "The more things change, the more they stay the same" (Watzlawick, et al. 1974). In fact, it seems that most systems employ negative feedback to protect themselves from being affected by outside influences. How then, do systems change, develop, or grow?

They contain some kind of positive feedback loop. Again, we are not referring to the colloquial use of the term, meaning to give someone positive strokes or compliments. Here, we mean that a small perturbation introduced into the system leads to a large system effect. Some examples include the growth of compound interest, rabbit populations, knowledge, personal power, and audio systems that howl at you. The audio system is diagramed in Figure 24.3.

**F I G U R E   24.3**

An Audio System That Howls

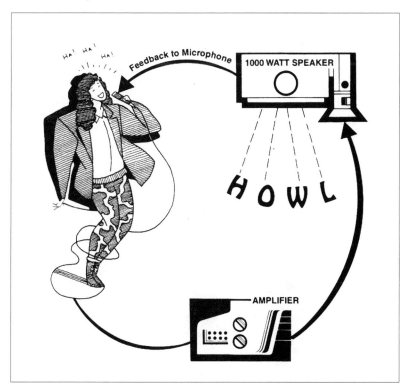

When you speak into the microphone, the sound of your voice is amplified and fed to the speakers. The microphone picks up the sound from the speakers, amplifies it, and a positive loop is created. You might ask why the system does not get louder and louder. There are always limits to growth. In the case of an electronic system, the amplifier can only produce so much power, so when the sound reaches that level, it can go no higher. Rabbit populations can grow only so far. They reach a point at which there is not enough food to feed all of them. They either have to move to new areas or begin to starve. Even compound interest might reach a limit. The bank can only pay interest on deposits if they can lend the money to someone, so if they reach a point at which no one wants to borrow the money you have deposited, they would no longer be able to pay you interest on it. Of course, you would have to be a very large depositor indeed for this to happen.

## BUILDING COMPLEX SYSTEMS

Every complex system that you will ever encounter is built from the two basic elements—positive and negative feedback loops. Because this is true, when you see two systems that have the same loop structure, you can expect them to behave

Positive loops would grow indefinitely if something didn't limit them.

in very similar ways. The beauty of this is that we can learn how a system behaves in one area and transfer that knowledge to systems of the same structure in other areas.

As I explained in the previous section, positive loops would grow indefinitely if something didn't limit them. In the case of rabbits, it is the food supply. Consider a similar system composed of bacteria. These single-cell organisms multiply by dividing. In the right environment, a cell will divide in about one half-hour. The two cells will themselves divide in another half-hour, so by then, you have four cells. This progression continues, so that you get 8, 16, 32, 64, 128, and so on. As incredible as it might seem, after only 10 hours, you will have more than a million cells!

This assumes that none of them die, of course. However, all living organisms do die, so to know how many bacteria you would have after a certain period, you must factor in the death rate. The overall system is shown in Figure 24.4.

**F I G U R E  24.4**

System for Bacteria Population Growth

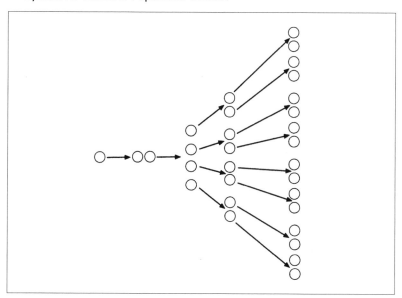

As you can see, the two loops work against each other. If 10 bacteria are born and 6 die, the net increase in population is 4. However, if 12 die for every 10 that are born, the population will gradually decline. The overall system behavior is determined by which loop is stronger or dominant.

This basic model can be applied to other populations. A city grows or declines in the same way that bacteria do. However, in addition to being born and dying, people also move into and away from cities, so the situation is more complicated. In this case, you might have four loops, as shown in Figure 24.5.

We might also ask what controls the rate at which loops operate. For example, in the case of population growth, we would ask what affects the birth and death rates. If the population is one of animals, death would be affected by the food supply, predators, and disease. For simplicity, we can begin by adding the effect of food alone, to get the diagram in Figure 24.6.

In the same way, we can add the effects of predators and disease, to arrive at the system shown in Figure 24.7.

**F I G U R E  24.5**

Growth of a City

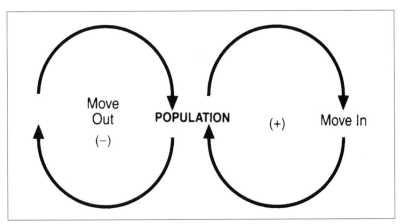

## F I G U R E   24.6

### Effect of Food Supply on Death Rates

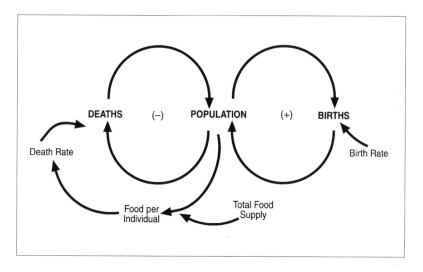

## F I G U R E   24.7

### Effects of Food, Predators, and Disease on Death Rates

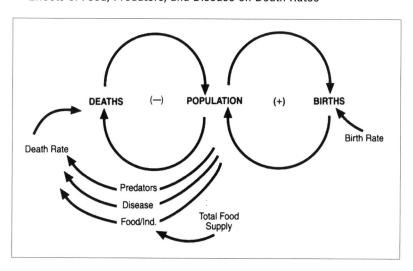

Is this everything? Not really. For animal populations, overcrowding introduces a significant factor (maybe the same is true of human populations too). For example, when rabbits get too crowded, they may go into shock and die at the slightest stimulus—a loud noise, the sight of an enemy, or even another friendly rabbit. They literally die of fright or excitement. This means that, if the other negative loops fail to control the population, the overcrowding loop takes over.

In addition, some animals use the amount of food or space to control population by moderating the actual birth rate. Considering all of these factors together, we can construct a diagram like the one in Figure 24.8.

**F I G U R E  23.8**

Major Factors Affecting Animal Populations

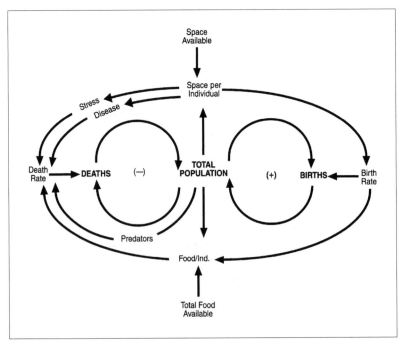

In this system, the loop that will eventually stop population growth depends on the particular situation. In some cases the loops all work together to control the positive loop. Sometimes a few do the major job and others are kept in reserve in case these fail.

One problem we have is that people sometimes intervene in a system to eliminate a negative feedback loop that they don't like. The next thing they know, a worse one takes its place. For example, if disease is reduced by medicine, and nothing is done to limit the birth rate, population might grow to the point where not enough food is available and famine occurs, which kills even more people. Even if the food supply is not a problem, we can already see the effects of people living longer

> Any change that affects the relationship between the positive and negative loops is going to alter the long-term behavior of the system.

because of improved health care. They now wind up in nursing homes or suffer Alzheimer's, which would not have struck them had they died younger.

Most systems will balance themselves if left alone, and will return to the balance point if disturbed. It is important to look for the balance point in complex systems. By understanding the nature of the positive and negative feedback loops, you can also differentiate between things that are going to affect the system only temporarily and things that will have a lasting effect. Any change—no matter how big—that does not change the important positive or negative loops of a system will be only temporary. Conversely, any change—no matter how small—that does affect the relationship between the positive and negative loops is going to alter the long-term behavior of the system.

From a practical point of view, this says that if we want to change a complex system, we must find a way to change the relationship between the loops that keep the system balanced. Otherwise, every change we try to make will be met with resistance by the system, which will just return to the status quo state.

That is a brief introduction to systems thinking. In the next chapter, we will look at ways to apply these ideas to projects.

# How to Apply Systems Thinking in Managing Projects

In the previous chapters, I showed how systems thinking can help us understand the dynamics of human interactions. Because project work is performed by people, it should be possible to apply systems concepts to the understanding and management of projects.

## FIXES THAT FAIL

Let's begin by considering a fairly common problem in projects: the work is falling behind schedule. It seems that the only thing to do is ask the person doing the work to increase his working hours each day—that is, to work a few hours of overtime to get back on track. He agrees. The first week, he works 12 hours a day and is making progress. The amount of work being done is definitely greater than what was previously accomplished. However, after a couple of weeks, you discover that he is making a lot of mistakes, and these must be corrected. Furthermore, his output is down from what it was the first week. In fact, you find that the amount of work he is turning out is just about equal to what he was doing in a normal 40-hour week before! You are actually losing, because he now has to spend time correcting the errors he has made, and this drops his output even more.

Something must be done.

You decide that, if overtime is not the answer, then you must obtain extra resources. You convince your boss to assign a new person to help. To your amazement, the work accomplished by both of them is barely the same as for one person working alone, and there are considerably more errors being made. What is going on?

You talk to your original team member, and he says, "It's very simple. The guy you gave me knows nothing about what I'm doing, so I spent most of Monday getting him on board. Then I found that he's making a lot of mistakes, so I had to help correct those, and I'm still having to work overtime to take care of training him and to correct all the errors. I would be better off with no help at all!"

This is an example of *fixes that fail*. Having the person work overtime initially worked, until the long-term effect of fatigue kicked in. Then the person started making more errors, which had to be corrected, which caused him to fall further behind, which required him to work harder, which caused more fatigue, and more errors, and on and on it goes. Then a helper was assigned to the project. The original worker had to train the helper, which dropped his productivity, which caused him to work harder, which made him more fatigued, and the helper made errors, which had to be corrected, which made him even more tired, and so on.

Another example. I know of a company, we'll call it Acme Electronics, that makes components that go in products manufactured by other companies. Occasionally, their customer has a problem with one of the components, and the design engineers are sent to the field to see if they can correct the problem. Because they are currently working on designing new components, that work comes to a standstill. They manage to correct the problem for the customer, and return to work.

Unfortunately, the deadline for completing the current component design has not changed, so they have fallen behind. The only solution is to work hard to try to catch up. The result is the same as described previously in this chapter—they do poor-quality work, which is not caught. The new component is released. The customer again has problems with the new part. The engineers are sent to the field to correct the problem. Current work comes to a standstill. They work hard to catch up, turn out another bad design, and the cycle begins all over again.

The common expression that describes this situation is firefighting. The engineers are doing a reasonable job of firefighting, but nothing is being done to prevent future fires.

## LEVELS OF UNDERSTANDING

There are numerous levels from which we can understand the world around us. Systems thinkers are concerned with four of these, as shown in Figure 25.1. At the level of *events* are things that occur on a day-to-day basis. Accidents happen, we go to work, eat lunch, perform a work task, or write a memo. In the case of the engineers, they correct a problem with a component—they put out a fire. This level is called *reactive*, because we are always reacting to the event rather than trying to control its occurrence.

At the next level are *patterns of events*. In the case of our engineers, we begin to notice that the same pattern keeps happening. Note that patterns can only be seen over a period of time. When we see patterns developing, we might be able to be *adaptive* in our response. We give the engineers training in firefighting, so that when they have a

We are often reacting to an event rather than trying to control its occurrence.

fire, they can extinguish it quickly. This still does nothing to prevent fires.

At the *systemic structure* level we begin to ask what causes the patterns of events to occur. This level is called *creative*, because we might be able to prevent fires if we can understand the patterns. This level is future-oriented. By preventing fires, we create a different future than the one that would have occurred normally. At this level, we might decide to set up a firefighting group, separate from the design engineers. This would free the engineers from any firefighting, so that they could concentrate on doing new designs really well, which over the long run should reduce the number of fires that break out.

The next tier is called the *shared vision* level. This level generates the structures that form patterns. This level is called *generative* and is truly future-oriented. At this level, we ask questions like, "What is the real role of design engineers? How should firefighting be handled? What trade-offs are we willing to make between resources devoted to design and those dedicated to firefighting?"

**F I G U R E  25.1**

Levels of Understanding

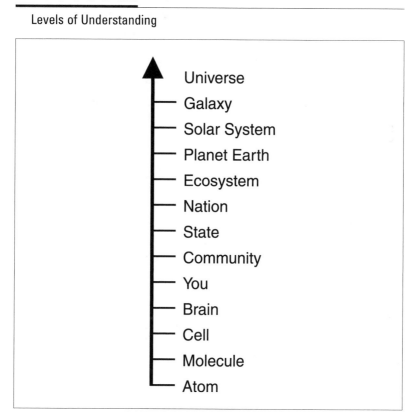

## THE TRAGEDY OF THE COMMONS

Complex systems have a lot of strengths, but they also are like everything else—you don't get anything for free. Complex systems also create their own set of problems. One of these is called the tragedy of the commons. In medieval England there were commons, or common pasture areas. This idea was brought to the United States by the colonists. Commons meant that all members of a community were entitled to graze their livestock there. The individual livestock owner soon begins to think, "The more cows I have, the better off I'll be, and because the grazing is free, I will increase my herd as fast as I can." This creates a positive feedback loop.

It also creates a situation that each individual is powerless to avoid. Each person tends to think the same way, so herds start growing. Soon they reach a point where the cows eat the grass faster than it can grow. Faced with nothing to eat, the animals crop the grass down to the roots, killing it, so that there is nothing at all to eat. Soon the cows are all starving and the entire village is faced with disaster.

Notice that it does no good for a single villager to voluntarily keep down the size of his herd. That just leaves more pasture for the others, who then have more incentive to add more cattle. Thus, the unselfish action will not prevent the disaster, and the person will just be poorer in the meantime, while his neighbors are prospering. The significant thing about this situation is that, if every person makes the best decision from his own point of view, everyone winds up worse off!

Peter Block has pointed out that *enlightened* self-interest would mean that every villager would do what is best for the village—not himself individually (Block, 2000). In doing so, he knows that he will benefit himself over the long run. Of course, it is very hard to get people to do this. People tend to look out for number one, never realizing that their actions will eventually destroy them. We see this with many of the environmental problems that are being created today.

But what does this have to do with project management? One of the significant aspects of project management is that we are always competing for scarce resources to get our jobs done. If we realized that our real self-interest lies in cooperation rather than competition, our project teams would function better. Instead, we sometimes get locked into win-lose conflicts over resources—each project manager wants to optimize his "herd," with no regard for the impact to other teams. From a systems point of view, anything that I do to help my organization in one area tends to help the entire system, and conversely, anything I do to hurt it hurts everyone.

I showed in Chapter 8 how we sometimes get locked into games without end, because we set up a move-countermove interaction. Now that you understand negative feedback loops, you can see that such a system tends to balance itself and resists being changed. As I said at the end of Chapter 22, systems tend to return to the balance point if disturbed, so if you try to reduce the conflict it just comes back after awhile. Unless you can interrupt the pattern—that is, disturb the negative feedback loop—the interaction will continue, unabated, forever! (Or until both parties get tired of it.)

## LIMITS TO GROWTH

In his book, *The Fifth Discipline,* Peter Senge (1990) presents a number of systems archetypes that appear over and over again in organizations, groups, and even in individual performance. One of these is the limits-to-growth model. This archetype is almost always found in situations where "growth bumps up against limits" (Senge, 1990, p. 96). Organizations grow for a while, then stop growing. Teams get better for a while, and then stop getting better. The same happens to individuals. Attempts to improve organizations through reengineering might succeed for awhile and then reach a limit.

This would certainly apply to project teams. When trying to improve processes in project teams, you might find that there are limits to the improvements you can achieve. We try to solve deadline problems by working longer hours, but, as I showed at the beginning of this chapter, the stress and fatigue begin to slow our work speed and reduce quality, thus reducing the benefit of the longer hours.

A limits-to-growth system has a structure like the one shown in Figure 25.2.

F I G U R E   25.2

Limits-to-Growth System Structure

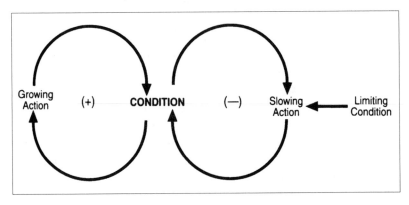

## SHIFTING THE BURDEN

This archetype is prevalent throughout government and corporate organizations. A problem causes symptoms that demand attention, but the underlying problem is difficult for people to address, either because it is obscure or costly to confront. So people shift the burden of the problem to other solutions. These are well-intentioned, easy fixes that seem efficient. However, the fixes just deal with the symptoms and leave the underlying problem unchanged.

One example of this at the personal level is that a person is overworked, possibly because the department is understaffed. She tries to juggle work, family, and her ongoing education, always running from one thing to another. When the workload increases beyond her capacity, the only real solution is to limit the workload. It might mean declining a promotion or prioritizing and making choices. Instead, she decides to juggle faster and tries to relieve her stress with alcohol or meditation, but neither provides a real solution. The problem persists, and so does the need for drinking.

We also see this in our attempts to deal with problem members of teams. Rather than dealing directly with the person, the manager tries to develop his human relations skills. Perhaps the HR department tries to intervene. They talk to the person, coach, counsel, and maybe "write him up." However, he persists in his problematic behavior. The real solution would be to remove him from the group (and probably the company), but no one wants to take that hard medicine, so the problem persists.

A system model for shifting the burden is shown in Figure 25.3.

**F I G U R E  25.3**

Shifting-the-Burden System Structure

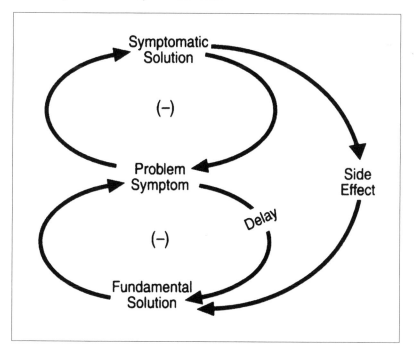

I hope these examples show how systems thinking could be useful to project managers. For in-depth treatment of systems in organizations, I know of no better source than Senge's book, *The Fifth Discipline* and a companion book entitled *The Fifth Discipline Fieldbook* (Senge, et. al, 1994). You might also want to subscribe to *The Systems Thinker Newsletter*. See the listing for Pegasus Communications in the Resource Appendix for information.

# 26

## CHAPTER

# Problem Solving in Projects

## FUNDAMENTAL CONCEPTS OF PROBLEM SOLVING

J. M. Juran (1989) defines a project as a problem scheduled for solution. Expanding on that definition, we can view a project as a job designed to solve a problem on a large scale. Furthermore, the way a problem is defined affects how it is solved, so it is important that a proper definition be established before any work is done. In addition, it is safe to say that many small problems exist to be solved in any large project, so it is impossible to separate problem solving from project management.

A related issue is that many decisions must be made throughout the life of a project, and how these are handled can determine whether a project is successful. For that reason, we need to hone our skills in problem solving and decision making if we are to be successful in managing projects.

## DECISIONS VERSUS PROBLEMS

Making a decision means trying to select the best alternative from a list that might be large or small. We often feel frustrated either because the list is so large that it is overwhelming or because only one choice seems to be available, and it is not very desirable.

A decision may be one step in solving a problem, or it may just be a choice that we must make. An example is selecting from a menu in a restaurant. It could be argued that making this choice is part of solving a problem, which is that we must eat to live. However, we usually don't call eating a problem, so we can say that our choice involves pure decision making.

> A *decision* is a choice of alternatives.

On the other hand, when the decision is part of solving a problem, it is one of several steps. The first step is to define

> A problem is a gap between where one is and where one would like to be, which is confronted by some obstacle that impedes movement to reduce the discrepancy or gap.

the problem; the next is to generate alternative courses of action that might be taken to solve it. Once this list is made, a choice from the alternatives can be made. This is the decision-making step. In other words, problem solving always involves decision making, but not the other way around.

Problems are often stated in terms of a desired goal. Lack of a desired goal is not a problem. An obstacle to attaining a desired goal constitutes a problem. Searching for ways to get around the obstacle constitutes problem solving. The proper statement of a problem is one that stimulates searching behavior.

Creativity consists in shifting our thinking from one obstacle to another that can be more easily overcome, rather than staying focused on finding a way to overcome a single obstacle.

## OPEN- AND CLOSE-ENDED PROBLEMS

It turns out that there are two kinds of problems, called open-ended and close-ended (grammatically, we should say closed-ended, but it is common in the literature to use *close* instead). An open- ended problem is one that has no single correct answer and has boundaries that can be challenged.

> A *close-ended* problem is one that has a unique solution.
>
> An *open-ended* problem is one that may have a number of solutions.

A close-ended problem, on the other hand, has a single right answer. Most close-ended problems are typified by math problems or situations in which something once worked and has quit.

Our educational system teaches us to find the *one right answer* to problems presented, implying, perhaps, that most problems are close-ended. Actually, it is very likely that *most* of the problems we encounter in life are open-ended, yet our educational bias makes us reluctant to challenge the boundaries of real-world problems. One way out of this dilemma is to always insist on finding the *second right answer!*

Problems encountered in projects may involve both open- and close-ended types. For example, if the process once worked but has become dysfunctional, we are dealing with a close-ended problem, since finding the cause of the dysfunction and fixing it involves a single solution. On the other

**F I G U R E   26.1**

Open- or Close-Ended Problems

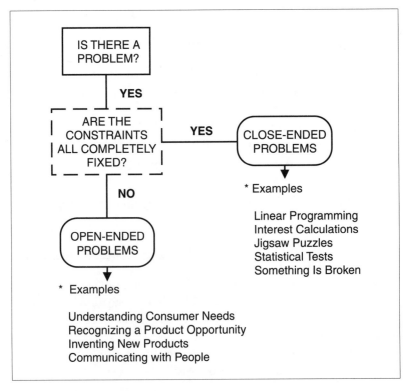

**T A B L E  26.1**

Differences between Open-Ended and Close-Ended Problems

| Open-Ended Problems | Close-Ended Problems |
|---|---|
| Boundaries may change during problem solving. | Boundaries are fixed. |
| Problem solving often involves production of novel and unexpected ideas. | The process has a predictable final solution. |
| The process may involve creative thinking of an unpredictable kind. | The process is usually conscious, controllable, and logically reconstructible. |
| Solutions are often outside the bounds of logic—they can neither be proved nor disproved. | Solutions are often provable and can be shown to be logically correct. |
| Direct, conscious efforts at stimulation of creative process may be difficult. | Procedures are known that directly aid in problem solving. |

hand, if the process is functioning correctly, but is to be improved, we may engage open-ended problem solving.

Figure 26.1 should help you determine whether you are dealing with an open- or close-ended problem. Table 26.1 details the differences between close- and open-ended problems.

# 27

# Solving Close-Ended Problems

## USING THE SCIENTIFIC METHOD TO DEFINE PROBLEMS

Before a problem can be solved, it must be defined. This seems clear enough, yet the educational system in the United States inadvertently produces students who are *solution-minded* rather than *problem-minded*. Throughout our schooling we are given problems to solve, and our teachers will generally accept only one right answer.

Then, when we leave school, we find that no one gives us the definition of the problem, and in many cases there is more than one right answer. For that reason, Americans tend to have difficulty with defining problems, and sometimes make the mistake of finding the right solution to the wrong problem.

> The way a problem is defined determines its solution possibilities.

Before a problem can be solved, it must be defined.

As was stated in Chapter 3, the first major step in managing a project is to define the problem to be solved by the project. Since most projects involve solving open-ended problems, the material in this chapter will be of limited usefulness at the problem definition stage. However, during implementation of the project, there will be many opportunities to apply the methods of solving close-ended problems.

The following story illustrates the importance of defining problems. I was having breakfast in a hotel one morning, and overheard two men talking at the table next to me. It soon became clear that one of them was a district sales manager for a large corporation and the other was one of his young salesmen. The sales manager was clearly unhappy with his staff, and was giving his salesman a lecture. It went like this:

"The company has spent a great deal of money developing product X," he said, "and none of you are selling it. If you guys don't get busy and start selling the product, I'm going to get myself some salesmen who can sell!"

Well, it is pretty obvious how he has defined the problem, isn't it? He has himself a group of poor salesmen. So if they don't get busy and start selling, he is going to get rid of them and get some who can sell.

Now I don't know about anyone else, but I don't think his problem is with his salespeople. After all, how can he have *all* bad ones? Doesn't it seem reasonable that he should have hired at least one good one—even by accident?

But he claims to have all bad ones.

Let's give him the benefit of the doubt for a moment and assume that he is correct, and that he has indeed hired all bad ones. Suppose he gets rid of all of them and hires new ones. What do you suppose he will have?

You bet! He'll end up with all bad ones again.

But the fact is, I suspect there is something wrong with the product, or the market has changed, or the pricing is wrong. If *none* of his salesmen can sell the product, it isn't likely to be the product. Nevertheless, he has defined the problem as people, and so the only solution open to him is to deal with the people.

This situation is more common than might be imagined. People simply make up their minds what the problem is and go about solving it, without conducting a proper problem analysis to be sure that their definition is correct. For close-ended problems, the best approach to defining the problem is to use what is commonly called the scientific method, which consists of the following steps:

- ◆ Ask questions
- ◆ Develop a plan of inquiry
- ◆ Formulate hypotheses
- ◆ Gather data to test those hypotheses
- ◆ Draw conclusions from hypothesis testing
- ◆ Test the conclusions

> **Attributes of a Good Problem Statement**
>
> A good problem statement should:
>
> ◆ Reflect shared values and a clear purpose
>
> ◆ Mention neither causes nor remedies
>
> ◆ Define problems and processes of manageable size
>
> ◆ List measurable characteristics whenever possible
>
> ◆ Be refined (if appropriate) as knowledge is gained

## SOLVING CLOSE-ENDED PROBLEMS WITH PROBLEM ANALYSIS

As was previously stated, close-ended problems have single solutions. Something used to work and is now broken. The remedy is to determine what has broken and repair it—a single solution. To solve close-ended problems, we use a general approach called *problem analysis*. The steps in analyzing a close-ended problem are presented in Figure 27.1.

### Identification

The first step in the problem analysis process is identification. "How do I know I have a problem?" As was previously stated, a problem is a gap between a desired state and a present state—confronted by an obstacle that prevents easy closure of the gap. When a process is involved, as in monitoring progress on a project, that gap can be a *deviation* from standard performance. When the critical ratio falls outside acceptable limits, it is a signal that a potential problem exists with the task in question. This is where problem analysis begins.

When dealing with deviations, we have to know the *norm*. How is the process supposed to behave? Some project

**F I G U R E   27.1**

Problem Analysis Steps

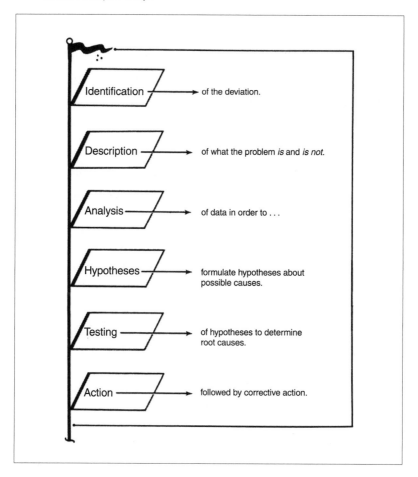

work will have a great deal more variability than others. For that reason, critical ratio limits for some tasks might be set tighter than others. Once the normal variability is known, we can determine if the deviation is significant, whether it is positive (performance is better than the norm) or negative (performance is worse than the norm).

**Making Glass**

Making glass is a nifty process. You melt sand to turn it into glass. Unfortunately, the process seems to be somewhat unreliable. Yields are often poor. A quality consultant went into a plant that had just achieved a yield of 85 percent. The people were ecstatic!

"How did you do it?" he asked.

"We don't know."

"Then how are you going to replicate it?" he asked.

In a more general sense, a problem is recognized because the *effects* produced are different from the normal outcomes expected in the process. Those effects might be a change in scrap level, higher or lower production, or a shift in customer purchases.

In order to correct for the deviation, we need to find its *cause*. For a desirable deviation, we must know the cause so it can be replicated. For an undesirable deviation, the cause must be remedied.

To determine the cause of the deviation, we move to the next step: *description* of the problem.

### Description Using Is/Is-Not Analysis and Stratification

Stratification and is/is-not analysis are ways to localize a problem by exposing underlying patterns. This analysis is done both before collecting data (so the team will know what kinds of differences to look for) and afterward (so the team can determine which factors actually represent the root cause).

To stratify data, examine the process to see what characteristics could lead to biases in the data. For example, could different shifts account for differences in the results? Are mistakes made by new employees very different from those made by experienced individuals? Does output from one machine have fewer defects than that from another?

Begin by brainstorming a list of the characteristics that could cause differences in results. Make

**stratum:** a layer.

data collection forms that incorporate those factors, and collect the data. Next look for patterns related to time or sequence. Then check for systematic differences between days of the week, shifts, operators, and so on.

The is/is-not matrix in Figure 27.2 is a structured form of stratification. It is based on the ideas of Charles Kepner and Benjamin Tregoe (1965).

## Analysis

Once stratified data have been collected, we need to analyze the differences to set the stage for formulating hypotheses about causes of the problem. The following questions are designed to help identify differences:

◆ What is different, distinctive, or unique between what the problem is and what it is not?

◆ What is different, distinctive, or unique between where the problem is and where it is not?

◆ What is different, distinctive, or unique between when the problem is seen and when it is not?

These questions are structured to help us determine what has changed about the process. If nothing had changed, there would be no problem. Our search should be limited to changes within the differences identified above. The following question can help keep us focused:

◆ What has changed about each of these differences?

## F I G U R E   27.2

### The Is/Is-Not Matrix

| | Is<br>Where, when, to what extent, or regarding whom does this situation occur? | Is Not<br>Where does this situation NOT occur, though it reasonably might have? | Therefore<br>What might explain the pattern of occurrence and nonoccurrence? |
|---|---|---|---|
| **Where**<br>The physical or geographical location of the event or situation. Where it occurs or is noticed. | | | |
| **When**<br>The hour/time of day/ day of week, month/ time of year of the event or situation. Its relationship (before, during, after) other events. | | | |
| **What Kind or How Much**<br>The type or category of event or situation. The extent, degree, dimensions, or duration of occurrence. | | | |
| **Who**<br>What relationships do various individuals or groups have to the situation/event? To whom, by whom, near whom, etc., does this occur? (Do not use these questions to place blame.) | | | |

Instructions: Identify the problem to be analyzed. Use this matrix to organize your knowledge and information. The answers will assist you in pinpointing the occurrence of the problem and in verifying conclusions or suspicions.

Noting the date of each change may also help us relate the start of the problem to some specific change that was made to the process.

## Formulation of Hypotheses

At the heart of the scientific method is the testing of hypotheses formulated on the basis of our data collection and analysis. A hypothesis is a guess or conjecture about the cause of the problem. At this point *all* reasonable hypotheses should be listed.

One of the most commonly used tools for formulating hypotheses is the Ishikawa or cause-effect diagram (Figure 27.3). It can be used separately or in conjunction with is/is-not analysis to help formulate hypotheses. The group technique employed will usually be brainstorming.

### F I G U R E  27.3

Ishikawa Diagram

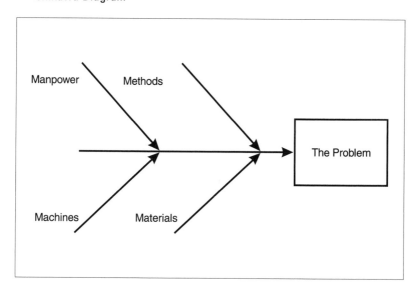

## Testing of Hypotheses

To test hypotheses, we first ask if the suspected cause can explain both sides of the problem description. That is, does the cause account for both the *is* and the *is-not* effects? If it cannot explain both, it is unlikely to be a real cause.

The testing method follows:

- Test each possible cause through the description, especially the sharp contrast areas
- Note all "only if" assumptions

The most likely cause will be the one that best explains the description or the one with the fewest assumptions. To be certain, you must now verify the hypothesis quickly and cheaply. One test is whether you can make the effects come and go by manipulating the factor that is supposedly causing the deviation. If you can, you have probably found the root cause.

## Action

At this point, there are three possible actions that might be taken. These are:

- **Interim action.** You buy time while the root cause of the problem is sought. This action is only a Band-aid™ to cover symptoms.

- **Adaptive action.** You decide to live with the problem or adapt yourself to it.

- **Corrective action.** You correct the actual cause. This is the only action that will truly solve the problem.

# 28 CHAPTER

# Solving Open-Ended Problems

## PROBLEM SOLVING THROUGH CREATIVE ANALYSIS

In solving project problems, it may be necessary to employ creative techniques to develop definitions, ideas, and so on. In particular, the problem being solved by the project itself is likely to be open-ended, requiring different methods than those presented in Chapter 27 for defining and solving close-ended problems. For close-ended problems, the scientific approach to analyzing data can be used. For open-ended problems, however, we need different methods. The techniques presented in this chapter are intended to help problem solvers develop good definitions of open-ended problems and apply a variety of idea-generating aids to solve it.

I should mention here that Edward de Bono (1992) is considered by many to be a leading expert on creative problem solving, and his book *Serious Creativity* covers the subject in more detail than this chapter can possibly do. I heartily recommend that the interested reader consult Dr. de Bono's works.

In solving project problems, it may be necessary to employ creative techniques to develop definitions, ideas, and solutions.

## REDEFINITIONAL PROCEDURES

The procedure outlined in Table 28.1 is designed to help you develop a good definition for an open-ended problem. However, it is only one approach, and others are presented below.

## THE GOAL ORIENTATION TECHNIQUE

Goal orientation is first of all an attitude and second, a technique to encourage that attitude. Open-ended problems are situations for which the boundaries are unclear, but in which there may be fairly well-defined needs and obstacles to progress.

The goal-oriented person tries to recognize the desired end state ("what I want") and obstacles ("what's stopping me from getting the result I want"). To illustrate the goal-orientation

**T A B L E   28.1**

Exercise to Develop a Good Problem Definition

1. Write down an open-ended problem which is important to you and for which you would like some answers that could lead to action. Take as long as you wish.

2. Complete the following statements about the problem you have chosen. Again, take your time. If you cannot think of anything to write for a particular statement, move on to the next one.

   ◆ There is usually more than one way of looking at problems. I could also define this one as . . .

   ◆ . . . but the main point of the problem is . . .

   ◆ What I would really like to do is . . .

   ◆ If I could break all laws of reality (physical, social, etc.), I would try to solve it by . . .

   ◆ The problem, put another way, could be likened to . . .

   ◆ Another, even stranger, way of looking at it might be . . .

3. Now return to your original definition (step 1). Write down whether any of the redefinitions have helped you see the problem in a different way.

technique, consider the problem outlined in Table 28.2. Note that each redefined goal has a different target audience: adults, kids, parents, schools. Each goal may solve a different facet of the problem. Note that, for problems with many causes, many solutions may be required.

## THE SUCCESSIVE ABSTRACTIONS TECHNIQUE

Suppose a company that makes lawn mowers is looking for new business ideas. The first definition of the problem is to "develop a new lawn mower." A higher level of abstraction is to define the problem as "develop new grass-cutting machines." An even higher level of abstraction yields "get rid of unwanted grass." The successive abstractions are shown in Table 28.3.

**T A B L E 28.2**

Goal Orientation Technique

---

*Original problem statement*
Adult illiteracy has reached alarming proportions. Ford Motor Company reports that it is having to train almost 25 percent of its workforce in basic reading, writing, and arithmetic, at considerable cost.

*Redefinitions*
1. (How to) efficiently and effectively teach adults to read.
2. (How to) keep kids from getting through school without being able to read.
3. (How to) get parents to take an interest in their kids so they will learn to read in school.
4. (How to) eliminate the influences that cause kids to take no interest in school.

**T A B L E 28.3**

Successive Abstractions

---

| Level | Example |
|---|---|
| Higher | Get rid of unwanted grass |
| Intermediate | Develop new grass-cutting machines |
| Lower | Develop new lawn mower |

Another definition of the problem, of course, might be to "develop grass that grows to a height of only $x$ inches above the ground." Such a definition would eliminate the need for the lawn mower and put the company in a different business.

## ANALOGY AND METAPHOR PROCEDURES

One of the really interesting approaches to describing problems is through analogy and metaphor. Such definitions increase the ways of looking at a problem and thus improve the chances of finding a solution. In brainstorming and other group settings, they are actually preferable to literal statements, since they tend to be extremely effective in stimulating creative thinking. For example:

- ◆ "How to improve the efficiency of a factory" is a down-to-earth statement.
- ◆ "How to make a factory run as smoothly as a well-oiled machine" is an analogical redefinition.
- ◆ "How to reduce organizational friction or viscosity" is a metaphoric definition.

## WISHFUL THINKING

Many left-brained, rational people do not appreciate the value of wishful thinking. However, wishful thinking can provide a rich source of new ideas. Edward de Bono, in his work on lateral thinking (1971), talks about an "intermediate impossible"—a concept that can be used as a stepping-stone between conventional thinking and realistic new insights. Wishful thinking is a great device for producing such "intermediate impossibles."

Rickards (1975) cites an example of a food technologist working on new methods of preparing artificial protein. As a fantasy, she considers the problem to be "how to build an artificial cow." Although the metaphor is wishful, it suggests that she might look closely at biological systems and perhaps look for a way of converting cellulose into protein, which is what takes place in nature.

Remember the statements from Table 28.1: "What I would really like to do is . . ." "If I could break all laws of reality, I would . . ." This too is thinking "out of the box."

> Many left-brained, rational people do not appreciate the value of wishful thinking. However, wishful thinking can provide a rich source of new ideas.

## NONLOGICAL STIMULI

One good way of generating ideas is through forced comparisons. Such comparisons are called nonlogical stimuli and can be used for developing ways to solve a problem or as an aid to redefinition. The dictionary is often a companion tool in this exercise. Table 28.4 illustrates the procedure.

## BOUNDARY EXAMINATION

When a problem is defined, the statement establishes the boundaries as one sees them. If we accept that these are open to modification, then the definition is only a starting point. Unfortunately, many problem solvers tend to treat boundaries as unchangeable. One way to demonstrate that boundaries can be changed is to examine a problem statement phrase-by-phrase for hidden assumptions. The following is an example:

**T A B L E  28.4**

Exercise in Nonlogical Stimuli

For this exercise, you will need paper, pencil, and a dictionary
1. Write down as many uses as you can think of for a piece of chalk.
2. When you can think of no more ideas, let your eyes wander to some object in your range of vision, which has no immediate connection to a piece of chalk.
3. Try to develop new ideas stimulated by the object.
4. Now repeat steps 2 and 3 with a second randomly selected object.
5. Open the dictionary and jot down the first three nouns or verbs that you see.
6. Try to develop new ideas stimulated by these words in turn.
7. Examine your ideas produced with and without stimuli for differences in variety (flexibility) and total numbers (fluency).

How to <u>improve</u> the performance of our <u>current engineering staff</u> in <u>managing projects.</u>

The underlined words can all be examined. Should we try to improve the performance of our staff, or should we perhaps appoint project managers who are separate from the engineering staff? Is it our staff who are not performing (through some innate problem), or is the system the cause of difficulty? Should the engineering staff be managing projects at all? Is it the management of projects that is the problem, or are we doing the wrong projects in the first place?

## REVERSALS

Sometimes the best way to do something is to not do it. By turning a problem upside down and examining the paradox that is created, we can sometimes see new approaches. For example, if a product has a weakness, try to make it a strength. The problem with many cold remedies is that they make the patient sleepy. Why not turn that *disadvantage* into an advantage? Thus, NyQuil™ was born. It was marketed as a *nighttime* remedy that could actually help the cold-sufferer get some sleep.

A food low in nutritive value becomes a diet food. A glue that won't stick permanently becomes the selling point for Post-it™ note paper. (The idea was rejected initially. Who needs such a thing? It was a number of years before 3-M decided to market the product, and it is hard to imagine the world without Post-it™ paper now. In fact, in conjunction with a white marker board, Post-it™ paper is a great tool for project planning.)

## Matrix Analysis

Matrix analysis is ideal for developing new product ideas. Suppose you wanted to investigate all possibilities for marketing training programs. You might then have a grid (matrix) that looks like Figure 28.1

> Nothing is more dangerous than an idea when it is the only one you have.
>
> –Emile Chartier

Each box (called an intersection) in the matrix represents a place to look for innovations. Thus, at the intersection "Retirees–Home Study" you might consider retirement activities that benefit from being taught in the home. At the intersection of "Trainer–Computer," you might develop a computer-based training program.

## Morphological Analysis

If you want to consider more than one or two variables, the matrix is not a very effective approach. Morphological analysis is probably better. As Miller (1986) says, this is a fancy title for a simple way to generate solutions to problems that

Matrix Analysis

| Delivery Method | Client Groups | | | |
|---|---|---|---|---|
| | Managers | Engineers | Trainers | Retirees |
| Seminars | | | | |
| Cassettes | | | | |
| Videos | | | | |
| Films | | | | |
| Home Study | | | | |
| Workshops | | | | |
| Computer | | | | |

have many variables. For example, to continue with our training programs, we might have to consider:

◆ Delivery method

◆ Course content

◆ Audience

◆ Location

Some of the topics that may fit into these categories are shown in Table 28.5.

Once the list is prepared, a single variable in each column is circled and the possibilities are considered. For example, suppose we circled *seminars, coping, factory workers,* and *nationwide.* The immediate ideas that come to mind are seminars

**T A B L E  28.5**

Morphology for Product Development

| Delivery Method | Content | Audience | Location |
|---|---|---|---|
| video | technical | college student | local |
| audio | behavioral | factory workers | foreign |
| workbooks | reading | managers | diff. state |
| films | writing | farmers | traveling |
| seminars | coping | housewives | same state |
| satellite | agriculture | school children | shipboard |
| computer | computer science | professionals | nationwide |
| mail | medical | paramedics | |

designed to help workers cope with being laid off during the recession. They might need help with the feelings of frustration and self-doubt that invariably accompany such situations, as well as training in how to prepare a résumé, conduct themselves in an interview, and conduct a job search.

## Attribute Listing

If you want to improve a procedure, product, or process, you might write down all the attributes or components and look for ways to improve any one or all of them.

For example, suppose you want to improve the project management process itself. It has the following attributes:

- Schedule
- Overall plan
- Project team
- Form of organization
- Control system
- Project manager

If you examine each of these attributes, you might ask how it can be improved. For example, how do you improve your scheduling methodology? Is your form of organization optimum? Is the control system functioning to keep the project on track?

## Alternative Scenarios

The two primary ways of exploring possibilities for the future are hypothetical situations and alternative scenarios. With hypothetical situations, you make up something and develop a solution for it. For example: "If a certain set of conditions existed, what would I do? To which of these conditions am I most vulnerable? What can I do about those vulnerabilities?"

Alternate scenarios are more comprehensive than hypothetical situations. They are qualitatively different descriptions of plausible futures. When long-range planning is based on a single forecast of trends, there is a big risk of "betting the farm" on that single forecast. Thinking through several scenarios is less risky and frees the problem solver to take more innovative actions.

Scenarios are developed for a particular problem. Your first task is to write a statement of the specific decision that must be made. Then, identify the major environmental forces that might influence the decision: technology, social values, economic growth, and so on. Next, build a scenario around the principal forces. Using information available to you, identify those plausible and qualitatively different possibilities for each force. Assemble the alternatives for each force into internally consistent "stories," with both a narrative and table of forces and scenarios.

## Forced or Direct Association

This approach is similar to nonlogical stimuli, discussed earlier in the chapter. New ideas can be generated by putting together two concepts that seemingly have nothing in common. For example, if we were trying to understand how to improve the performance of a work group, we might ask, "How is this group like a roller coaster?" The following list might result:

+ **tracks**   We stay on track, but the tracks just go up and down and around in a circle. All we seem to be doing is making ourselves sick.

+ **cars**   The cars are designed to keep us from falling out. Maybe we aren't taking enough risks.

+ **speed**   We aren't going anywhere, but we're getting there pretty fast.

+ **control**   The person controlling the roller coaster just started it going and went on a break. Who's in control here, anyway?

With these ideas, we might identify ways to respond to the situation.

## Design Tree

Another term for design tree is "mind map." This approach has been used for many years to illustrate associations of ideas. For example, one author has a book on writing that makes use of mind maps. You begin by writing a single word—representing the issue you want to deal with—then draw a circle around it. Next you list all the ideas that come to mind, connect them to the first word with lines, and continue by examining each new word in turn for the ideas it might trigger. Figure 28.2 illustrates the approach with the word "transportation."

## F I G U R E   28.2

Design Tree for Transportation

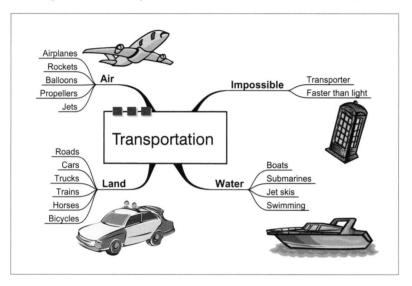

# 29

## CHAPTER

# Managing Decision Making in Project Teams

### THE DILEMMA—INDIVIDUAL OR TEAM DECISION?

Every project manager occasionally must deal with the question, "When should decisions be made by the team and when by an individual?" If all decisions are made by consensus, you will spend all of your time making decisions and get very little work done. On the other hand, if you make an autonomous decision when the team should have been involved, you will spend your time regretting it. This chapter presents guidelines on when a decision should be autonomous and when it should be a consensus or team decision.

### THE NATURE OF DECISIONS

Certainly there are times when consensus decision making is valid and other times when autonomous decisions should be made. The question is: When do you do which? To answer this question, you need to understand the characteristics of decisions. Potentially, every decision has two components or dimensions. One is whether there is some quantitative way in which one choice is better than another. We

> **decision:** A choice made from among several alternatives.

will call this the merit dimension. The other is whether people affected by the decision will accept it. This is the acceptance dimension.

Of course, if you are making a decision that affects no one but yourself, then the acceptance dimension is automatically covered, since, presumably, if you make the decision, you accept it. This is clearly not the case if other people are involved.

It is possible for a decision to involve merit and/or acceptance. For example, if you are trying to choose a stock in which to invest, there is hardly any acceptance issue to deal with. The decision is almost entirely a merit issue.

> An effective decision is one that considers both merit and acceptance dimensions, when appropriate. This can be specified as:
>
> $$ED = f(M, A)$$
>
> which reads, "An effective decision is a function of merit and acceptance."

The situation changes, however, if you are picking restaurants rather than stocks. Suppose you assume that several restaurants have equally good food (merit). One restaurant is Thai, another is Chinese, and a third is American. If you want to take a group out for lunch, there are likely to be acceptance issues to deal with.

In practice, both issues affect most decisions. Someone who likes both Thai and Chinese food may very well say that the two restaurants are not really equal in quality. As a rule, she tells you, the Thai restaurant has better food. Since she likes both Thai and Chinese food, acceptance is not an issue, but merit is.

Another factor that influences how decisions are made is time. If a decision must be made in a hurry, you generally can't afford long, drawn-out group consensus. But you can't ignore the acceptance issue, either. What do you do? You might—in the case of choosing a restaurant—ask who would object to each one. The choice with the fewest objections would be the one you go to. It isn't perfect, but it might be the most satisfactory approach in this case.

## DECISION-MAKING GUIDELINES

### When Merit Is Most Important

One thing that should be clear at this point is that merit issues should be dealt with by those qualified to judge. If I know nothing about choosing good stocks, I had better get some expert advice. That is what financial advisers are for. Similarly, let us suppose that I am managing a project to design a nuclear reactor containment vessel. It turns out that a wide array of structural steels are available. The question is: Which one is best?

The question (a merit issue) concerns me, since a wrong choice could lead to disaster. How should this decision be made? Should I get the entire team to reach a consensus? Or should I make the decision myself, since the buck stops with me if there is a problem? Or should I delegate this choice to someone in the team who is an expert in properties of structural materials?

The answer is obvious, isn't it? An expert should make the decision. Why involve the entire team when most people know nothing about materials? What will they add to it?

Is there an acceptance issue involved? Only in the sense that the members of the team are probably concerned that the decision be a valid one, and if they know it has been made by an expert (and possibly reviewed by another expert), they are likely to be satisfied with it.

## When Acceptance Is Most Important

Now consider the case in which my friends and I are trying to decide where to have a dinner party. Even though there are merit issues, this is largely an acceptance issue. The only way to maximize the probability that everyone will accept the final decision is if each person has input to it. This means a consensus.

## When Merit and Acceptance Are Both Important

Finally, consider the situation in which both merit and acceptance are issues. This may, in fact, be the most typical case. Do we want a group to deal with expert issues that it knows nothing about? Certainly not. In this case, we want an expert to deal with the merit question. The expert should help people understand some of those issues and let them have input to implementation concerns. This is called the *consultative* approach.

Consider this example. A family wants to buy a new car. The wife is an automotive engineer, the husband is an artist, and the children are both boys, aged 15 and 17. Like their father, they tend to be artistic in their temperament, and what is important to them is that the car be *classy!* Their mother, on the other hand, wants to buy a car that has technical integrity, good economic performance, and serviceability, and she is much less concerned with the appearance of the car than they are.

Using the consultative approach, Mom selects several cars that she judges to be about equal, according to her technical merit criteria. The men can then choose the one that they like best, according to their artistic appearance criteria. Of course, if they hate all of Mom's selections, then more negotiating may have to take place.

To summarize, then, here are the rules for handling group decision making:

| When the issue is | The decision should be |
| --- | --- |
| M/A (largely merit) | Made by an expert |
| A/M (largely acceptance) | Made by consensus |
| A&M (combination of both) | Made by consultation |

## THE EFFECT OF TIME ON DECISION APPROACHES

If a decision must be made in a very short time, you can't afford long, drawn-out group discussions. For the M/A situation, there is no problem, as this is an autonomous decision anyway. It is the A/M and A&M cases that are the problem. For those decisions that would be normally made by consensus (A/M), the group would have to use some time-reducing strategy. Maybe people will all agree to flip a coin or draw choices from a hat or just vote, with majority rule being accepted. The same may be true for consultation (A&M), or the expert may make the choice and inform the group of the reasons for that choice.

## WHAT IS CONSENSUS?

One dictionary that I consulted defines consensus as "general agreement or majority will." I don't like the "majority will" connotation, because majority vote leads to trouble when you need the full support of the group. On the other hand, "general agreement" may be taken to mean that the entire group agrees on an issue. Naturally, this is virtually impossible to achieve when the issues are tough. So why not just vote—use majority rule? After all, isn't that the democratic way?

It may be, but it has its drawbacks. In project teams, you want all members to support decisions that affect them (else there is no acceptance issue), and voting often does not achieve this result. In fact, it may have quite an opposite effect. A school superintendent said to me once, "Now I understand why we always have problems. We regularly vote on important issues. Then I find, later in the school year, that some of my principals aren't supporting what was decided, and when I mention this, they say, 'Yes, but you remember, I didn't vote for it, either.'"

Exactly! When people don't vote *for* something, they feel no obligation to support it. Worse yet, they may continue to actively fight it, or look for opportunities to say, "I told you it was a dumb idea." Neither response is good for team camaraderie—or performance.

So if majority rule doesn't work, and it is impossible to get everyone to agree, then we're sunk. Is that it? Well, not necessarily. You just have to define consensus differently. You want all team members to be able to say, "While I don't entirely agree with the majority opinion, I hear you and understand your position. Furthermore, I think you've given me a fair hearing. And I can fully *support* the majority position." There is the key—the word *support*. If the person will support the majority position, that is often the best you can do.

Suppose, however, you have a team member who says, "Not only can I not agree with you, but I certainly am not willing to support you. I think it's a dumb idea." If you need this person's support, you definitely have a problem. What do you do?

There are four possibilities. One is to persuade the person that the majority position is correct. A second is to select another course of action that everyone can support. A third is to go the way the dissenter thinks is best. A fourth is to throw the person off the team. Each has a downside. Persuading the dissenter that the majority is correct may gain outward compliance without inner conviction. Or it may truly convince the person that the majority position is correct even when it

> There is the key—the word SUPPORT. If
> the person will support the majority
> position, that is often the best you can do.

is wrong. History is littered with examples of the majority being wrong. "Mob rule" is not a popular or positive term.

The second alternative is often a good one. Most of the problems that teams deal with have many possible solutions. If a choice can be made that everyone can live with—even though it is not the one preferred by the majority—then the situation is resolved in a way that gains the support of all team members. I know the argument can be made that the majority solution is the optimum one, so why cave in and implement a less effective approach just because one person is against it? My answer is: a less-than-optimum solution that can be made to work is better than an optimum one that may never see the light of day. Clearly, there is no way to say that this is always the best approach. Every situation is different and must be handled in context.

The third option, which is to go the way of the dissenter, has merit when the dissenter is suggesting an approach that may be a paradigm shift. Any new paradigm is likely to seem strange to most people. So if the dissenter is presenting a different paradigm, it is worth considering with an open mind.

The final option, kicking the dissenter off the team, should be regarded as a last resort. If you remove too many people from your team because they resist majority opinion, no one is going to want to join up. Sometimes, however, people are assigned to a project team who simply do not fit. In that case, especially if their full support and contributions are vital to the success of the group, you may have no choice but to take them off the team. This is a soul-searching step, one that should never be taken lightly. Instead, you must always "weigh the good of the many against the good of the one," as Spock said on *Star Trek*.

## AVOIDING FALSE CONSENSUS AND GROUPTHINK

### False Consensus

Remember the Abilene Paradox from Chapter 4? Jerry Harvey, a professor at George Washington University, told the story years ago to illustrate the false consensus effect (Harvey, 1988).

The story points out that the family drives 180 miles round-trip to Abilene for a mediocre lunch, when no one really wanted to go. They fell into the "silence-means-consent" trap.

Now for the important point. Harvey says it is tempting to see the situation as a failure to manage agreement, but *it is really a failure to manage disagreement!* If a poll had been taken on whether everyone really wanted to go, and if a climate existed in which people felt free to say no, then they would not have gone to Abilene.

> In false consensus, everyone agrees, because no one voices any dissent.

Note, however, that people operating in groups do not always feel free to express dissent. In some teams, a dissenter is called out for not being a team player, and is told "Don't rock the boat." Under those conditions, people learn to be very tentative in their opinions, feeling out the group before being willing to say what they *really think*. When *everyone* is playing the same game, it becomes very difficult to find out what anyone really thinks.

## Groupthink

Similar to false consensus is the phenomenon called *groupthink* by Irving Janis (Janis & Mann, 1977). This takes place when a group leader expresses a preference for a particular course of action and the group accepts it, regardless of its merits. Thomas Becket, Archbishop of Canterbury, was murdered in Canterbury Cathedral on December 29, 1170, after King Henry II was heard to remark: "Who

> **groupthink:** The acceptance by an entire group of a decision or course of action suggested by the leader, without questioning its merits.

will rid me of this meddlesome priest?" Henry later claimed that it was simply a complaint, an expression of frustration—so the story goes—but those who heard him took it as something he wanted carried out. Leaders who deliberately "think out loud" are sometimes unaware of their power to manufacture consensus.

Numerous incidents of groupthink have been written about in modern times. A prime example is Admiral Kimmel's suggestion to his staff that an intelligence report on the Japanese plan to bomb Pearl Harbor was a smokescreen. By the time the bombs were falling, it was too late.

There is a standard way of dealing with groups that will reduce the probability of either false consensus or groupthink happening in a team. This procedure was originally recommended by Irving Janis and Leon Mann (Janis and Mann, 1977).

1. The leader should carefully avoid expressing a preferred course of action in the initial stages of a group's discussion.

2. The group should be asked to offer options in a brainstorming fashion—that is, with no evaluation during the idea-generation phase.

3. Once evaluation begins, *all* members should be encouraged to play the role of critical evaluator—looking at the potential risks and consequences of a particular option, no matter who offered it as a possibility. Such criticism as is offered should deal with issues, not personalities. That is, an idea should never be labeled "dumb," or any other derogatory term, since this tends to attack the person who suggested it. Rather, the person should say, "I have a concern with this option for this reason," and then state the reason.

4. An attempt should be made to reach a consensus decision, using the rule above that everyone should be willing to support the majority position even if they don't totally agree with it.

5. If time permits, a final check should be made a day later, so that people have time to "sleep on it." If concerns occur to them overnight, they should bring them back to the group to consider.

It is clear that this procedure takes a lot of time, and so is reserved for critical issues only. It should not be used for routine decisions.

# 30

CHAPTER

# Developing Project Managers

## THE NEED FOR DEVELOPMENT

There seems to be a prevailing belief in the United States that if you are good at *doing* something, then you can manage other people doing that same work. Since 1981, when I entered the training and consulting business, I have talked to thousands of people who were put into management positions and given no training in how to manage. In fact, the same thing happened to me, and I know firsthand the fallacy of the implicit assumption.

I personally believe that this lack of skills is one of the major causes of project failure. So this chapter is intended to tell project managers what kinds of skills they need, and how to go about acquiring them.

## SKILLS NEEDED BY PROJECT MANAGERS

Following is a list of the primary areas of knowledge and/or skills needed by project managers. There may be other skills specific to the job, but these are the broad-based areas. For example, if you are doing contracting, you need to know the details of how contracts work in your area and how to administer them.

| | |
|---|---|
| Planning | Decision making |
| Problem solving | Conflict management |
| Goal setting | Data analysis |
| Negotiation skills | Leadership skills |
| Oral communications | Written communication |
| Interviewing | Coaching/counseling |
| Group dynamics | Team building |
| Quality function deployment | Listening skills |
| Total quality management | Scheduling methods |
| Concurrent engineering | Earned-value analysis |
| Time management | |

## WHAT IS MOST IMPORTANT?

I am frequently asked what skill is most important, and I have no hesitancy in answering, "People skills." A project manager who can't deal with people is going to have a lot of trouble. The director of a large construction group told me that he had to remove one of his project managers and put him in a job where he didn't have to work with people. The fellow knew construction. He knew how to plan. But he constantly made people angry, and the director was spending far too much of his own time smoothing ruffled feathers.

I am frequently asked what skill is most important, and I have no hesitancy in answering, "People skills."

As I said in Chapter 1, people skills are placed at the bottom of the pyramid representing a project management system simply because they are the foundation that holds up everything else. Nevertheless, these are undervalued by most organizations. Every year I teach about 40 three-day seminars in planning, scheduling, and control, and only about 4 in leading, managing, and facilitating project teams. It seems that companies still see no bottom-line relevance in these "soft skills," so they won't pay for their people to attend them.

Yet I don't believe I have ever seen a project fail because the project manager didn't know how to put together a PERT schedule. I *have* seen many projects get into serious trouble because of interpersonal issues. Perhaps one of these days managers will wake up and realize that people need training in this area, simply because the skills aren't being taught in schools.

## PERSONAL CHARACTERISTICS OF PROJECT MANAGERS

Over the years I have asked members of project teams what they expect of their project managers. Here are the responses I received:

| | |
|---|---|
| Good listener | Mutual ownership |
| Supportive | Buffer to rest of organization |
| Organized | Visible leadership |
| Clears roadblocks | Technical knowledge |
| Mutual respect | Fair |
| Team builder | Flexible |
| Knows own limitations | Open-minded |
| Sense of humor | Delegates |
| Gives feedback | Honest/trustworthy |
| Good decision maker | Understanding |
| Follows up | Challenges team to do well |
| Shares experience | Knows strengths/weaknesses of team members |

Clearly, this list is a tall order for any one individual to fill. My suggestion is that you take stock. Be aware of the need to have other members of your team support you in the areas you feel are weaker than others.

### Thinking Styles

No doubt, everyone has heard about left-brain, right-brain orientations in thinking. Left-brain thinkers are more analytical, logical, and sequential in their thinking than are right-brain thinkers. These folks are more parallel thinking, intuitive, and global.

In his studies of how people think, Ned Herrmann (1995) found that the left-right dichotomy did not go far enough to explain thinking differences, and he postulated another axis based on cerebral-limbic thinking. When this dimension is added, four quadrants emerge to yield four different thinking styles.

The instrument that measures these styles is the Herrmann Brain Dominance Instrument (HBDI), and the respondent receives a profile like the one shown in Figure 30.1. In this profile, scores range from 1 (most preferred) to 3 (least preferred). There is no such thing as a 0 score, since everyone uses all four styles to some degree. Note also that the instrument measures *preferences,* not skills or abilities. Herrmann believed that the preference for a way of thinking

**F I G U R E  30.1**

HBDI Profile of Thinking Styles

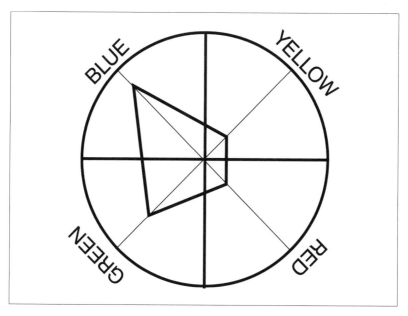

was based on brain chemistry or genetics. Whether this is true or not, the preferences are very real. To date, more than 1 million people have taken the HBDI, and most find that the measures represent them fairly well. Seldom does anyone say, "That's just not me!"

People with strong quadrant A preferences tend to be very logical, analytical, technical, mathematical, and problem solving in orientation. They are attracted to tasks and jobs that allow them to think in these ways. Engineers, financial analysts, and others tend to cluster in this quadrant.

The B quadrant involves thinking in organizational, administrative, conservative, controlled, and planning ways. People who have a preference for this thinking style are often managers, administrative assistants, and so on.

C quadrant thinkers have an interpersonal, emotional, musical, spiritual, and talker orientation. Many of them become teachers, counselors, and other human services workers.

Finally, people who endorse the D quadrant prefer artistic, holistic, imaginative, synthesizing, and conceptualizing ways of thinking. This is clearly the quadrant for creative types—artists, sculptors, and so on. People who tend toward AB preferences see D quadrant thinkers as a bit "flaky," as not having their feet planted firmly on the ground.

Is there a *best* profile? No.

Is there a best profile for a specific job? Perhaps.

The HBDI is an excellent instrument for counseling individuals about career choices, and it is administered only under the guidance of a certified practitioner.[1] The profile is accompanied by a write-up on the meaning of the results,

---

[1] The HBDI is available on the Lewis Institute Web site at www.lewisinstitute.com. We are beginning a study at the institute to determine how various profiles affect performance in project management. Check our Web site for periodic updates on the results. If your organization would be interested in participating in the study, you can contact us at the Web site.

and is best reviewed with the practitioner by phone or in person. However, the Herrmann group stresses strongly that the HBDI was not designed as a selection instrument, and cautions against using it for that purpose unless the inventory is validated by a skilled psychometrician.

One application of the HBDI that is now well documented is its use in putting together teams. A team should collectively represent a "whole brain," meaning that if you overlay the profiles of all members of the team, they will form a composite profile that shows preferences in all four quadrants. If a team is "out of balance"—if it has a strong aversion to one of the quadrants—issues requiring thinking in that area may not be handled very well.

## NONCREDIT TRAINING IN PROJECT MANAGEMENT

Many individuals, universities, and other organizations offer seminars and workshops in project management. These range from one-day to week-long sessions. The one-day programs are limited to an overview of project management, and most participants come away with only a conceptual understanding upon completion of the course. It takes at least three days to cover the fundamentals of planning, scheduling, and control in enough depth that students can apply what they have learned. Programs are best when they contain some group and individual exercises, which permit students to test their understanding of principles through application to a classroom problem. In addition, case studies are helpful for allowing group discussion and for testing the application of principles in hypothetical situations.

Many project management programs offer a certificate in project management. Following is the curriculum offered by the Lewis Institute, and it is representative of those provided by most schools. Contact the short-course or continuing-education department at your local university to find out if it offers such programs.

## Project Management: Tools, Principles, Practices

This course provides the necessary skills to plan, schedule, and control projects of all kinds. Tools provided include work breakdown structures, critical path/PERT scheduling, earned-value analysis, and much more.

## How to Lead, Manage, and Facilitate Project Teams

The missing area for many project managers, this program fills the gap, offering practical skills for dealing with the "people problems" that cause many projects to fail.

## How to Manage Risks and Contracts

These are major sources of difficulties for project managers in all kinds of projects. This program provides guidance in how to handle all aspects of these two subject areas.

## How to Communicate, Influence, and Negotiate Effectively

Project managers are universally faced with a basic problem—they have considerable responsibility and little authority. This program will enable managers to get things done even when they have no authority!

## Project Simulation Workshop

This three-day workshop allows new and experienced project managers to practice their skills in a safe environment. The class is divided into four teams, each of which has to plan, schedule, and build part of a diorama. The instructors assist each team in scheduling its subproject with Microsoft Project software, and the construction phase is given over to tracking and progress reporting, so that actuals can be compared with estimates. This is the ideal way to learn by doing.

For people taking these courses over the Web, the simulation workshop is replaced with a capstone project, in which students manage a real project and submit their documentation to the instructor for review. This is, of course, the ultimate learn-by-doing approach.

## FOREIGN LANGUAGE TRAINING

For project managers who are involved in international work, learning a second language may be necessary. There are basically two approaches: classroom and self-learning. Classroom programs usually involve intense "doses" of training over perhaps a one-month period. While they are effective, they are also expensive, typically costing in the thousands of dollars.

Self-learning programs rely on language tapes or records. A number of providers exist, and if you have the self-discipline, this method works. However, most programs rely on rote learning through "overlearning," as it is called, which means that you repeat, repeat, repeat, ad nauseam.

A much more effective approach was developed by Dr. Paul Pimsleur. He based his method on a principle from learning theory, which is that learning is more effective if a stimulus is presented to the learner at *unequal intervals*, rather than equal ones. Dr. Pimsleur developed his courses using this method, which he called *graduated interval recall*. As it turns out, the most effective approach is to present the stimulus in intervals of 2, 4, 8, 16, 256 time units. So, for example, if you were trying to learn how to say "potato" in German, you would be presented with the German word, which is *kartoffel*. About two minutes later, the instructor would ask, "Do you remember how to say 'potato' in German?" You would be given a chance to respond, and regardless of whether you got it right, the native speaker would say the word *kartoffel*, which would either verify your correct response or provide a memory jogger for you. Then about four minutes later, the same steps would be repeated. This would be done again in eight minutes, then sixteen, and again on a later tape, so that by the time you have had the stimulus word presented at least five times, in graduated intervals, it has gone from short-term memory to long-term memory. In other words, you know the word for potato now.

What this means is that the method makes learning virtually painless. You can work on the language in your car, on a plane, etc., because the instructions are given in your native language, making a book unnecessary. (In fact, a book is undesirable. A language is auditory, not visual, and it is far more effective to learn entirely through the ears than through the eyes. Once you can speak the language, reading and writing are easily mastered.) See the Pimsleur entry in "Resources."

## PUTTING IT ALL TO WORK ON THE JOB

Developing one's skills and abilities is a lifelong process. The process is most effective when it is self-directed and proactive. Learning by simply behaving like a sponge is not the most effective strategy for an adult. Rather, an active, seeking-out method has been found to be the best.

There is one barrier to learning new behavioral skills: the reaction of your employees. If you start managing them differently, they are going to feel uncomfortable, because they can no longer predict you. To deal with their discomfort, they will try to pull you back into the old patterns.

In order to minimize the impact of your own subordinates on your new behavior, it helps to discuss with them the changes you want to make. This will keep them from experiencing such an abrupt change in your behavior. Ask for their support and suggest that they discuss their feelings with you when they notice new behavior on your part. One of the best ways to neutralize resistance is to talk about it!

As a method of developing your skills in project management, the following procedure will help you deal with ongoing self-development.

- Identify the skill(s) you wish to improve or acquire
- Assess your current level of ability using the scale below—draw a *circle* around the number that represents your **present** level of skill:

| Absent | Low | Moderate | High | Very High |
|:------:|:---:|:--------:|:----:|:---------:|
| 0 | 1 | 2 | 3 | 4 |

- Decide what level you **want** the skill to be, and draw a *box* around the level on the scale above
- List some of the resources available to help you improve your skills in the area identified
- Engage in the learning experience you identified above
- Reassess your skills to determine if the learning objective was met

# RESOURCES AND REFERENCES

# CHECKLISTS FOR MANAGING PROJECTS

## PROJECT PLANNING

1. A problem statement has been written for the project.
2. The project mission has been communicated to all participants.
3. Risks have been identified and contingencies developed when possible.
4. Project strategy has been tested for $P, C, T, S$ feasibility.
5. Force-field analysis is satisfactory.
6. Consequences have been analyzed and are acceptable.
7. The ultimate purpose of the project is understood by all team members.
8. At least one of the $P, C, T, S$ variables is estimated, rather than all four being dictated.
9. Clear definition(s) of project performance requirements exist.
10. Adequate criteria exist for measuring achievement of performance targets.

11. The work breakdown structure has been developed to levels sufficient to permit estimates of cost, time, and resource requirements at desired accuracy.

12. The WBS has been reviewed with

   ◆ Client

   ◆ Contributors

   ◆ Senior management

13. Schedule milestones have been established with planned reviews.

14. A task-level schedule has been developed against the WBS in network form.

15. The critical path has been identified.

16. The critical path allows the required end date to be met.

17. The critical path has been examined to determine if it is realistic.

18. A Gantt chart has been developed to be used as a working tool.

19. Resource allocation has been checked to ensure that no one is overloaded.

20. Resources are not allocated at more than 80 percent productivity.

21. Resource conflicts with other projects have been eliminated or resolved.

22. The control system has been designed.

23. Measures of progress have been established.

24. People who must implement the project plan participated in preparing it.

25. The plan is at the right level of detail (neither too much nor too little).

26. Estimates are based on recorded data for similar tasks when possible.

27. Padding of estimates has been done aboveboard.
28. Padding is acceptable to management.
29. The project plan has been reviewed in a sign-off meeting.
30. The project notebook has been signed off by all stakeholders.
31. Concerns raised in the sign-off meeting have been addressed to the satisfaction of everyone.
32. The plan contains the following:

    ◆ Problem statement

    ◆ Mission statement

    ◆ Project strategy

    ◆ Project objectives

    ◆ QFD analysis or other means of identifying customer needs

    ◆ SWOT analysis

    ◆ Statement of project scope

    ◆ List of deliverables and other contractual requirements

    ◆ End-item specifications to be met

    ◆ A work breakdown structure

    ◆ Both milestone and task-level schedules

    ◆ Resource requirements

    ◆ Control system, including change control procedures

    ◆ Major contributors in the form of a linear responsibility chart

    ◆ Risk analysis with contingencies

    ◆ Statements of work as required

33. Resource allocations include deductions for vacations, holidays, sick leave, and so on.

34. Cost estimates include travel and living expenses as required.

35. Costs for project security are included as appropriate.

36. Plans include time for reviews, meetings, approvals, and so on.

37. All physical facilities are expected to be available.

38. Testing facilities are adequate.

39. Steps have been taken to ensure availability of new hires as required.

40. All project team members are qualified for their work.

41. Any required training of team members has been budgeted and provided for.

42. Any political problems that could affect this project have been identified and can be handled.

43. Arrangements have been made to promote free and open communication among all members of the team.

44. Members have been collocated as necessary to facilitate communication. When physical collocation is not possible, *virtual* collocation has been arranged.

45. Vendors have been required to submit their own project plans to ensure that all deliveries can be met.

46. Boundaries have been preestablished for change control.

47. The system has provided that all project revisions be distributed to all appropriate individuals/departments/parties.

48. Chart-of-account numbers have been set up for all project work.

**49.** Schedules and charts of accounts are traceable to the work breakdown structure.

**50.** Unbudgeted project expenditures must be approved by the project manager.

**51.** Functional managers must inform the project manager before reassigning personnel to other jobs.

**52.** Critical ratios have been established to aid project monitoring.

**53.** A system is in place to revise the project budget both upward and downward when appropriate.

**54.** All team members have personal plans for conducting their part of the project work.

**55.** Variance limits have been established for all contributors.

**56.** Bonus/penalty arrangements have been applied to vendors as needed.

**57.** A vendor certification program is followed to ensure vendor capability.

**58.** Critical future events have been evaluated for project impact.

**59.** Resource usage has been smoothed as much as possible.

**60.** The initial plan does not require significant overtime to meet initial schedule dates.

**61.** All deliverables (schedules, reports, etc.) have been identified for each milestone.

**62.** Performance specs have been written and agreed upon by all stakeholders.

**63.** Government regulations (and others) have been identified and cited in the project plan.

64. For product design projects, representatives from manufacturing have been included on the team.

65. The *real* customer has been consulted in order to pin down requirements.

66. SWOT analysis is based on data, rather than strictly personal biases or other subjective factors.

67. Team members have been selected whose individual needs will be met through participation in the project (when possible).

68. A project termination procedure has been developed.

69. Team members have been convinced of the value of the project goals.

70. Controls are not so rigid that they stifle innovation.

71. Project planning has been based on reviews of previous records for similar programs.

72. Unique physical resources (such as test equipment) have been entered into the schedule so bottlenecks can be spotted.

73. Required resources that do not yet exist have been identified as risks to project success.

74. Roles and responsibilities of each team member have been clearly defined.

75. Procedures for doing work have been developed by participants and approved by managers.

76. No performance specifications greater than required have been asked for.

77. Tasks with durations greater than four to six weeks have been subdivided to avoid back-end loading.

78. Parallel critical paths have been eliminated when possible.

79. Network diagrams have been checked for logic violations.

80. Functional managers in matrix projects have resource-loading diagrams to support their ability to staff projects.

81. Projects that span long periods have been budgeted to account for inflation.

82. Exit criteria have been established to define completion of each project phase.

## PROJECT EXECUTION

1. Meetings are scheduled on a regular basis to review progress.

2. An auditor has been assigned for all audits.

3. Estimates of progress on nonquantifiable work are checked by an independent party.

4. Estimates of work remaining are not just linear projections—unless those can be justified.

5. Causes of delays and other problems have been explained in progress reports and documented in the project notebook.

6. Impact of scope changes has been explained to stakeholders and approved.

7. Impact of unexpected resource shortages has been computed and explained.

8. All team members have been trained in earned-value analysis.

9. Meetings have been scheduled for the project team to look at improving its work processes.

10. Transfer or termination of a team member has been coordinated with his or her replacement.

11. When coordination is impossible, the predecessor has left written instructions for his or her successor.

12. Progress reports show "red flags" for situations that are expected to have serious impact on project performance.

13. Monitoring of outside vendors is periodic.

14. Progress payments to vendors are based on earned-value analysis.

15. Team reviews are facilitated by an independent party.

16. Action plans are in place to address the outcomes of team review meetings.

17. Action assignments have been made to follow up team meetings.

18. Time worked is logged daily by contributors to the project.

19. All hours worked on a project are tracked back to the project, including nonpaid overtime hours.

20. Competition is kept to a minimum within the project team.

21. When concurrent engineering or concurrent project management is applied, frequent coordination meetings are held to keep everyone informed.

22. Corrective action for off-target tasks has been developed and approved.

23. Progress reports are distributed in appropriate increments.

24. The expression "If it ain't broke, don't fix it" is repeatedly challenged.

25. There are no penalties for performance that is better than the plan.

26. A climate of open discussion and inquiry exists in the project team.

27. Team members are encouraged to provide "early warnings" about developing problems.

28. The project manager keeps *all* team members as fully informed as possible.

29. Decisions are made at the lowest possible level in the project.

30. Consensus decisions are made when appropriate, but not *every* time a decision is required.

31. A structured problem-solving approach is employed.

32. Taguchi methods are applied in design projects.

33. Functional managers are kept informed of changes that may impact them.

34. When the project is a disaster, the project manager has a current résumé ready.

35. When no contingency exists for a risky task, precautions are taken to minimize the risk.

36. Critical path activities are managed so that they complete *at least* on time, and earlier if possible.

37. Tasks with float are completed at the earliest times possible. Float is reserved to handle unforeseen problems.

38. Memos to team members require RSVP to ensure that they were received.

39. Deliverables are used as milestone measures.

40. Actual project costs compare well with planned costs.

41. Personnel problems (absenteeism, turnover, etc.) are addressed in a positive way, rather than being ignored.

42. Decisions made by the project manager are accepted without complaint.

43. Morale in the team seems to be good.

44. Change procedures are being followed.

45. The customer is involved and aware of project status.

46. Upper management is aware of project status.

## SOFTWARE QUALITY

1. All next-in-line parties have been involved in planning the project to ensure that their needs will be met.
2. When appropriate, privacy, security, and audit matters have been taken into account in the design.
3. Adequate plans have been developed to ensure that the architecture of the system is correct.
4. Testing has been assigned to an independent test group for objectivity.
5. Technical standards (for design, coding, etc.) are being followed.
6. The documentation is complete, understandable, and accurate, as certified by an independent auditor.
7. Primary deliverables are of satisfactory quality.
8. Deliverables meet customer requirements, as certified by the customer.

## PROJECT CHANGE PROCEDURE

1. There is a documented change procedure for the project.
2. Provision is made for handling requests for clarification and interpretation of existing documents.
3. Change requests are approved by the appropriate parties, with complete visibility by the project manager.
4. All change requests are evaluated for project impact, and stakeholders are informed of the impact before a change is approved.
5. Resources allocated to the project are changed as necessary to accommodate project changes.
6. All changes are documented and stored in the project notebook.

## SOFTWARE INSTALLATION AND CONVERSION

1. Conversions are audited by an independent party to ensure quality.
2. An adequate recovery system exists in case data are lost during conversion.
3. Plans exist for maintenance of the new system.
4. Installation has been planned to have minimum impact on users.
5. New equipment and supplies required for the conversion have been identified and ordered.
6. Installation plans have been developed for new equipment.
7. A training program has been developed to ensure user capability with the new system.
8. A fall-back plan is in place in the event of conversion problems.
9. Arrangements have been made with outside service providers to ensure an on-time conversion.

## WORKING CONDITIONS

1. Adequate work space has been provided for all team members.
2. Lighting, temperature control, noise level, privacy, and safety issues have been addressed.
3. Adequate storage space exists.
4. A conference facility exists for team meetings.
5. Clerical support has been provided at adequate levels.
6. Provision has been made to stock adequate supplies.

# RESOURCES FOR PROJECT MANAGERS

## ASSOCIATIONS

Following is a listing of some of the professional associations that may be of interest to project managers. Contact information is provided. No endorsement is offered as to whether a source is worthwhile.

**American Management Association**
135 West 50th Street
New York, NY 10020
Tel: 212-586-8100

**American Society for Training and Development**
1630 Duke Street
Alexandria, VA 22313
Tel: 703-683-8100

**Engineering Management Society of**
**Institute of Electrical and Electronic Engineers**
345 East 47th Street
New York, NY 10017-2366
Tel: 212-705-7900

**Internet**
Secretariat
Internet/CRB Switzerland
Zentralstrasse 153
Zurick CH 8003 Switzerland

**National Management Association**
2210 Arbor Boulevard
Dayton, OH 45439-1580
Tel: 513-294-0421

**Project Management Institute**
Four Campus Boulevard
Newtown Square, PA 19073-3299
Tel: 610-356-4600
FAX: 610-356-4647
Internet: www.pmi.org

## MAGAZINES AND JOURNALS

*La Cible: Le Journal du management de projet*
Association Francophone de Management de Projet
3, rue Françoise 75001 Paris
Tel: 42-36-36-37
FAX: 42-36-36-35

*CrossTALK: The Journal of Defense Software Engineering*
A free journal available at www.STSC.Hill.AF.Mil/

*Finnish Project Management Journal*
Editor-in-Chief, Associate Professor Karlos Artto
Helsinki University of Technology
P.O. Box 9500
02015 HUT, Finland
Tel: 358-9451-4751
FAX: 358-9451-3665
Internet: Karlos.Artto@hut.fi

### *International Journal of Project Management*
Elsevier Science Ltd.
The Boulevard
Langford Lane Kidlington
Oxford OX5 1GB
Tel: 44 (0) 1865 843 010
e-mail: cdhelp@elsevier.co.uk

### *Project Management Journal*
### *and PMNETwork*
Project Management Institute Communications Office
323 West Main Street
Sylva, NC 28779 USA
Tel: 704-586-3715
e-mail: pmnetwork@aol.com

## NEWSLETTERS

### *ALLPM Today!*
Internet: www.ALPM.com
A free project management services vendor newsletter of
ALL project management, an Internet Project Management
resource center.

### *Project News*
Balcombe Associates
Freepost (HR140)
Dilwyn, Herefordshire
Tel: 44 (0) 1544-388 848
FAX: 44 (0) 1544-388 400
e-mail: balcombe@pnews.kc3ltd.co.uk

### *Successful Project Management*
Management Concepts
Internet: www.mgmtconcepts.com

## WEB SITES OF INTEREST

Because the Web is growing exponentially, any listing is out of date almost before it reaches publication. These addresses should get you started, and provide links to other sites of interest. All Web addresses begin with http://www.

    pmforum.org
    lewisinstitute.com
    pmi.org

## OTHER ORGANIZATIONS

Following is a list of sources of information, books, and professional associations that may be helpful in managing projects. Not all are specifically aimed at project management, but you may find them helpful.

### Air Academy Press, LLC
Steve Schmidt
1155 Kelly Johnson Boulevard, Ste. 105
Colorado Springs, CO 80920
Tel: 719-531-0777  FAX: 719-531-0778
This group offers a *very practical* seminar on design of experiments, as well as training in statistical process control. The materials are first-class.

### The Business Reader
P.O. Box 41268
Brecksville, OH 44141
Tel: 216-838-8653
FAX: 216-838-8104
A mail-order bookstore specializing in business books. If it's on business, the chances are it's here.

## CRM Films
2215 Faraday Avenue
Carlsbad, CA 92008
Tel: 800-421-0833
A good source of films for training, including *Mining Group Gold, The Abilene Paradox,* and many others.

## The Lewis Institute, Inc.
302 Chestnut Mountain Drive
Vinton, VA 24179
Tel: 540-345-7850
FAX: 540-345-7844
e-mail: jlewis@lewisinstitute.com
LII offers a certificate series in project management, together with courses for project team members. Related courses are also available.

## MindWare
6142 Olson Memorial Highway
Golden Valley, MN 55422
Tel. 800-999-0398
FAX: 612-595-8852
The store for the other 90 percent of your brain, with an attractive catalog listing. A source of tools, books, and other materials to enhance learning and creativity in organizations.

## Pegasus Communications
P.O. Box 943
Oxford, OH 45056-0943
Tel: 800-636-3796
FAX: 905-764-7983
Publishers of *The Systems Thinker,* a monthly newsletter, as well as videos by Russell Ackoff and Peter Senge, among others.

**Pimsleur International**
30 Monument Square
Concord, MA 01742
Tel: 800-658-8989
Producers of foreign language training tapes based on the
Pimsleur method.

## FORMS FOR MANAGING PROJECTS

A number of forms for managing projects are available online
at www.lewisinstitute.com. These can be downloaded in pdf
format or in Word and WordPerfect format. Some spread-
sheets are also available.

# GLOSSARY

## A GLOSSARY OF PROJECT MANAGEMENT TERMS

**activity**   The work or effort needed to achieve a result. It consumes time and usually consumes resources.

**activity description**   A statement specifying what must be done to achieve a desired result.

**activity-on-arrow**   A network diagram showing sequence of activities, in which each activity is represented by an arrow, with a circle representing an **event** at each end.

**activity-on-node**   A network diagram showing sequence of activities, in which each activity is represented by a box or circle (that is, a **node**) interconnected with arrows to show precedence of work.

**authority**   The legitimate power given to a person in an organization to use resources to reach an objective and to exercise discipline.

**backward-pass calculation**   Working backward through a network from the latest event to the beginning event to calculate event late times. Cf. **forward-pass calculation**.

**calendars**   The arrangement of normal working days, together with nonworking days (holidays, vacations, etc.) and special work days (overtime periods), used to determine dates on which project work will be completed.

**change order**   A document that authorizes a change in some aspect of a project.

**control**   The practice of monitoring progress against a plan so that corrective steps can be taken when a deviation from plan occurs.

**CPM**   acronym for **critical path** method. A network diagraming method that shows the longest series of activities in a project, thereby determining the earliest completion time for the project.

**crashing**   An attempt to reduce activity or total project duration, usually by adding resources.

**critical path**   The longest sequential path of activities that are absolutely essential for completion of the project.

**dependency**   A relationship in which the next task or group of tasks cannot begin until preceding work has been completed.

**deviation**   Any variation from planned performance. The deviation can be in terms of schedule, cost, performance, or **scope** of work. Deviation analysis is the heart of exercising project control.

**dummy activity**   A zero-duration element in a network showing a logic linkage. A dummy does not consume time or resources, but simply indicates precedence.

**duration**   The time it takes to complete an activity.

**earliest finish**   The earliest time that an activity can be completed.

**earliest start**   The earliest time that an activity can be started.

**estimate**   A forecast or guess about how long an activity will take, how many resources will be required, or how much it will cost.

**event**  A point in time. cf. **activity.** An event is binary—either achieved or not—whereas an activity can be partially complete. An event can be the start or finish of an activity.

**feedback**  Information derived from observation of project activities that is used to analyze the status of the job and take corrective action if necessary.

**float**  A measure of how much an activity can be delayed before it begins to affect the project finish date.

**forward-pass calculation**  Determining the **earliest start** time for each activity in a network diagram. cf. **backward-pass calculation.**

**free float**  The amount of time that an activity can be delayed without affecting succeeding activities.

**Gantt chart**  A bar chart that indicates the time required to complete each activity in a project. It is named for Henry L. Gantt, who developed a complete notational system for displaying progress with bar charts.

**hammock activity**  A single activity that actually represents a group of activities. It "hangs" between two events and is used to report progress on the composite that it represents. See also **activity; event.**

**histogram**  A vertical bar chart, typically showing **resource allocation** levels over time in a project.

**i-j notation**  A system of numbering each **node** in an **activity-on-arrow** network. The i-node is always the beginning of an activity, while the j-node is always the finish.

**inexcusable delays**  Project delays that are attributable to negligence on the part of the contractor and that may incur penalty payments.

**latest finish**  The latest time that an activity can be finished without extending the end date for a project.

**latest start**   The latest time that an activity can start without extending the end date for a project.

**learning curve**   The time it takes people to learn an activity well enough to achieve optimum performance. The learning curve must be factored into estimates of activity durations in order to achieve planned completion dates.

**leveling**   An attempt to smooth the use of resources, whether people, materials, or equipment, to avoid large peaks and valleys in their usage.

**life cycle**   The phases that a project goes through from concept to completion. The nature of the project changes during each phase.

**matrix organization**   A method of drawing people from functional departments within an organization for assignment to a project team, but without removing them from their physical location. The project manager in such a structure is said to have *dotted-line* **authority** over team members.

**milestone**   An event of special importance, usually representing the completion of a major phase of project work. Reviews are often scheduled at milestones.

**most likely time**   The most realistic time estimate for completing an activity under normal conditions.

**negative float or slack**   A condition in a network in which the *earliest time* for an event is actually later than its *latest time*. Also called *slack*. This happens when the project has a constrained end date, which is earlier than can be achieved, or when an activity uses up its float and is still delayed.

**node**   An **event** in a network.

**PERT**   Acronym for program evaluation and review technique. PERT makes use of network diagrams, as does **CPM**, but in addition applies statistics to activities to estimate the probabilities of completion of project work.

**pessimistic time**   Roughly speaking, the *worst-case* time to complete an activity. The term has a more precise meaning as defined in the **PERT** literature.

**phase**   A major component or segment of a project.

**precedence diagram**   See **activity-on-node**.

**queue**   Waiting time.

**resource allocation**   The assignment of people, equipment, facilities, or materials to a project. Unless adequate resources are provided, project work cannot be completed on schedule, and resource allocation is a significant component of project scheduling.

**resource pool**   A group of people who can generally do the same work, so that they can be chosen randomly for assignment to a project.

**risk**   The possibility that something can go wrong and interfere with the completion of project work.

**scope**   The magnitude of work that must be done to complete a project.

**statement of work**   A description of work to be performed.

**subproject**   A small project within a larger one.

**time now**   The current calendar date from which a network analysis, report, or update is being made.

**time standard**   The time allowed for the completion of a task.

**variance**   Any deviation of project work from what was planned. Variance can be around costs, time, performance, or project **scope**.

**work breakdown structure**   A method of subdividing work into smaller and smaller increments to permit accurate estimates of durations, resource requirements, and costs.

# REFERENCES AND SUGGESTED READING

Ackoff, Russell. *Ackoff's Fables: Irreverent Reflections on Business and Bureaucracy.* New York: Wiley, 1991.

Ackoff, Russell. *The Art of Problem Solving.* New York: Wiley, 1978.

Ackoff, Russell. *Creating the Corporate Future.* New York: Wiley, 1981.

Ackoff, Russell. *The Democratic Corporation.* New York: Oxford University Press, 1994.

Adams, James L. *Conceptual Blockbusting: A Guide to Better Ideas,* 2d ed. New York: W. W. Norton, 1979.

Adams, John D. (Editor) *Transforming Leadership: from Vision to Results.* Alexandria, VA: Miles River Press, 1986.

Adler, Nancy J. *International Dimensions of Organization Behavior.* Cincinnati, Ohio: South Western.

Ailes, Roger. *You Are the Message: Secrets of the Master Communicators.* Homewood, IL: Dow Jones-Irwin, 1988.

Albrecht, Karl. *The Northbound Train.* New York: AMACOM, 1994.

Archibald, R. D., and R. L. Villoria *Network-Based Management Systems (Pert/cpm).* New York: Wiley, 1967.

Argyris, Chris. *Overcoming Organizational Defenses: Facilitating Organizational Learning.* Boston: Allyn and Bacon, 1990.

Axelrod, Robert. *The Evolution of Cooperation*. New York: Basic Books, 1984.

Barker, Joel A. *Future Edge*. New York: William Morrow, 1992.

Barker, Joel A. *Wealth, Innovation & Diversity*. Videotape. Carlsbad, CA: CRM Learning, 2000.

Bauer, Eugene E. *Boeing: The First Century*. Enumclaw, Washington: TABA Publishing, 2000.

Bedi, Hari. *Understanding the Asian Manager*. Singapore: Heinemann Asia, 1992.

Beer, Stafford. *Brain of the Firm*, 2d ed. New York: Wiley, 1981.

Bennis, Warren G. *Managing the Dream: Reflections on Leadership and Change*. Cambridge, MA: Perseus, 2000.

Bennis, Warren G., and Burt Nanus *Leaders: The Strategies for Taking Charge*. New York: Harper & Row, 1985.

Benveniste, Guy. *Mastering the Politics of Planning*. San Francisco: Jossey-Bass, 1989.

Barnhart, Robert K. *The Barnhart Concise Dictionary of Etymology: The Origins of American English Words*. New York: Harper Collins, 1995.

Blanchard, Benjamin S. *Engineering Organization and Management*. Englewood Cliffs, NJ: Prentice-Hall, 1976.

Blake, Robert, and Jane Mouton. *The Managerial Grid*. Houston: Gulf Publishing, 1964.

Block, Peter. *The Empowered Manager*, 2nd ed. San Francisco: Jossey-Bass, 2000.

Bodanis, David. *E=mc²: A Biography of the World's Most Famous Equation*. New York: Walker & Company, 2000.

Brooks, F. P. *The Mythical Man-Month: Essays on Software Engineering*. Reading, MA: Addison-Wesley, 1975.

Bunker, Barbara Benedict, and Billie T. Alban. *Large Group Interventions: Engaging the Whole System for Rapid Change.* San Francisco: Jossey-Bass, 1997.

Burns, James McGregor. *Leadership.* New York: Harper & Row, 1978.

Buzan, Tony. *The Mind Map Book.* New York: NAL/Dutton, 1996.

Carlzon, Jan. *Moments of Truth.* New York: Perennial, 1987.

Chen, Yanping, and Francis N. Arko. *Principles of Contracting for Project Management.* Arlington, VA: UMT Press, 2003

Cialdini, Robert B. *Influence: The Power of Persuasion,* revised edition. New York: Quill, 1993.

Cleland, David I., and William R. King, Editors. *Project Management Handbook.* New York: Van Nostrand Reinhold, 1983.

Covey, Stephen. *The 7 Habits of Highly Effective People.* New York: Fireside Books, 1989.

Crosby, Philip. *Quality Is Free.* East Rutherford, NJ: Signet, 1980.

de Bono, Edward. *New Think.* New York: Avon Books, 1971.

de Bono, Edward. *Serious Creativity.* New York: Harper, 1992.

de Bono, Edward. *Six Thinking Hats.* Boston: Little, Brown & Co., 1985.

Deming, Edwards. *Out of the Crisis.* Cambridge, MA: Massachusetts Institute of Technology, 1986.

Dimancescu, Dan. *The Seamless Enterprise: Making Cross Functional Management Work.* New York: Harper, 1992.

Downs, Alan. *Corporate Executions: The Ugly Truth About Layoffs: How Corporate Greed Is Shattering Lives, Companies, and Communities.* New York: AMACOM, 1995.

Drucker, Peter F. *Management: Tasks, Responsibilities, Practices.* New York: Harper & Row, 1973, 1974.

Dyer, Wayne. *You'll See It When You Believe It.* New York: Avon Books, 1989.

Eisenstein, Paul A. "How Toyota's Kentucky Operations Mix People, Processes to Be Best." *Investor's Business Daily,* 12/4/2000.

Fleming, Q. W. *Cost/Schedule Control Systems Criteria.* Chicago: Probus, 1988.

Fleming, Quentin W., and Joel M. Koppelman. *Earned Value Project Management.* Upper Darbey, PA: Project Management Institute, 1996.

Fortune, Joyce, and Geoff Peters. *Learning from Failure: The Systems Approach.* Chichester, England: Wiley, 1998.

Frame, J. Davidson. *Managing Projects in Organizations.* San Francisco: Jossey-Bass, 1995.

Frame, J. Davidson. *The New Project Management,* 2d ed. San Francisco: Jossey-Bass, 2002.

Frame, J. Davidson. *Project Finance: Tools and Techniques.* Arlington, VA: UMT Press, 2003.

Frankl, Viktor. *Man's Search for Meaning,* 3d ed. New York: Touchstone, 1984.

Freiberg, Kevin, and Jackie Freiberg. *Nuts! Southwest Airlines' Crazy Recipe for Business and Personal Success.* New York: Broadway Books, 1996.

Gardner, Howard. *Frames of Mind: The Theory of Multiple Intelligences.* New York: Basic Books, 1993.

Garten, Jeffrey E. *The Mind of the CEO.* New York: Basic Books, 2001.

Gause, Donald, and Gerald Weinberg. *Exploring Requirements: Quality Before Design.* New York: Dorset House Publishing, 1989.

George, Michael. *Lean Six Sigma: Combining Six Sigma Quality with Lean Production Speed.* New York: McGraw-Hill, 2002.

George, Michael. *Lean Six Sigma for Service.* New York: McGraw-Hill, 2003.

Goldratt, Eliyahu M. *Critical Chain.* Great Barrington, MA: The North River Press, 1997.

Graham, Robert J. and Randall L. Englund, *Creating an Environment for Successful Projects.* San Francisco: Jossey-Bass, 1997.

Hammer, Michael, and James Champy. *Reengineering the Corporation.* New York: Harper Business, 1993.

Hancock, Graham. *Fingerprints of the Gods.* New York: Crown, 1995.

Harry, Mikel, and Richard Schroeder. *Six Sigma: The Breakthrough Management Strategy Revolutionizing the World's Top Corporations.* New York: Currency, 2000.

Harvey, Jerry B. *The Abilene Paradox: And Other Meditations on Management.* San Diego: University Associates, 1988.

Heller, Robert. *Achieving Excellence.* New York: DK Publishing, 1999.

Heller, Robert, and Tim Hindle. *Essential Manager's Manual.* New York: DK Publishing, 1998.

Herrmann, Ned. *The Creative Brain.* Lake Lure, NC: Brain Books, 1995.

Herrmann, Ned. *The Whole Brain Business Book.* New York: McGraw-Hill, 1996.

Hersey, Paul, and Kenneth Blanchard. *Management of Organizational Behavior: Utilizing Human Resources,* 4th ed. Englewood Cliffs, NJ: Prentice Hall, 1981.

Hiebeler, Robert, Thomas Kelly, and Charles Ketteman. *Best Practices: Building Your Business with Customer-Focused Solutions.* New York: Simon and Schuster, 1998.

Highsmith, III, James A. *Adaptive Software Development.* New York: Dorset House, 2000.

Ittner, Christopher D., and David F. Larckner. "A Bigger Yardstick for Company Performance." London: *The Financial Times,* 10/16/2000.

Janis, Irving, and Leon Mann. *Decision Making.* New York: The Free Press, 1977.

Johnson, Spencer. *Who Moved My Cheese?* New York: G. P. Putnam's Sons, 1998.

Jones, Russel A. *Self-Fulfilling Prophecies.* Hillsdale, NJ: Lawrence Erlbaum, 1977.

Kaplan, Robert, and David Norton. *The Balanced Scorecard: Translating Strategy Into Action.* Harvard Business School Press, 1996.

Kayser, Tom. *Mining Group Gold.* New York: McGraw-Hill, 1995.

Keane. *Productivity Management: Keane's Project Management Approach for Systems Development,* 2d ed. Boston: Keane Associates (800-239-0296), 1995.

Keirsey, David. *Please Understand Me II.* Del Mar, CA: Prometheus Nemesis Book Company, 1998.

Kepner, Charles H., and Benjamin B. Tregoe. *The Rational Manager.* Princeton, NJ: Kepner-Tregoe, Inc., 1965.

Kerzner, Harold. *In Search of Excellence in Project Management.* New York: Van Nostrand, 1998.

Kerzner, Harold. *Project Management: a Systems Approach to Planning, Scheduling, and Controlling,* 5th ed. New York: Van Nostrand, 1995.

Kiemele, Mark J., and Stephen R. Schmidt. *Basic Statistics: Tools for Continuous Improvement,* 3d ed. Colorado Springs, CO: Air Academy Press, 1993.

Knight, James A. *Value-Based Management: Developing a Systematic Approach to Creating Shareholder Value.* New York: McGraw-Hill, 1998.

Knowles, Malcolm. *Self-Directed Learning.* New York: Association Press, 1975.

Koch, Richard. *The 80/20 Principle.* New York: Doubleday, 1998.

Kohn, Alfie. *Punished by Rewards.* Mariner Books, 1999.

Kouzes, James M., and Barry Z. Posner. *The Leadership Challenge: How to Get Extraordinary Things Done in Organizations.* San Francisco: Jossey-Bass, 1987.

Kuhn, Thomas. *The Structure of Scientific Revolutions.* Chicago: University of Chicago Press, 1970.

Leider, Richard J. *Life Skills: Taking Charge of Your Personal and Professional Growth.* Paramus, NJ: Prentice Hall, 1994.

Leider, Richard J. *The Power of Purpose: Creating Meaning in Your Life and Work.* San Francisco: Berrett Koehler, 1997.

Lerner, Michael. *The Politics of Meaning.* Reading, MA: Addison-Wesley, 1996.

Lewis, James P. *Fundamentals of Project Management,* 2d ed. New York: AMACOM, 2001.

Lewis, James P. *Mastering Project Management.* New York: McGraw-Hill, 1998.

Lewis, James P. *Project Leadership.* New York: McGraw-Hill, 2002.

Lewis, James P. *Project Planning, Scheduling and Control*, 3d ed. New York: McGraw-Hill, 2000.

Lewis, James P. *The Project Manager's Desk Reference*, 2d ed. New York: McGraw-Hill, 2000.

Lewis, James P. *The Project Manager's Pocket Survival Guide*. New York: McGraw-Hill, 2003.

Lewis, James P. *Team-Based Project Management*. Baltimore, MD: Beard Books, 2004.

Lewis, James P. *Working Together*. New York: McGraw-Hill, 2002.

Lewis, James P., and Louis Wong. *Accelerated Project Management*. New York: McGraw-Hill, 2004.

Lewis, James, and Robert E. Dudley. *The McGraw-Hill Guide to the PMP Exam*. New York: McGraw-Hill, 2005.

MacMillan, Ian C., and Rita Gunther McGrath. "Corporate Ventures: Maximising Gains." London: *Financial Times*, 10/16/2000.

Maidique, Modesto, and Billie Jo Zirger. *The New Product Learning Cycle*. Research Policy. (Cited in Peters, 1987).

Maier, Norman R. F. *Psychology in Industry*. Boston: Houghton Mifflin, 1955.

Maloney, Lawrence D. "For the Love of Flying." *Design News*, Vol 51, Number 5, March 4, 1996.

March, James, and Herbert Simon. *Organizations*. New York: Wiley, 1966.

Maslow, Abraham. *Motivation and Personality*, 2d ed. New York: Harper & Row, 1970.

McCartney, Scott. "Out of the Blue: How Two Pacific Nations Became Oceanic Aces of Air-Traffic Control." *The Wall Street Journal*, Friday, December 29, 2000.

McClelland, David. *Power: The Inner Experience.* New York: Halsted Press, 1975.

McGraw, Phillip. *Life Strategies: Doing What Works, Doing What Matters.* New York, Hyperion, 1999.

Michalko, Michael. *Thinkertoys.* Berkeley, CA: Ten Speed Press, 1995.

Miller, William C. *The Creative Edge: Fostering Innovation Where You Work.* Reading, MA: Addison-Wesley, 1986.

Mintzberg, Henry. *Mintzberg on Management.* New York: The Free Press, 1989.

Moder, Joseph J., Cecil R. Phillips, and Edward W. Davis. *Project Management with CPM, PERT, and Precedence Diagraming,* 3d ed. New York: Van Nostrand, 1983.

Morrison, Terri, Wayne A. Conaway, and George A. Borden. *Kiss, Bow or Shake Hands.* Holbrook, MA: Adams Media Corporation, 1994.

Mouzelis, N. P. "Bureaucracy," *The New Encyclopaedia Britannica,* 15th ed., Macropaedia 3, 1974.

Nadler, Gerald and Shozo Hibino. *Breakthrough Thinking.* Rocklin, CA: Prima Publishing, 1990.

NASA. *100 Rules for Project Managers.*

Nellore, Rajesh. "R&D Structures to Keep the Focus on Products." London: *Financial Times,* 12/11/2000.

von Oech, Roger. *A Whack on the Side of the Head.* New York: Warner, 1983.

von Oech, Roger. *A Kick in the Seat of the Pants.* New York: Warner, 1986.

Packard, Vance. *The Pyramid Climbers.* New York: McGraw-Hill, 1962.

Page, Rick. *Hope Is Not a Strategy.* New York: McGraw-Hill, 2003.

Pasmore, William. *Designing Effective Organizations: The Sociotechnical Systems Perspective.* New York: Wiley, 1988.

Patterson, Marvin. *Accelerating Innovation: Improving the Processes of Product Development.* New York: Van Nostrand Reinhold, 1993.

Peter, Lawrence J. *The Peter Principle.* New York: William Morrow & Co., 1969.

Peters, Tom. *Liberation Management.* New York: Knopf, 1992.

Peters, Tom. *Thriving on Chaos.* New York: Knopf, 1987.

Peters, Tom. "The WOW Project." *Fast Company* , May 1999.

Peters, Tom, and Bob Waterman. *In Search of Excellence.* New York: Warner Books, 1982.

Pinto, Jeffrey K. *Power and Politics in Project Management.* Upper Darby, PA: Project Management Institute, 1996.

Pinto, Jeffrey K., Editor. *The Project Management Institute Project Management Handbook.* San Francisco: Jossey-Bass, 1998.

Ray, M., and R. Myers. *Creativity in Business.* Garden City, NY: Doubleday, 1986.

Rickards, Tudor. *Problem Solving through Creative Analysis.* Epping, Essex, England: Gower Press, 1975.

Rosen, Robert H. *Leading People: The 8 Proven Principles for Success in Business.* New York: Penguin Books, 1996.

Rosenthal, R., and L. Jacobson. *Pygmalion in the Classroom.* New York: Holt, Rinehart, and Winston, 1968.

Saaty, Thomas L. *Decision Making for Leaders.* Pittsburgh: RWS Publications, 1995.

Sabbagh, Karl. *Twenty-First Century Jet.* New York: Scribner, 1996.

Schuster, John P., Jill Carpenter, and Patricia Kane. *The Power of Open-Book Management.* New York: Wiley, 1996.

Senge, Peter. *The Fifth Discipline.* New York: Doubleday, 1990.

Senge, Peter. Interview in *Fast Company,* May 1999.

Smith, Hyrum W. *The 10 Natural Laws of Successful Time and Life Management.* New York: Warner Books, 1994.

Smith, Preston G., and Donald G. Reinertsen. *Developing Products in Half the Time.* New York: Van Nostrand, 1995.

Stacey, Ralph D. *Complexity and Creativity in Organizations.* San Francisco: Berrett-Koehler, 1996.

Steiner, Claude. *Scripts People Live By,* 2d ed. New York: Grove Weidenfeld, 1990.

Sugimoto, T. *Estimation on the Project Management Workload.* In "Proceedings of the International Conference on Project Management," Singapore, 31 July to 2 August, 2002.

Sykes, Charles. *A Nation of Victims: The Decay of the American Character.* New York: St. Martin's Press, 1992.

Sykes, Charles. *Dumbing Down Our Kids.* New York: St. Martin's Press, 1995.

Treacy, Michael, and Fred Wiersema. *The Discipline of Market Leaders.* Reading, MA: Addison-Wesley, 1995.

Trompenaars, Fons, and Peter Wolliams. *Business Across Cultures.* Chichester, England: Capstone.

Vroom, Victor, and Arthur Jago. *The New Leadership.* Englewood Cliffs, NJ: 1988.

Vroom, Victor, and Phillip Yetton. *Leadership and Decision Making.* Pittsburgh: University of Pittsburgh Press, 1973.

Walpole, Ronald E. *Introduction to Statistics,* 2d ed. New York: Macmillan, 1974.

Watzlawick, Paul, John Weakland, and Richard Fisch. *Change: Principles of Problem Formulation and Problem Resolution.* New York: Norton, 1974.

Weisbord, Marvin. *Productive Workplaces.* San Francisco: Jossey Bass, 1987.

Weisbord, Marvin, editor. *Discovering Common Ground: How Future Search Conferences Bring People Together to Achieve Breakthrough Innovation, Empowerment, Shared Vision, and Collaborative Action.* San Francisco: Berrett-Koehler, 1992.

Weisbord, Marvin, and Sandra Janoff. *Future Search: An Action Guide to Finding Common Ground in Organizations and Communities.* San Francisco: Berrett-Koehler, 1995.

Wheatley, Margaret. *Leadership and New Science.* San Francisco: Berrett-Koehler, 1992.

White, Gregory L. "In Order to Grow, GM Finds That the Order of the Day Is Cutbacks." *The Wall Street Journal,* Monday, December 18, 2000.

Wilson, Larry. *Changing the Game.* Fireside, 1988.

Wing, R. L. *The Tao of Power.* New York: Doubleday, 1986.

Wysocki, Robert K. *Effective Project Management,* 2d ed. New York: Wiley, 2000.

Wysocki, Robert K., and James P. Lewis. *The World-Class Project Manager.* Boston: Perseus Books, 2000.

Young, S. David, and Stephen F. O'Byrne. *EVA® and Value-Based Management.* New York: McGraw-Hill, 2001.

Zander, Rosamund Stone, and Benjamin Zander. *The Art of Possibility.* Boston: Harvard Business School Press, 2000.

# INDEX

# ABOUT THE AUTHOR

**James P. Lewis, Ph.D.** is an experienced project manager who now teaches seminars on the subject throughout the United States, England, and the Far East. His solid, no-nonsense approach is largely the result of the 15 years he spent in industry, working as an electrical engineer engaged in the design and development of communication equipment. He held various positions, including Project Manager, Product Engineering Manager, and Chief Engineer, for Aerotron, Inc. and ITT Telecommunications, both of Raleigh, NC. He also was a Quality Manager for ITT Telecom, managing a department of 63 quality engineers, line inspectors, and test technicians.

While he was an engineering manager, he began working on a doctorate in organizational psychology, because of his conviction that a manager can only succeed by developing good interpersonal skills.

Since 1980, Dr. Lewis has trained over 30,000 supervisors and managers in Argentina, Canada, England, Germany, India, Indonesia, Malaysia, Mexico, Singapore, Sweden, Thailand, and the United States. He has written articles for *Training and Development Journal, Apparel Industry Magazine,* and *Transportation and Distribution Magazine,* and is the author of *Mastering Project Management, Project Planning, Scheduling and Control, Fourth Edition, Working Together: The 12 Principles Employed by Boeing Commercial Aircraft to Manage Projects, Teams, and the Organization, Project Leadership,* and *The Project Manager's Survival Guide,* and coauthor with Louis

Wong of *Accelerated Project Management*, published by McGraw-Hill, and *Fundamentals of Project Management, Second Edition; How to Build and Manage a Winning Project Team;* and *Team-Based Project Management*, published by the American Management Association. He is coauthor, with Bob Wysocki, of *The World-Class Project Manager*, published by Perseus in 2001. The first edition of *Project Planning, Scheduling and Control* has been published in a Spanish edition, and the AMACOM book *Fundamentals of Project Management* has been published in Portuguese and Latvian. Several of his books have also been published in Chinese, and *Project Leadership* has been translated into Spanish and Russian.

He has a B.S. in Electrical Engineering and a Ph.D. in Psychology, both from NC State University in Raleigh. He is a member of the Project Management Institute. He is also a certified Herrmann Brain Dominance Instrument practitioner.

He is president of The Lewis Institute, Inc., a training and consulting company specializing in project management, which he founded in 1981. He is a member of the Project Management Institute and the American Society for Training and Development.

Jim was married to the former Lea Ann McDowell for 35 years, and he lives in Vinton, Virginia, in the Blue Ridge Mountains. Although he has no biological children, he has four exchange student daughters, Yukiko Bono of Japan, Katarina Sigerud of Sweden, Susi Mraz of Austria, and Stephanie Woilier from France.